The Beat Generation FAQ

All That's Left to Know About the Angelheaded Hipsters

Rich Weidman

Backbeat
Books

An Imprint of Hal Leonard Corporation

Copyright © 2015 by Rich Weidman
All rights reserved. No part of this book may be reproduced in any form, without written permission, except by a newspaper or magazine reviewer who wishes to quote brief passages in connection with a review.

Published in 2015 by Backbeat Books
An Imprint of Hal Leonard Corporation
7777 West Bluemound Road
Milwaukee, WI 53213

Trade Book Division Editorial Offices
33 Plymouth St., Montclair, NJ 07042

All images are from the author's collection unless otherwise noted.

The FAQ series was conceived by Robert Rodriguez and developed with Stuart Shea.

Printed in the United States of America

Book design by Snow Creative Services

Library of Congress Cataloging-in-Publication Data is available upon request.

ISBN 978-1-61713-601-6

www.backbeatbooks.com

The Beat Generation FAQ

Dedicated to the memory of my grandfather, Professor T. E. Maki,
who told me to "endeavor to persevere"

Contents

Acknowledgments

My interest in literature dates back to an eleventh-grade reading of William Golding's *Lord of the Flies* in James Ketchen's class at Northeast High School in Oakland Park, Florida. Thanks, Mr. Ketchen! I went on to study English literature at Stetson University under the tutelage of such legendary professors as Michael Raymond, C. Carter Colwell, and Wayne Dickson, each of whom I owe a debt of gratitude.

A special shout-out goes to my wife, Nadine, and kids, Hailey and Dylan, who provided encouragement and patience as I spent countless hours at my desk grinding out the book. Once again, I would like to thank my mom and dad, as well as my brother, Boyd, and my sister, Tracy, for their support during my Beat Generation odyssey over the past year.

The book itself would not have been completed in a timely manner if it hadn't been for the assistance of my good friend, Jack Thompson, the brilliant architect of the "database" and frequent collaborator on offbeat projects since that fateful day in high school when we gave a desperate, CliffsNotes-inspired presentation of Upton Sinclair's *The Jungle*. Since then, Jack and I have worked on several Internet projects, including Alternative Reel, Forgotten Movie Classics, and the upcoming Wrestle Cinemania: The Definitive Guide to Grappling in the Movies.

During the summer of 2014, my wife and I flew out to San Francisco for both our twentieth wedding anniversary and a Beat Generation fact-finding mission. I would like to thank the staff at the Beat-inspired Hotel Bohème (www.hotelboheme.com), which lies in the heart of North Beach, for their amazing hospitality, as well as Jerry Cimino of the Beat Museum (www.kerouac .com) for showing us around the facility and recommending the fascinating Beat Generation walking tour. By the way, a trip to the Beat Museum is an absolute must if you are interested in the Beats!

In addition, I would like to thank Pat Barmore and Pete Gallagher of the Friends of the Jack Kerouac House, as well as Dale Nichols, owner of the Flamingo Sports Bar, one of Jack Kerouac's favorite hangouts in St. Petersburg, Florida. The Flamingo hosts a "Jack Kerouac Night" twice a year that features poetry readings and live music from the likes of great singer-songwriter Ronny Elliott ("Jack's St. Pete Blues"). Thanks also to Summer Rodman of the Kerouac Project (www.kerouacproject.org) in Orlando, Florida.

I would also like to extend my appreciation to my editor at Backbeat Books, Bernadette Malavarca; my agent, Robert Lecker of the Robert Lecker Agency; and Robert Rodriguez, the founder of the FAQ series.

Last but not least, I would like to thank my supervisors at Westgate Resorts—Robert Jensen and Denise Brookfield—for tolerating my frequent absences during the writing of this book.

Introduction

id you know . . .

- Jack Kerouac's first draft of his landmark 1957 novel, *On the Road*—typed on a 120-foot scroll of tracing paper—was purchased by Indianapolis Colts owner Jim Irsay in 2001 for $2.43 million?
- Not only did author William S. Burroughs's grandfather perfect the adding machine, leading to the eventual creation of the Burroughs Corporation, but his uncle, Ivy Lee, is today considered the "Father of Public Relations"?
- Speaking at the 1960 Republican convention in Chicago, former President Herbert Hoover denounced the "communist front, and the beatniks and the eggheads" for destroying the social fabric of the country?
- The star-studded lineup at the famous hippie gathering known as the Human Be-In in 1967 featured not only Timothy Leary but also influential Beat Generation writers Allen Ginsberg, Lawrence Ferlinghetti, Gary Snyder, and Michael McClure?
- Neal Cassady's long-lost, stream-of-consciousness-style "Joan Anderson Letter," which strongly influenced the writing style of *On the Road*, was discovered in a neglected box of stored documents from a defunct publishing firm in the fall of 2014?

These fascinating tidbits and thousands of others can be discovered throughout *The Beat Generation FAQ*, a comprehensive, informative, and entertaining look at the offbeat personalities and cutting-edge works that shaped this fascinating cultural and literary movement that was born in the 1940s, took shape in the early 1950s, skyrocketed into the national consciousness in the late 1950s, and helped spawn the hippie counterculture in the 1960s.

Disillusioned with the repression and conformity encompassing post–World War II life in the United States, the Beats actively sought more creative alternatives to the mind-numbing banality of modern culture. Beat Generation writers were no strangers to controversy: Both Allen Ginsberg's landmark, prophetic poem, "Howl" (1956), and Burroughs's groundbreaking novel, *Naked Lunch* (1959), led to obscenity trials, while *On the Road* was blamed by the establishment for corrupting the nation's youth and continues to this day to serve as a beacon of hipster culture and the bohemian lifestyle. In fact, the Beat Generation as a whole served to extend a collective "fuck you" to the establishment with their controversial works and even more contentious lifestyles.

The Beats shared a vision for the creation of a new type of literature, one that escaped the boundaries of academia (and the formalism evident in the modernist poetry of such luminaries as T. S. Eliot) and used a more natural language forged by the inspiration of the spontaneity and improvisational nature of jazz music and abstract expressionism (a style of writing Kerouac labeled "spontaneous prose"). In order to find greater meaning in life, Beat Generation writers experimented not only with language but also with spirituality, art, drugs, sexuality, and unconventional lifestyles.

Although the movement as a whole flamed out quickly in the early 1960s—replaced by the onset of the hippie counterculture—the Beat Generation definitely staked its claim on the nation's consciousness and has had a long-lasting influence on a variety of artistic and cultural spheres, as highlighted in *The Beat Generation FAQ*. Interest in the Beat Generation continues to be strong with the recent releases of such Beat-related feature films as *Howl* (2010), *Big Sur* (2013), *On the Road* (2013), and *Kill Your Darlings* (2013).

I first discovered the Beat Generation as a teenager after reading the influential 1980 Jim Morrison biography, *No One Here Gets Out Alive*, which listed works that had influenced "The Lizard King," such as *On the Road*. So after reading *On the Road* three times straight through, I turned to *Naked Lunch* and other key works of the Beat Generation, as well as several biographies of Kerouac and Burroughs. I moved on to other writers influenced by the Beats, such as Ken Kesey, and ended up writing my college senior thesis, "The American Romance Tradition in *One Flew Over the Cuckoo's Nest*," on this topic.

During my college break in the summer of 1988, I found myself painting houses in Boston and was fortunate enough to attend "An Evening of Poetry and Music to Honor Jack Kerouac" in the author's hometown of Lowell, Massachusetts, a lively event that featured poetry reading and music by Ginsberg, Ferlinghetti, Robert Creeley, Michael McClure, and keyboardist Ray Manzarek of the Doors, along with several local poets. It was rather jolting to witness Ginsberg, who had sported a scruffy beard and beads during the height of the counterculture, take the stage in a suit and tie like some Madison Avenue ad executive—but when the poet launched into an inspired reading of "Howl," it was easy to imagine the amazing impact the landmark poem had made when it was first unleashed on American society at the Six Gallery Reading in San Francisco in 1955.

Fast forward more than twenty-five years to the summer of 2014, as my wife and I traveled across the country to San Francisco and stayed at the Beat-inspired Hotel Bohème in the heart of bustling North Beach, the famous Beat Generation enclave during the 1950s. As we wandered the streets of North Beach, evidence of the Beat Generation's legacy was everywhere, from City

Lights Bookstore and Vesuvio Café to Jack Kerouac Alley and Caffe Trieste, as well as the incredible Beat Museum.

As we made the arduous "trek" up Grant Avenue toward Bob Kaufman Alley near Coit Tower, I got to thinking about how new generations of young readers, writers, and adventurers continually receive inspiration and guidance from the Beat writers who once roamed these streets and raised hell in these bars. Truly, the Beat Generation endures. As Ken Kesey has remarked, "We have to keep this little flame going and pass it on. All it takes is one person." If you are reading this sentence right now and want to delve headlong into the Beat Generation, that person could be you.

Angelheaded Hipsters

Major Figures of the Beat Generation

The Beat Generation consisted of a group of creative individuals from a variety of diverse backgrounds who shared common interests but had extremely diverse writing styles. In addition to the literary giants of the Beat Generation—Jack Kerouac (*On the Road*), Allen Ginsberg ("Howl"), and William S. Burroughs (*Naked Lunch*)—several other individuals made important contributions, such as Neal Cassady, the inspiration for "Dean Moriarty" in *On the Road*; "Rimbaudian Beat muse" Lucien Carr, who introduced Kerouac, Ginserg, and Burroughs to each other; ex-con Gregory Corso, the youngest of the Beat writers; Lawrence Ferlinghetti, the "elder statesman" of the Beat Generation and cofounder of City Lights Bookstore; John Clellon Holmes, author of the first Beat novel, *Go* (1952); Herbert Huncke, Times Square denizen who introduced the word "beat" to the group; and Gary Snyder, the so-called "Poet Laureate of Deep Ecology."

Jack Kerouac (1922–69)

Allen Ginsberg once referred to Jack Kerouac as the "new Buddha of American prose." Kerouac was born Jean-Louis Lebris de Kerouac on March 12, 1922, to working-class Catholic, French-Canadian parents Gabrielle and Leo Kerouac in Lowell, Massachusetts. Tragically, Kerouac's older brother, Gerard, died at the age of nine of rheumatic fever in 1926, a definitive event the author would later chronicle in his 1963 novel, *Visions of Gerard*. Kerouac, who didn't learn to speak English fluently until he was six years old (his nickname was "Ti Jean," or "Little Jean"), also had an older sister named Caroline ("Nin"). A gifted high school athlete in both track and football, Kerouac scored the winning touchdown in a legendary game against Lawrence dubbed the "Turkey Day Classic" on Thanksgiving Day 1938. Kerouac's high school sweetheart, Mary Carney, was later immortalized in his 1959 novel, *Maggie Cassidy*.

Often referred to as the "Father of the Beat Generation," Jack Kerouac published an immense body of work, including *On the Road* (1957), the defining work of the Beat movement.

Photo by John Cohen/Courtesy of Getty Images

Kerouac's early literary influences included Thomas Wolfe (*Look Homeward, Angel*), Walt Whitman (*Leaves of Grass*), Jack London (*The Call of the Wild*), and Mark Twain (*Huckleberry Finn*). Kerouac attended Columbia University briefly on a football scholarship. At Columbia, Kerouac met Allen Ginsberg and William S. Burroughs through their mutual friend Lucien Carr. During World War II, Kerouac served briefly in the merchant marine (he wrote an early novel based on his experiences called *The Sea Is My Brother*) and US Navy. Between 1947 and 1950, Kerouac and Neal Cassady made a series of cross-country trips that would serve as the basis for his most popular novel, *On the Road* (1957).

A true literary icon, Kerouac published an immense body of work, including the Wolfe-inspired *The Town and the City* (1950) and *On the Road* (1957), the defining work of the Beat Generation, which features such classic lines as "the only people for me are the mad ones, the ones who are mad to live, mad to talk, mad to be saved, desirous of everything at the same time." Upon the publication of *On the Road*, Kerouac became a celebrity overnight. According to his good friend, the author John Clellon Holmes, Kerouac "didn't object to being famous, but he realized he wasn't famous—he was notorious." Indeed, most critics from that moment on focused on Kerouac's novels as part of a social movement instead of considering the essence of the writing itself.

Other major writings in Kerouac's so-called "Duluoz Legend" (his fictional alter ego was known as "Jack Duluoz") include *The Dharma Bums* (1958), *The Subterraneans* (1958), *Doctor Sax* (1959), *Maggie Cassidy* (1959), *Big Sur* (1962), and *Desolation Angels* (1965). Kerouac famously remarked, "My work comprises one vast book like Proust's . . . seen through the eys of poor Ti Jean (me), otherwise known as Jack Duluoz." Kerouac also wrote books of poetry, most popularly *Mexico City Blues* (1959), which is made up of 242 "choruses."

Kerouac was married three times: to Edie Parker, to Joan Haverty (who gave birth to his only child, Jan Kerouac), and to Stella Sampas. Kerouac died on October 21, 1969, in St. Petersburg, Florida, of a gastrointestinal hemorrhage after years of excessive drinking. Kerouac is buried in Edson Cemetery in his hometown of Lowell. His epitaph reads, "He Honored Life." A new granite marker was added to the gravesite in 2014 with the inscription "The Road is Life" from *On the Road*.

Essential Reading: *The Town and the City* (1950), *On the Road* (1957), *The Dharma Bums* (1958), *The Subterraneans* (1958), *Doctor Sax* (1959), *Maggie Cassidy* (1959), *Mexico City Blues* (1959), *Tristessa* (1960), *Big Sur* (1962), *Desolation Angels* (1965), *Vanity of Duluoz* (1968), *Visions of Cody* (1972).

Allen Ginsberg (1926–97)

"Under the burden of solitude, under the burden of dissatisfaction . . . the weight of the world is love." An innovative and highly influential poet best known for his epic, "Howl," one of the principal works of the Beat Generation, Ginsberg served as a major advocate of the other Beat writers. According to fellow poet Lawrence Ferlinghetti, "There wouldn't have been any Beat Generation without Allen Ginsberg, who, besides being a genius poet, was a genius publicist." In *On the Road*, Jack Kerouac called Ginsberg ("Carlo Marx") "the sorrowful poetic con-man with the dark mind." Irwin Allen Ginsberg was born on June 3, 1926, in Newark, New Jersey, to Naomi and Louis Ginsberg, second-generation Russian-Jewish immigrants. An active member of the Communist Party, Naomi struggled with mental illness for most of her life, while Louis was a high school English teacher and published poet. Eugene, Ginsberg's older brother, was named after labor agitator Eugene V. Debs. Ginsberg first discovered Walt Whitman as a student at East Side High School in Newark, and the so-called "Bard of Democracy" remained a major influence throughout his life (he later paid

The author of "Howl," one of the landmark works of the Beat Generation, Allen Ginsberg later became a major figure in the 1960s counterculture movement, as well as a leading advocate of other Beat writers.   *Photo by Michiel Hendryckx/Wikimedia Commons*

tribute to Whitman in one of his most memorable poems, "A Supermarket in California").

An above-average student, Ginsberg received a scholarship from the Young Men's Hebrew Association of Paterson to Columbia University and studied English under such influential professors as Lionel Trilling, Mark Van Doren, and Raymond Weaver. Through his friendship with Lucien Carr, Ginsberg eventually met Jack Kerouac and William S. Burroughs. In the summer of 1948, Ginsberg had a "Blakean vision," where he claimed to hear the voice of English Romantic poet William Blake, after which he dedicated his life to poetry. Ginsberg spent eight months at the Columbia Presbyterian Psychiatric Institute.

In a truly landmark event in the history of American poetry, Ginsberg read his poem "Howl" for the first time at the legendary Six Gallery Reading, which ushered in the San Francisco Poetry Renaissance, on October 7, 1955. The publication of *Howl and Other Poems* by City Light Publishers (No. 4 in the Pocket Poets Series) resulted in a heavily publicized obscenity trial that turned into a victory for freedom of expression and against censorship. Naomi spent her last years in a series of mental hospitals and endured both electroshock treatments and a lobotomy. She died in Pilgrim State Hospital in 1956. Ginsberg wrote one of his greatest works, the long autobiographical poem "Kaddish," for his mother.

During the late 1950s, Ginsberg and his lover, Peter Orlovsky, resided in Paris at the "Beat Hotel," which was home to William S. Burroughs and Gregory Corso, along with a diverse variety of other writers and artists. During the 1960s, Ginsberg served as a bridge between the Beat Generation and the counterculture, diving headlong into the psychedelic movement where he befriended Timothy Leary, Ken Kesey, and the Merry Pranksters. Ginsberg was also at the forefront of the antiwar movement and was arrested in the riots during the notorious 1968 Democratic National Convention in Chicago. Ginsberg was crowned King of the May by Czech students in Prague on May Day 1965 and was promptly deported by Czech authorities. According to Kenneth Rexroth in his 1971 book *American Poetry in the Twentieth Century*, "Ginsberg is the only one of his immediate associates who outgrew the nihilistic alienation of the Beat Generation and moved on to the positive counter culture which developed in the Sixties."

Ginsberg cofounded with Anne Waldman the Jack Kerouac School of Disembodied Poetics at the Naropa Institute (a Buddhist university) in Boulder, Colorado, in 1974, the same year he won the National Book Award for his poetry collection *The Fall of America: Poems of These States*. A member of the American Academy of Arts and Letters, Ginsberg was awarded the medal of Chevalier de l'Ordre des Arts et Lettres by the French Minister of Culture in 1993. A tireless advocate for personal freedom, nonconformity, and the search for enlightenment throughout his entire life, Ginsberg died of liver cancer in New York City on April 5, 1997. He is buried in Gomel Chesed Cemetery in Newark, New Jersey. According to Mikal Gilmore in *Stories Done* (2009), "As much as Presley, as much as the Beatles, Bob Dylan, or the Sex Pistols, Allen Ginsberg helped set loose something wonderful, risky, and unyielding in the psyche and dreams of our times."

Essential Reading: *Howl and Other Poems* (1956), *Kaddish and Other Poems* (1961), *Reality Sandwiches* (1963), *The Fall of America: Poems of These States* (1972), *Death and Fame: Last Poems 1993–1997* (1999).

William S. Burroughs (1914–97)

No less than Norman Mailer once declared William S. Burroughs "the only American writer who may be conceivably possessed by genius." Jack Kerouac referred to Burroughs as "the greatest satirical writer since Jonathan Swift." Burroughs's various pseudonyms and nicknames include "William Lee," "El Hombre Invisible," "Cosmonaut of Inner Space," "Godfather of Punk," and

"Elvis of American Letters." In addition, the so-called "Godmother of Punk," Patti Smith, dubbed Burroughs "the Father of Heavy Metal."

William Seward Burroughs was born on February 5, 1914, to Laura Lee (the daughter of James Wideman Lee and Emma Eufaula Ledbetter, and a direct descendant of Robert E. Lee) and Mortimer Burroughs in St. Louis, Missouri. He had one brother, Mortimer Burroughs Jr. His grandfather perfected the adding machine, leading to the creation of the Burroughs Adding Machine Company (later known as the Burroughs Corporation). Burroughs later remarked in a 1965 *Paris Review* interview that "my grandfather . . . didn't exactly invent the adding machine, but he invented the gimmick that made it work . . . And it gave me a little money, not much, but a little." In addition, Burroughs's uncle, Ivy Lee, is today considered the "Father of Modern Public Relations."

As a youth, Burroughs attended the Los Alamos Ranch School for Boys. Burroughs's early literary influences included Jack Black (*You Can't Win*), Oswald Spengler (*The Decline of the West*), Louis-Ferdinand Celine (*Journey to the End of the Night*), Thomas De Quincey (*Confessions of an English Opium Eater*), and Alfred Korzybski (*Science and Sanity*). Burroughs, who reportedly kept a pet ferret in his dorm room, received his bachelor of arts degree in English literature ("for lack of interest in any other subject") from Harvard University in 1936. In 1937, Burroughs married Ilse Herzfeld Klapper, so she could flee the Nazi regime in Germany.

At the onset of World War II, Burroughs tried to join the army but was declared unfit for active duty in 1942. Burroughs spent the World War II years in a series of "strange wartime jobs," such as bartender, exterminator, reporter, and factory worker. He eventually made his way to New York City, and through Lucien Carr, an old friend from St. Louis, he befriended Allen Ginsberg and Jack Kerouac. In 1944, Burroughs met Times Square hustler Herbert Huncke, rolled drunks in the subway, and became a morphine addict. Burroughs would later figure prominently in several of Kerouac's novels, including *The Town and the City* ("Will Dennison"), *On the Road* ("Old Bull Lee"), *The Subterraneans* ("Frank Carmody"), *Desolation Angels* ("Bull Hubbard"), and *Vanity of Duluoz* ("Wilson Holmes Hubbard"). In 1951, Burroughs accidentally shot and killed his common-law wife, Joan Vollmer, during a drunken William Tell act in Mexico City. In 1953, Ace Books published Burroughs's first novel, *Junkie*, which was subtitled *Confessions of an Unredeemed Drug Addict*.

Burroughs's highly controversial novel, *Naked Lunch*, was published by Olympia Press in Paris in 1959, and introduced the world to such bizarre and legendary characters as Dr. Benway, Clem Snide the Private Asshole, the Paregoric Kid, Pantopon Rose, the Gimp, the Vigilante, Captain Everhard,

Dr. "Doodles" Rindfest, the Rube, Placenta Juan the After Birth Tycoon, Dr. "Fingers" Schafer the Lobotomy Kid, Clem and Jody, Autopsy Ahmed, Hepatitis Hal, and "Fats" Terminal. His other major writings include *The Soft Machine* (1961), *The Ticket That Exploded* (1962), *Nova Express* (1964), *The Wild Boys: A Book of the Dead* (1971), *Exterminator!* (1973), *Port of Saints* (1980), *The Place of Dead Roads* (1984), *Queer* (1985), *The Western Lands* (1987), and *My Education: A Book of Dreams* (1995), among others. In a 1965 *Paris Review* interview, Burroughs remarked, "All of my work is directed against those who are bent, through stupidity or design, on blowing up the planet or rendering it uninhabitable."

When he wasn't writing books or experimenting with the effect of different drugs, Burroughs dabbled in Scientology but later rejected it as "a series of manipulative gimmicks." His diverse range of interests over the years included Aztec history, Mayan codices, Reich's orgone box, Korzybski's semantics, space travel, Egyptian burial rituals, shotgun art, and cats (he even wrote a tribute to his felines in 1986 called *The Cat Inside*). As far as political affiliation, Burroughs once described himself as an "unaffiliated conservative anarchist." Marshall McLuhan once noted that Burroughs attempted "to reproduce in prose what we accommodate every day as a commonplace aspect of life in the electric age."

Burroughs lived in Tangier during the mid-50s and then relocated to Paris, where he resided at the "Beat Hotel" with fellow Beat writers Ginsberg, Peter Orlovsky, and Gregory Corso. It was here that Burroughs became interested in the cut-up style of writing by his friend Brion Gysin. During the 1960s and early 1970s, Burroughs lived in London. Burroughs returned to New York City in 1974, where he lived in a windowless apartment known as "The Bunker."

Burroughs, who moved into a stone farmhouse five miles outside of Lawrence, Kansas, in 1982, was voted into the American Academy of Arts and Letters the following year. In 1981, Burroughs appeared on *Saturday Night Live* and was introduced by actress Lauren Hutton as "the greatest living American writer." He also found time to appear in roles in several cult movies, such as "Father Murphy the Junkie Priest" in *Drugstore Cowboy* (1989) and "Man in Barn" in *Twister* (1989), as well as doing ads for Nike in the early 1990s. Burroughs died of a heart attack in Lawrence, Kansas, on August 2, 1997.

Essential Reading: *Junkie* (1953), *Naked Lunch* (1959), *The Soft Machine* (1961), *The Yage Letters* (1963, with Allen Ginsberg), *The Last Words of Dutch Schultz* (1970), *Exterminator!* (1973), *Cities of the Red Night* (1981), *Queer* (1985), *The Adding Machine: Selected Essays* (1986), *The Western Lands* (1987), *My Education: A Book of Dreams* (1995)

Neal Cassady (1926–68)

"I became the unnatural son of a few score of beaten men." Best known as the model for the legendary character "Dean Moriarty" from Jack Kerouac's 1957 novel, *On the Road*, street hustler, con man, womanizer, drifter, and dreamer Neal Cassady would later provide a bridge between the Beat Generation and the 1960s counterculture when he served as the bus driver (nicknamed "Speed Limit") for Ken Kesey and the Merry Pranksters as they made their way across the United States in a bus called "Further" during the summer of 1964, promoting the use of psychedelic drugs. Cassady was born in Salt Lake City, Utah, on February 8, 1926, to Maude Jean (Scheuer) and Neal Marshall Cassady. He grew up in the skid row section of Denver, Colorado, with his alcoholic father after his parents separated. For a while father and son shared a tiny space in a flophouse with a double amputee named Shorty (as Cassady described vividly in his memoir *The First Third*, which was published posthumously in 1971).

A juvenile delinquent, Cassady stole approximately five hundred cars before his twenty-first birthday, according to legend. Cassady was arrested for possession of stolen tires in 1944 and sentenced to twelve months in the Colorado State Reformatory. During his prison stint, he started reading the Harvard Classics, particularly enamored of the work of Voltaire and Francis Bacon. In 1946, Cassady married sixteen-year-old LuAnne Henderson. In December 1946, the couple stole a car from LuAnne's uncle and headed to New York City to visit Cassady's friend Hal Chase, a student at Columbia University, who introduced them to Jack Kerouac. Through Kerouac, Cassady met Allen Ginsberg, who was immediately smitten, and the two soon began a sexual relationship (Ginsberg later referred to Cassady as a "secret hero . . . cocksman and Adonis of Denver" in his poem "Howl"). Kerouac and Cassady embarked on a series of cross-country trips between 1947 and 1950 that would serve as the basis for *On the Road*.

Cassady's frantic lifestyle and stream-of-consciousness-style letters to Kerouac helped move Kerouac from the straightforward narrative style of *The Town and the City* to the "spontaneous prose" of *On the Road*. In one such letter, dated January 7, 1948, Cassady wrote Kerouac, "Art is good when it springs from necessity. This kind of origin is the guarantee of its value: there is no other." Cassady married his second wife, Carolyn Robinson, in 1948. Carolyn's turbulent relationship with Neal (as well as her well-documented affair with Kerouac) was depicted in her 1990 memoir, *Off the Road: Twenty Years with Cassady, Kerouac and Ginsberg*. In addition to "Dean Moriarty" in *On the Road*, Cassady inspired a number of characters in Kerouac's novels, most notably as "Cody Pomeray" in *The Dharma Bums* (1958), *Visions of Cody* (1960), *Big Sur* (1962), and *Desolation Angels* (1965). Cassady ended up serving a two-year stint in San Quentin State Prison for marijuana possession in the late 1950s. In the early 1960s, Cassady met Kesey and soon became a fixture within his group of Merry Pranksters, as detailed in Tom Wolfe's riveting 1968 book, *The Electric Kool-Aid Acid Test.*

On February 4, 1968, totally burnt out and exhausted, Cassady was found collapsed beside a railroad track and later died in San Miguel de Allende, Mexico, just four days shy of his forty-second birthday. A drug-fueled Cassady reportedly had decided to count the nails in the railroad ties between towns. According to legend, his last words were "sixty-four thousand nine hundred and twenty-eight." Cassady's cremated remains were sent to Carolyn in a box, and they remain with the Cassady family today. Kesey's 1980 short story "The Day After Superman Died," which is featured in his 1985 book *Demon Box*, features a vivid, albeit fictionalized, depiction of Cassady's final hours. Directed by Noah Buschel (*The Missing Person*) and starring Tate Donovan, the little-seen drama *Neal Cassady*, which was released in 2007, featured the tagline "Going on the road made him a legend. Now he just has to live it down." The Beat Museum in North Beach, San Francisco, hosts an annual "Neal Cassady Birthday Bash" in early February.

Essential Reading: *The First Third* (1971), *Neal Cassady: Collected Letters, 1944–1967* (2005).

Lucien Carr (1925–2005)

Central to the Beat movement (although never a published author), Lucien Carr was part of the early Beat crowd that centered on Columbia University in the early to mid-1940s. Frequently described as both handsome and brilliant, Carr was the one who introduced Allen Ginsberg to Jack Kerouac. He then introduced Ginsberg and Kerouac to William S. Burroughs, whom he had known growing up in St. Louis, Missouri. Carr shared his affinity for both German philosopher Friedrich Nietzsche (1844–1900) and visionary French poet Arthur Rimbaud (1854–91) with Ginsberg. The self-destructive Rimbaud sought out experience and embraced anarchism, alcohol, drugs, and violence. At the age of nineteen, Rimbaud completed his farewell to literaure, *Une saison en enfer* (*A Season in Hell*). It was Rimbaud who, in a famous 1871 letter, defined the role of the poet as visionary: "A poet makes himself a visionary through a long, boundless, and systemized disorganization of all the senses. All forms of love, of suffering, of madness: he searches himself, he exhausts within himself all poisons and preserves their quintessences." Inspired by Rimbaud, Carr and Ginsberg discussed the creation of a "New Vision"—centered on unexpurgated self-expression and transformation of the world through art.

In *The Awakener: A Memoir of Kerouac and the Fifties* (2009), Helen Weaver, who had a rather tumultuous two-month affair with Kerouac during the mid-1950s, described Carr as "witty, sarcastic, a brilliant talker and a devout drinker and hell-raiser whose Bible was Rimbaud's *Une saison en enfer*." In one of his journal entries, as quoted in the 2012 book *The Voice Is All: The Lonely Victory of Jack Kerouac* by Joyce Johnson, Kerouac described a typical night hanging out with Carr as involving fights, dances, "pukings from balconies," and "half-expirings from alcoholic surfeit." According to legend, Carr once rolled Kerouac home in a beer barrel after a booze-soaked evening on the town.

However, Carr had an unwanted admirer, his former Boy Scout troop leader from St. Louis, David Kammerer, who was sixteen years older than Carr and reportedly "stalking" him (although the true nature of their relationship appears to have been much more complicated than that). Kammerer, who was also a childhood friend of Burroughs, followed Carr to New York City and continued to pester him there. Ostensibly in self-defense to ward off one of Kammerer's sexual advances, Carr ended up killing Kammerer in 1944 by stabbing him with a Boy Scout knife in Riverside Park and throwing his body into the Hudson River. Carr spent two years in the Elmira Reformatory for the killing of Kammerer.

Upon his release from prison, Carr went to work for United Press International in New York, where he later became an editor, and retired from their Washington bureau in the late 1980s. Although Carr remained in touch with his friends from the former Beat circle, for the most part he kept his distance. He was particularly loyal to Kerouac, whose inscription of Carr's copy of *Big Sur* reads, "To Lucien my dearest friend & compatriot in alcoholic sorrow & sorrow otherwise." Carr died of bone cancer in Washington, DC, in 2005. Carr's son, Caleb, is the author of the bestselling book *The Alienist* (1994).

Carr appeared as "Kenny Wood" in Kerouac's 1950 novel, *The Town and the City*, and "Damion" in his 1957 novel, *On the Road*. In addition, Kerouac and Burroughs collaborated on a 1945 novel, *And the Hippos Were Boiled in Their Tanks*, a highly fictionalized account of the Kammerer killing that remained unpublished until 2008. The 2013 movie *Kill Your Darlings*, which was directed by John Krokidas and starred Dane DeHaan as Carr, presented a similar fictionalized account of the Carr/Kammerer case.

Gregory Corso (1930–2001)

"Standing on a street corner waiting for no one is power." Allen Ginsberg called Gregory Corso "a rascal poet Villonesque and Rimbaudian" and described his poetry as "pure velvet, close to John Keats for our time." The youngest of the first generation of Beat writers, Corso was described by City Lights editor Nancy Peters as "the most important of the beat poets . . . a really true poet with an original voice, probably the most lyrical of those poets." Gregory Nunzio Corso was born at St. Vincent's Hospital (where Dylan Thomas died in 1953) in Greenwich Village, New York City, on March 26, 1930, to teenage immigrant parents. Corso's mother mysteriously abandoned him the following year, and he ended up in a series of foster homes and youth centers. At the age of seventeen, Corso was sent to prison for three years, where he began reading classic literature and history. He also discovered the poetry of Percy Bysshe Shelley, who remained a lifelong influence. Corso's poem "I Held a Shelley Manuscript" was written in Houghton Library at Harvard University.

Upon his release from prison in 1950, Corso headed back to Greenwich Village and met Ginsberg at the Pony Stable Inn, a lesbian bar. Ginsberg read some of Corso's poetry and encouraged him to write more. Through Ginsberg, Corso also became friends with Kerouac, who described him as "a tough young kid from the Lower East Side who rose like an angel over the rooftops." Corso's first book of poetry, *The Vestal Lady on Brattle and Other Poems*, was published in 1955. In the late 1950s, Corso relocated to Paris and resided in an attic room at the legendary "Beat Hotel," whose famous residents included Ginsberg and William S. Burroughs. In 1958, City Lights published Corso's first major work, *Gasoline*, in its critically acclaimed Pocket Poets Series. Corso dedicated the poetry collection to "the angels of Clinton Prison who, in my seventeenth year, handed me, from all the cells surrounding me, books of illumination." Corso once remarked that the poetry from *Gasoline* came to him "from a dark river within."

Corso's book *Mindfield: New and Selected Poems* was published in 1989. In his foreword to *Minefield*, Ginsberg wrote, "Gregory Corso's an aphoristic poet and a poet of ideas . . . Corso's handling of ideas is unique, as in various one-word title poems . . . Corso is a poet's Poet, his verse pure velvet, close to John Keats for our time." Corso served as a regular visiting faculty member at the Jack Kerouac School of Disembodied Poetics at the Naropa Institute, where he can be seen in the 1986 documentary *What Happened to Kerouac?* He also had a cameo as an "Unruly Stockholder" in *The Godfather III* (1990) and appeared as a hotel deck clerk in the low-budget independent film *What About Me* (1993).

Corso died on January 17, 2001, in Robbinsdale, Minnesota. Rock poet Patti Smith wrote upon Corso's death: "The fresh light pours. The boys from the road steer him on. But before he ascends into some holy card glow, Gregory, being himself, lifts his overcoat, drops his trousers, and as he exposes his poet's rump one last time, cries, 'Hey man, kiss my daisy.' Ahh Gregory, the years and petals fly." A fascinating documentary, *Corso: The Last Beat*, was released in 2009 and features an emotional reunion between Corso and his long-lost mother.

Essential Reading: *The Vestal Lady on Brattle and Other Poems* (1955), *Gasoline* (1958), *Bomb* (1958), *The Happy Birthday of Death* (1960), *Mindfield: New and Selected Poems* (1989).

Lawrence Ferlinghetti (1919–)

"Poetry is the shadow cast by our streetlight imaginations." Known as the "elder statesman" of the Beat Generation (although he never considered himself a Beat writer!), poet and publisher Lawrence Ferlinghetti opened City Lights Bookstore in 1953 with Peter D. Martin in the heart of North Beach, San Francisco. Ferlinghetti also published many Beat writers through City Lights Publishers' highly influential Pocket Poets Series, such as Allen Ginsberg's landmark *Howl and Other Poems* in 1956. Lawrence Monsanto Ferlinghetti was born on March 24, 1919, in Yonkers and spent his early childhood in France. Among his literary influences were T. S. Eliot, Ezra Pound, Gertrude Stein, James Joyce, and Thomas Wolfe. Ferlinghetti received his bachelor of arts degree in journalism from the University of North Carolina in 1941. He went on to receive a master of arts degree from Columbia University and a PhD from the Sorbonne. During World War II, Ferlinghetti served in the US Naval Reserve and was sent to Nagasaki, Japan, just six weeks after the atomic bomb destroyed the city (an event that turned him into a lifelong pacifist and antiwar activist).

In 1953, Ferlinghetti and Martin (son of labor agitator and anarchist Carlo Tresca) started *City Lights* magazine and opened City Lights Books—the first paperback bookstore in the United States—in San Francisco, California. Ferlinghetti launched City Lights Publishers in 1955. After publishing *Howl and Other Poems*, Ferlinghetti and City Lights bookstore manager Shig Murao were arrested on obscenity charges and later acquitted during a highly publicized trial that proved to be a landmark victory in the fight for freedom of expression and against censorship in the United States. Originally published in 1958, Ferlinghetti's *A Coney Island of the Mind* (the book's title was taken from Henry Miller's 1947 work *Into the Night Life*) has been translated into nine languages, and there are approximately one million copies in print. The collection contains some of Ferlinghetti's most famous poems, including "Constantly Risking Absurdity," "I Am Waiting," and "Junkman's Obbligato," among others.

Ferlinghetti was fictionalized as "Lorenzo Monsanto" in Jack Kerouac's 1962 novel, *Big Sur* (which depicts Kerouac's stay at Ferlinghetti's cabin in Bixby Canyon). He also served as a featured presenter at the Human Be-In, the prelude to the "Summer of Love," on January 14, 1967. Ferlinghetti's fourth book of poems, *The Secret Meaning of Things: Assassination Raga* was read on the night of Robert Kennedy's funeral, June 8, 1968, at a "mammoth poetry reading" in San Francisco's Nourse Auditorium. He also appeared in *The Last Waltz*, the 1978 documentary directed by Martin Scorsese that featured the farewell concert of the Band.

In addition, Ferlinghetti was instrumental in the creation of Jack Kerouac Alley, which lies between City Lights Bookstore and Vesuvio Café in North Beach, San Francisco. In 1994, the City of San Francisco named a street in Ferlinghetti's honor, and he was also selected first Poet Laureate of San Francisco in 1998. In 2003, Ferlinghetti was elected to the American Academy

Cofounder of City Lights Bookstore in San Francisco Lawrence Ferlinghetti published many Beat writers through his highly influential Pocket Poets Series, as well as his own highly acclaimed work, such as *A Coney Island of the Mind* (1958), one of the most popular books of poetry ever published in the United States.   *Photo by Nat Farbman/ Courtesy of the LIFE Picture Collection/Getty Images*

of Arts and Letters. Directed by Christopher Felver, the documentary *Ferlinghetti: A Rebirth of Wonder*, was released in 2009.

Essential Reading: *Pictures of the Gone World* (1955), *A Coney Island of the Mind* (1958), *Starting from San Francisco* (1967), *The Secret Meaning of Things* (1970), *These Are My Rivers: New and Selected Poems, 1955–1993* (1993).

John Clellon Holmes (1926–88)

"Each stolen moment is like a withering rose caught at the superb beauty of its decline, death already dreadfully kissing it." An early spokesman for the Beat Generation and author of the first Beat novel, *Go* (1952), John Clellon Holmes was born in Holyoke, Massachusetts, on March 12, 1926, to Elizabeth Franklin Emmons and John McClellan Holmes. A close friend of Jack Kerouac, Holmes was occasionally referred to as the "quiet Beat" since he was more of an observer of the early Beat scene rather than an active participant. It was actually Holmes who first heard Kerouac casually remark in conversation in 1948, "You know, this is really a beat generation." Holmes's article "This Is the Beat Generation" appeared in the *New York Times Magazine* on November 16, 1952, and helped popularize the term, which he credited to Kerouac.

In *Go* (original title: *The Daybreak Boys*), Holmes (as the rather demure "Paul Hobbes," who is "paralyzed by the vision of unending lovelessness") profiles his encounters with Kerouac ("Gene Pasternak"), Neal Cassady ("Hart Kennedy"), Allen Ginsberg ("David Stofsky"), and William S. Burroughs ("Will Dennison"), as well as Herbert Huncke ("Albert Ancke"), LuAnne Henderson ("Dinah"), Bill Cannastra ("Bill Agatson"), and Al Hinkle ("Ed Schindel"). *Go* presents a world of wild all-night parties, drunken antics, casual drug use, and eccentric characters related in a somewhat detached style. Hart/Neal is his usual manic self in *Go*, spouting out such classic lines as "Lotsa weed tonight and crazy music! You dig that, woman?" The book also relates the tragic story of "wild man" Cannastra, who was killed in a bizarre New York City subway accident in 1950.

The character "Tom Saybrook," who appears briefly in Kerouac's 1957 novel, *On the Road*, is said to be based on Holmes: "Tom is a sad, handsome fellow, sweet, generous, and amenable; only once in a while he suddenly has fits of depression and rushes off without saying a word to anyone." Holmes's other works included his 1958 novel, *The Horn* (considered the definitive jazz novel of the Beat Generation), *Get Home Free* (1964), *Nothing More to Declare* (1967), and *The Bowling Green Poems* (1977), among others. Lawrence Lipton in his 1959 book, *The Holy Barbarians*, referred to *The Horn* as "a sensitive treatment of jazz musicians, perhaps the best that has been done by anybody so far." Holmes lectured at Yale University in 1959, at the Writers' Workshop at the State University of Iowa in 1963, and at Brown University in 1971. In addition, he was a longtime professor at the University of Arkansas, where he established a creative writing program. Holmes died of cancer in 1988 at the age of sixty-two. A March 31, 1988, *New York Times* obituary for Holmes quoted him as remarking, "As a man, I am a pacifist by nature who views violence and fanaticism of any stripe as the enemies of life. As I have gotten older, I have found that a warm-hearted scepticism towards existence is the surest road to maturity."

Essential Reading: *Go* (1952), *The Horn* (1958), *Gone in October: Last Reflections on Jack Kerouac* (1985).

Herbert Huncke (1915–96)

In a September 13, 1947, letter, Jack Kerouac confided to Neal Cassady, "Huncke is the greatest storyteller I know." Although his literary output was extremely limited, Herbert Huncke, an unapologetic hustler, petty thief, dope fiend, and frequent prison inmate, first initiated the young writers who would make up the core of the Beat Generation to the netherworld of Times Square. He also introduced them to the term "beat" (an old carny term used by many jazz musicians of the day meaning "beaten down," "exhausted," and/or "hopeless"). Huncke would later appear as a down-and-out character in several Beat novels, such as John Clellon Holmes's *Go* ("Ancke"), William S. Burroughs's *Junkie* ("Herman," who gives narrator "William Lee" his first shot of morphine), and Jack Kerouac's *On the Road* ("Elmo Hassel"), among other works. Huncke is also referenced in Allen Ginsberg's landmark poem "Howl" (getting released from Rikers Island).

Herbert Edwin Huncke was born in Greenfield, Massachusetts, on January 9, 1915, to Marguerite Bell and Herbert Spencer Huncke, but grew up in Chicago. A high school dropout, Huncke spent several years as a hobo, hitchhiking and riding the rails throughout the country during the Great Depression. He arrived in New York City in 1939 at the age of twenty-four and became a regular on the Forty-Second Street scene (while his friends called him "the Mayor of Forty-Second Street," the cops referred to him as "the Creep"). During World War II, Huncke joined the merchant marine and traveled around the world (it is even said that he scored morphine on the beach at Normandy three days after the invasion). Back in New York City, Huncke befriended Dr. Alfred Kinsey and even recruited subjects among the denizens of Times Square who would discuss the intimate details of their sex lives for the famous Kinsey study of sexual behavior. In a July 3, 1948, journal entry, Kerouac wrote, "Hunkey scares me because he has been the most *miserable* of men, jailed & beaten and cheated and starved and sickened and homeless, and still he knows there's such a thing as love."

Huncke's notebook writings were published by Diane di Prima's Poet's Press as *Huncke's Journal* in 1964. Huncke also published a collection of stories called *The Evening Sun Turned Crimson* (1980) and *Guilty of Everything* (1990), a straightforward autobiography full of the colorful characters he encountered during his travels, such as a freak show "hermaphrodite" named Elsie John and Little Jack Melody, an ex-con with mob ties. Published in 1998, *The Herbert Huncke Reader* features the full texts of *Huncke's Journal* and *The Evening Sun Turned Crimson*, as well as excerpts from *Guilty of Everything*, and an eclectic selection of unpublished letters and diary entries. In "Courtroom Scene," Huncke embarks on an extended rant after being busted for drugs shortly after getting out of jail: "I wanted to kill myself. Thoughts of disgust, anger, frustration, confusion, and a complete physical let-down had me exhausted . . . Fuck my writing. Fuck me. Fuck the world. Jail again—motherfucker. Why? Why? Why? Actually whose business but my own if I use drugs or poison?"

In addition, Huncke is featured in several Beat documentaries, including *Burroughs: The Movie* (1983), *What Happened to Kerouac?* (1986), *The Beat Generation: An American Dream* (1987), and *Huncke and Louis* (1999), which depicts the "long, tumultuous friendship" between Huncke and his longtime companion, the photographer Louis Cartwright, who was stabbed to death in 1994. Huncke lived out his last years in a small room in the legendary Chelsea Hotel in New York City (Jerry Garcia of the Grateful Dead paid his rent). He died of congestive heart failure on August 8, 1996, at the age of eighty-one. Lydia Lunch—poet, author, actress, singer, and founding member of Teenage Jesus and the Jerks—called Huncke the "unsung hero of the literary underground," who was "a mesmerizing storyteller," and "THE original Beat."

Essential Reading: *Guilty of Everything: The Autobiography of Herbert Huncke* (1990), *The Herbert Huncke Reader* (1998).

Gary Snyder (1930–)

A Pulitzer Prize–winning poet, environmental activist, essayist, and lecturer, Gary Snyder is sometimes referred to as the "Poet Laureate of Deep Ecology," while fellow poet Lawrence Ferlinghetti referred to him as the "Thoreau of the Beat Generation." Stewart Brand, founder of the Whole Earth Catalog, remarked in the *CoEvolution Quarterly* (Issue No. 4, 1974) that "Gary Snyder's poetry addresses the life-planet identification with unusual simplicity of style and complexity of effect." Snyder was born on May 8, 1930, in San Francisco, and grew up in the Pacific Northwest, spending much of his time enjoying the outdoors. He received a dual degree in anthropology and literature from Reed College in Portland, Oregon, in 1951. While at Reed College, Snyder roomed with fellow poets Philip Whalen and Lew Welch. Looking back on his Reed College experience, Snyder remarked in his 1980 book, *The Real Work: Interviews & Talks 1964–1979*, "I was in an atmosphere that challenged me and pushed me to the utmost, which was just what I needed. They wouldn't tolerate bullshit, made me clean up my prose style, exposed me to all varieties of intellectual positions and gave me a territory in which I could speak out my radical politics and get arguments and augmentations on it. It was an intensive, useful experience."

After graduation, Snyder headed to the Bay Area, started studying Zen Buddhism, spent his summer as a fire lookout in the Pacific Northwest, and joined the so-called San Francisco Renaissance. Snyder was among six poets who took part in the famous Six Gallery Reading on October 7, 1955. Snyder was in the unenviable position of having to follow Allen Ginsberg, who had just read "Howl" to a stunned audience. However, Snyder reportedly performed admirably with his spirited reading of "A Berry Feast."

Snyder and Jack Kerouac became good friends and hiked Matterhorn Peak in California together. Snyder, who had served as a fire lookout for two summers on Crater Mountain in 1952 and Sourdough Mountain in 1953, encouraged Kerouac to try it out. Kerouac based the character "Japhy Ryder" in his 1958 novel *The Dharma Bums* on Snyder. An idealistic, meditative vagabond, Ryder spouts off such lines as "You and I ain't out to bust anybody's skull, or cut someone's throat in an economic way, we've dedicated ourselves to prayer for all sentient beings and when we're strong enough we'll really be able to do it, too, like the old saints. Who knows, the world might wake up and burst out into a beautiful flower of Dharma everywhere." Snyder also appeared as "Jarry Wagner" in Kerouac's 1965 novel, *Desolation Angels*.

Snyder lived in Japan where he studied Zen Buddhism between 1956 and 1964. His first book, *Riprap*, was published in 1959 and drew on his experiences as a forest lookout. Snyder and poet Joanne Kyger were married from 1960 to 1965. Snyder's 1974 book of poetry, *Turtle Island*, won the Pulitzer Prize for poetry. He received an American Book Award for *Axe Handles* (1983). In *A Place in Space* (1995), Snyder wrote, "The marks of Buddhist teaching are impermanence, no-self, the inevitability of suffering and connectedness, emptiness, the vastness of mind, and a way to realization." Snyder was elected a Chancellor of the Academy of American Poets in 2003 and received the 2012 Wallace Stevens Award for lifetime achievement by the Academy of American Poets. He has also taught creative writing at the University of California, Davis, and was featured in John J. Healy's 2010 documentary, *The Practice of the Wild*, which made its debut at the fifty-third San Francisco International Film Festival.

Essential Reading: *Riprap* (1959), *Myths & Texts* (1960), *The Back Country* (1967), *Turtle Island* (1974), *The Real Work: Interviews & Talks 1964–1979* (1980), *The Practice of the Wild* (1990), *Danger on Peaks* (2005), *Back on the Fire: Essays* (2007).

2

A Path to Paradise

Defining Characteristics of the Beat Generation

Writers of the Beat Generation for the most part shared a common sensibility that encompassed a rejection of conventional values and a free-flowing writing style that invoked the rhythms of jazz and the romantic legacy of spontaneity. In 1982, Allen Ginsberg published "A Definition of the Beat Generation" in *Friction* No. 1 (Winter 1982) that summarized the "essential effects" of the Beat Generation as: spiritual liberation, sexual revolution, liberation of the world from censorship, demystification and/or decriminalization of cannabis and other drugs, evolution of rhythm and blues into rock and roll as a high art form, spread of ecological consciousness, respect for land and indigenous peoples and creatures, opposition to the military-industrial machine civilization, and the development of a "second religiousness" within an advanced civilization. According to William S. Burroughs in a 1986 interview with *New Letters*, "The Beat movement was more sociological than literary. Of course, the Beat writers have something in common, but not a great deal from a literary point of view, despite a certain continuity of ideas." In an interview that appeared in *Beat Writers at Work* (1999), Lawrence Ferlinghetti remarked, "Most of the tenets of the counterculture of the sixties were first annunciated by the Beat writers: the first stirrings of ecological consciousness, the first movement towards Far Eastern philosophy, Buddhism, pacifism, the first use of psychedelics to expand consciousness since Poe and Fitzhugh Ludlow [American author of *The Hasheesh Eater*, 1857]."

Experimental Writing Styles

The Beat writers opened up the possibilities of literature at a time when the American literary landscape had been dominated for years by modernist poets such as T. S. Eliot, Ezra Pound, and E. E. Cummings. Heavily influenced by the poetry of William Blake, Walt Whitman's *Leaves of Grass*, and William

Carlos Williams's *Paterson*, Allen Ginsberg employed a free verse style that emphasized his natural poetic voice and the uninhibited free expression of ideas. J. D. McClatchy, editor of the *Yale Review*, called Ginsberg "a bard in the old manner—outsized, darkly prophetic, part exuberance, part prayer, part rant."

Jack Kerouac believed in a theory of "spontaneous prose," where the novelist or poet wrote whatever came to mind, "all first-person, fast, mad, confessional," much like the improvisation evident in jazz music. His most experimental novel, *Visions of Cody*, blended stream-of-consciousness narrative with taped transcripts of conversations between Kerouac and Neal Cassady, who served as the inspiration for "Dean Moriarty," the hero of *On the Road*.

The spontaneity evident in many early works of the Beat Generation was directly influenced by the style of jazz prevalent in the 1940s and 1950s known as bebop. Released in 2012, *Beat Generation Jazz* features the music of legendary bebop pioneers, including Charlie Parker, Dizzy Gillespie, Thelonious Monk, and others.   *Author's collection*

Kerouac remarked, "By not revising what you've already written, you simply give the reader the actual workings of your mind during the writing itself: you confess your thoughts about events in your own unchangeable way" (*Conversations with Kerouac*, 2005). Kerouac even wrote an essay about the spontaneous prose method titled "Belief and Technique for Modern Prose" (first published in *Evergreen Review*, 1959), which listed thirty "essentials," such as "Write in recollection and amazement for yourself." Ironically, Kerouac was also known for relying on his notebooks and journals, which he carried everywhere, as well as making careful revisions to his manuscripts.

William S. Burroughs moved from the straightforward narratives of his early novels *Junkie* and *Queer* to the fragmentary "routines" of *Naked Lunch*, followed by the cut-up novels that make up the Nova Trilogy (*The Soft Machine*, *Nova Express*, and *The Ticket That Exploded*). According to Burroughs in a 1965 *Paris Review* interview, "It is unfortunately one of the great errors of Western thought, the whole either/or proposition. You remember [Alfred] Korzybski and his idea of non-Aristotelian logic. Either/or thinking is just not accurate thinking. That's not the way things occur, and I feel the Aristotelian construct is one of the great shackles of Western civilization. Cut-ups are a movement toward breaking this down."

The Beats also thrived on collaboration, such as Burroughs and Kerouac working on their famous hardboiled novel, *The Hippos Were Boiled in Their Tanks* (written in 1945 but not published until 2008), based on Lucien Carr's killing of David Kammerer. Burroughs and Ginsberg collaborated on *The Yage Letters* (1963), while Kerouac and composer David Amram held jazz poetry readings in the late 1950s. Starting in the 1980s, poet Michael McClure took the stage with keyboardist Ray Manzarek of the Doors on a self-described "musical mind expanding journey of their creations" (recorded for posterity in the 2012 CD *Piano Poems: Live in San Francisco*). Last but not least, Burroughs, Brion Gysin, Gregory Corso, and South African poet Sinclair Beiles collaborated on the 1960 cut-up work *Minutes to Go*.

Autobiographical, Confessional Poetry and Prose

The Beats departed from the strict formalism of American modernism poetry and moved toward autobiographical, confessional poetry and prose. Nearly everything Jack Kerouac wrote was autobiographical, although embellished and shaped through many revisions. In fact, Kerouac only reluctantly changed names at the request of his publishers in order to avoid litigation.

In his author's note to *Big Sur* (1962), Kerouac wrote, "My work comprises one vast book like Proust's except that my remembrances are written on the run instead of afterwards in a sick bed. Because of the objections of my early publishers I was not allowed to use the same personae names in each work. *On the Road, The Subterraneans, The Dharma Bums, Doctor Sax, Maggie Cassidy, Tristessa, Desolation Angels, Visions of Cody*, and the others including this book *Big Sur* are just chapters in the whole work which I call The Duluoz Legend. In my old age I intend to collect all my work and re-insert my pantheon of uniform names, leave the long shelf full of books there, and die happy. The whole thing forms one enormous comedy, seen through the eyes of poor Ti Jean (me), otherwise known as Jack Duluoz, the world of raging action and folly and also of gentle sweetness seen through the keyhole of his eye."

Ginsberg's landmark poem "Howl," which was published by City Lights in *Howl and Other Poems* (1956), highlights a variety of real-life incidents, including Herbert Huncke's release from Rikers Island Prison, Bill Cannastra's bizarre death in a subway accident, Tuli Kupferberg's leap off the Manhattan Bridge in a failed suicide attempt, and Carl Solomon throwing potato salad in a Dadaesque gesture during a college lecture, among many others. He also refers to Neal Cassady as "N.C."—"the secret hero of these poems."

Much of William S. Burroughs's early work is semi-autobiographical, including his novels *Junkie* (1953) and *Queer* (written in the early 1950s but not published until 1985). Interestingly, Burroughs's work is nearly devoid of any mention of his common-law wife, Joan Vollmer, or any of the other major Beat writers, such as Jack Kerouac or Allen Ginsberg. Burroughs, who appears as the anonymous "William Lee" in many of his writings, also served as the inspiration for "Old Bull Lee" in *On the Road.*

Anarchic Individualism

The Beat Generation evolved out of a malaise toward the widespread conformity and repression characterized by post–World War II America. The Beats in general rejected traditional American middle-class values in search of individual freedom—quite daring in the era of McCarthyism. In his Zen Buddhism–inspired 1958 novel, *The Dharma Bums*, Jack Kerouac wrote, "Colleges being nothing but grooming schools for the middleclass non-identity which usually finds its perfect expression on the outskirts of the campus in rows of well-to-do houses with lawns and television sets in each living room with everybody looking at the same thing and thinking the same thing at the same time while the Japhies of the world go prowling in the wilderness." Poet Jack Micheline later took the quest for individualism one step farther, accusing Beat writers themselves of becoming the establishment: "I never thought creativity had anything to do with publishers or art galleries!

It's a private fucking thing. Between me and my muse. Between me and my spirit. What's it got to do with Ferlinghetti? Or any of these other cocksuckers? . . . I'm not a critic of the establishment, I'm anti-establishment. There's a difference. I'm anti-Ginsberg. Ginsberg *is* the establishment."

Quest for Authentic Experience

Cold War disillusionment led the Beat Generation writers on a quest for authentic experience in the increasingly rigid air of conformity that overtook the United States during the 1950s. The Beats were aspiring to a "New Vision" as outlined by Lucien Carr and Allen Ginsberg at Columbia University during the early 1940s that "assumed the death of square morality and replaced that meaning with belief in creativity," according to Ginsberg (*The Beats: From Kerouac to Kesey*, 2007). According to William S. Burroughs, "The people in the Beat movement—myself, Gregory Corso, Allen, Jack Kerouac—we were quite different artistically. But we were together in the simple concept of openness and expanding awareness." In an interview, Gary Snyder remarked, "I don't think people are going to get their values off the Internet. I think they're going to have to get their values in communities with their peers, with their workmates, and form their agenda that way . . . What about some young person who simply watches TV six hours a day? What picture do they form of the world?"

Deliberate Rootlessness

In a 1934 article for *Fortune* magazine titled "The Great American Roadside," writer James Agee commented, "We are restive entirely for the sake of restiveness. Whatever we may think, we move for no better reason than for the plain unvarnished hell of it. And there is no better reason." The freedom of the open road provides one of the most enduring images of Jack Kerouac's 1957 novel, *On the Road*, which in some aspects was simply an outgrowth of the hobo literature prevalent in the United States during the early decades of the twentieth century. In her introduction to *Desolation Angels* (1995 edition), Joyce Johnson wrote, "[Kerouac] was a man without a home, stopping off in different places, then moving on. I think he always fantasized that in some new destination he might find a balance between his craving for novelty and companionship and the reclusive side of his nature."

Early classics of hobo literature include *The Road* (1907) by Jack London, in which the author of *The Call of the Wild* wrote, "Perhaps the greatest charm of tramp-life is the absence of monotony. In Hobo Land the face of life is

The restiveness and thirst for adventure exemplified in Jack Kerouac's 1957 novel, *On the Road*, hearkened back to the widespread proliferation of hobo literature during the early twentieth century, such as Jack Black's *You Can't Win* (1926), which also influenced the writings of William S. Burroughs.   *Author's collection*

protean—an ever changing phantasmagoria, where the impossible happens and the unexpected jumps out of the bushes at every turn of the road. The hobo never knows what is going to happen the next moment; hence, he lives only in the present moment. He has learned the futility of telic endeavor, and knows the delight of drifting along with the whimsicalities of Chance."

Other classics of hobo literature include *Life and Adventures of A-No. 1: America's Most Celebrated Tramp* (1910) by Leon Ray Livingston, *Tramping on*

Life: An Autobiographical Narrative (1922) by Harry Kemp, *Beggars of Life* (1924) by Jim Tully, *You Can't Win* (1926) by Jack Black (which captivated a young William S. Burroughs and influenced his writings), *Waiting for Nothing* (1935) by Tom Kromer, *Sister of the Road: The Autobiography of Boxcar Bertha* (1937) "as told to" Ben Reitman, and *Bound for Glory* (1943) by Woody Guthrie, among others.

Although Kerouac himself immortalized hitchhiking in *On the Road*, by the early 1950s, the activity had started to lose its appeal, as evidenced in the creepy 1953 film noir *The Hitch-Hiker*, which was directed by Ida Lupino. The tagline asked, "Who'll be his *next* victim . . . YOU?" In his 1962 novel, *Big Sur*, Kerouac depicts a failed attempt at hitchhiking: "This is the first time I've hitch hiked in years and I soon begin to see that things have changed in America, you can't get a ride anymore."

Other iconic works of American road literature include *Travels with Charley* (1962) by John Steinbeck, *The Electric Kool-Aid Acid Test* (1968) by Tom Wolfe, *Fear and Loathing in Las Vegas: A Savage Journey to the Heart of the American Dream* (1971) by Hunter S. Thompson, *Zen and the Art of Motorcycle Maintenance* (1974) by Robert M. Pirsig, *Blue Highways* (1982) by William Least Heat-Moon, and *The Lost Continent: Travels in Small-Town America* (1989) by Bill Bryson.

Affinity with Outlaw Culture

After reading the classic hobo tale *You Can't Win* (1926) by Jack Black as a youth, William S. Burroughs became fascinated with the world of small-time criminals. Street hustler and drug addict Herbert Huncke served as a "Virgil" for Burroughs and other early Beat writers, introducing them to the lower depths of the underworld culture of Times Square during the early 1940s. Along with Phil White (the inspiration for "Sailor" in *Naked Lunch*), Burroughs would "roll drunks" in the New York City subways. In the 1960s, Ken Kesey, along with his Merry Pranksters, carried on the outlaw tradition, remarking, "If society wants me to be an outlaw, then I'll be an outlaw and a damned good one—that's something people need. People at all times need outlaws" (*Hippie*, 2005).

The Outlaw Bible of American Literature (2004), which was edited by Alan Kaufman, Barney Rosset, and Neil Ortenberg, features excerpts from the very best of outlaw culture, including *Naked Lunch* (Burroughs), *On the Road* (Jack Kerouac), *Baby Driver* (Jan Kerouac), *Last Exit to Brooklyn* (Hubert Selby Jr.), *How to Talk Dirty and Influence People* (Lenny Bruce), *Cool Hand Luke* (Donn Pearce), *The Basketball Diaries* (Jim Carroll), *Pimp* (Iceberg Slim), *Drugstore Cowboy* (James Fogle), *Leaving Las Vegas* (John O'Brien), and others.

Indifference to Materialism

Jack Kerouac once stated, "Everything belongs to me because I'm poor." In *Jack's Book* (1978), Joyce Johnson remarked that Kerouac "had very little money. He was one of those people who knew how to live on nothing. He really just owned the clothes on his back." In *The Holy Barbarians* (1959), Venice Beach poet Lawrence Lipton wrote, "In a society geared to the production of murderous hardware and commodities with built-in obsolescence for minimum use at maximum prices on an artificially stimulated mass consumption basis, poverty by choice is subversive . . ." According to poet Jack Micheline in a 1997 *Chiron* interview, "The people are totally seduced in this nation. I'm looking for the rare human being. Most people give up everything just to stay alive. They work at jobs they don't like. They kiss the boss's ass, whom they despise. They compromise everything beautiful in life, just to stay alive. This is true capitalism. You can be mediocre and be a millionaire. This country is afraid of people who have their own mind. If you're poor, you're supposed to be a sheep or a clone. God bless the animals."

According to Neeli Cherkovski in *Whitman's Wild Children* (1989), "Compressed into 'Howl' is an anthem, hardly muted by the passing of time, to the poet's friendship with people who felt dispossessed by the emerging post–World War II dream of America. Ginsberg did not buy the package of goods offered by the emerging consumerism the country was experiencing, nor could postwar optimism about a healthy economy placate yearnings for a greater sense of freedom."

Self-Exploration Through Drug Use

The early Beat circle that centered on and around Columbia University in the early 1940s experimented with drugs such as marijuana, morphine, and especially Benzedrine. William S. Burroughs expertly (and disturbingly!) chronicled his descent into the underworld drug culture of New York, New Orleans, and Mexico City in his first published novel, *Junkie* (1953). It was actually Herbert Huncke ("Herman" in *Junkie*) who gave Burroughs his first shot of morphine. Of course, *Naked Lunch* (1959) further explores the horrors of drug addiction in nightmarish detail. Burroughs portrayed "Old Tom the Junkie Priest" in Gus Van Sant's 1989 cult film, *Drugstore Cowboy*.

Allen Ginsberg was one of the first participants in Timothy Leary's psychedelic experiments at Harvard University, and eventually recruited Burroughs and Jack Kerouac, who were both less than enthusiastic. In the 1960s, Ginsberg was an outspoken advocate for the legalization of marijuana. Kerouac reportedly wrote his novellas *The Subterraneans* on Benzedrine in just three days and *Tristessa* on morphine. After becoming the notorious "King of the Beatniks" with the success of *On the Road* in 1957, Kerouac gradually descended into the throes of alcoholism, as depicted in his 1962 novel, *Big Sur*. In 1963, Burroughs and Ginsberg collaborated on *The Yage Letters* (1963), which features correspondence based on Burroughs's 1953 travels through South America in search of the hallucinogenic drug.

Ecological Consciousness

Through their poetry, essays, and social activism, the Beats helped intro-duce ecology and environmentalism to mainstream America. In a 2014 *San Francisco Examiner* interview, poet Michael McClure remarked, "We were environmentalists, though there were times when we talked about the environment and audiences booed us . . . I remember falling in love with the wildflowers, the beauty of the ocean and Mount Tam, and I remember growing to hate all the wars. Roads were narrower then, traffic was lighter; the natural world seemed so close. Then houses crawled up all the hills, and there were more and more people, more cars, more everything. I belong to a generation that wasn't trained by the computer. I read a lot of books. I still do."

Known as the "Poet Laureate of Deep Ecology," Gary Snyder is the Beat writer perhaps most often associated with environmental concerns. Snyder's Pulitzer Prize–winning book, *Turtle Island* (1974), features some of his best ecological poems and essays. In *Turtle Island*, Snyder wrote, "We have it within our deepest powers not only to change our 'selves' but to change our culture. If man is to remain on earth he must transform the five-millenia-long urban-izing civilization tradition into an ecologically-sensitive harmony-oriented wild-minded scientific-spiritual culture." Snyder's deep compassion for the environment can also be witnessed in his 1980 book of ecological speeches and interviews, *The Real Work: Interviews and Talks 1964–1979*. Bruce Cook, the author of *The Beat Generation* (1971), has remarked, "If Ginsberg is the Beat movement's Walt Whitman, Gary Snyder is the Henry David Thoreau."

In his 1991 novella, *Ghost of a Chance*, William S. Burroughs lamented the destruction of the Amazon rainforests: "All going, to make room for more and more devalued human stock, with less and less of the wild spark, the priceless ingredient—energy into matter. A vast mudslide of soulless sludge."

Interest in Eastern Religion

The Beats, especially Jack Kerouac, Allen Ginsberg, Gary Snyder, Philip Whalen, Michael McClure, and Diane di Prima, were heavily influenced by the study of Buddhism and always thought of themselves as spiritual seekers. Ginsberg even referred to Kerouac as the "new Buddha of American prose" in the dedication to "Howl," while Snyder studied Zen Buddhism in Japan for many years during the late 1950s and 1960s, and Whalen actually became a Zen Buddhist monk in the 1970s. Snyder was influenced by both Zen scholar D. T. Suzuki (*An Introduction to Zen Buddhism*, 1934) and Eastern philosopher Alan Watts (*The Way of Zen*, 1957).

Of course, Kerouac's 1958 novel, *The Dharma Bums*, highlights the main character "Ray Smith" (Kerouac's alter ego) as he searches for enlightenment with the help of his Zen Buddhist buddy, "Japhy Ryder" (poet Gary Snyder). Although fascinated with Buddhism, Kerouac stayed true to his Catholic roots and even remarked in *Satori in Paris* (1966), "I'm not a Buddhist, I'm a Catholic revisiting the ancestral land that fought for Catholicism against impossible odds yet won in the end." Written in the 1950s but not published until 1999 by City Lights, Kerouac's book *Some of the Dharma* features "notes on Buddhist study and practice, poems, haiku, conversations, prayers, meditations, journal entries, sketches, stories, thoughts on writing, fragments of letters, epiphanies and more."

In 1974, Ginsberg cofounded with Anne Waldman the Jack Kerouac School of Disembodied Poetics at the Naropa Institute (now known as Naropa University), a Buddhist-inspired, student-centered liberal arts university in Boulder, Colorado. In addition to Ginsberg and Waldman, Burroughs, di Prima, Gregory Corso, and Peter Orlovsky all taught at the Jack Kerouac School at one time or another.

Michael McClure's Zen poems were included in the 1999 collection *Touching the Edge*, which was subtitled *Dharma Devotions from the Hummingbird Sangha*. In addition, spirited analysis of the relationship between Buddhism and the Beat Generation can be found in the 1981 book *How the Swans Came to the Lake: A Narrative History of Buddhism in America* by Rick Fields, an early instructor at the Jack Kerouac School of Disembodied Poetics.

3

Just the Froth Riding on a Wave

Beat Generation Influences

Unique among literary movements, the Beat writers were influenced not only by authors such as the English Romantic poets (especially William Blake and Percy Bysshe Shelley), Walt Whitman (*Leaves of Grass*), Fyodor Dostoevsky (*Notes from Underground*), William Carlos Williams (*Paterson*), and Thomas Wolfe (*Look Homeward, Angel*), but also by such eclectic sources as pulp magazines (particularly *The Shadow*); Surrealism; Jack Black's classic of hobo literature, *You Can't Win* (1926); jazz music (especially bebop); and Abstract Expressionism.

Romanticism

The English Romantic poets of the late eighteenth and early nineteenth centuries rebelled against the intellectualism of the Enlightenment—cultivating individualism and favoring more natural, emotional, and personal artistic themes—in a similar way that the Beats rejected the formalism of the American modernist poets. In addition to Percy Bysshe Shelley and William Blake, English Romantic poets included William Wordsworth, Samuel Taylor Coleridge, Lord Byron, and John Keats. Famous works of the Romantic era include *The Marriage of Heaven and Hell* (Blake), *Ozymandias* (Shelley), *The Rime of the Ancient Mariner* (Coleridge), *Don Juan* (Lord Byron), and "Ode on a Grecian Urn" (Keats). In his preface to *Lyrical Ballads* (1798), a collection of poems by Wordsworth and Coleridge, Wordsworth defined poetry as "the spontaneous overflow of powerful feelings" that "takes its origin from emotion recollected in tranquility."

Shelley (1792–1822), remained a strong influence on Gregory Corso throughout his life, and the Beat poet is actually buried at the foot of Shelley's grave at the Protestant Cemetery in Rome, Italy. Author Bruce Cook even went so far as to call Corso an "urchin Shelley" in his 1971 book, *The Beat Generation*.

In 1954, Corso moved to Cambridge and spent most of his time in Harvard University's Widener Library reading Shelley and other Romantic poets. In addition, Ginsberg acknowledged the influence of Shelley's "Adonais" on his poem "Kaddish." Fellow Beat poet Michael McClure compared Ginsberg's "Howl" to Shelley's 1813 poem "Queen Mab."

However, Ginsberg's main influence among the English Romantic poets was Blake. Ginsberg considered Blake to be a prophet, and his "Blakean vision" in 1948 proved to be a major turning point in his life. When Ginsberg first met McClure at a party in San Francisco, the two engaged in a long discussion of Blake. McClure said, "I was writing poems in the style of Blake when I was seventeen . . . I used to dream I was Blake!" The poetry of William Blake later proved influential to songwriters Bob Dylan and Jim Morrison of the Doors, as well as filmmaker Jim Jarmusch. Ginsberg and Dylan even recorded two Blake songs together: "Nurse's Song" and "The Tyger." In Jarmusch's 1995 existential western, *Dead Man*, the main character portrayed by Johnny Depp is named "William Blake."

Walt Whitman

"I sound my barbaric yawp over the roofs of the world." With his spirited celebration of individualism and nature, Walt Whitman would have fit right in with the Beat Generation. According to Nancy J. Peters, writer, publisher and co-owner of City Lights Bookstore, the Beat writers "were part of a sizable postwar generation that propelled American literature and culture in a radical new direction . . . Walt Whitman's democratic spirit had been unloosed in the land, with compelling prose and poetry—spontaneous, audacious, candid, and accessible." Along with Thomas Wolfe, Walt Whitman was one of Jack Kerouac's earliest influences. Kerouac even wrote an essay titled "Whitman: A Prophet of the Sexual Revolution" for one of Alfred Kazin's literature courses at the New School in 1948. Published in *Howl and Other Poems* in 1956, Allen Ginsberg's "A Supermarket in California," one of his most popular poems, served as a tribute to Whitman upon the centennial of the first edition of *Leaves of Grass*.

In a 2008 interview with *Beatdom*, Neeli Cherkovski remarked, "'Song of the Open Road,' one of Whitman's greatest poems, resonates, of course with Jack Kerouac's *On the Road*. [Charles] Bukowski once wrote . . . that Allen Ginsberg has been the most awakening force in American poetry since Walt Whitman. He was writing specifically of Ginsberg's 'Howl.'" According to Gary Snyder (*The Real Work*, 1980), "What I read Whitman for is inspiration. He's inspiring. I love to read 'The Song of the Open Road,' or 'By Blue

Ontario's Shores,' or 'Passage to India'—I love to read 'em aloud, to a small audience. He's a good *communal* poet in that way."

Whitman was born on Long Island, New York, on May 31, 1819. *Leaves of Grass* was first published with just twelve poems in 1855 at Whitman's own expense, but the poet continued revising and enlarging his masterpiece right up to his death (the so-called "Deathbed Edition" of the book was published in 1891, a year before he died). Upon reading the book, author Ralph Waldo Emerson sent Whitman a letter on July 21, 1855, exclaiming, "I find [*Leaves of Grass*] the most extraordinary piece of wit and wisdom that America has yet contributed . . . I greet you at the beginning of a great career." (Lawrence Ferlinghetti used these same words when he dropped Ginsberg a note, asking him if he could publish *Howl and Other Poems* in his Pocket Poets Series.) Whitman went ahead and published Emerson's letter (without his consent!) in the *New York Tribune* in order to promote the book.

However, *Leaves of Grass* had its fair share of critics, such as the *Boston Intelligencer*, which declared the book a "heterogeneous mess of bombast, egotism, vulgarity, and nonsense. The author should be kicked from all decent society as below the level of a brute—it seems he must be some escaped lunatic, raving in pitiable delirium." The *Cincinnati Commercial* called Whitman "the laureate of the empty deep incomprehensible." The publishing history of *Leaves of Grass* mirrored *Howl and Other Poems* in that both books faced controversy and attempts at censorship. In 1882, *Leaves of Grass* was banned in Boston after Boston district attorney Oliver Stevens, who claimed that it was "obscene literature," demanded that some of the poems be excised in the next edition. Of course, Whitman refused.

Known as the "Bard of Democracy," acclaimed nineteenth-century poet Walt Whitman celebrated American individualism in his epic book of poetry, *Leaves of Grass*, a work that strongly influenced many of the young Beat writers, especially Allen Ginsberg and Jack Kerouac.

Photo by George C. Cox/Library of Congress/Wikimedia Commons

In *Scratching the Beat Surface* (1982), Michael McClure wrote, "I believe that the cosmic scale of Whitman's 'Song of Myself,' the experience seed of *Leaves of Grass*, was already manifest and was demonstrated within visionary precepts. The awareness that we are without proportion, and that living beings are proportionless, seemed natural. We who felt deeply in the cold fifties were monists and animists. The fifties were most distinguished in the mental field by the creative energy of the artists and poets, and by the war neurosis of the country at large."

Fyodor Dostoevsky

The impact of great nineteenth-century Russian novelist Fyodor Dostoevsky (1821–81), who is sometimes considered to be the "Father of Existentialism," can be found throughout the works of the Beat writers, especially Jack Kerouac, who shared his enthusiasm for both Dostoevsky and Thomas Wolfe with others in the Beat circle during the 1940s. Dostoevsky's major works include *Notes from Underground* (1864), *Crime and Punishment* (1866), *The Idiot* (1869), *The Possessed* (1872), and *The Brothers Karamazov* (1880), among others. According to Ginsberg in a 1983 interview, "We, meaning Kerouac, myself, and Burroughs, all read a lot of Russian literature, Dostoevsky particularly. The first sort of meeting of minds that Kerouac and I had was over the fact that we both read Dostoevsky's *Idiot*. And we identified with Alyosha and Myshkin. And Burroughs was very interested in [Dostoevsky's] nutty-man confessional."

While working on his first published novel, *The Town and the City*, Kerouac wrote in his journal (June 19, 1947), "I concluded that Dostoevsky's wisdom is the highest wisdom of the world, because it is not only Christ's wisdom, but a Karamazov Christ of lusts and glees." In a March 1950 journal entry, Kerouac stated that "the greatness of Dostoevsky lies in his recognition of human love." In an interview that appeared in *Jack's Book*, John Clellon Holmes commented that Kerouac "had a tremendously free and easy feeling about Dostoevsky. He treated it like reality. So we would talk about characters as if they were real. We'd spend whole nights saying, 'Kirillov wouldn't say that, he'd say *this*,' and we'd invent whole conversations and scenes."

Kerouac later consciously modeled his 1958 novella, *The Subterraneans*, on Dostoevsky's 1864 novel, *Notes from Underground*, calling it "a full confession of one's most wretched and hidden agonies after an affair of any kind. The prose is what I believe to be the prose of the future, from both the conscious top and the unconscious bottom of the mind, limited only by the limitations of time flying by as our mind flies by with it." Last but not least, in their famous psychiatric hospital meeting, Ginsberg introduced himself as "Myshkin" from *The Idiot*, and Carl Solomon replied that he was "Kirillov" from *The Possessed*.

Pulp Magazines

Jack Kerouac, Allen Ginsberg, and William S. Burroughs all acknowledged the influence of pulp magazines (named because of the cheap wood pulp paper used to print them) on their later work. Pulp magazines (a.k.a. "pulps") were extremely popular during the 1920s and 1930s, such as *Amazing Stories, The Shadow, Doc Savage, Weird Tales, Black Mask, Planet Stories, Dime Detective, Flying Aces, Marvel Tales, Spicy Detective,* and *Unknown,* among others. A March 1936 issue of *The Shadow* featured the tagline "How Did The Shadow Defeat Horrible Murder Plans of Witch Doctor?" A 1939 promotional advertisement for *The Shadow* exclaimed, "The Shadow, scourge of the underworld, nemesis of crime, blasting his way through the evil machinations of master minds to justice! Mystery and action, packed with suspense and thrills, in every issue. A complete book-length novel; short detective stories, codes, crime problems, and other features pack every issue of this powerful mystery magazine."

Kerouac's 1959 fantasy novel, *Doctor Sax,* served as a tribute to the pulp magazine characters (especially "The Shadow") he had loved as a child growing up in Lowell, Massachusetts. The author even adapted the book as a screenplay that was never filmed. In *Doctor Sax,* Kerouac wrote, "On Saturday night I was settling down alone in the house with magazines, reading *Doc Savage* or the *Phantom Detective* with *his* masky rainy night—*The Shadow Magazine* I saved for Friday night, Saturday morning was always the world of gold and rich sunlight."

In a 1957 interview with the *Village Voice,* Kerouac named the then-unpublished *Doctor Sax* as his best book, describing it as "a kind of Gothic fairy tale, a myth of puberty, about some kids in New England playing around in this empty place when a shadow comes out at them, a real shadow." In addition, Burroughs's first published novel, *Junkie* (1953), was written in the confessional style of the pulp magazines under the pseudonym "William Lee" and even featured the subtitle *Confessions of an Unredeemed Drug Addict,* along with a sensational, pulp-style front cover. Burroughs singled out *Black Mask, Weird Tales,* and *Amazing Stories* among the pulps he read in his youth.

Director Quentin Tarantino paid tribute to the pulp craze with the title of his 1994 *Pulp Fiction* (the original title being *Black Mask*). Tarantino has remarked that he originally intended "to do a *Black Mask* movie—like that old detective story magazine . . . it kind of went somewhere else" (*Filmmaker Magazine,* Summer 1994).

Surrealism

Surrealist Marcel Duchamp once remarked, "I tell them that the tricks of today are the truths of tomorrow." The psychoanalytic work of Sigmund Freud and Carl Jung paved the way for Surrealism (the term was originally coined by poet Guillaume Apollinaire in 1917), which was founded in Paris by a small group of writers and artists. In 1924, Andre Breton published the *Le manifeste du surréalisme* ("The Manifesto of Surrealism") in which he defined Surrealism as "psychic automatism in its pure state, by which one proposes to express—verbally, by means of the written word, or in any other manner—the actual functioning of thought." The Surrealist circle included a diverse array of artists, such as Max Ernst, Jean Arp, Man Ray, Joan Miró, and Salvador Dali.

San Francisco–born poet Philip Lamantia is the Beat writer most closely associated with Surrealism. His first encounter with Surrealism occurred at a Salvador Dali retrospective at the San Francisco Museum of Art, followed by a Joan Miró exhibition. Lamantia's first surrealist poems were featured in the Spring 1943 issue of *View: A Magazine of the Arts*, published by artist and writer Charles Henri Ford. A fifteen-year-old high school dropout at the time, Lamantia moved to New York City and became assistant editor at *View*. Lamantia soon became acquainted with Breton, the "Pope of Surrealism," who he thought was "the most important poet and mind of the century."

Breton was so impressed with Lamantia—describing him as "a voice that rises once in a hundred years"—that he published him in the experimental Surrealist magazine *VVV* in 1944. Lamantia documented his encounters with Breton in "Poem for Andre Breton," which is included in *Bed of Sphinxes: New & Selected Poems 1943–1993* (City Lights Books, 1997). Lamantia's Surrealistic style is evidenced in the poem "I Am Coming," which includes such imagery as "the wavering moon," "valleys of beautiful arson," and "men eating wild minutes from a clock."

Lamantia soon moved back to San Francisco and introduced Surrealist poetry to other Beat writers. According to Lawrence Ferlinghetti, Lamantia was "the primary transmitter of French Surrealist poetry in this country. He was writing stream-of-consciousness Surrealist poetry and he had a huge influence on Allen Ginsberg. Before that, Ginsberg was writing rather conventional poetry. It was Lamantia who turned him on to Surrealist writing. Then Ginsberg wrote 'Howl'" (*SFGate*, March 11, 2005). Michael McClure called Lamantia "a poet of the imagination" whose poetry was "hyper-personal visionary Surrealism." Other Beat poets influenced by Surrealism include Gregory Corso, Bob Kaufman, and Ted Joans, whose motto was "Jazz is my religion, and Surrealism is my point of view."

Jack Black, Author of *You Can't Win* (1926)

In his groundbreaking work of hobo literature, *You Can't Win* (1926), Jack Black wrote, "Looking back at it, it seems to me that I was blown here and there like a dead leaf whipped about by the autumn winds till at last it finds lodgment in some cozy fence corner." A legendary hobo, opium addict, convict, and professional thief who specialized in safe cracking, Jack Black (no relation to the *School of Rock* star) wrote the gritty, bestselling autobiography, which strongly influenced a young William S. Burroughs.

The book, which immerses readers in a colorful world of freight hoppers, hobo jungles, seedy rooming houses, pool parlors, and opium dens, is full of memorable characters, such as "Salt Chunk Mary," "Montana Blacky," the "Sanctimonious Kid," "Foot-and-a-half George," "Irish Annie," and "Rebel George," among many others. To Black, the extended "Johnson Family" of bums and thieves maintained their dignity by keeping their word and minding their own business. Black's final words of wisdom? "All I can say with certainty is that kindness begets kindness, and cruelty begets cruelty. You can make your choice and reap as you sow."

Among those individuals Black dedicates *You Can't Win* to is "that dirty, drunken, disreputable, crippled beggar, 'Sticks' Sullivan, who picked the buckshot out of my back—under the bridge—at Baraboo, Wisconsin." *You Can't Win* is full of colorful slang words, such as "yegg" (safe cracker), "Dr. Hall" (alcohol), "yaffled" (arrested), and "skookum house" (jail). Born in Vancouver, British Columbia, in 1871, Black claimed his childhood hero was the outlaw Jesse James. After the success of *You Can't Win*, Black wrote a screenplay called *Salt Chunk Mary* in the early 1930s and then disappeared for good. According to rumors, he committed suicide by drowning.

In 1988, *You Can't Win* was republished by Amok Books (billing it as a "lost classic of American road literature") with a foreword by Burroughs and cover illustration by visionary apocalyptic artist Joe Coleman. More of Coleman's fascinating *You Can't Win* illustrations can be found in the 1994 book *Cosmic Retribution: The Infernal Art of Joe Coleman*. In his foreword to *You Can't Win*, Burroughs waxed nostalgic for "a chapter of specifically American life that is now gone forever. Where are the hobo jungles, the hop joints, the old rod-riding yeggs, where is Salt Chunk Mary? As another thief, Francois Villon, said, 'Where are the snows of yesteryear?' In the words of poets and writers, in the pictures of painters."

The impact of *You Can't Win* is evident in several of Burroughs's novels, most prominently *Junkie* (1953), which was subtitled *Confessions of an Unredeemed Drug Addict*. In addition, Burroughs wrote an essay about *You Can't Win* titled "The Johnson Family" that appeared in *The Adding Machine: Selected*

Essays (1986). In 2000, *You Can't Win* was republished by AK Press and again included an introduction by Burroughs. Actor Michael Pitt starred in a 2015 film adaptation of *You Can't Win* directed by Robinson Devor.

William Carlos Williams

Highly influential American modernist poet William Carlos Williams was born on September 17, 1883, in Rutherford, New Jersey. Williams attended Horace Mann School (where Jack Kerouac would later study for a year) in New York City, where he first began publishing poetry. He met Ezra Pound while both were students at the University of Pennsylvania. Williams worked as a family physician and wrote poetry in his spare time. The first book in Williams's five-volume masterpiece, *Paterson*, a free-verse poem of life in New Jersey, was published in 1946. Fellow poet Randall Jarrell remarked that "the subject of *Paterson* is: How can you tell the truth about things?—that is, how

A major influence on Allen Ginsberg, modernist poet William Carlos Williams (*Paterson*) wrote the introduction to *Howl and Other Poems* (1956), which included the famous line "Hold back the edges of your gowns, Ladies, we are going through hell." *Author's collection*

can you find a language so close to the world that the world can be represented and understood by it?" Williams, who famously coined the phrase "No ideas but in things," received the National Book Award for Poetry in 1950.

Allen Ginsberg considered Williams a mentor and asked him to write an introduction to his first published book of poetry, the landmark *Howl and Other Poems* (1956). Williams had known Ginsberg as a young poet in Paterson when he was "mentally much disturbed by the life which he had encountered about him." According to Williams, Ginsberg "was always on the point of 'going away,' where it didn't seem to matter: he disturbed me. I never thought he'd live to grow up and write a book of poems. His ability to survive, travel, and go on writing astonishes me. That he has gone on developing and perfecting his art is no less amazing to me . . . Now he turns up fifteen or twenty years later with an arresting poem. Literally he has, from all the evidence, been through hell." Williams concluded the introduction with the famous line "Hold back the edges of your gowns, Ladies, we are going through hell."

Williams's book *Kora in Hell: Improvisations* was published as No. 7 in City Lights Publishers' Pocket Poets Series in 1957. In his 1965 novel, *Desolation Angels*, Kerouac wrote, "And the next day Irwin [Allen Ginsberg] carts me and Simon and Raphael off in bus to Rutherford New Jersey to meet William Carlos Williams the old great poet of 20th Century America." Williams died on March 4, 1963, and was buried in Hillside Cemetery in Lyndhurst, New Jersey. He was posthumously awarded the 1963 Pulitzer Prize for Poetry for *Pictures from Brueghel and Other Poems*.

Thomas Wolfe

"I think the true discovery of America is before us. I think the true fulfillment of our spirit, of our people, of our mighty and immortal land, is yet to come." One of the most acclaimed American novelists of the early twentieth century—a literary giant once discussed in the same breath as Ernest Hemingway and William Faulkner—and a major influence on Beat writers such as Jack Kerouac and Allen Ginsberg, Thomas Wolfe is nearly forgotten today outside of college English literature departments and in his home state of North Carolina. Thomas Clayton Wolfe was born on October 3, 1900, in Asheville, North Carolina. His mother ran a boardinghouse called the "Old Kentucky Home." Wolfe attended the University of North Carolina at Chapel Hill at the age of fifteen. His masterpiece, *Look Homeward, Angel* (1929), presents a colorful portrayal of his hometown (which he refers to as "Altamont" in the novel) and life at the boardinghouse (known as "Dixieland" in the novel). In *Look Homeward, Angel*, Wolfe wrote, "We are the sum of all the moments of our lives—all that is ours is in them: we cannot escape or conceal it . . . Fiction is not fact, but fiction is fact selected and understood, fiction is fact arranged and charged with purpose."

Wolfe's other major works include *Of Time and the River* (1935), *The Web and the Rock* (1939), and *You Can't Go Home Again* (1940). Writer and political activist V. F. Calverton called Wolfe "the prose Walt Whitman of the twentieth century," as quoted in *Thomas Wolfe: An Illustrated Biography* (2006) by Ted Mitchell. Author Sinclair Lewis praised Wolfe as well in the March 3, 1935, issue of *Time* magazine, remarking that "he may have a chance to be the greatest American writer . . . In fact I don't see why he should not be one of the greatest world writers." Malcolm Cowley in the *New Republic* stated that Wolfe was "the only contemporary writer who can be mentioned in the same breath as Dickens and Dostoevsky."

Wolfe did have his critics, such as Hemingway, who called him "the over-bloated Li'l Abner of literature," as quoted in *Look Homeward: A Life of Thomas Wolfe* (2003) by David Herbert Donald. Author Evan Hughes in *Literary Brooklyn* (2011) stated, "Some detractors noted right away that *Look Homeward,*

Jack Kerouac's earliest writings, especially his first published book, *The Town and the City*, revealed the influence of Thomas Wolfe (*Look Homeward, Angel*), one of the most acclaimed American novelists of the early twentieth century. The Thomas Wolfe Memorial in Asheville, North Carolina, celebrates the author's life and work.   *Courtesy of Abe Ezekowitz/Wikimedia Commons*

Angel is overlong, shapeless, and often bombastic and grandiose." According to Donald Newlove in his 1981 memoir *Those Drinking Days*, "Another manic gargantuan, Thomas Wolfe got me drunk on life, gave me a larger-than-life appetite for drunkenness and led me into lonesome drinking for the sheer glow of it." Wolfe died of tuberculosis in 1938, just eighteen days short of his thirty-eighth birthday.

Neal Cassady started reading Wolfe while serving time at the Colorado State Reformatory in 1944–45, remarking that he was a "great" writer. Kerouac shared Cassady's enthusiasm for Wolfe's work and wrote in his January 11, 1948, journal entry: "Am reading Thomas Wolfe's 'Home Again' and am struck by the simplicity, humbleness, and beauty of his perfectly mature soul in his later years, 35 & 36. This is something only 'aging' can produce, as in good Bourbon. American critics are blind to Wolfe's perfect maturity, especially to the simple and magical tone of it." In fact, Kerouac's first novel, *The Town and the City* (1950), was written in Wolfe's sweeping prose style full of extensive descriptive passages. In a 1968 *Paris Review* interview, Kerouac remarked, "Hemingway was fascinating, the pearls of words on a white page giving you an exact picture . . . but Wolfe was a torrent of American heaven and hell that opened my eyes to America as a subject in itself."

Wolfe also had influence over the writers of the New Journalism movement of the 1960s and 1970s, such as Tom Wolfe (no relation) and Hunter S. Thompson. Wolfe, the author of *The Electric Kool-Aid Acid Test* (1968), remarked in a 1991 *Paris Review* interview, "As soon as I was old enough I became a tremendous fan of Thomas Wolfe and remain so to this day. I ignore his fluctuations on the literary stock market." Hunter S. Thompson reportedly took "fear and loathing" from a line in Wolfe's novel *The Web and the Rock* for the title of his 1971 book *Fear and Loathing in Las Vegas: A Savage Journey to the Heart of the American Dream.*

According to historian Douglas Brinkley in his 2008 book, *The Majic Bus: An American Odyssey*, "Some critics tend to belittle Thomas Wolfe's immense, landmark literary achievement, often by calling him an adolescent writer or an American primitive. Those deluded critics say that just because he was possessed of genius doesn't mean he wrote great novels . . . As a writer Wolfe's strengths are America's strengths; his weaknesses are America's weaknesses."

Jazz Music

In the first published Beat novel, *Go* (1952), John Clellon Holmes wrote, "In this modern jazz, they heard something rebel and nameless that spoke for them, and their lives knew a gospel for the first time. It was more than music; it became an attitude toward life." The style of jazz known as bebop or simply

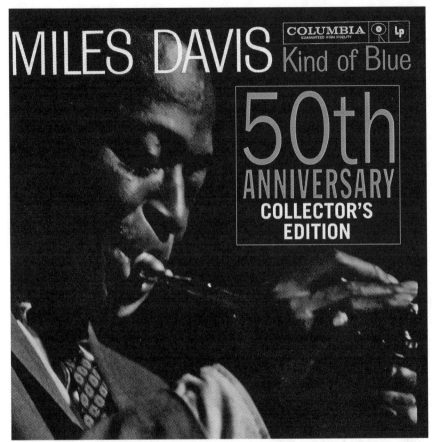

Jack Kerouac and other Beat writers often acknowledged the influence of the spontaneous style of jazz on their writing. However, when asked what he thought of the Beats, jazz great Miles Davis referred to it as "more synthetic white shit."   *Author's collection*

bop that influenced the Beat writers had evolved in the early to mid-1940s and was characterized by fast tempo, instrumental virtuosity, and improvisation. Legendary bebop pioneers include John Coltrane, Charlie Parker, Dizzy Gillespie, Miles Davis, and Thelonious Monk, among others. Among bebop standards are Gillespie's "Salt Peanuts" (1941), Parker's "Anthropology" (1946), and Monk's "Round Midnight" (1944), among many others.

Jack Kerouac's *On the Road* is full of enthusiastic references to jazz (for instance, he refers to tenor saxophonist Lester Young as "that gloomy, saintly goof in whom the history of jazz was wrapped"), and according to Ann Charters in *The Portable Beat Reader* (1992), "The word 'beat' was primarily in use after World War II by jazz musicians and hustlers as a slang term meaning down and out, or poor and exhausted. The jazz musician Mezz Mezzrow combined it with other words like 'dead beat.'" Composer David Amram, who worked with jazz greats such as Gillespie, Lionel Hampton, and Charles Mingus, collaborated with Kerouac on the first-ever jazz/poetry reading in New York City in 1957. Introducing *Mexico City Blues* (1959), his landmark jazz-inspired poem composed of 242 "choruses," Kerouac wrote, "I want to be considered a jazz poet blowing a long blues in an afternoon jam session on Sunday. I take 242 choruses; my ideas vary and sometimes roll from chorus to chorus or from halfway through a chorus to halfway into the next."

According to Anthony Bianco in *Ghosts of 42nd Street: A History of America's Most Infamous Block* (2004), Times Square denizen Herbert Huncke "not only frequented the jazz clubs clustered on 52nd Street but also socialized with Billie Holiday and the saxophonists Charlie Parker and Dexter Gordon. According to one account, Huncke was so close to Gordon that they used to break into cars together and sell stolen fur coats to prostitutes in Harlem." Beat poet Ted Joans even roomed with Parker briefly in the mid-1950s and upon Parker's death on March 12, 1955, started the famous "BIRD LIVES" graffiti campaign throughout New York City.

According to Lawrence Lipton in *The Holy Barbarians* (1959), "Everything the shamans of jazz do is legendary material for the beat: the gargantuan user, the cat who kicked it, the martyr-hero who died of it. Dead, he becomes, like Charley Bird Parker, a cult hero on the order of James Dean and Dylan Thomas . . . The hip cats among the holy barbarians will tell you they have no desire for the heavy stuff, but their curiosity about it is boundless, and if you listen to them talking about it you will not fail to notice their admiration for jazz musicians who are known to use heroin in heroic doses."

In a 1968 *Paris Review* interview, Kerouac remarked, "Yes, jazz and bop, in the sense of a, say, a tenor man drawing a breath and blowing a phrase on his saxophone, till he runs out of breath, and when he does, his sentence, his statement's been made . . . That's how I therefore separate my sentences, as breath separations of the mind." However, when rock journalist Al Aronowitz asked Miles Davis what he thought of the Beats, the jazz great told him it was just "more synthetic white shit."

Abstract Expressionism

An outgrowth of Surrealism, Abstract Expressionism (a.k.a. the New York School or Action Painting) opened up art's possibilities in post–World War II America. The Abstract Expressionist artists were a loosely associated group of unconventional artists that included Jackson Pollock, Willem de Kooning, Franz Kline, Robert Motherwell, Mark Rothko, William Baziotes, Adolph Gottlieb, Richard Prousette-Dart, Clyfford Still, and Barnett Newman. Just as the Beat writers explored unconventional writing techniques and subject matter, the Abstract Expressionists significantly departed from conventional painting techniques. Both groups burst onto the scene in the late 1940s and early 1950s, and were full of outsiders who challenged the orthodoxy of the day in their respective fields.

Many of the Abstract Expressionist artists gathered at the same hangouts in New York City as the Beats, such as the Cedar Tavern, which first opened its doors in 1866 at 24 University Place. According to Bill Morgan in *Beat Generation in New York* (2001), "At one point Kerouac was barred from the Cedar Tavern for urinating into an ashtray or sink (depending on conflicting accounts). Jackson Pollock was banned around the same time for kicking in the men's room door."

Considered the foremost Abstract Expressionist, Pollock (1912–56) was born in Cody, Wyoming. He studied with the famous regionalist painter Thomas Hart Benton and married artist Lee Krasner. Known for his unique style of drip painting, Pollock once remarked, "When I am *in* my painting, I am not aware of what I'm doing." *Time* magazine sardonically referred to him as "Jack the Dripper" in a notorious 1956 article titled "The Wild Ones." An alcoholic prone to fits of depression, an inebriated Pollock died after his car crashed into a tree just a mile from his home on August 11, 1956, at the age of forty-four. According to Grove Press publisher Barney Rosset in *Beat Writers at Work* (1999), "If you asked Pollock about the Beats, he wouldn't have known what the hell you were talking about . . . Pollock didn't read the Beats. Pollock didn't read anything. Neither did de Kooning. They were artists; they weren't writers."

A 2000 film, *Pollock*, starred Ed Harris in the title role, as well as Marcia Gay Harden, Jennifer Connelly, Robert Knott, Bud Cort, Sada Thompson, and Molly Regan. In addition, the hilarious 2006 documentary *Who the #$&%Is Jackson Pollock?* concerns a seventy-three-year-old female truck driver who buys a $5 painting in a thrift shop and later discovers it may actually be a Jackson Pollock worth millions.

4

Caught in a Square World

The Emergence of the Beat Generation

Columbia University played a crucial role in bringing key members of the Beat Generation together in the early 1940s. Jack Kerouac received a football scholarship to Columbia, where he met Allen Ginsberg and Lucien Carr. It was Carr who introduced the group to William S. Burroughs, a childhood friend of David Kammerer (Carr later infamously killed Kammerer, allegedly in self-defense). Another one of Kerouac's Columbia friends, Hal Chase, introduced him to Neal Cassady, who would later serve as the model for "Dean Moriarty" in *On the Road*. Burroughs in turn introduced the group to the Times Square "underworld" through Herbert Huncke. It was also at Columbia University that some of the Beat writers came into contact with influential professors, such as Mark Van Doren and Lionel Trilling, who served as Ginsberg's mentor. Early unpublished Beat writings during this period include *And the Hippos Were Boiled in Their Tanks* (Kerouac/Burroughs) and *The Sea Is My Brother* (Kerouac).

The Columbia University Crowd

The early origins of the Beat Generation can be traced to the campus of Columbia University in the early 1940s. Kerouac initially attended Horace Mann School during 1939–40 and befriended Henri Cru, who would later served as the model for "Remi Boncoeur" in *On the Road*. The following year, Kerouac entered Columbia on a football scholarship under legendary coach Lou Little, who later appeared as the character "Lu Libble" in Kerouac's 1959 novel *Maggie Cassidy*. Initially determined to study to become a labor lawyer, Ginsberg met Lucien Carr at Columbia in 1943, and the two like-minded intellectuals discussed the poetry of French symbolist poet Arthur Rimbaud and formulated the need for a "New Vision" against the stilted conservatism entrenched within the university culture. According to Ginsberg, "The new vision assumed the death of square morality and replaced that meaning with belief in creativity."

Carr later introduced Ginsberg to William S. Burroughs and David Kammerer, who was infatuated with Carr. Kammerer and Burroughs had been classmates in St. Louis, Missouri. Kerouac met Carr at the West End Bar near the campus. Through Burroughs's friendship with Herbert Huncke, the early Beat circle became exposed to the Times Square underworld. Burroughs also shared his wisdom with the others by directing them to such influential books as Oswald Spengler's *The Decline of the West* and Alfred Korzybski's *Science and Sanity*. Wild parties and all-night gab sessions were commonplace at the apartment shared by Edie Parker (Kerouac's future wife) and Joan Vollmer (Burroughs's future common-law wife). The sixth-floor apartment was located at 421 West 118th Street, just a block away from Columbia.

Founded in 1754, Columbia is a historic Ivy League university located in the heart of New York City. Illustrious faculty members in the early 1940s included literary critic and author Lionel Trilling (who served as Ginsberg's mentor) and poet, writer, and critic Mark Van Doren, who won the 1940 Pulitzer Prize for Poetry for his *Collected Poems 1922–1938*.

The Beats at War

Although it often appears that the early Beat circle was apathetic and oblivious to World War II while they spent hours partying in New York City jazz clubs and staying up all night popping Benzedrine, several Beats served their country during the war (although none in combat roles). Jack Kerouac joined the merchant marine during the summer of 1942 and shipped out of Boston on the *SS Dorchester* bound for Greenland. Other Beat writers who served in the merchant marine include Gary Snyder, Bob Kaufman, Herbert Huncke, and Carl Solomon. Kerouac used his brief experiences in the merchant marine as the basis of an early novel, *The Sea Is My Brother*, which was not published until 2011. Billed as "The Lost Novel," it received mixed reviews. In 1943, Kerouac joined the US Navy but was honorably discharged on psychiatric grounds after just ten days of active duty.

In 1942, William S. Burroughs joined the US Army, which classified him as infantry. His mother reportedly pulled some strings to get him released from duty. Lawrence Ferlinghetti joined the navy and rose to the position of lieutenant commander. Stationed in Nagasaki, Japan, at war's end, he witnessed the destructive effects of the atomic bomb. He later wrote, "Anyone who saw Nagasaki would suddenly realize that they'd been kept in the dark by the United States government as to what atomic bombs can do." The horrifying images of Nagasaki led Ferlinghetti to become a pacifist and lifelong antiwar activist.

Killing of David Kammerer

The sensational killing of David Kammerer by Lucien Carr, a key member of the early Beat scene, led to a highly publicized trial. At the time, Carr was a Columbia University sophomore who had introduced Allen Ginsberg, Jack Kerouac, and William S. Burroughs to each other. Kammerer, who had known both Carr and Burroughs in St. Louis, became infatuated with Carr and followed him to New York City, where he became a fringe member of the crowd, barely tolerated by the others. According to Edie Parker in her memoir *You'll Be Okay* (2007), "I always felt that David was creepy and might as well have had cloven hooves and horns growing out of thick, curly red hair. He was the dark cloud that hovered over our lives."

On August 13, 1944, Carr and Kerouac made an unsuccessful attempt to ship out of New York City to Paris on a merchant ship. They ended up getting drunk at one of their frequent haunts, the West End Bar. Kammerer later caught up with Carr and the drinking continued. During a drunken argument in Riverside Park around 3:00 a.m. on August 14, 1944, Carr killed Kammerer by stabbing him in the heart multiple times with his Boy Scout knife. Carr then methodically weighted Kammerer's body down with rocks and dumped it into the Hudson River.

Carr quickly sought out Burroughs, who advised him to turn himself in, claim self-defense, and get a good lawyer. Kerouac helped Carr dispose of the murder weapon, as well as Kammerer's eyeglasses. Then they went to a movie theater and watched *The Four Feathers* (1939) several times. Later that afternoon, Carr decided to turn himself in. The local newspapers printed sensational stories about the crime with titles such as "Columbia Student Kills Friend and Sinks Body in Hudson River" (*New York Times*, August 17, 1944) and "Student Accused as 'Honor' Slayer" (*New York Daily News*, August 17, 1944). After the fatal stabbing, both Kerouac and Burroughs were held as material witnesses on $500 bonds. Burroughs's father posted bail, but Kerouac's father was so upset that he refused to bail him out. Kerouac promised to marry Edie Parker if she paid the $500 bond. The couple got married in a quick ceremony in the jail and then moved to Edie's hometown of Grosse Pointe, Michigan. Kerouac got restless after a couple of months and headed back to New York City. Parker annulled the marriage in 1946.

Carr spent his time in police custody reading the poetry of Arthur Rimbaud and William Butler Yeats. At the trial, Carr claimed self-defense and was charged with second-degree murder. He later pled guilty to first-degree manslaughter and served a two-year term at the Elmira Correctional Facility (a.k.a. "The Hill") in upstate New York. Kerouac and Burroughs collaborated on a fictionalized account of the Kammerer killing titled *And the Hippos Were Boiled in Their Tanks*, which was not published until 2008. In addition, James Baldwin's second novel, *Giovanni's Room* (1956), was partly inspired by the tragedy. In a *Paris Review* interview, Baldwin remarked that he was "fascinated by the trial." The 2013 film *Kill Your Darlings* is also based on the killing. Kammerer was buried in Bellefontaine Cemetery, which also serves as the final resting place of Burroughs, in St. Louis, Missouri. His marker simply reads, "DAVID EAMES KAMMERER 1911–1944."

And the Hippos Were Boiled in Their Tanks

A straightforward World War II–era detective novel, *And the Hippos Were Boiled in Their Tanks* was a collaborative effort on the part of Jack Kerouac and William S. Burroughs, who based their work on the sordid true-life tale of their close friend Lucien Carr's killing of David Kammerer during a drunken fight in August 1944. Written in 1945 (at a time when both writers were unknown and unpublished), the rather pedestrian work gained legendary status as a "lost novel" until it was finally published in 2008 by the Estate of Jack Kerouac and the William S. Burroughs Trust—at which time many reviewers wondered what all the fuss had been about.

More of a historical artifact than anything else, the hard-boiled, heavily fictionalized account features alternating chapters written by bartender/detective "Will Dennison" (Burroughs) and merchant seaman "Mike Ryko" (Kerouac). The cast of characters includes "Phillip Tourian" (Carr), "Ramsey Allen" (Kammerer), "Janie" (Kerouac's future wife Edie Parker), and "Babs Bennington" (Carr's then-girlfriend, Celine Young). When not focused on the actual crime itself, the book does capture a sense of the bohemian lifestyle of the characters, the endless parties, sexual antics, and experimentation with drugs. Interestingly, the coauthors changed the actual circumstances of the murder, having Tourian kill Allen with a hatchet and then throw his body off the roof of a warehouse.

The strange book title was allegedly taken from a radio report Burroughs heard about a circus fire (perhaps alluding to the tragic Hartford circus fire on July 6, 1944). In a 1968 *Paris Review* interview, Kerouac remarked, "Burroughs and I were sitting in a bar one night and we heard a newscaster saying . . . 'and so the Egyptians attacked blah blah . . . and meanwhile there was a great fire in the zoo in London and the fire raced across the fields and

The White Horse Tavern in Greenwich Village in New York City served as a hangout for Beat writers, as well as other notable bohemian writers and artists. Kerouac was eighty-sixed from the bar on at least one occasion, and Welsh poet Dylan Thomas reportedly had his last drink there before dying at the age of thirty-nine.

Photo by Phyllis Twachtman/ New York World-Telegram/ Wikimedia Commons

the hippos were boiled in their tanks! Goodnight everyone!' That's Bill, he noticed that. Because he notices them kind of things."

In a 1974 interview included in the 2000 book *Conversations with William S. Burroughs*, which was edited by Allen Hibbard, Burroughs remarked, "Kerouac and I wrote a book . . . It wasn't very good." In his essay "Remembering Jack Kerouac," published in *The Adding Machine: Selected Essays* (1986), Burroughs stated that "in 1945 or thereabouts, Kerouac and I collaborated on a novel that was never published. Some of the material covered in this lost opus was later used by Jack in *The Town and the City* and *Vanity of Duluoz*. At that time, the anonymous grey character of William Lee was taking shape: Lee, who is there just so long and long enough to see and hear what he needs to see and hear for some scene or character he will use 20 or 30 years later in his writing."

In a review of *Hippos* for the *New York Times* (November 10, 2008), critic Michiko Kakutani wrote, "None of these one-dimensional slackers are remotely interesting as individuals, but together they give the reader a sense of the seedy, artsy world Kerouac and Burroughs inhabited in New York during the war years." According to a review in the *Guardian* (December 5, 2008), "Neither Burroughs nor Kerouac is at his best here, but *Hippos* has value as a testament to their latent talent." *Kirkus Reviews* (November 1, 2008) wryly noted, "When the manuscript made the rounds back in 1945, it found no publisher, for reasons that will soon become apparent to the reader, and ended up in a filing cabinet. Its publication will (possibly) benefit American literature. More likely it will benefit agents and estates."

Greenwich Village Scene

Attracted by low rent and the neighborhood's rich bohemian history, Beat writers and avant-garde artists alike descended upon Greenwich Village during the 1940s and 1950s. William S. Burroughs lived for a time at 69 Bedford Street in the Village during the early 1940s just down the street from Chumley's, a popular tavern and former speakeasy popular with writers such as Eugene O'Neill, John Dos Passos, Edna St. Vincent Millay, John Steinbeck, William Faulkner, E. E. Cummings, and others. Opened in 1938, Café Society nightclub in Greenwich Village featured a slew of notable performers, including Miles Davis, John Coltrane, Billie Holiday, Charlie Parker, Count Basie, Lester Young, Art Tatum, and others. Other favorite Beat hangouts in the Village included the San Remo, Cedar Street Tavern, the Gaslight, Gerde's, Café Wha?, the Figaro, the Hip Bagel, and the White Horse Tavern. Washington Square Park also became a main gathering place for folk singers and writers alike.

Bob Dylan arrived in the Village in 1961 and quickly became a fixture on the folk club scene there. *New York Times* folk critic Robert Shelton announced Dylan's official arrival when he wrote on September 29, 1961, "A bright new face in folk music is appearing at Gerde's Folk City . . . Resembling a cross between a choir boy and a beatnik, Mr. Dylan has a cherubic look and a mop of tousled hair he partly covers with a Huck Finn black corduroy cap. His clothes may need a bit of tailoring, but when he works his guitar, harmonica or piano and composes new songs faster than he can remember them, there is no doubt that he is bursting at the seams with talent." *Village Voice* photographer Fred W. McDarrah (1926–2007) documented the Beat scene in Greenwich Village and later published many of his images in the 1985 book *Kerouac and Friends: A Beat Generation Album*.

Allen Ginsberg (right) and longtime companion Peter Orlovsky (second from left) hanging out near the Kettle of Fish bar on MacDougal Street in Greenwich Village in 1959.
Photo by Fred W. McDarrah / Getty Images

Times Square Underworld

Commonly referred to as "the Crossroads of the World" and "Center of the Universe," Times Square in the 1940s was a bustling commercial intersection that captured the imagination of the early Beat scene. For instance, Allen Ginsberg remarked, "The new social center has been established on Times Square—a huge room lit in brilliant fashion by neon glare and filled with slot machines, open day and night. There all the apocalyptic hipsters in New York eventually stopped, fascinated by the timeless room." In his first published novel, *The Town and the City* (1950), Jack Kerouac expertly depicted the Times Square of the 1940s: "He wandered into Times Square. He stood on the sidewalk in the thin drizzle falling from dark skies. He looked about him at the people passing by—the same people he had seen so many times in other American cities on similar streets: soldiers, sailors, the panhandlers and drifters, the zoo-suiters, the hoodlums, the young men who washed dishes in cafeterias from coast to coast, the hitchhikers, the hustlers, the drunks, the battered lonely young Negroes, the twinkling little Chinese, the dark Puerto Ricans, and the varieties of dungareed young Americans in leather jackets who were seamen and mechanics and garagemen everywhere."

The Beat persona most commonly associated with Times Square, Herbert Huncke, first arrived here in 1939. In his 1990 autobiography, *Guilty of Everything*, Huncke wrote, "When I first arrived in New York I was stone broke and like every other young kid who hits the city broke I went directly to 42nd Street. I hadn't known anything about Time Square except the name . . . I soon became acquainted with many of the regular habitués Russian Blackie, who I joined with as part of the crowd that hung around the cafeterias, Bickford's, Chase's, Hector's, the Automat; Detroit Redhead, who I'd known well as a popular Times Square prostitute in the '40s and who eventually married—becoming last I heard, the typical suburban matron, active in the PTA; and typical young cats who hustled the Street for a living."

A Blakean Vision

During a furious masturbation session while reading "Ah, Sunflower" by English Romantic poet William Blake in his East Harlem apartment during the summer of 1948, twenty-six-year-old Allen Ginsberg claimed he heard the voice of Blake instructing him to "cultivate the terror, get right into it." According to Ginsberg, he then experienced a series of visions and "the top of my head came off, letting in the rest of the universe." Although Ginsberg asserted that no drugs were involved during this bizarre experience, he later admitted to using drugs in later efforts to recapture the feelings inspired by the vision. According to Ginsberg, "I was never able to figure out whether I was having a religious vision, a hallucinatory experience, or what, but it was the deepest 'spiritual' experience I had in my life, and determined my karma as poet. That's the key pivotal turnabout of my own existence."

An English poet, painter, printmaker, and mystic, Blake (1757–1827) was misunderstood by his contemporaries, who believed he was insane for his idiosyncratic views. Blake published a number of classic works during his lifetime, such as *Songs of Innocence* (1789), *Songs of Experience* (1794), and *Jerusalem* (1820), which was his longest single work. Utilizing prose, poetry, and illustrations, Blake's *The Marriage of Heaven and Hell* was written in imitation of biblical books of prophecy and featured powerful lines such as "The road of excess leads to the palace of wisdom." Also known for his apocalyptic illustrations, Blake was painting watercolors for an edition of Dante's *Divine*

Comedy that he worked on up to the day of his death. Blake was buried in an unmarked grave at Bunhill Fields in London. In 1957, a memorial was erected for Blake and his wife, Catherine, in the Poet's Corner of Westminster Abbey.

Ginsberg had been first exposed to the poetry of Blake through William S. Burroughs, who also gave him copies of William Butler Yeats's *A Vision* and Oswald Spengler's *The Decline of the West*. In 1970, MGM Records released *Songs of Innocence* by William Blake, tuned by Allen Ginsberg (listen at your own risk!). The track list includes "The Shepherd," "The Echoing Green," "The Lamb," "The Little Black Boy," "The Blossom," "The Chimney Sweeper," "The Little Boy Lost," "The Little Boy Found," "Laughing Song," and "Holy Thursday." *Songs of Experience* includes "Nurse's Song," "The Sick Rose," "Ah, Sunflower," "The Garden of Love," "London," "The Human Abstract," "To Tirzah," and "The Grey Monk."

The Town and the City

Jack Kerouac's first published novel, *The Town and the City* (1950), was written in the highly descriptive style of Thomas Wolfe and in a much more conventional form than his later, more experimental works. The book's tepid reception deeply discouraged Kerouac, who would not have another major work published until the *On the Road* breakthrough in 1957. According to author/historian Douglas Brinkley in his introduction to *Windblown World: The Journals of Jack Kerouac 1947–1954* (2004), "Kerouac was driven to write *The Town and the City* by the grief he experienced at the death of his father, Leo, from stomach cancer in early 1946." Kerouac sat down at his mother's table and was so dedicated in his quest to write the "Great American Novel" that Allen Ginsberg nicknamed him "The Wizard of Ozone Park." In a July 1947 journal entry, Kerouac wrote, "My father's life was so rich and so deep that I still spend days absorbed in its details, which could fill a book. My father did not die blankly leaving life to be fulfilled, if at all, by his children. He fulfilled it, just as I want to fulfill it in my way, sincerely."

The Town and the City focuses on the experiences of young "Peter Martin" in the small town of "Galloway, Massachusetts" (Kerouac's hometown of Lowell). When Martin arrives in New York City to attend college on a football scholarship, he makes acquaintances with other key figures in the early Beat scene, including "Leon Levinsky" (Allen Ginsberg), "Will Dennison" (William S. Burroughs), "Mary Dennison" (Joan Vollmer), "Kenneth Wood" (Lucien Carr), "Waldo Meister" (David Kammerer), "Judie Smith" (Edie Parker), and last but not least, "Junky" (Herbert Huncke). In the book, Meister falls from the window of Wood's apartment (in reality, Carr knifed Kammerer and threw his body into the Hudson River).

Kerouac began writing *The Town and the City* as early as 1945, and in 1948 sent the completed 1,100-page manuscript to Wolfe's publisher, Charles Scribner's Sons, but they passed on the novel. Columbia University professor Mark Van Doren recommended the novel to Robert Giroux at Harcourt Brace the following year. Kerouac received a $1,000 advance against royalties. He used the name "John Kerouac" for the book, which was eventually published on March 2, 1950, to mixed reviews and sold poorly. Kerouac dedicated the novel to Giroux, who rejected all of the subsequent novels the author sent him over the years (including *On the Road*).

In a March 5, 1950, review of *The Town and the City* for the *New York Times*, critic John Brooks called it a "big, rambling first novel" with early scenes that "tend to be overly idyllic in content and wordy" and a "Dostoevskyian view of New York City life" that is "powerful and disturbing." Brooks concluded that "Like Wolfe, to whom he seems to owe much, Mr. Kerouac tends to overwrite. Admirably, however, he avoids imposing a false thematic framework on his material, pinning everything by force to 'lostness' or 'loneliness.' His is the kind of novel that lets life lead where it will. More often than not, the depth and breadth of his vision triumph decisively over his technical weaknesses." The *Saturday Review* criticized the novel as being "radically deficient in structure and style," while the *New Yorker* referred to it as "ponderous, shambling . . . tiresome." *Newsweek* called Kerouac "the best and most promising of the young novelists whose first works have recently appeared."

In his 1959 book, *The Holy Barbarians*, Lawrence Lipton remarked, "[Kerouac's] first published novel, *The Town and the City* . . . is a sensitive picture of the life it depicts—the dope addict, the beat poet, the criminal hangers-on—but its style, except in the dialogue, is still conventional. In short, Kerouac has still to master his idiom." *Library Journal* (February 15, 1950) called it "a first novel of moral strength. Recommended, but not for the faint-hearted." According to *Catholic World* (April 1950), *The Town and the City* was "an incoherent novel adolescent in its philosophy, that could stand more editing."

Some of the more vitriolic reviews left Kerouac feeling totally disillusioned. For instance, in his March 1, 1950, journal entry, Kerouac lamented, "That I spent 4 years abandoning the joys of normal youthful life, to make a serious contribution to American literature, and the result is treated like a cheap first novel—which it certainly is not—(in spite of my apparent 'success')—that my Town & City, poor as it is in spots, but over-all serious, not frivolous—should be bandied about by frivolous reviewers who do the same thing day after day on countless novels of all kinds . . . I'm so confused I don't care to finish the sentence. Apparently nothing is 'significant' except a portrait of themselves insofar as commuter-middle-class reviewers are concerned." Interestingly, in his inscription to Carolyn Cassady's copy of *The Town and the City*, Kerouac apologized for getting drunk at Neal Cassady's birthday and vowed that "it'll never happen again."

"This Is the Beat Generation"

John Clellon Holmes was rather a peripheral outsider to the burgeoning Beat scene in New York City as a whole even though Jack Kerouac remained one of his closest friends. After Holmes published what is considered to be the first Beat Generation novel, *Go*, in 1952, his article "This Is the Beat Generation" appeared in the *New York Times Sunday Magazine* (November 16, 1952) and formally introduced the term "beat" to the world.

In Holmes's view, the "lust for freedom" of this new postwar generation "led to black markets, bebop, narcotics, sexual promiscuity, hucksterism, and Jean-Paul Sartre." Holmes compared the Beat Generation with the Lost Generation of the 1920s ("caught up in the romance of disillusionment") and concluded that "the wild boys of today are not lost" since they "were brought up in those ruins and no longer notice them. They drink to 'come down' or to 'get high,' not to illustrate anything. Their excursions into drugs or promiscuity come out of curiosity, not disillusionment." According to Holmes, "*How* to live seems to them much more crucial than *why*."

Holmes added, "For the wildest hipster, making a mystique of bop, drugs and the night life, there is no desire to shatter the 'square' society in which he lives, only to elude it. To get on a soapbox or write a manifesto would seem to him absurd . . . [The Beat Generation's] ability to keep its eyes open, and yet avoid cynicism; its ever-increasing conviction that the problem of modern life is essentially a spiritual problem; and that capacity for sudden wisdom which people who live hard and go far possess, are assets and bear watching." Although Holmes's widely read article on the Beat Generation quickly faded from view, it set the stage for the total frenzy surrounding the publication of Kerouac's *On the Road* almost exactly five years later in 1957. Coincidentally, *On the Road* received widespread attention based on a glowing review in the *New York Times* by Gilbert Millstein, who had originally asked Holmes to write his 1952 article on the Beat Generation.

Origins of the Word "Beat"

According to legend, it was actually Forty-Second Street hustler, drug addict, and petty thief Herbert Huncke who introduced the word "beat" to the group of aspiring writers that would make up the core of the Beat Generation. Huncke and his Times Square cronies had picked up on the old carny term, which indicated "beaten down." Huncke later commented, "I meant beaten. The world against me." However, to Jack Kerouac, "beat" had more of a spiritual or mystical connotation, as in "beatitude." During a discussion between Kerouac and John Clellon Holmes in 1948 concerning the Lost Generation of writers, such as Ernest Hemingway and F. Scott Fitzgerald, Kerouac casually remarked, "You know, this is really a beat generation."

Other Beat writers chimed in with their own definition of beat, such as Gregory Corso, who wrote in his 1959 essay "Variations on a Generation" that "by avoiding society you become separate from society and being separate from society is being BEAT." In his foreword to *The Beat Book* (1996), Allen Ginsberg wrote, "The phrase 'Beat generation' arose out of specific conversation between Jack Kerouac and John Clellon Holmes in 1948 . . . Herbert Huncke . . . introduced them to what was then known as 'hip language.' In that context, the word 'beat' is a carnival, 'subterranean' (subcultural) term—a term much used then in Times Square: 'Man, I'm beat,' meaning without money and without a place to stay.' . . . So 'beat' was interpreted in various circles to mean emptied out, exhausted, and at the same time wide-open and receptive to vision."

In 1959, the editors of the *Random House Dictionary* solicited Kerouac for a historical definition of the "Beat Generation" and he replied: "Members of the generation that came of age after World War II, who, supposedly as a result of disillusionment stemming from the Cold War, espouse mystical detachment and relaxation of social and sexual tensions." Looking back from his vantage point in the 1960s, a more bitter Kerouac remarked in a 1968 *Paris Review* interview, "Oh the Beat generation was just a phrase I used in the 1951 written manuscript of *On the Road* to describe guys like Moriarty who run around the country in cars looking for odd jobs, girlfriends, kicks. It was thereafter picked up by West Coast Leftist groups and turned into a meaning like 'Beat mutiny' and 'Beat insurrection' and all that nonsense; they wanted some youth movement to grab on to for their own political and social purposes."

As writer, editor and co-owner of City Lights Bookstore Nancy J. Peters concluded in her foreword to Bill Morgan's *Beat Atlas* (2011), "The term Beat Generation is catchy and the name caught on with the press. But 'beat' is an ambiguous word—beaten down? dead beat? beatific? The writers themselves were never consistent in defining it."

5

Find Your Place

Legendary Beat Haunts

Early Beat activity centered on Greenwich Village, the all-night cafeterias and dive bars of Times Square, the smoky jazz joints of Harlem, and other New York City locales before spreading across the United States all the way to North Beach in San Francisco and eventually throughout the world to places like Mexico City, Mexico; Paris, France (home to the legendary "Beat Hotel"); and Tangier, Morocco—the model for "Interzone" in *Naked Lunch* that William S. Burroughs referred to as "the prognostic pulse of the world." Many of the most memorable settings in Jack Kerouac's *On the Road* are big cities, particularly New York, Denver, and San Francisco (where Ginsberg gave his first public reading of "Howl" in 1956), but also Los Angeles, New Orleans, and Mexico City.

Lowell

"I was going home in October. Everybody goes home in October." In his first published novel, *The Town and the City* (1950), Jack Kerouac wrote, "Follow along to the center of the town, the Square, where at noon everybody knows everybody else." Kerouac was referring to his hometown of Lowell, Massachusetts, a historic mill town nestled on the banks of the Merrimack River, where he was born on March 12, 1922, at 9 Lupine Road in the Centralville neighborhood. Several of Kerouac's other novels are set in Lowell, such as *Maggie Cassidy* (1959), *Doctor Sax* (1959), *Visions of Gerard* (1963), and *The Vanity of Duluoz* (1968). A young Kerouac spent hours at the Lowell Public Library (now known as the Pollard Memorial Library) and was a football and track star at Lowell High School. Another favorite Lowell haunt for Kerouac in later years was Nicky's Bar at 110 Gorham Street (now the site of Ricardo's Café Trattoria—billed as "A Taste of Italy and a Side of Jazz"). Kerouac is buried in Edson Cemetery, which also lies on Gorham Street.

Dedicated in June 1988, the Kerouac Commemorative Memorial in Eastern Canal Park Park in downtown Lowell features eight triangular marble columns with inscriptions from Kerouac's five novels set in Lowell, as well as

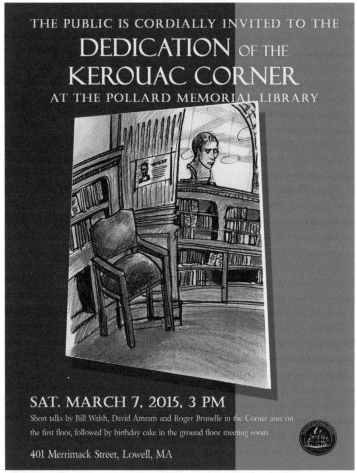

THE PUBLIC IS CORDIALLY INVITED TO THE

DEDICATION OF THE
KEROUAC CORNER
AT THE POLLARD MEMORIAL LIBRARY

SAT. MARCH 7, 2015, 3 PM
Short talks by Bill Walsh, David Amram and Roger Brunelle in the Corner area on the first floor, followed by birthday cake in the ground floor meeting room

401 Merrimack Street, Lowell, MA

Jack Kerouac's hometown of Lowell, Massachusetts, the setting for several of his novels, periodically honors its native son with various accolades, such as the new Kerouac Corner at the Pollard Memorial Library.

Author's collection

selections from his works *On the Road, Mexico City Blues, Lonesome Traveler,* and *Book of Dreams.* Poets Allen Ginsberg and Lawrence Ferlinghetti were among those present at the dedication of the memorial, which was designed by artist Ben Woitena. "For the Kerouac Commemorative I sought images which sculpturally communicate and honor his philosophy of life and the genius of his literary talent," remarked Woitena on his official website at www.benwoitenasculptor.com. The park earned an American Institute of Architects Citation for Excellence in Urban Design in 1990.

Founded in 2005, the Jack and Stella Kerouac Center for the Public Humanities at the University of Massachusetts Lowell serves as the home for the Kerouac Writer-in-Residence program, the Kerouac Conference on Beat Literature, Kerouac scholarships, and the New England Poetry Conference. An annual event held each October, Lowell Celebrates Kerouac! offers tours, documentary screenings, and readings. However, unfortunately, there is as of yet no museum devoted to Kerouac in his hometown.

Sometimes referred to as the "Birthplace of the American Industrial Revolution," Lowell boasts an estimated population of more than 108,000 people, making it the fourth-largest city in Massachusetts behind Boston, Worcester, and Springfield. Although Lowell faced some serious economic and social problems in the 1990s, as documented in the 1995 HBO documentary *High on Crack Street: Lost Lives in Lowell*, the downtown area has bounced back dramatically. Lowell also is the birthplace of artist James Abbott McNeill Whistler (1834–1903), as well as Academy Award–winning actresses Bette Davis (1908–89) and Olympia Dukakis. Interestingly, Whistler would later claim St. Petersburg, Russia, as his birthplace, even going as far as to declare, "I shall be born when and where I want, and I do not choose to be born in Lowell."

New York City

New York City can truly lay claim to being the "Birthplace of the Beat Generation." It was there, in and around the environs of Columbia University, in 1944 that Jack Kerouac, Allen Ginsberg, and William S. Burroughs met each other through mutual friend Lucien Carr. In late 1946, Neal Cassady and his teenage bride, LuAnne, made their way from Denver to New York City to visit Cassady's friend Hal Chase, who eventually introduced him to Jack Kerouac and the rest of the early Beat circle.

Fascinated with criminal behavior, Burroughs soon descended into the Times Square underworld with help from hustler, drug addict, and small-time criminal Herbert Huncke. The Angle Bar on the corner of Forty-Third and Eighth was a "favorite of Manhattan low-lifes," according to one source. One of the favorite Beat hangouts, the White Horse Tavern, is still open at 567 Hudson Street in Greenwich Village. Kerouac was eighty-sixed from the White Horse several times, according to legend. In *Desolation Angels*, Kerouac wrote about how he discovered "Go Home Kerouac" scrawled on the bathroom wall at the White Horse. Built in 1880, the White Horse Tavern is certified as a National Poetry Landmark by the Academy of American Poets. Dylan Thomas drank his last shot of whiskey there and famously exclaimed, "I've had eighteen straight whiskies. I think that's the record." A plaque commemorating Thomas's last visit to the White Horse hangs above the bar. Another legendary Beat hotspot that remains open is the Café Wha? at

115 MacDougal Street, where Kerouac and Ginsberg reportedly held poetry readings and folk singer Bob Dylan made his New York debut. Other famous musicians who performed there include Jerry Lee Lewis, Little Richard, Richie Havens, the Velvet Underground, and Jimi Hendrix.

Another popular Beat gathering spot was the now-defunct San Remo Café at 93 MacDougal Street. In his 1958 novella, *The Subterraneans*, Kerouac described the San Remo crowd as "hip without being slick, intelligent without being corny, they are intellectual as hell and know all about Pound without being pretentious or saying too much about it. They are very quiet, they are very Christlike." On at least one occasion in the late 1950s, Kerouac was beaten badly outside the Sam Remo. The Beats also enjoyed congregating in Washington Square Park, the site of the notorious "Beatnik Riot" on April 9, 1961, when hundreds of folk musicians descended upon the park to protest having their permits to perform there revoked by city officials. The New York Police Department arrived with billy clubs to kick them out, and several arrests were made. The incident was captured in Dan Drasin's seventeen-minute documentary, *Sunday* (1961). The Washington Square Diner at 150 West Fourth Street is the former site of the Pony Stable Inn, a lesbian bar where Ginsberg met Gregory Corso for the first time.

When Burroughs returned to New York City in 1974 after living for twenty-six years abroad in Tangier, Paris, and London, he holed up in "The Bunker," a three-room apartment converted from the locker room of a gymnasium at 222 Bowery in the heart of the Lower East Side and just around the block from the legendary CBGB music club. During the late 1970s, Burroughs cultivated his new image as the "Godfather of Punk." Bill Morgan's 2001 book, *Beat Generation in New York: A Walking Tour of Jack Kerouac's City*, serves as the definitive guide to the history of Beat Generation activities in the Big Apple.

Denver

In *On the Road*, Jack Kerouac exclaimed, "Here I was in Denver . . . I stumbled along with the most wicked grin of joy in the world, among the bums and beat cowboys of Larimer Street." As the hometown of Neal Cassady, as well as a frequent stopping point for Jack Kerouac and Allen Ginsberg, Denver figures prominently in the Beat legend. Cassady grew up in the Larimer Street skid row district (long since gentrified) with his alcoholic father, Neal Sr., as described in his memoir, *The First Third* (published posthumously in 1971). Jazz legends such as Duke Ellington, Billie Holiday, Dizzy Gillespie, Miles Davis, and many others performed in the nightclubs within Denver's Five Points neighborhood (nicknamed "The Harlem of the West"), which lies approximately one mile northeast of downtown. The fabled Cervantes' Masterpiece Ballroom at 2637 Welton Street still hosts live entertainment.

Several bars the Beats used to frequent are still open, such as Charlie Brown's Bar & Grill (980 Grant Street) and My Brother's Bar (2376 Fifteenth Street, Denver's oldest bar and reportedly Cassady's favorite hangout). A letter Cassady wrote to a friend from the Colorado Reformatory asking him to pay off his tab at My Brother's Bar hangs on a wall in the bar. The Tattered Cover Book Store, which boasts an extensive selection of Beat-related literature, features three locations in the greater Denver Metro area: 2526 East Colfax Avenue, 1628 Sixteenth Street, and 9315 Dorchester Street (Highlands Ranch). Just outside of Denver in Wheat Ridge lies Mt. Olivet Cemetery, which serves as the final resting place for "Old Dean Moriarty" himself, Neal Cassady Sr. The unmarked grave is located in section 26, block 5, lot 6, grave 9.

New Orleans

In addition to its historic role as the birthplace of jazz, New Orleans holds a special place in Beat lore. For example, poet Bob Kaufman, the quintessential jazz poet known as the "black American Rimbaud," was born here on April 18, 1925, one of fourteen children. Kaufman later claimed that his grandmother practiced voodoo. In addition, William Burroughs and his common-law wife, Joan Vollmer; her daughter from a previous marriage, Julie; and their son, Billy Jr., lived at 509 Wagner Street in Algiers, Louisiana, across the river from New Orleans during 1948–49. The house, which Burroughs purchased for $7,000, featured a sagging wooden porch. Burroughs was deep into his heroin addiction at the time and spent most of day sitting in a rocking chair.

In his first published novel, *Junkie* (1953), Burroughs described New Orleans as "a stratified series of ruins. Along Bourbon Street are ruins of the 1920s. Down where the French Quarter blends into Skid Row are ruins of an earlier stratum: chili joints, decaying hotels, oldtime saloons with mahogany bars, spittoons, and crystal chandeliers. The ruins of 1900." In *Naked Lunch* (1959), he called New Orleans "a dead museum." Jack Kerouac detailed a rather chaotic visit to Burroughs ("Old Bull Lee') at the house in *On the Road* (1957). However, Burroughs later described Kerouac's account of the visit as highly fictionalized, especially the description of an "orgone box" in the front yard. In Burroughs's essay "My Experiences with Wilhelm Reich's Orgone Box" in *The Adding Machine* (1986), he wrote, "When [Kerouac] visited me I was living in Algiers, across the river from New Orleans, in a little house laid out like a railroad flat and raised up on the marshy lot by concrete blocks. In Algiers I had practically no front yard at all, and was far too busy with a habit to build an accumulator."

In the spring of 1949, Burroughs was arrested in New Orleans while trying to score drugs and the family fled to Mexico City before the trial. A historical marker was erected in front of Burroughs's Algiers house in 2007 that reads: "William S. Burroughs House . . . Residence from 1948 to 1949 of William S. Burroughs . . . World renowned author of *Naked Lunch*, *Junky*, *Queer* and other works. Jack Kerouac visited this location on January 21, 1949, and describes the house in his book *On the Road*: 'It ran clear around the house; by moonlight with the willows it looked like an old southern mansion that had seen better days.' The house was built in 1916 by Steven A. Eross."

Known as New Orleans's "oldest living beatnik," Robert Cass was a poet and essayist who published *Climax: A Creative Review* in *Jazz Spirit* in 1955 and 1956 from the bar A Quaterite Place at 733 Bourbon Street. *Climax* featured the work of such writers as Lawrence Lipton and Judson Crews. Cass was referred to as a "handsome blond adventurer" in Diane di Prima's 1969 book, *Memoirs of a Beatnik*.

Jon and Louise "Gypsy Lou" Webb founded the avant-garde literary magazine *The Outsider* in an apartment in the French Quarter of New Orleans in the early 1960s. During the day, Gypsy Lou sold paintings on a street corner. The first two books published by Loujon Press were by Charles Bukowski: *It Catches My Heart in Its Hands* (1963) and *Crucifix in Deathhand* (1965). Bukowski, who frequently corresponded via letters with the Webbs, also received *The Outsider*'s first annual "Outsider of the Year" Award in 1962. Bukowski himself referred to his brief time in New Orleans during a ten-year period of wandering in his 1975 novel, *Factotum*: "living on two five-cent candy bars a day for weeks at a time in order to have leisure to write . . . But starvation, unfortunately, didn't improve art . . . The myth of the starving artist was a hoax."

Loujon Press also published works by Jack Kerouac, Lawrence Ferlinghetti, Allen Ginsberg, William S. Burroughs, Langston Hughes, Diane di Prima, and Henry Miller (*Order and Chaos Chez Hans Reichel* and *Insomnia, or the Devil at Large*), as well as the artwork of Noel Rockmore (1928–95). The fascinating story of Loujon Press is highlighted in the 2007 biography *Bohemian New Orleans: The Story of the Outsider and Loujon Press* by Jeff Weddle, as well as the 2007 documentary *The Outsiders of New Orleans: Loujon Press*. The film's soundtrack features the talents of legendary New Orleans jazz trumpeter Punch Miller (1894–1971).

Mexico City

In his introduction to *Queer*, William S. Burroughs wrote, "In 1949, [Mexico City] was a cheap place to live, with a large foreign colony, fabulous whorehouses and restaurants, cockfights and bullfights, and every conceivable diversion. A single man could live well there for two dollars a day." On the run from the law after getting busted for drugs in New Orleans, Burroughs and his common-law wife, Joan Vollmer, arrived in Mexico City in the fall of 1949. Burroughs quickly befriended another junky, "Old Dave" Tesorero, who taught him the ways of the drug underworld in Mexico City. It was in Mexico City where Burroughs started writing *Junk*, an autobiographical novel that depicts his drug experiences and was eventually published as *Junky* under the pseudonym "William Lee" in 1953. Tesorero would appear as "Old Ike" in *Junky*. Burroughs also worked on a narrative documenting his withdrawal from heroin, along with his pursuit of a twenty-one-year-old Mexico City College student named Lewis Marker, which would eventually be published as *Queer* in 1985.

On September 6, 1951, Burroughs accidentally killed Joan, who is buried in the Panteon Americano cemetery in Mexico City. Released on bail, Burroughs headed to South America in search of the powerful hallucinogen yage. Burroughs's correspondence with Allen Ginsberg during his quest for yage in the Amazon rainforest would first be published as *The Yage Letters* in 1963. During the summer of 1955, Jack Kerouac lived in Mexico City, where he wrote *Mexico City Blues*. In addition, Kerouac's novella *Tristessa*, which was published in 1960, depicted his doomed relationship with a drug-addicted Mexican prostitute, who "is so high all the time, and sick, shooting ten grams of morphine per month,—staggering down the city streets yet so beautiful people keep turning and looking at her—Her eyes are radiant and shining."

San Francisco

In *On the Road*, Jack Kerouac wrote, "It seemed like a matter of minutes when we began rolling in the foothills before Oakland and suddenly reached a height and saw stretched out ahead of us the fabulous white city of San Francisco on her eleven mystic hills with the blue Pacific and its advancing wall of potato-patch fog beyond, and smoke and goldenness of the late afternoon of time." Bustling North Beach in San Francisco serves as a living legacy to the Beat Generation. Visitors can still browse through the stacks at City Lights Bookstore, which was founded in 1953 by poet Lawrence Ferlinghetti, who published Allen Ginsberg's *Howl and Other Poems* through his Pocket Poets Series in 1956. City Lights Bookstore has been designated a National Poetry Landmark by the Academy of American Poets.

Jack Kerouac Alley separates City Lights Bookstore from Vesuvio Café, which first opened its doors in 1948. Neal Cassady stopped at Vesuvio for a few drinks right before heading to the landmark 1955 poetry reading at the

The colorful mural *Vida y suenos de la canada Perla* (*Life and Dreams of the Perla River Valley*) adorns the side of City Lights Bookstore, which has been designated a National Poetry Landmark by the Academy of American Poets.   *Photo by Romain Fliedel/Wikimedia Commons*

Six Gallery. According to legend, Kerouac drank himself into a stupor at Vesuvio on the night that he was supposed to meet *Tropic of Cancer* author Henry Miller at his Big Sur home. The walls of Vesuvio are crammed with Beat-related memorabilia. The cocktail menu at Vesuvio features a "Jack Kerouac" (rum, tequila, orange, and cranberry juice with a squeeze of lime), as well as a "Kenneth Rexroth" (Maker's Mark, ginger, Peychaud's Bitters, and orange) and a "Swinging Beat" (Stoli Vodka, Pama Pomegranate, Cointreau, and fresh lime). Hardcore drinkers will appreciate the fact that Vesuvio is open 365 days a year from 6:00 a.m. until 2:00 a.m.!

Another Beat hangout, Caffe Trieste, was founded in 1956 by Italian immigrant and aspiring opera singer Giovanni "Papa Gianni" Giotta. The jukebox here features opera tunes only. Academy Award–winning director Francis Ford Coppola reportedly wrote the script for *The Godfather* at Caffe Trieste. Across Columbus Avenue from Vesuvio lies another eclectic drinking spot, Specs' Twelve Adler Museum Café. Richard "Specs" Simmons opened the bar in 1968 and filled it to the rafters with unusual artifacts he collected during his travels. Around the corner from Specs' lies the Beat Museum (www.kerouac .com), which was founded by Jerry Cimino in 2003 and features a wealth of

Beat-related artifacts and memorabilia, as well as rare books, T-shirts, CDs, and DVDs. It is a must-stop for any Beat aficionado visiting San Francisco.

Up near Coit Tower at the top of Telegraph Hill lies Bob Kaufman Alley (formerly Harwood Alley), a tribute to the San Francisco poet known as the "black American Rimbaud." At 3119 Fillmore Street is the former site of the Six Gallery, home to the famous poetry reading on October 7, 1955, where Ginsberg gave his first public reading of "Howl." Although the Six Gallery has been replaced by a furniture store, a plaque documents the famous location. Nestled in the heart of North Beach, Hotel Bohème on Columbus Avenue was originally built in the 1880s and was extensively renovated in the early 1990s. According to the hotel's official website (www.hotelboheme.com), "The Boheme was specially designed to reflect the culture and taste of late fifties North Beach. The hotel's interiors and design are reminiscent of the bohemian style and flavor the area was famous for during the heyday of the Beat era." Allen Ginsberg often stayed here when visiting North Beach in his later years.

North Beach is also home to Coppola's American Zoetrope Studios, which is housed in the historic, flatiron-style Sentinel Building (a.k.a. Columbus Tower, one of the few surviving structures of the 1906 San Francisco earthquake) at the corner of Columbus and Kearny. The European-style Café Zoetrope can be found on the first floor of the Sentinel Building. Sadly, defunct former Beat hangouts in North Beach include the Co-Existence Bagel Shop on Grant Avenue (which Kaufman immortalized in his poem "Bagel Shop Jazz"), the Cellar (a bustling club that featured jazz and poetry readings) at 574 Green Street, and the Place (an underground bohemian club famously home to "Blabbermouth Night") on Grant Avenue.

Venice Beach

Located just fourteen miles west of Los Angeles, funky and laid-back Venice Beach was a favorite haunt for Beat writers in Southern California during the 1950s. In his 1959 guide to beatnik culture in Southern California, *The Holy Barbarians*, Beat poet Lawrence Lipton referred to Venice as "a horizontal, jerry-built slum by the sea, warm under a semitropical Pacific sun on a Sunday afternoon." Born in Lodz, Poland, Lipton (1898–1975) was a well-known Beat poet and the father of James Lipton, who became the host of *Inside the Actors Studio*. Visionary Abbot Kinney (1850–1920) founded Venice Beach in 1905 as an upscale beach resort with sixteen miles of manmade canals, as well as beachfront homes and shops. However, Venice Beach never evolved into the upscale paradise envisioned by its founder and became known instead as the "Coney Island of the Pacific" for its plethora of amusement attractions. By the mid-1960s, Venice had become totally rundown, but offered the enticement of low rents and cheap eateries. The bohemian crowd moved to Venice Beach in droves.

In the 1950s and 1960s, Venice Beach became a hub of Beat activity centered on writers such as Lipton, Stuart Z. Perkoff, John Thomas, Philomene Long, Tom Sewell, John Haag, Saul White, Frank T. Rios, Tony Scibella, and others. Beat hangouts in Venice Beach included the Gas House, which was owned by hipster Eric "Big Daddy' Nord and served as the setting for several scenes in the cult horror film *The Hypnotic Eye* (1960). Opened by Perkoff in 1958, the Venice West Café at 7 Dudley Avenue served as one of the main Beat hangouts in Venice. In a 1965 *Los Angeles Times* interview, Lipton lamented, "The Venice West Beat scene was the most promising attempt ever made to bring avant-garde culture to Southern California, and it was murdered by self-righteous, puritanical busybodies and hostile police."

According to poet David Meltzer, "Lipton, who was an older guy who looked like any one of my Jewish uncles—balding, thick horn rims, cigar-chopping, and a spoken-word evangelist before his time. He'd play reel-to-reel tapes of himself and other Venice poets declaiming their verse. Lipton's stuff was kind of corny to me, and the Venice scene seemed more like the Hollywood B-movie version of Beatsville. Perkoff was, hands down, the major poet there, and his work bears it out." Venice Beach poet John Thomas and his wife, Philomene Long, collaborated on *LA Exile: A Guide to Los Angeles Writing 1932–1998* (1999). For a definitive history of the Venice Beach Beat scene, look no farther than *Venice West: The Beat Generation in Southern California* (1993) by John Arthur Maynard.

Desolation Peak

During the summer of 1956, a thirty-four-year-old Jack Kerouac hitchhiked from San Francisco and spent sixty-three days as a US Forest Service fire lookout atop 6,102-foot Desolation Peak in the Mount Baker National Forest in Whatcom County, Washington. A two-way radio to the ranger station was Kerouac's only contact with the outside world. Kerouac's solitary stay (his salary was just $230 a month) provided material for his novels *The Dharma Bums* (1958) and *Desolation Angels* (1965), as well as the short story "Alone on a Mountaintop" in *Lonesome Traveler* (1960). It was Kerouac's friend, Beat poet and Buddhist scholar Gary Snyder (the model for "Japhy Ryder" in *The Dharma Bums*) who had suggested the fire lookout position to Kerouac. Snyder himself had worked as a fire lookout for two summers on nearby Crater Mountain in 1952 and Sourdough Mountain in 1953. In addition, San Francisco Renaissance poet Philip Whalen had also served as a fire lookout in the North Cascades during the early 1950s. All three writers studied Zen Buddhism and followed ninth-century Chinese poet Hanshan's lead when he wrote, "Who can leap the world's ties / And sit with me among the white clouds?"

Legendary photographer, surveyor, and cartographer Lage Wernstedt, who served with the US Forest Service for thirty-five years, first climbed Desolation Peak in 1926. Today, hardy visitors can follow Kerouac's footsteps with a strenuous hike up to Desolation Peak, which is accessible by trail twenty-three miles from the nearest road or via a one-hour boat ride up Ross Lake and then seven miles of trail. The trailhead lies about three hours from Seattle. Built in 1933, the fourteen-by-fourteen historic fire lookout at Desolation Peak that briefly served as Kerouac's home is listed on the National Historic Lookout Register, a cooperative effort of the US Forest Service, Forest Fire Lookout Association, state agencies, and other private groups to recognize historic fire lookouts throughout the United States. The Desolation Peak fire lookout remains one of the most remote active lookouts in the United States. In the distance lie the twin peaks of 8,071-foot Hozomeen Mountain, which Kerouac described as "the void." Other surrounding peaks include Jack Mountain, Mount Prophet, Eldorado Peak, Three Fools Peak, Snowfield Peak, and Luna Peak.

Billed as "the story of the birth of a wilderness ethic," John Suiter's 2003 book *Poets on the Peaks: Gary Snyder, Philip Whalen and Jack Kerouac* profiles the three writers during their fire-lookout summers in the North Cascades during the 1950s utilizing majestic images and previously unpublished letters and journals, as well as interviews with Snyder and Whalen.

Tangier

In his introduction to *Naked Lunch* (1959), William S. Burroughs wrote, "I lived in one room in the Native Quarter of Tangier. I had not taken a bath in a year nor changed my clothes or removed them except to stick a needle every hour in the fibrous grey wooden flesh of terminal addiction. I never cleaned or dusted the room . . . I did absolutely nothing. I could look at the end of my shoe for eight hours. I was only roused to action when the hourglass of junk ran out." Burroughs moved to the Villa Muniria in Tangier, Morocco, in 1955 and began working on *Naked Lunch* (where Tangier morphs into the nightmarish "Interzone"). According to Burroughs in *The Adding Machine* (1986), "For the first time in my life I began writing full-time and the material from which *Naked Lunch* was later abstracted and a good deal of the material that went into *The Soft Machine* and *The Ticket That Exploded* was produced at this time." Burroughs also befriended author Paul Bowles (*The Sheltering*

Sky), and his wife, Jane, also an author and playwright, who had been living in Tangier since the late 1940s. *The Sheltering Sky* had been first published in 1949 with the rather lurid tagline "An Exciting Bestseller of a Daring Woman Who Became a Harem Wife."

In one instance, Bowles lent Burroughs a first edition of *The Angel in the Alcove* by Tennessee Williams. According to Burroughs in *With William Burroughs* (1981), "I was on junk at the time and I dripped blood all over it, and Paul was furious. It should be quite a collector's item—first edition, and with my blood all over it." In his 1972 autobiography, *Without Stopping*, Bowles wrote, "During my convalescence a tall thin man came to see me, brought by a Tangier acquaintance. His name was William Burroughs, and he had just written a book entitled *Junkie* and sold it directly to a paperback company; this was the first time I had heard of anyone doing such a thing . . . His manner was subdued to the point of making his presence in the room tentative. I recalled having seen him before from time to time, walking in the street, not looking to right or left." It was Bowles who introduced Burroughs to Brion Gysin "because I thought they would get on well together. I was right: eventually they became inseparable."

Between 1956 and 1958, Burroughs had several visitors, including Allen Ginsberg, Peter Orlovsky, Jack Kerouac, and Alan Ansen, who helped him type the manuscript. In a letter to Lucien Carr, Kerouac remarked that Burroughs had "gone insane" and "his new book is best thing of its kind in the world (Genet, Celine, Miller, etc.) & we might call it WORD HOARD . . . His message is all scatological homosexual super-violent madness." Jane Bowles thought that Ginsberg was a "complete madman" because he called once asking for her husband by introducing himself as "Allen Ginsberg, the Bop poet," and asking her if she believed in God. When Paul Bowles finally met Ginsberg he was with Orlovsky and Ansen "collecting the typed pages of a work in progress by Burroughs which had been lying on the floor of Bill's basement room these many months. Often I had looked at the chaos of sheets of yellow paper being trampled underfoot, thinking that he must like to have them there, otherwise he would have picked them up . . . I liked Ginsberg for being honest and dedicated, but Jane found him insensitive because he mentioned William Carlos Williams' recent stroke and its unfortunate results upon his ability to work" (*Without Stopping*, 1972).

Burroughs departed Tangier for Paris in 1959 to take up residence in the "Beat Hotel." In 1985, the author returned to Tangier for a visit and commented, "To me the town was hardly recognizable—the Parade Bar was closed, and with the exception of my old friend Paul Bowles, there was almost no one still there from the late 1950s."

Paris

During the late 1950s and early 1960s, the rundown "Beat Hotel" at 9 rue Git-le-Coeur on the Left Bank in Paris was home to Beat writers William S. Burroughs, Gregory Corso, Allen Ginsberg, and Peter Orlovsky, as well as an eclectic assortment of jazz musicians, prostitutes, artists, and writers. In fact, the forty-two-room hotel (which didn't even have a proper name!) barely met the minimum health and safety standards of the day, and cost ten francs a night (about fifty US cents). The "Beat Hotel" was run by a rather eccentric proprietor by the name of Madame Rachou. According to photographer Harold Chapman in a 2012 interview with Michael Limnios at www.blues.gr.com, "Madame Rachou used to spy on everybody and controlled everybody with an iron hand. Some artists couldn't pay the rent so Madame Rachou took paintings instead and had a huge store in her cellar." After Madame Rachou sold the hotel, the artwork was burned "in an act of unspeakable vandalism," according to Chapman.

It was at the "Beat Hotel" where Burroughs completed *Naked Lunch* (it was published by Olympia Press in Paris in 1959) and learned the so-called "cut-up technique" from his good friend—the artist and writer Brion Gysin—that would influence so much of his later work, including his Nova Trilogy (comprising *The Soft Machine*, *The Ticket That Exploded*, and *Nova Express*). Gysin later developed (along with mathematician Ian Sommerville) the

Dedicated in 2009, a plaque outside the former site of the legendary "Beat Hotel" at 9 rue Git-le-Coeur in Paris honors seven of its most famous occupants: Brion Gysin, Harold Norse, Gregory Corso, Allen Ginsberg, Peter Orlovsky, Ian Sommerville, and William S. Burroughs.   *Photo by Monceau/Wikimedia Commons*

Dreamachine, a stroboscopic flicker device used to produce visual stimuli or "sober hallucinations," at the hotel. Ginsberg worked on portions of his landmark poem "Kaddish" about his mother, Naomi, while residing at the hotel. Corso lived in a tiny room in the hotel's attic and penned several of his most famous poems, including "Bomb." Author Harold Norse wrote an experimental cut-up novel, *Beat Hotel*, while residing at the "Beat Hotel."

Through it all, Chapman documented Beat activity at the "Beat Hotel" with his black-and-white photography, calling the experience both "Dada" and "surreal." Chapman later published two photography books documenting the period: *Beat Hotel* (1984) and *Beats in Paris* (2001).

While residing at the "Beat Hotel," the Beat writers often frequented the legendary Shakespeare and Company bookstore, which was opened in 1951 by brilliant, eccentric, and cantankerous American expatriate George Whitman (1913–2011), who referred to his business as a "den of anarchists disguised as a bookstore." Whitman, who was totally passionate about books and lived in a tiny apartment above the bookstore, inherited the rights to use the name "Shakespeare and Company" from Sylvia Beach, who owned the original Shakespeare and Company (1919–41), a favorite of such renowned writers as Ernest Hemingway, Gertrude Stein, and James Joyce (Beach published the first edition of *Ulysses* in 1922).

Whitman, who himself befriended such famous authors as James Baldwin, Samuel Beckett, Lawrence Durrell, Richard Wright, Anaïs Nin, and Henry Miller, allowed young writers, artists, and total strangers to actually crash at the bookstore in exchange for working odd jobs there (he would regularly cook his guests a signature batch of pancakes that tasted like they were mixed with cleaning products as roaches scrambled around nearby). A sign over one of the doorways in the bookstore stated Whitman's philosophy: "Be Not Inhospitable to Strangers Lest They Be Angels in Disguise."

Currently owned and operated by Whitman's daughter, Sylvia, Shakespeare and Company to this day serves as the "sister store" of Lawrence Ferlinghetti's City Lights Bookstore in San Francisco. Whitman passed away in 2011 at the age of ninety-eight and is buried at Père Lachaise Cemetery along with the likes of Oscar Wilde, Marcel Proust, Frederic Chopin, Victor Hugo, Colette, Gertrude Stein, Guillaume Apollinaire, and Jim Morrison. Whitman and his famous bookstore were profiled in the fascinating 2003 documentary *Portrait of a Bookstore as an Old Man*. Directed by Benjamin Sutherland and Gonzague Pichelin, the film made its debut on the Sundance Channel. Whitman's unconventional personality shines through in this brief (fifty-two-minute running time) but fascinating documentary, such as when he throws some of his infamous tantrums and cuts his own hair using a candle flame!

The "Beat Hotel" closed its doors for good in 1963. Burroughs headed to London and in a 1965 *Paris Review* interview commented, "To me, Paris is now one of the most disagreeable cities in the world. I just hate it. The food is uneatable . . . The French have gotten so nasty and they're getting nastier and nastier." The former "Beat Hotel" location is now occupied by the four-star Relais du Vieux Paris. A brass plaque located outside the hotel was erected in 2009 and lists the following names: "B. Gysin, H. Norse, G. Corso, A. Ginsberg, P. Orlovsky, I. Sommerville, W. Burroughs."

6

A Point of No Return

The San Francisco Renaissance

The West Coast "wing" of the Beat Generation featured such talented writers as Kenneth Rexroth, Michael McClure, Robert Duncan, William Everson (a.k.a. Brother Antoninus), Philip Whalen, Bob Kaufman, Lew Welch, Philip Lamantia, Kenneth Patchen, Kirby Doyle, and others. However, it must be said that there was a thriving poetry scene in San Francisco for many years before the landmark Six Gallery Reading on October 7, 1955. In a *Jacket* magazine interview, Whalen remarked, "In 1955 Ginsberg and Kerouac showed up, and we began 'the revolution'—which had been started by Robert Duncan and Jack Spicer and everybody earlier on. We were all carpetbaggers, which did not sit well with the locals." According to Everson, "Here we were all being tagged San Francisco or beat poets in 1955, which made no sense, and a lot of people resented it, but it did bring new attention to the scene" (*William Everson: The Life of Brother Antoninus*, 1988).

Kenneth Rexroth (1905–82)

"Against the ruin of the world, there is only one defense—the creative act." Poet, critic, translator, pacifist, philosophical anarchist, painter, mentor, and elder statesman of the San Francisco Renaissance Kenneth Rexroth was known as the "Father of the Beats" (although he hated that label and in fact did not consider himself a Beat writer at all). Kenneth Charles Marion Rexroth was born in South Bend, Indiana, on December 22, 1905. Orphaned at the age of fourteen, Rexroth moved to Chicago to live with his aunt. It was in Chicago where Rexroth discovered the anarchist movement and turned to social activism. A high school dropout, Rexroth traveled across the country, supporting himself through a series of jobs such as cook, meat packer, clerk, reporter, and soda jerk. Rexroth eventually made his way to San Francisco in the late 1920s.

A conscientious objector during World War II, Rexroth actively assisted Japanese-American internees. Rexroth's first collection of poems, *In What Hour*, was published in 1940, followed by *The Phoenix and the Tortoise* in 1944.

Most of Rexroth's work can be classified as "erotic poetry." In a 1958 interview (published on the *Jacket* magazine website at www.jacketmagazine.com), Rexroth commented, "What I try with my own stuff is to work the poem to a slow climax through a series of quiet painful dissonances." In the late 1940s, Rexroth became a host on the radio station KPFA and started promoting the poetry of up-and-coming writers such as William Everson, Philip Whalen, Lawrence Ferlinghetti, and Denise Levertov. Rexroth also helped organize and served as master of ceremonies for the landmark Six Gallery poetry reading on October 7, 1955, where Allen Ginsberg first introduced "Howl" to the world.

Rexroth was caricatured as "Reinhold Cacoethes" in Jack Kerouac's 1958 novel, *The Dharma Bums*. In a 1958 interview, Rexroth remarked, "I have no interest in Kerouac whatsoever. I've done my stint for him. As far as I'm concerned, Kerouac is what Madison Avenue wants a rebel to be. That isn't my kind of rebel." In his 1959 book, *Bird in the Bush/Obvious Essays*, Rexroth wrote, "The Beat Generation may once have been human beings—today they are simply comical bogies conjured up by the Luce publications." Rexroth moved to Santa Barbara, California, in 1968 and taught at the University of California, Santa Barbara, until 1974 when he was awarded a Fulbright scholarship to study in Japan. In 1975, Rexroth received the Copernicus Award from the Academy of American Poets in recognition of his lifetime of work and contribution to poetry as a cultural force. Rexroth, who was married four times (to Andree Dutcher, Marie Kass, Marthe Larsen, and Carol Tinker, respectively), died on June 6, 1982. He is buried in Santa Barbara Cemetery on a cliff overlooking the sea.

Kenneth Patchen (1911–72)

"Flowers alternate with her eyes as we journey through these prodigal catacombs." A pioneer of painted poems (many of which were published posthumously in the 1984 collection *What Shall We Do Without Us*) and jazz poetry, Kenneth Patchen was also a pacifist and mainstay of the San Francisco poetry scene. Patchen was born in Niles, Ohio, on December 13, 1911. He moved to Wisconsin after high school and attended the University of Wisconsin briefly before dropping out to travel the country, working odd jobs along the way. In 1934, Patchen married Miriam Oikemus and the couple moved to Greenwich Village for several years, during which time he published his first collection of poetry, *Before the Brave*, in 1936.

In 1942, Patchen collaborated with composer John Cage on a radio play, *The Radio Wears a Slouch Hat*. He also wrote a series of experimental novels, including *The Journal of Albion Moonlight* (1941) and *The Memoirs of a Shy*

Pornographer (1945). Novelist Henry Miller (*Tropic of Cancer*) was an early supporter of Patchen's work and even wrote a long essay titled *Patchen: Man of Anger and Light* (which was published in 1946). During the 1950s, Patchen was known for reading his poetry to the accompaniment of jazz music, including a memorable performance with the Chamber Jazz Sextet in 1957. Patchen was a major influence on Beat writers such as Lawrence Ferlinghetti and Allen Ginsberg but later derided the media hype surrounding the Beat Generation as a "freak show."

Patchen struggled with crippling back pain for most of his adult life due to a spinal injury, and a botched surgery in 1959 left him almost completely bedridden for the rest of his life. In 1967, Patchen received an award for his "life-long contribution to American letters" from the National Foundation on the Arts and Humanities. *The Collected Poems of Kenneth Patchen* was published the following year to positive reviews, including one by David Meltzer, who called him "one of America's great poet-prophets" and compared his work to that of Walt Whitman and William Blake. In a *Gargoyle* magazine interview, Patchen remarked, "People who say they love poetry and don't buy any are a bunch of cheap sons-of-bitches." When Patchen died on January 8, 1972, in Palo Alto, California, his wife, Miriam, remarked, "He looked like someone who had been homeless for three thousand years."

Lawrence Ferlinghetti wrote a tribute poem called "Elegy on the Death of Kenneth Patchen." Singer-songwriter Jimmy Buffett has acknowledged that Patchen was the inspiration for his song "Death of an Unpopular Poet," which appeared on his 1973 album, *A White Sport Coat and a Pink Crustacean*, and ends with the lines "And everybody wonders / Did he really lost his mind / No, he was just a poet who lived before his time." In a December 1976 *High Times* interview, Buffett remarked, "I was watching Walter Cronkite one night and he had a little blurb on there that Kenneth Patchen had died. That surprised me, because hardly anybody ever heard of Patchen except in small circles. He was one of my favorite poets."

William Everson (1912–94)

Often referred to as a "prophetic visionary," William Oliver Everson (a.k.a. Brother Antoninus) was born in Sacramento, California, on September 10, 1912. He attended Fresno State College briefly before dropping out. In 1933, Everson entered the Civilian Conservation Corps, where he worked on building roads in Sequoia National Park and encountered the work of Robinson Jeffers, whereupon "suddenly the whole inner world began to tremble" (Everson would later write several critical studies of Jeffers: *Robinson Jeffers: Fragments of an Older Fury* in 1968 and *The Excesses of God: Robinson Jeffers as a*

Religious Figure in 1988). Everson published his first book of poetry, *These Are the Ravens*, in 1935.

After registering with the draft board as an anarchist and pacifist during World War II, Everson was sent to a work camp for conscientious objectors in Waldport, Oregon, called Camp Angel (poet Kenneth Patchen was also residing there at the time). During his time at Camp Angel, Everson wrote a volume of poems called *The Residual Years*. After the war, Everson made his way to San Francisco, where he was mentored by Kenneth Rexroth. According to Everson (*Talking Poetry* interview, 1987), "Rexroth got the thing started in San Francisco, then Ginsberg took it back east and sold it to *Time*." Everson joined the Dominican Order in 1951 in Oakland and took the name "Brother Antoninus" (he was later tagged with the nickname "Beat Friar").

Everson left the Dominican Order in 1969 and married his third wife, Susanna Rickson. He was diagnosed with Parkinson's disease in the early 1970s. Everson served as a poet-in-residence at the University of California, Santa Cruz (UCSC), during the 1970s and 1980s, founded the Lime Kiln Press at UCSC, and lived in a rustic cabin known as "Kingfisher Flat." In the fall of 1977, *Sequoia*, the Stanford University literary magazine, published a "William Everson/Brother Antoninus Issue." A gifted literary theorist, Everson published *Archetype West: The Pacific Coast as a Literary Region* in 1976. Everson founded a small press through which he printed his own work, as well as that of Robinson Jeffers and others.

Everson was named Artist of the Year by the Santa Cruz County Arts Commission in 1991. Suffering from advanced-stage Parkinson's disease and sipping from a bottle of Jack Daniel's, Everson read his poetry to the standing-room-only crowd. Everson died at the age of eighty-one on June 3, 1994, at his Kingfisher Flat cabin. Black Sparrow Press released a three-volume series, *The Collected Poems of William Everson: Volume 1: The Residual Years, 1934–1948; Volume 2: The Veritable Years, 1949–1966;* and *Volume 3: The Integral Years, 1966–1994*.

Robert Duncan (1919–88)

Kenneth Rexroth referred to Robert Duncan as "one of the most accomplished, one of the most influential" of the postwar American poets. Michael McClure remarked of Duncan, "I was amazed by his clarity of perception and his ability to express himself and to be concise." Although Lew Welch admitted that "Duncan's work is very beautiful," he also thought his poems were "utterly useless and will not have any heirs. And it will not go anywhere." Born Edward Howard Duncan in Oakland, California, on January 7, 1919, he was put up for adoption when he was six months old (his mother had died in childbirth). Duncan attended the University of California, Berkeley (1936–38), and later briefly attended the experimental Black Mountain College in North Carolina. In 1941, Duncan received a psychiatric discharge from the Army after declaring his homosexuality. Duncan wrote a landmark essay titled "The Homosexual in Society," which was published in the March 1944 issue of *Politics*, a journal edited by Dwight Macdonald.

In 1944, Duncan edited the *Experimental Review* in New York but returned to San Francisco the following year and befriended poet Kenneth Rexroth, who introduced him to the poetry of Edith Sitwell and H. D. (Hilda Doolittle). Duncan's first book of poetry, *Heavenly City Earthly City*, was published in 1947. In 1951, Duncan met artist Jess Collins (1923–2004), who became his lifetime companion and collaborator, providing illustrations for many of his books. In his essay "The Truth and Life of Myth," Duncan wrote, "The poetic imagination faces the challenge of finding a structure that will be the complex story of all the stories felt to be true, a myth in which something like the variety of man's experience of what is real may be contained." Duncan's other works include *The Opening of the Field* (1960), *Roots and Branches* (1964), and *Bending the Bow* (1968). In 1985, Duncan received the National Poetry Award.

Duncan died on February 3, 1988. An expanded edition of Michael Rumaker's classic study, *Robert Duncan in San Francisco*, was published by City Lights Publishers in 2013, and is billed as "both a portrait of the premier poet of the San Francisco Renaissance and a fascinating account of gay life in late 1950s America."

Philip Whalen (1923–2002)

Upon hearing of his friend Philip Whalen's death, Gary Snyder remarked, "He was a poet's poet . . . His intelligence and skill is very subtle and very deep. There are many poets who feel in his debt" (*SFGate*, June 27, 2002). A celebrated poet, Zen Buddhist, and major figure in the San Francisco Renaissance, Whalen was born in Portland, Oregon, on October 20, 1923. After serving in the US Army Air Corps, Whalen attended Reed College in Oregon on the GI Bill and roomed with both Gary Snyder and Lew Welch. Whalen reminded Snyder of Dr. Samuel Johnson since "his humor was dry, witty, ironic and learned." While attending Reed, Whalen studied calligraphy with acclaimed calligrapher Lloyd J. Reynolds. He reportedly became interested in Zen Buddhism after Snyder lent him several books on the subject by D. T. Suzuki.

After graduation, Whalen headed to the San Francisco Bay Area and was one of the six poets at the historic Six Gallery Reading on October 7, 1955. Whalen's poems "Sourdough Mountain Lookout" and "2 Variations: All

About Love" appeared in the landmark poetry anthology *The New American Poetry 1945–1960* (1960), which was edited by Donald Allen. Whalen also inspired several of Jack Kerouac's characters, including "Warren Coughlin" in *The Dharma Bums* and "Ben Fagin" in *Big Sur*. Like both Kerouac and Snyder, Whalen served as a fire lookout in the Cascade Mountains, where (quite unlike Kerouac) he thrived in solitude, filling up several notebooks and journals with his writing.

Whalen published more than a dozen books of poetry, including *Like I Say* (1960), *Memoirs of an Interglacial Age* (1960), *On Bear's Head* (1969), and *Canoeing up Cabarga Creek* (1996), as well as two novels, *You Didn't Even Try* (1967) and *Imaginary Speeches for a Brazen Head* (1972). Whalen's memoir, *The Diamond Noodle*, was published in 1980. Whalen's work is also featured in *The Portable Beat Reader* (1992), which was edited by Ann Charters. Whalen studied Buddhism in Japan during the mid-1960s. Upon returning to the United States, Whalen became a student of Zentatsu Richard Baker. Ordained as a Zen Buddhist priest in 1973, Whalen became head monk of Dharma Sangha in Santa Fe, New Mexico, in 1984, and then served as abbot of the Hartford Street Zen Center in San Francisco. Whalen died on June 26, 2002, at the age of seventy-eighty after a long illness.

Bob Kaufman (1925–86)

Robert Garnell Kaufman was born on April 18, 1925, in New Orleans, Louisiana, to a black Roman Catholic mother and a German-Jewish pool hall operator father. He ran away from home at the age of thirteen and eventually joined the merchant marine. Kaufman ended up in New York City in the early 1940s and studied literature at the New School, where he met both Allen Ginsberg and William S. Burroughs.

Known as the "American Rimbaud," poet Bob Kaufman was honored posthumously with the naming of Bob Kaufman Alley near Coit Tower in San Francisco.   *Author's collection*

Inspired by both Surrealism and jazz music, Kaufman developed a large following in France, where he was known as the "American Rimbaud." Kaufman moved to North Beach in San Francisco in 1958 and resided there for most of the rest of his life. Kaufman began reciting his spontaneous poetry in the bars and coffeehouses (including the famed Co-Existence Bagel Shop), as well as the streets of San Francisco—earning the moniker "The Original Bebop Man." In fact, *San Francisco Chronicle* columnist Herb Caen later remarked that he had Kaufman in mind when he coined the word "beatnik" in 1958. According to Caen, in the obituary for Kaufman that appeared in the *Los Angeles Times* (January 14, 1986), "It was a combination of the beat poets like him and Sputnik (the first Soviet satellite) that typified the era and gave me the word."

Inspired by both surrealism and jazz music, Bob Kaufman earned the moniker of "Original Bebop Man" for his spirited reciting of spontaneous poetry on the streets of San Francisco.
Author's collection

Kaufman was one of the founders of *Beatitude* magazine in 1959, along with Allen Ginsberg, A. D. Winans, William Margolis, and John Kelly. He also had a small role in the 1960 underground film *The Flower Thief*, which was shot by Ron Rice in North Beach and also featured Taylor Mead and Eric "Big Daddy" Nord. In 1961, Kaufman was nominated for Great Britain's prestigious Guinness Award (losing out to T. S. Eliot). According to Jack Micheline in a 1997 *Chiron Review* interview, "Bob Kaufman was a true jazz poet. He was more musical. He figured in the rhapsody of bop and jazz." Despondent over the assassination of President John F. Kennedy, Kaufman took a Buddhist vow of silence that lasted until the end of the Vietnam War. On that day, he recited his poem "All Those Ships That Never Sailed." Kaufman's books of poetry include *Solitudes Crowded with Loneliness* (1965), *Golden Sardine* (1966), *Watch My Tracks* (1971), and *The Ancient Rain: Poems 1956–1978* (1981).

According to writer Neeli Cherkovski in *Whitman's Wild Children* (1989), "Kaufman was committed to oral poetry. Much of his work survives because his wife, Eileen, wrote it down as he spontaneously recited it. *Golden Sardine* is filled with poems written on scraps of paper, rescued by Kaufman's friends ... His last book, *The Ancient Rain*, came to fruition because of the care given by Raymond Foye [of Hanuman Books] to gathering all of the poet's unpublished writings from paper scraps, napkins, old tape recordings, and singed manuscripts retrieved from Kaufman's burned-out hotel room. Kaufman himself would have nothing to do with the shaping of the book."

Frequently homeless, Kaufman also battled drug addiction for a number of years. He died of emphysema at the age of sixty on January 12, 1986, and his ashes were scattered onto San Francisco Bay. A street in San Francisco was renamed "Bob Kaufman Alley" in his honor. According to *The Outlaw Bible of American Poetry* (1999), "Kaufman was a street poet, a people's poet, a poet's poet. He was a multi-ethnic poet, an African American poet, a Beat poet, a surrealist poet, a jazz poet, a poète maudit, a New Orleans poet, a San Francisco poet."

Lew Welch (1926–71)

No one talks about Lew Welch anymore, but he deserves to be better remembered. Welch was born Lewis Barrett "Lew" Welch Jr. in Phoenix, Arizona, on August 16, 1926, and attended Reed College in Portland, Oregon, where he roomed with poets Gary Snyder and Philip Whalen. He became coeditor of the school's literary magazine and wrote his senior thesis on Gertrude Stein. William Carlos Williams, Sherwood Anderson, and Ernest Hemingway were also among his early influences. After graduating from Reed College, Welch headed to New York City and became a copywriter for an ad agency (he reportedly came up with the slogan "RAID KILLS BUGS DEAD"). Welch then attended the University of Chicago, where he studied philosophy and English before joining Montgomery Ward's advertising department.

Welch returned to California after getting a transfer to the Oakland office of Montgomery Ward and quickly became involved in the San Francisco literary scene. His work was included in the groundbreaking 1960 anthology *The New American Poetry*. Jack Kerouac based the character "Dave Wain" from his

GARY SNYDER
JOANNE KYGER • TOM KILLION
AND SURPRISE GUESTS
HONOR BEAT ICON
LEW WELCH

celebrating the new edition of

RING OF BONE
SELECTED POEMS
by Lew Welch
with a new foreword by Gary Snyder

published by City Lights

Lew Welch was a brilliant poet, legendary
among his Beat peers. In 1971, he
disappeared leaving behind a suicide
note. *Ring of Bone* collects poems, songs,
and even a few drawings, documenting the
full sweep of his creative output, from his
early years until just before his disappearance.
First published by legendary poetry editor
Donald Allen, this expanded edition
includes a new foreword from close friend,
Gary Snyder, a biographic timeline, and a
statement of poetics gleaned from Welch's
own writing.

Join Gary Snyder and friends as they pay
tribute to Lew Welch.

This event is free and open to the public

THURSDAY • JULY 12, 2012 • 6:00 P.M.
SAN FRANCISCO PUBLIC LIBRARY
100 LARKIN STREET • SAN FRANCISCO

Beat poet Lew Welch disappeared without a trace in 1971. A new
edition of his celebrated body of work was published as *Ring of Bone:
Collected Poems of Lew Welch* in 2012 with a foreword by Gary Snyder.
Author's collection

1962 novel, *Big Sur*, on Welch, who was at the time in a relationship with poet
Lenore Kandel ("Ramona Swartz" in the novel). From 1965 to 1970, Welch
taught a poetry workshop as part of the Extension program of the University
of California, Berkeley. Welch had a common-law relationship with Magda
Cregg and was stepfather to her son Hugh Anthony Cregg III, who later
became famous as musician Huey Lewis of Huey Lewis and the News (choosing his stage name to honor Welch).

Throughout his life, Welch suffered from frequent bouts of depression and heavy drinking. On May 23, 1971, Welch left Gary Snyder's
house in the Sierra Nevadas with a revolver. Snyder found a suicide note in

Welch's truck that read: "I never could make anything work out right and now I'm betraying my friends. I can't make anything out of it—never could. I had great visions but never could bring them together with reality. I used it all up. It's all gone." His body was never found. One of the last poems Welch wrote was called "Song of the Turkey Buzzard," which eerily foreshadowed his disappearance.

Several of Welch's works were published posthumously, such as *How I Work as a Poet* (1973), *Trip Trap* (1973, with Jack Kerouac and Albert Saijo), and *How I Read Gertrude Stein* (1996). Welch was also the subject of a critical study published in 1979 by Aram Saroyan titled *Genesis Angels: The Saga of Lew Welch and the Beat Generation*. City Lights published *Ring of Bone: Collected Poems by Lew Welch* in 2012 with a foreword by Gary Snyder, who commented, "Lew Welch writes lyrical poems of clarity, humor, and dark probings . . . jazz musical phrasings of American speech is one of Welch's clearest contributions." In addition, the Geisel Library of the University of California, San Diego, holds a selection of Welch's papers.

Philip Lamantia (1927–2005)

In 2005, Nancy Peters, writer/editor and co-owner of City Lights Books, said of her late husband, the poet Philip Lamantia, "He found in the narcotic night world a kind of modern counterpart to the gothic castle—a zone of peril to be symbolically or existentially crossed." Allen Ginsberg called Lamantia "an American original, soothsayer even as Poe, genius in the language of Whitman, native companion and teacher of myself."

Lamantia was born in San Francisco, California, on October 23, 1927, to Sicilian immigrants. He became fascinated with Surrealism as a young teenager after viewing a retrospective exhibition of Salvador Dali and Joan Miró at the San Francisco Museum of Art, and his work was first published in *View: A Magazine of the Arts* in 1943 (he was just fifteen at the time and soon started working at *View* as an assistant editor) and in the influential Surrealist magazine *VVV* in 1944. Lamantia soon met Andre Breton, who called him "a voice that rises once in a hundred years." His first book of poetry, *Erotic Poems* (the title was suggested by Kenneth Rexroth), was published the following year. According to Lamantia, "On the West Coast—Berkeley and San Francisco—there was an extraordinary convergence of poets, painters, ex-conscientious objectors, and radical anarchists—rebels of all stripes. Kenneth Rexroth was the central figure, with Robert Duncan and Bill Everson connecting the two generations."

A key member of the San Francisco Renaissance, Lamantia participated in the Six Gallery Reading on October 7, 1955, choosing to read the prose poems of his recently deceased friend, John Hoffman. According to Lawrence Ferlinghetti, "Philip was a visionary like [William] Blake, and he really saw the whole world in a grain of sand . . . He was the primary transmitter of French Surrealist poetry in this country . . . He was writing stream-of-consciousness Surrealist poetry, and he had a huge influence on Allen Ginsberg. Before that, Ginsberg was writing rather conventional poetry. It was Philip who turned him on to Surrealist writing. Then Ginsberg wrote 'Howl'" (*SFGate*, 2005).

Michael McClure called Lamantia "a poet of the imagination . . . He was highly original—I'd call his poetry hyper-personal visionary Surrealism—and he was thrilling to be around. Everybody would sit around and listen to him all night. The flow of his imagination was a beautiful thing." In a review of Lamantia's *Selected Poems, 1943–1966*, in the *New York Times Book Review*, Tom Clark remarked that Lamantia's "poems are about rapture as a condition. They are spiritual and erotic at the same time. Bright and dark, the enclosed polarities of devotion. St. Teresa and Rimbaud." Lamantia inspired the character "Francis DaPavia" in Jack Kerouac's *The Dharma Bums* and *Tristessa*, and "David D'Angeli" in *Desolation Angels*. His surrealistic poetry can be found in such volumes as *The Blood of the Air* (1970), *Becoming Visible* (1981), *Meadowlark West* (1986), and *Bed of Sphinxes: New and Selected Poems 1943–1993* (1997).

Lamantia died of heart failure on March 7, 2005, in San Francisco at the age of seventy-seven. In his obituary for Lamantia in *SFGate*, Jesse Hamlin called him "a widely read, largely self-taught literary prodigy whose visionary poems—ecstatic, terror-filled, erotic—explored the subconscious world of dreams and linked it to the experience of daily life."

Kirby Doyle (1932–2003)

A fixture of the North Beach literary scene whose work has unfortunately faded into obscurity over the years, Kirby Doyle was born Stanton Doyle in San Francisco on November 27, 1932. An army veteran, Doyle started writing poetry while studying art at San Francisco State University. Doyle was heavily influenced by the Romantic poets, mainly John Keats. He soon befriended other San Francisco writers, such as Kenneth Rexroth, Robert Duncan, and Lew Welch.

In the Spring 1958 issue of *Chicago Review* devoted to San Francisco Renaissance writers, Doyle's poems appeared alongside the work of Jack Kerouac, Allen Ginsberg, and Lawrence Ferlinghetti. He was also featured in the 1960 anthology *The New American Poetry*. According to poet Michael McClure, Doyle was "an original Beat, loose-jointed, with a great laugh. His poetry was beautiful stuff." Doyle's friend and fellow writer Neeli Cherkovski called his verse "poetry without boundaries that—in clear, concise, musical language—expressed something timeless about the human condition." Venice Beach Beat poet Philomene Long remarked that "Doyle's work always startled me—like being fed lightning."

During the 1960s, several of Doyle's poems were published by the Communication Company, the publishing arm of the Diggers—the hippie activist group based in Haight-Ashbury in San Francisco. Former Digger Peter Coyote later remarked that Doyle's "mental life was prodigious, magnetic in the pull it exerted on his consciousness, drawing him, over the years, farther and farther from the rest of us." Doyle's first novel, *Happiness Bastard* (1968), was written using a single roll of paper—the same way Kerouac wrote *On the Road*. McClure later remarked, "The novel that he wrote, before it was butchered by its publisher, was the most grotesque and hilarious novel I'd seen. It was rich and autobiographical, and each person had become a cartoon character." Doyle also wrote a collection of love poems, *Sapphobones* (1966); an unpublished epic poem, "Pre American Ode"; and an unpublished novella, *White Flesh*.

Doyle's other works include *Ode to John Garfield* (1967), *Angel Faint* (1968), *The Collected Poems of Kirby Doyle* (1983), *After Olson* (1984), *The Questlock: Gymnopaean of A. Dianaei O'Tamal* (1987), *Lyric Poems* (1988), and *Crime, Justice & Tragedy and Das Erde Profundus* (1989). Doyle can be heard reading from *Angel Faint* on *Howls, Raps & Roars: Recordings from the San Francisco Poetry Renaissance* (1993). Doyle suffered from alcoholism and drug addiction for most of his life. In his later years, Doyle was treated at Laguna Honda Hospital for dementia and the effects of diabetes. He died on April 5, 2003, at the age of seventy.

Michael McClure (1932–)

"This was still a time of cold, gray silence, but inside the coffeehouses of North Beach, poets and friends sensed the atmosphere of liberation." Allen Ginsberg once referred to Michael McClure's poetry as "a blob of protoplasmic energy," while Jack Kerouac called McClure's long poem "Dark Brown" the "most fantastic poem in America." A critically acclaimed Beat poet, novelist, playwright, and songwriter, McClure was born on October 20, 1932. McClure's early influences included Percy Bysshe Shelley, John Keats, Walt Whitman, and William Blake. In fact, Gary Snyder later stated McClure was "closer to Blake than anybody else writing." At the age of twenty-two, McClure gave his first poetry reading at the legendary Six Gallery on October 7, 1955, the night that Allen Ginsberg first read "Howl." He chose to read the poem "For the Death of 100 Whales." According to McClure, "I overcame my own shyness when I read at the Six Gallery . . . when we all put our toes to the line in the sand. That was a pivotal moment in a life punctuated by pivotal moments."

McClure's first book of poetry, *Passage*, was published the following year. McClure served as the model for "Pat McLear" in Jack Kerouac's novel *Big Sur*. McClure famously read a selection from his collection of poetry *Ghost Tantras* (1964) to lions at the San Francisco Zoo. In a later interview, McClure remarked, "I read and they roared. We roared together." McClure's controversial play, *The Beard*, made its debut at the Actor's Workshop Theatre in San Francisco in December 1965 and provoked several high-profile censorship battles. The play depicts a fictional encounter between outlaw Billy the Kid and actress Jean Harlow. The San Francisco Police Department secretly taped one of the performances and raided the venue on August 8, 1966, arresting both of its stars, Billie Dixon and Richard Bright, and charging them with "lewd or dissolute conduct in a public place." The charges were later dropped.

On January 14, 1967, McClure read his poetry at the Human Be-In, which drew approximately twenty thousand attendees, in Golden Gate Park. McClure also cowrote the song "Mercedes Benz" with Janis Joplin. In addition, he was a close friend of Doors lead singer Jim Morrison and did much to help promote "The Lizard King" as a poet (the *Los Angeles Times* once characterized McClure as the "role model for Jim Morrison"). He also wrote the afterword to the seminal 1980 Morrison biography, *No One Here Gets Out Alive*, which was written by Jerry Hopkins and Danny Sugerman. Author and Beat historian Barry Miles referred to McClure as "the Prince of the San Francisco Scene," while actor Dennis Hopper once remarked, "Without McClure's roar there would have been no Sixties."

McClure has appeared in several films, including as a Hell's Angel in Norman Mailer's *Beyond the Law* (1968), as well as Peter Fonda's *The Hired Hand* (1971) and Martin Scorsese's 1978 documentary, *The Last Waltz* (reading a selection from *The Canterbury Tales*). In 1982, McClure published *Scratching the Beat Surface*, a book of essays. For many years, McClure toured extensively with Doors keyboardist Ray Manzarek. McClure continues to perform his poetry at festivals, colleges, and clubs throughout the United States.

7

State of Revolt

The Legendary Six Gallery Reading

One of the landmark events in Beat Generation history, the Six Gallery Reading took place on October 7, 1955, in San Francisco and featured poetry readings by Allen Ginsberg (who read "Howl" in public for the first time), Gary Snyder, Michael McClure, Philip Lamantia (who read poems of his late friend John Hoffman), and Philip Whalen before a crowd of approximately one hundred, including a drunkenly exuberant Jack Kerouac, who later remarked, "So here comes Snyder with a bottle of wine . . . and here comes Whalen, and here comes what's his name . . . Rexroth . . . and everybody . . . and we had the poetry renaissance of San Francisco" (*Paris Review*, Summer 1968).

History of the Six Gallery

Founded in 1954 by a group of six artists and writers that included Wally Hedrick, Deborah Remington, John Ryan, Jack Spicer, David Simpson, and Hayward King, the Six Gallery at 3119 Fillmore Street was opened on the former site of an auto repair shop that had been converted into the King Ubu Gallery by artist Jess Collins and his longtime companion, the poet Robert Duncan, in 1952. The only female among the founders, Remington (1930–2010), a renowned abstract painter and descendent of the Western artist Frederic Remington, was born in Haddonfield, New Jersey, and attended classes at the Philadelphia School of Industrial Art. She received her bachelor of fine arts in 1955 from the San Francisco Art Institute.

According to Bill Morgan in *The Beat Generation in San Francisco: A Literary Tour* (2003), "On [Six Gallery] opening day they displayed a toilet in the front window with a draft notice suspended over it. During the McCarthy era and the Korean War, this was a daring gesture, and the police showed up immediately, forcing them to remove the installation." A 1957 exhibition mailer for the Six Gallery stated, "The Six Gallery was established in September 1954 with the intention that there might exist in the San Francisco area some outlet for the works of local artists who had heretofore been met with varying

Neal Cassady, who served as the model for "Dean Moriarty" in *On the Road*, reportedly stopped for a drink at Vesuvio Café before attending the Six Gallery Reading. Today, the walls of Vesuvio are covered with Beat-related memorabilia.   *Author's collection*

degrees of indifference, disinterest, or hostility by the larger commercial galleries and museums of art, where the concern seems to lie less with local, contemporary artists, than with others who have perhaps already established themselves."

Wally Hedrick

One of the cofounders of the Six Gallery in San Francisco, Wally Hedrick (1928–2003) was instrumental in helping to organize the famous Six Gallery Reading on October 7, 1955. An idiosyncratic and prolific artist in the Surrealist and Dada tradition, Hedrick was heavily involved in helping shape the San Francisco art scene in general. Born in Pasadena, California, Hedrick, who received his BFA degree in Art from the California School of Fine Arts (now known as the San Francisco Art Institute) in 1955, is known for his pioneering artworks in Pop Art, psychedelic light art, mechanical kinetic sculpture, junk/assemblage sculpture, and Funk Art. Hedrick would later be dubbed the "Godfather of Funk Art" for his use of found materials such as beer cans, broken TV sets, and other junkyard artifacts in his sculptures. One of Hedrick's crushed beer can sculptures was shaped in a pyramid that he called "American Everest." In a 1974 interview for the Smithsonian Archives of American Art, Hedrick stated, "What interests me is to take garbage and make it into art, kind of ironic art."

As soon as the Six Gallery opened in 1954, it quickly evolved into a focal point for countercultural activity. By the following year, Hedrick had become official director of the Six Gallery, which served not only as an art gallery but also as a gathering place for unconventional writers throughout the Bay Area. In a 2004 interview, Hedrick remarked, "In San Francisco in the late '40s, early '50s, there was no venue for artists like us, or anybody really. There were a couple of galleries that showed contemporary work, but they were sort of holdovers from the Depression. [The Six Gallery] was very successful. People were starting to get recognized."

In regard to the Six Gallery Reading, Hedrick had first approached Ginsberg to organize a reading the year before, but Ginsberg did not feel like he was ready (that is, until he completed his first draft of "Howl"). During the reading itself, Hedrick and Jack Kerouac collected change from the audience to buy jugs of wine. In the late 1950s, Hedrick was actually hired by Vesuvio Café (located adjacent to City Lights Bookstore in North Beach) to sit in the window fully decked out as a beatnik—complete with a bushy beard, turtleneck, and sandals—while creating his improvisational paintings and drawings.

Hedrick taught at various institutions over the years, such as the San Francisco Art Institute; San Francisco Academy of Art; San Francisco State University; University of California, Davis; San Jose State; and the College of Marin. The Grateful Dead's Jerry Garcia studied with Hedrick at the San Francisco Art Institute as a teenager. According to Garcia in the 2005 book *Jerry Garcia: The Collected Artwork*, "Wally taught me that art is not only something you do, but something you are."

An antiwar activist, Hedrick protested US military actions abroad from the Vietnam War to the Iraq War. Hedrick was married to visual artist Jay DeFeo between 1954 and 1969. DeFeo is best known for her painting "The Rose," which took eight years to create and weighed approximately 2,300 pounds. Hedrick died of congestive heart failure on December 17, 2003, in Bodega Bay, California, at the age of seventy-three.

Rexroth—Master of Ceremonies

It was quite appropriate that the so-called "father" of the San Francisco Renaissance, Kenneth Rexroth, served as master of ceremonies at the Six Gallery Reading. Rexroth was well known among the poetry circles and held a popular open house in his apartment on Friday evenings that would draw an eclectic group of poets, artists, filmmakers, and anarchists. Allen Ginsberg had first met Rexroth in 1954 with a letter of introduction provided by William Carlos Williams.

Ginsberg's powerful reading of "Howl" reportedly reduced Rexroth to tears. In Kerouac's rendition of events featured in his 1958 novel, *The Dharma Bums*, "Between poets, Rheinhold Cacoethes, in his bow tie and shabby old coat, would get up and make a little funny speech in his snide funny voice and introduce the next reader: but as I say come eleven thirty when all the poems were ready and everybody was milling around wondering what had happened and what would come next in American poetry, he was wiping his eyes with his handkerchief." Because of his role mentoring the younger Beat poets and helping to organize the Six Gallery Reading, Rexroth was later dubbed the "Father of the Beat Generation," although he truly despised the label. He later remarked, "I've never understood why I'm [considered] a member of the avant-garde . . . I [just] try to say, as simply as I can, the simplest and most profound experiences of my life."

Lamantia's Reading

In a January 26, 1955, letter to Surrealist poet Philip Lamantia, author Henry Miller exclaimed, "You will probably be our greatest living poet since Whitman." However, Lamantia was odd man out at the Six Gallery Reading since he decided to read the prose poems of his friend, John Hoffman, instead of his own poems. Hoffman had died under mysterious circumstances in Mexico in 1951.

In his 1988 book, *Emergency Measures: An Autobiographical Miscellany*, Carl Solomon described Hoffman as a "friend of Gerd Stein, etc, also Philip Lamantia and Chris Maclaine, both California poets. Blond, handsome, bespectacled, long hair. Spaced out quality that amused many people. Girl friend blonde girl named to Mexico in 1950. Experimented with peyote. Died of mononucleosis while in Mexico. Poems highly regarded by avant-garde connoisseurs." William S. Burroughs referred to Hoffman as "one of those junkies in Mexico."

According to Lamantia, "John Hoffman, who died in Mexico at the age of twenty-five, was the poet whose poems I read at the Six Gallery Reading, and who was characterized by Carl Solomon in Ginsberg's quote from 'The Myth of John Hoffman' . . . John Hoffman had a wonderful definition: 'The hipster is a romantic idea.'" In 2008, City Lights published "two long-lost books from the classic Beat period" in a single volume through its Pocket Poets Series: *Tau* by Lamantia and *Journey to the End* by Hoffman.

McClure's Reading

In a 2013 *San Francisco Examiner* interview, Michael McClure commented, "I overcame my own shyness when I read at the Six Gallery in 1955 with Ginsberg, Gary Snyder and Philip Lamantia—when we all put our toes to the line in the sand. That was a pivotal moment in a life punctuated by pivotal moments." McClure first met Allen Ginsberg in early 1955 at a party in San Francisco given in honor of W. H. Auden's poetry reading at the museum and embarked on a spirited discussion of William Blake.

McClure had been involved in a staged reading of Robert Duncan's play *Faust Foutu* at the Six Gallery during the summer of 1955 that had gotten the attention of Wally Hedrick, who asked the young poet if he would like to read at the upcoming poetry reading, and he replied, "Absolutely." He later ran into Ginsberg, who was having trouble setting up the reading and asked

Michael McClure's reputation as one of the leading poets of the San Francisco Renaissance skyrocketed after his participation in the Six Gallery Reading, and he later branched out into writing novels, plays, and songs (including collaborations with both Jim Morrison and Ray Manzarek of the Doors).

Photo by Gloria Graham/Wikimedia Commons

McClure for help. According to McClure, "I knew Philip Lamantia quite well. I knew Kenneth Rexroth from going through his salons. In the meantime Allen met—I think a week or two before the night of the reading—Gary Snyder and Philip Whalen. They had been roommates at Reed and joined up in San Francisco again . . . So that's how the Six Gallery reading came about."

At the Six Gallery, McClure followed Lamantia and read the following poems: "For the Death of 100 Whales," "Nightwards the Ravishing," "Point Lobos Animism," "Mystery of the Hunt," and "Poem." The five poems made up McClure's first book of poetry, *Passage,* which was published by small press publisher Jonathan Williams in 1956. In *Whitman's Wild Children,* Neeli Cherkovski wrote, "McClure's poem on the whale slaughter was the result of having read an article in *Time* about the killing of what were described as 'savage sea cannibals' by GIs at the request of the Icelandic government because the mammals were destroying thousands of dollars worth of fishing nets."

According to McClure, the eclectic crowd at the Six Gallery Reading comprised "painters, North Beach Pre-Beats, members of the Anarchist Workman's Circle, elderly women professors with tacky fur coats, and just about anyone that intuited that this was going to be an event . . . All of us felt that we were speaking what people in the audience were feeling. It was a time to say things. These were extremely radical poems—radical even now—and we certainly didn't get tamer as time went on." McClure concluded that "in all of our memories no one had been so outspoken in poetry before—we had gone beyond a point of no return—and we were ready for it, for a point of no return. None of us wanted to go back to the gray, chill, militaristic silence, to the intellective void—to the land without poetry—to the spiritual drabness. We wanted to make it new and we wanted to invent it and the process of it as we went into it. We wanted voice and we wanted vision."

Whalen's Reading

According to Philip Whalen, "And so, anyhow, there were various moves and switches and whatnot, and in 1955 Ginsberg and Kerouac showed up, and we began . . . the revolution . . . which had been started by Robert Duncan and Jack Spicer and everybody earlier on, and we were all carpetbaggers, which did not sit well with the locals." Whalen had served as a fire lookout (Gary Snyder had helped him land the gig) in the Mount Baker National Forest during the summer of 1955 and then headed back to San Francisco. It was Snyder who invited Whalen to join the other poets at the Six Gallery Reading. It was here that Whalen met Allen Ginsberg and Jack Kerouac for the first time.

At the Six Gallery, Whalen read his poem "Plus Ça Change," which the *Los Angeles Times* described as "a put-down of the reticence of the age." Ginsberg described Whalen as "a strange fat young man from Oregon—in appearance a Zen Buddist Bodhisattva—[who] read a series of very personal relaxed, learned mystical-anarchic poems. His obvious carelessness for his reputation as a poet, his delicacy and strange American sanctity is evident in his poetry, written in rare post Poundian assemblages of blocks of hard images set in juxtapositions, like haikus."

Ginsberg Reads "Howl"

One of the first things Allen Ginsberg did when he arrived in San Francisco was seek out poet Kenneth Rexroth, whose open house gatherings on Friday nights had become legendary. Rexroth introduced Ginsberg to Gary Snyder.

Ginsberg had created a postcard to advertise the Six Gallery Reading event that stated, "Six poets at the Six Gallery. Kenneth Rexroth, M.C. Remarkable collection of angels all gathered at once in the same spot. Wine, music, dancing girls, serious poetry, free satori. Small collection for wine and postcards. Charming event." At the Six Gallery Reading, Ginsberg performed second to last that evening and brought down the house with his first public reading of "Howl." By most accounts, Ginsberg was visibly intoxicated and somewhat nervous but gained confidence throughout the reading, responding to the enthusiastic crowd (which included Jack Kerouac shouting "Go!" at the end of each line).

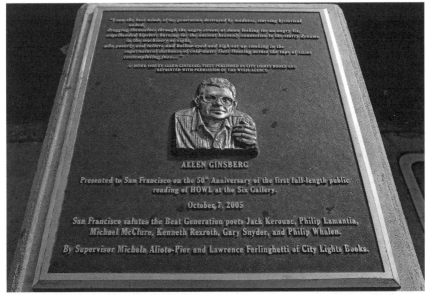

A plaque outside the former Six Gallery in San Francisco commemorates the famous poetry reading on October 7, 1955, that featured Allen Ginsberg's first public reading of the landmark poem "Howl."   *Author's collection*

According to Michael McClure, "People left after [the "Howl" reading] completely blown away. It was very immediately a revelation." Snyder later remarked, "I remember walking away from the Six Gallery, in San Francisco, after Allen's first reading of 'Howl,' saying, 'Poetry will never be the same. This is going to change everything.' It was the beginning of the Beat Generation and, in a sense, the defining moment in all of our literary careers."

Howl and Other Poems was published as the fourth book in City Lights' Pocket Poets Series the following year. On November 14, 1981, Ginsberg, dressed in a suit and tie, gave a reading of "Howl" at Columbia University to celebrate the twenty-fifth anniversary of the Six Gallery Reading to a sold-out crowd. Ginsberg had been introduced by Anne Waldman, who described the poem as the product of "postwar materialist paranoid doldrums."

Snyder's Reading

Snyder read last at the Six Gallery, and he had a hard act to follow: Ginsberg had just finished his first public reading of "Howl" in front of the transfixed crowd. After waiting for the crowd to settle down, Snyder launched into his Zen Buddhism–inspired poem "A Berry Feast."

"A Berry Feast" was later featured in the landmark No. 2 issue of *Evergreen Review* in 1957 along with poems and stories by Kenneth Rexroth, Brother Antoninus, Robert Duncan, Lawrence Ferlinghetti, Michael McClure, Josephine Miles, Jack Spicer, Philip Whalen, Allen Ginsberg, Jack Kerouac, and others. The poem can also be found in Snyder's 1967 book, *The Back Country*. According to McClure, "Equally well-received was Gary Snyder, bearded and laughingly intense, reading his nature poems of logging and forest fire, huckleberries and bear shit on the trail, love-making and the trickster god Coyote. Gary knew at first breath how to read words of his lore directly into the ears of the cheering listeners."

The choice of poems was appropriate for Snyder, who would later be known as the "Poet Laureate of Deep Ecology." Snyder once remarked, "As a poet I hold the most archaic values on earth . . . the fertility of the soil, the magic of animals, the power-vision in solitude, the terrifying initiation and rebirth, the love and ecstasy of the dance, the common work of the tribe. I try to hold both history and the wilderness in mind, that my poems may approach the true measure of things and stand against the unbalance and ignorance of our times." In 1956, Snyder left the United States for a twelve-year residence abroad, mostly in Japan, where he continued his studies in Zen Buddhism.

Kerouac's Role

Declining to read at the event, Kerouac detailed his version of the events that transpired at the Six Gallery Reading in his 1958 novel, *The Dharma Bums*, as he followed "the whole gang of howling poets" to the venue on "the night of the birth of the San Francisco Poetry Renaissance." Kerouac gathered a collection for wine among "the rather stiff audience" and returned "with three huge gallon jugs of California Burgundy."

According to Kerouac's depiction in *The Dharma Bums*, the entire audience was drunk by the time "Alvah Goldbrook" (Ginsberg) started reading his poem "Wail" ("Howl") and "old Rheinhold Cacoethes" (Kenneth Rexroth) "the father of the Frisco poetry scene was wiping tears in gladness." After the reading, everyone drove "to Chinatown for a big fabulous dinner." According to Rexroth, "By the time the second poet on the program started reading—that was Lamantia—Kerouac was already banging his big gallon jug of wine on the floor just to show his enthusiasm. Kerouac used to carry those gallons of port around the same way F. Scott Fitzgerald carried a flask."

Six Gallery Legacy

The Six Gallery Reading served to energize the Beat Generation and establish San Francisco as a center for countercultural activity that would blossom in the 1960s. According to Gary Snyder in *The Real Work* (1980), it "was a curious kind of turning point in American poetry. It succeeded beyond our wildest thoughts. In fact, we weren't even thinking of success; we were just trying to invite some friends and potential friends, and we borrowed a mailing list from the art gallery and sent out maybe two hundred postcards. Poetry suddenly seemed useful in 1955 San Franciscio. From that day to this, there has never been a week without a reading in the Bay Area."

No photos, film, or sound recordings exist of the legendary poetry reading. Although the Six Gallery is long gone and the former site of the venue now serves as a furniture store, a commemorative plaque was dedicated on October 7, 2005, to celebrate the fifieth anniversary of the reading. The plaque features the first lines of "Howl" and the image of a young Allen Ginsberg, followed by the lines "Presented to San Francisco on the 50th Anniversary of the first-full length public reading of HOWL at the Six Gallery . . . October 7, 2005 . . . San Francisco salutes the Beat Generation poets Jack Kerouac, Philip Lamantia, Michael McClure, Kenneth Rexroth, Gary Snyder, and Philip Whalen . . . By Supervisor Michela Alioto-Pier and Lawrence Ferlinghetti of City Lights Books."

8

Angels of the World's Desire

With its powerful opening lines about "the best minds" that were "destroyed by madness," Allen Ginsberg's landmark poem "Howl" truly helped define a generation. The poem, which strongly bears the influence of Walt Whitman's *Leaves of Grass*, marked a turning point not only in the history of the Beat Generation but also within American literature in general. The unexpurgated content of the poem—including obscene language, the frank depiction of homosexuality, and references to drug use and criminality—led to a highly publicized obscenity trial in 1957 that helped pave the way for the publication of other works considered objectionable and was considered a major victory in the battle against censorship in the United States.

Background

In the summer of 1954, Ginsberg was staying at the Cassadys' house in San Jose, California, until the day that Carolyn walked in on him giving Neal a blowjob. Carolyn demanded that Ginsberg pack his bags and leave but was kind enough to lend him $20 and drop him off in Berkeley. Ginsberg eventually moved to San Francisco and got a job with a market research firm, but was soon laid off. It was around this time that Ginsberg met his lifelong companion, Peter Orlovsky, through the artist Robert LaVigne.

Living off his unemployment benefits in a first floor apartment at 1010 Montgomery Street in North Beach, Ginsberg reportedly started writing the first drafts of "Howl" during 1954–55. He showed his first attempts to Kenneth Rexroth, who called them too "stilted" and "academic." According to Ginsberg, in "Notes Written on Finally Recording Howl" (*Deliberate Prose*,

2000), "I thought I wouldn't write a poem, but just write what I wanted to without fear, let my imagination go, open secrecy, and scribble magic lines from my real mind—sum up my life—something I wouldn't be able to show anybody, writ for my own soul's ear and a few other golden ears."

"Howl" revealed the influenced of Walt Whitman (1819–92) and William Carlos Williams (1883–1963), as well as English poet Christopher Smart (1722–71), William Blake's prophetic books, and the "spontaneous prose" of Jack Kerouac. From the outset, it is clear that Ginsberg intended the poem to be a performance piece. The poem is dedicated to Carl Solomon, a fellow patient he had befriended at the Columbia Psychiatric Institute. In 2008, Peter Orlovsky suggested that the title of the poem may have originated when he and Ginsberg took a moonlit stroll and Orlovsky sang a rendition of Hank Williams's "Howlin' at the Moon." However, Ginsberg stated in his dedication that the title was suggested by Kerouac.

Part I

With one of the most memorable and quotable opening lines in the history of American poetry concerning "the best minds of my generation," Part I of "Howl" is drawn from Ginsberg's personal experiences, including his expulsion from Columbia University for writing an expletive on a dirty dorm window and his Blakean vision, as well as his memories of the individuals he encountered, such as Neal Cassady, Herbert Huncke, and Bill Cannastra. Madness as a response to an increasingly mechanized society is a central theme. Ginsberg typed Part I "madly in one afternoon, a tragic custard-pie comedy of wild phrasing, meaningless images for the beauty of abstract poetry of mind running along making awkward combinations like Charlie Chaplin's walk, long saxophone-like chorus lines I knew Kerouac would hear *sound* of—taking off from his own inspired prose line really a new poetry."

Part II

Ginsberg got high on peyote in his Nob Hill apartment and "saw an image of the robot skullface of Moloch in the upper stories of a big hotel glaring into my window." Weeks later he got high again and "the visage was still there in red smoky downtown metropolis." Ginsberg wandered down Powell Street muttering "Moloch Moloch" and claims he wrote Part II of the poem "nearly intact" in a cafeteria at the Drake Hotel, "deep in hellish vale." Part II describes the state of industrial civilization ("Moloch," which is repeated forty times), excessive mechanization that serves to destroy the human spirit. According to Ginsberg ("Notes Written on Finally Recording Howl"), "Here

Allen Ginsberg's vision of "Moloch" in his landmark poem "Howl" was inspired by a peyote vision he had of the Sir Francis Drake Hotel in San Francisco.   *Photo by Gideon Wright/Wikimedia Commons*

the long line is used as a stanza form broken into exclamatory units punctuated by a base repetition, Moloch."

The term "Moloch" referred to both the Biblical idol in Leviticus to whom the Canaanites sacrificed children, and the name of an industrial, demonic figure in Fritz's Lang's classic 1927 silent film *Metropolis*. Critic Roger Ebert called *Metropolis* "one of the great achievements of the silent era, a work so audacious in its vision and so angry in its message that it is, if anything, more powerful today than when it was made." Poet Lawrence Ferlinghetti later remarked in a 2002 ACLU interview, "It is not the poet but what he observes which is revealed as obscene. The great obscene wastes of 'Howl' are the sad wastes of the mechanized world, lost among atomic bombs and insane nationalism."

Part III

Part III of "Howl" is directly addressed to Carl Solomon, and the Columbia Presbyterian Psychological Institute where they met is referred to as

"Rockland" in the poem. According to Ginsberg ("Notes Written on Finally Recording Howl"), "The rhythmic paradigm for Part III was conceived and half-written same day as the beginning of 'Howl,' I went back later and filled it out. Part I, a lament for the Lamb in America with instances of remarkable lamb-like youths; Part II names the monster of mental consciousness that preys on the Lamb; Part III a litany of affirmation of the Lamb in its glory . . . The structure of Part III, pyramidal, with a graduated longer response to the fixed base."

Footnote

According to Ginsberg, "The last part of 'Howl' was really an homage to art but also in specific terms an homage to Cezanne's method, in a sense I adapted what I could to writing; but that's a very complicated matter to explain." The footnote is characterized by the repetitive use of the word "Holy." According to Ginsberg, "I remembered the archetypal rhythm of Holy Holy Holy weeping in a bus on Kearny Street, and wrote most of it down in notebook there . . . I set it as 'Footnote to Howl' because it was an extra variation of the form of Part II."

References

Sprinkled generously throughout "Howl" are references to Ginsberg's friends and acquaintances, as well as events, both inspirational and tragic, from his life. In Part I of "Howl," Ginsberg alludes to his Blakean vision in 1948, which revealed to him the interconnectedness of all existence, and he also writes about the incident at Columbia where he was suspended from school for writing obscenities on a dirty dorm window. Ginsberg also references the deaths of poet John Hoffman in Mexico and Bill Cannastra, an early member of the Beat circle in New York City, who was decapitated in a bizarre subway accident; as well as poet, artist, anarchist, and Fugs cofounder Tuli Kupferberg's failed suicide attempt, where he jumped off the Manhattan Bridge; and Ginsberg's mother, Naomi, who suffered from paranoid schizophrenia. Ginsberg also comments on the insatiable sexual appetite of "N.C." (Neal Cassady), and Carl Solomon's Dadaesque gesture of throwing potato salad during a college lecture. Other allusions in Part I include Herbert Huncke's release from prison, among others. In addition, Ginsberg name-dropped popular Beat hangouts in New York City, such as Bickford's (an all-night cafeteria) and Fugazzi's.

Ginsberg's use of "Moloch" in Part II of the poem references the Bible, specifically the book of Leviticus. Ginsberg's Moloch-inspired vision came to him after he got high on peyote and viewed the Sir Francis Drake Hotel in San Francisco. In Part III, Ginsberg directly addresses Carl Solomon and uses "Rockland" to represent the Columbia Presbyterian Psychological Institute where they were both patients. Ginsberg references the shock treatment Solomon received. In the footnote, Ginsberg directly alludes to Solomon, Cassady, Peter Orlovsky, Lucien Carr, Jack Kerouac, Herbert Huncke, and William S. Burroughs, adding "Holy" before each of their names.

City Lights Pocket Poets Series

After Allen Ginsberg's landmark reading of "Howl" at the Six Gallery on October 7, 1955, City Lights Bookstore owner and publisher Lawrence Ferlinghetti sent him a telegram that stated, "I greet you at the beginning of a great career" (the same verbiage Ralph Waldo Emerson had directed toward Walt Whitman upon the publication of his masterpiece, *Leaves of Grass*, in 1855). Ferlinghetti then asked, "When do I get the manuscript?"

Ferlinghetti had launched his Pocket Poets Series in 1955 with his own book of poetry, *Pictures of the Gone World*, followed by Kenneth Rexroth's translation of *Thirty Spanish Poems of Love and Exile* (1956), and Kenneth Patchen's *Poems of Humor and Protest* (1956). He later claimed to have gotten the idea for the design of the books in the Pocket Poets Series from Patchen's early edition of *An Astonished Eye Looks Out of the Air* (1945). *Howl and Other Poems* was published in 1956 as No. 4 in the Pocket Poets Series (Ginsberg completed Part II and the footnote specifically for the poem's publication). In addition to "Howl," the collection included several other poems, such as "A Supermarket in California," "Sunflower Sutra," and "America." According to Ferlinghetti (quoted on the official City Lights website, www.citylights .com), "As long as there is poetry, there will be an unknown; as long as there is an unknown there will be poetry. The function of the independent press (besides being essentially dissident) is still to discover, to find the new voices and give voices to them." Several other of Ginsberg's works were published through the Pocket Poets Series, such as *Kaddish and Other Poems* (1961), *Reality Sandwiches* (1963), *The Fall of America: Poems of These States 1965–1971* (1972), *Mind Breaths: Poems 1972–1977* (1977), and *Plutonian Ode and Other Poems 1977–1980* (1982).

Today, the Pocket Poets Series numbers more than sixty volumes and features a diverse range of works, including Marie Ponsot's *True Minds* (1956), Denise Levertov's *Here and Now* (1957), Gregory Corso's *Gasoline* (1958), Robert Duncan's *Selected Poems* (1959), Nicanor Parra's *Anti-Poems* (1960), Frank O'Hara's *Lunch Poems* (1964), Philip Lamantia's *Selected Poems 1943–1966* (1967), Bob Kaufman's *Golden Sardine* (1967), Pablo Picasso's

Hunk of Skin (1968), Diane di Prima's *Revolutionary Letters* (1971), Jack Kerouac's *Scattered Poems* (1971), Anne Waldman's *Fast Speaking Woman* (1975), Peter Orlovsky's *Clean Asshole Poems & Smiling Vegetable Songs* (1978), Philip Lamantia's *Becoming Visible* (1981), Pier Paolo Pasolini's *Roman Poems* (1986), Ernesto Cardenal's *From Nicaragua With Love* (1986), and Vladimir Mayakovsky's *Listen!* (1991), among many others.

A fundraiser for the Seattle Poetics LAB (SPLAB), the annual Allen Ginsberg Poetry Marathon celebrates the life and work of the legendary Beat poet with poetry readings, special guests, writing exercises, and Beat-related films.   *Author's collection*

"From the beginning," Ferlinghetti states in the mission statement on City Lights' website, "the aim was to publish across the board, avoiding the provincial and the academic. I had in mind rather an international, dissident, insurgent ferment. What has proved most fascinating are the continuing cross-currents and cross-fertilizations between poets widely separated by language or geography, from France to Germany to Italy to America North and South, East and West, coalescing in a truly supra-national poetic voice."

Reception

In a September 2, 1956, article published in the *New York Times Book Review* titled "West Coast Rhythms," critic Richard Eberhart singled out "Howl" as "the most remarkable poem of the young group" of poets who made up the Beat Generation. M. L. Rosenthal in the *Nation* (February 23, 1957) wrote that Ginsberg "has brought a terrible psychological reality to the surface with enough originality to blast American verse a hair's breadth forward in the process." According to the *New York Post*, "Howl" was nothing more than a "glorification of madness, drugs, and homosexuality" that reveled in its own "contempt and hatred for anything and everything generally deemed healthy, normal, or decent." Writing in the *New Republic*, (September 16, 1957), notorious Beat critic Norman Podhoretz claimed that "Howl" celebrated "dope addicts, perverts and maniacs," while Frederick Eckman in *Poetry* (September 1957) remarked, "It's a very shaggy book, the shaggiest I've ever seen."

In a May 29, 1956, letter to Ginsberg, Lionel Trilling (his former professor at Columbia University) wrote, "I'm afraid I have to tell you that I don't like the poems at all. I hesitate before saying that they seem to me quite dull, for to say of a work which undertakes to be violent and shocking that it is dull is, I am aware, a well known and all too easy device. But perhaps you will believe that I am being sincere when I say they are dull. They are not like Whitman—they are all prose, all rhetoric, without any music . . . There is no real voice here."

"Howl" on Trial

Allen Ginsberg's landmark collection of poetry, *Howl and Other Poems*, was first published on November 1, 1956, through the Pocket Poets Series from City Lights Books. The unexpurgated content of the poem—including obscene language, frank depictions of homosexuality, and references to drug use and criminality—led customs officials to seize 520 copies of the book on March 25, 1957.

In June 1957, City Lights Bookstore manager Shigeyoshi Murao was arrested for selling two copies of the book to undercover San Francisco police officers. City Lights owner Lawrence Ferlinghetti was also thrown in jail for publishing the book. According to Murao in his vivid account, "Footnotes to My Arrest for Selling Howl," he "was fingerprinted, posed for mug shots and locked in a drunk tank. The cell smelled like piss. There was a piss-stained mattress on the floor." As for Ginsberg, he was traveling in Europe at the time and reportedly enjoying every bit of his sudden notoriety. Ferlinghetti and

The enduring influence of "Howl" is evident in the many related annual celebrations, such as the lively Howl Festival held at the Shambhala Meditation Center of San Antonio.   *Author's collection*

Murao faced charges that they "did willfully and lewdly print, publish and sell obscene and indecent writings." The obscenity trial that followed ("The People of the State of California vs. Lawrence Ferlinghetti") would later be considered a landmark battle for freedom of expression.

The trial judge was Clayton W. Horn (who regularly taught a Sunday school Bible class), while the prosecutor was Ralph McIntosh, who called for an outright ban on the book. Arguing for the defense were ACLU attorneys J. W. Ehrlich and Albert Bendich, who called several expert witnesses to defend the book, such as San Francisco Renaissance poet Kenneth Rexroth, later known (much to his chagrin!) as the "Elder Statesman of the Beat Generation." The widely publicized trial drew national attention and even ended up in the pages of *Life* magazine. Judge Horn released his decision on October 3, 1957, stating, "I do not believe that 'Howl' is without redeeming social importance. The first part of 'Howl' presents a picture of a nightmare world; the second part is an indictment of those elements in modern society destructive of the best qualities of human nature; such elements are predominantly identified as materialism, conformity, and mechanization leading toward war. The third part presents a picture of an individual who is a specific representation of what the author conceives as a general condition. 'Footnote to Howl' seems to be a declamation that everything in the world is holy, including parts of the body by name. It ends in a plea for holy living."

Significantly, the "Howl" decision came down just several months after the landmark Roth vs. United States case, where Supreme Court Justice William Brennan famously declared, "All ideas having even the slightest redeeming social importance—unorthodox ideas, controversial ideas, even ideas hateful to the prevailing climate of opinion—have the full protection of the guaranties, unless excludable because they encroach upon the limited area of more important interests."

According to an account of the "Howl" trial in the *San Francisco Chronicle*, "The judge's opinion was hailed with applause and cheers from a packed audience that offered the most fantastic collection of beards, turtlenecked shirts and Italian hairdos ever to grace the grimy precincts of the Hall of Justice." Published in 2006 upon the fiftieth anniversary of *Howl and Other Poems*, the book *Howl on Trial: The Battle for Free Expression* (edited by Bill Morgan and Nancy J. Peters) offers the definitive account of the "Howl" trial. In his introduction to *Howl on Trial*, Ferlinghetti remarked, "To me [Shig] was the real hero of this tale of sound and fury, signifying everything." The events of the "Howl" trial are depicted in the 2010 film *Howl*, which was directed by Rob Epstein and Jeffrey Friedman, and stars James Franco as Ginsberg and Andrew Rogers as Ferlinghetti.

Legacy

The publication of *Howl and Other Poems* in 1956 and the subsequent obscenity trial scored a major victory in the battle for freedom of expression and against censorship. According to poet John Giorno in a Fall 2008 *Bomb* magazine interview, "It's not that it's such a great poem—it's that it miraculously mirrored the moment of 1956, and the late '50s and early '60s, and that it resonated through the world in an extraordinary way." Poet Jack Micheline remarked in a 1998 *Chiron Review* interview that the publication of "Howl" "opened up a lot of peoples' minds and gave a lot of people the courage to be themselves . . . *Howl* was the spark that set things off."

The earliest known recording of Ginsberg reading "Howl" was made at Reed College, Portland, Oregon, on February 14, 1956. Ginsberg and Gary Snyder (Reed College graduate, 1951) visited the campus during a hitchhiking trip through the Pacific Northwest. Ginsberg read all of Part 1 of "Howl," and several other poems, all of which were recorded. Ginsberg was again recorded reading "Howl" on March 18, 1956, at the Town Hall Theatre in Berkeley, California. In addition, Ginsberg reportedly made a pilgrimage to French poet Charles Baudelaire's grave at Cimetière du Montparnasse in Paris, where he placed a copy of *Howl and Other Poems*. According to Bill Morgan in the *Beat Atlas* (2011), "Allen Ginsberg vowed to read his masterpiece, 'Howl,' in every state in the Union at least once, and he managed to achieve that goal before his death in 1997." Beat photographer Gordon Ball took a famous, ironic photo of a group of young cadets at the Virginia Military Institute reading "Howl" in a class in 1991.

Edited by Jason Shinder, *The Poem That Changed America: "Howl" Fifty Years Later* was published in 2006 to mark the fiftieth anniversary of the poetry book's publication. *The Poem That Changed America* features essays by Frank Bidart, Andrei Codrescu, Vivian Gornick, Phillip Lopate, Daphne Merkin, Rick Moody, Robert Pinsky, and Luc Sante. According to Sante, "Reading 'Howl' aloud or reciting it you could feel the poem giving you supernatural powers, the ability to punch through brick walls and walk across rooftop to rooftop."

9

Under the Burden of Solitude

The Essential Works of Allen Ginsberg

T he amazing impact of "Howl" has tended to overshadow Ginsberg's extensive body of work as a whole. However, collections such as *Kaddish and Other Poems* (1961), the poet's tribute to his mother, Naomi, who suffered from schizophrenia, and *The Fall of America: Poems of These States* (1972), which won the National Book Award for Poetry, are stellar examples of the outstanding nature of his later work. According to Ginsberg, "Poetry is not an expression of the party line. It's that time of night, lying in bed, thinking what you really think, making the private world public, that's what the poet does" (*Gargoyle* magazine, 1978).

Kaddish and Other Poems (1961)

Allen Ginsberg's mother, Naomi, died in 1956 in Pilgrim State Hospital after struggling with mental illness most of her life. Written in two parts, Ginsberg's epic poem "Kaddish" serves as an elegy for his mother and her struggles. Most of the poem was reportedly written on Benzedrine at the "Beat Hotel" in Paris. The word *Kaddish* refers to the mourning prayer or blessing in Judaism. In Part I of "Kaddish," Ginsberg reflects on his mother's life as a young Russian immigrant. In Part II, Ginsberg delves into Naomi's mental illness, which involved intense paranoia. "Kaddish" also serves as a meditation on death and Ginsberg's relationship to Judaism.

Kaddish and Other Poems 1958–1960 was published by City Lights in 1961 as No. 14 in its Pocket Poets Series. "Kaddish" was also referred to as "Kaddish for Naomi Ginsberg (1894–1956)" and titled in the table of contents as "Kaddish: Proem, narrative, hymmnn, lament, litany & fugue." Ginsberg also wrote a screenplay based on "Kaddish." Robert Frank, who directed the landmark Beat film *Pull My Daisy* (1959), wanted to direct the film, but he couldn't raise money for the project. A special fiftieth-anniversary edition of

Allen Ginsberg reportedly embarked on "Howl" while living in a first floor apartment at 1010 Montgomery Street in North Beach. An outstanding collection of Ginsberg memorabilia can be found at the Beat Museum in San Francisco.   *Author's collection*

Kaddish and Other Poems was published in 2010 with documents and letters related to the poem's composition, as well as Naomi's paintings and previously unpublished family photographs.

Empty Mirror: Early Poems (1961)

In his 1974 book, *Out of the Vietnam Vortex: A Study of Poets and Poetry Against the War*, author James F. Mersmann wrote, "*Empty Mirror* records the beginning of Ginsberg's search for wholeness and authenticity." Published by Totem Press, *Empty Mirror* features a dedication "To Herbert E. Huncke for his Confessions," as well as an introduction by William Carlos Williams.

In his introduction, Williams wrote, "This young Jewish boy, already not so young any more, has recognized something that has escaped most of the modern age, he has found that man is lost in the world of his own head. And that the rhythms of the past have become like an old field long left unploughed and fallen into disuse. In fact they are excavating there for a new industrial plant. There the new inferno will soon be under construction . . . Here the terror of the scene has been laid bare in subtle measures, the pages are warm with it. The scene they invoke is terrifying more so than Dante's pages, the poem is not suspect, the craft is flawless." Highlights of *Empty Mirror* include "Fyodor" (a tribute to Dostoevsky), "A Meaningless Institution" (about the poet's experience at a psychiatric hospital in the late 1940s), "Marijuana Notation," "A Poem on America," "Paterson," "The Blue Angel" (about actress Marlene Dietrich), and "Gregory Corso's Story."

Reality Sandwiches (1963)

Dedicated to Gregory Corso, *Reality Sandwiches* was published in 1963 as No. 18 in City Lights Publishers' Pocket Poets Series. The title was derived from "On Burroughs' Work," one of the poems featured in the collection that was written in San Jose, California, in 1954 that mentions "naked lunch." The poems were written between 1953 and 1960 and show Ginsberg at his early, energetic best.

Among the poems included in *Reality Sandwiches* are "My Alba," "The Green Automobile" (a tribute to Neal Cassady), "Siesta in Xbalba," "Love Poem on Theme by Whitman," "Malest Cornifici Tuo Catullo," "Dream Record: June 8, 1955" (a haunting poem that details an encounter with the ghost of Joan Vollmer), "A Strange New Cottage in Berkeley," "My Sad Self," "I Beg You Come Back & Be Cheerful," and "To An Old Poet in Peru" (written during Ginsberg's 1960 trip to South America and later translated into Spanish by Peruvian poet Antonio Cisneros).

In a review of *Reality Sandwiches* for the June 1964 issue of *Poetry* magazine, A. R. Ammons wrote, "The poems in this volume date from 1953 to 1960, poems both before and after 'Howl.' They mostly lack the desperately earnest cry for truth and the sung-tension accuracy of Ginsberg at his best."

Planet News (1968)

City Lights published *Planet News* in 1968 as No. 23 in its Pocket Poets Series. Many of the poems in this collection were written during Ginsberg's extensive travels with Peter Orlovsky between 1961 and 1967 to India, Japan, Europe, and Africa. A City Lights ad for *Planet News* exclaimed: "Celestial vulgar humor! Solemn experience! Black & Whitman ride again! Hare Krishna! Waves of Queer Bliss! An ecological thrill!" The diverse collection of poems in *Planet News* includes "Television was a Baby Crawling Toward the Deathchamber," "This Form of Life Needs Sex," "Death News" (about the death of Ginsberg's mentor, William Carlos Williams), "Why is God Love, Jack?" (addressing Jack Kerouac), "After Yeats," "I Am a Victim of Telephone," "Kral Majales" (about being elected "The King of May" in Czechoslovakia),

"First Party at Ken Kesey's with Hell's Angels," "Wichita Vortex Sutra" (a classic antiwar poem), "City Midnight Junk Stains," and "Wales Visitation," among others.

In a May 17, 1969, review for *Rolling Stone*, John Grissim Jr. wrote, "*Planet News* is a beautiful experience in sharing one man's vision of humanity." In his article "The Last Antiwar Poem" (the *Nation*, November 27, 2006), which profiled "Wichita Vortex Sutra," Rolf Potts stated that the poem "reads like a prophetic and final antiwar poem, an elegy for the power of language in an age of competing information."

The Fall of America: Poems of These States (1972)

Ginsberg shared with Adrienne Rich the National Book Award for Poetry for *The Fall of America: Poems of These States, 1965–1971*, which was published as No. 30 in City Lights Publishers' Pocket Poets Series. More political in tone than some of his earlier works, the poems in this collection cover a wide range of topics, from the Vietnam War, the 1968 Democratic National Convention, and the Apollo 11 moon landing to the deaths of Che Guevara and Neal Cassady ("Elegy for Neal Cassady" and "On Neal's Ashes").

According to critic Michael Rogers in *Rolling Stone* magazine (April 12, 1973), "*The Fall of America* chronicles the last days of the crumbling fascist empire, state by state, town by town, from the center of Chicago to the padded seats of a jetliner to the flowering hills of Big Sur." In the *New York Times* review of *The Fall of America* (April 15, 1973), critic Helen Vendler wrote, "An addictive sociability coexists now in Ginsberg with a pall of solitude; willed prophecy inhabits a religious void; and of empty necessity topographical descriptions supersedes familial drama."

In his controversial acceptance speech for the National Book Award that was delivered by Peter Orlovsky at Alice Tulley Hall, Lincoln Center, New York, on April 18, 1974, Ginsberg wrote, "Poem book *Fall of America* is time capsule of personal national consciousness during American war-decay recorded 1965 to 1971 . . . Watergate is a froth on the swamp: impeachment of a living president does not remove the hundred billion power of the military nor the secret billion power of the police state apparatus. Any president who would try to curb power of the military-police would be ruined or murdered." Ginsberg concluded, "There is no longer any hope for the salvation of America proclaimed by Jack Kerouac and others of our Beat Generation, aware and howling, weeping and singing Kaddish for the nation decades ago, 'rejected yet confessing out the soul.' All we have to work from now is the vast empty quiet space of our own consciousness. AH! AH! AH!"

Mind Breaths (1978)

Mind Breaths was published in 1978 as No. 35 in City Lights Publishers' Pocket Poets Series and contains poems written between 1972 and 1977. Among the poems in the collection are "Ayers Rock Uluru Song," "Under the World There's a Lot of Ass," "On Neruda's Death" (about Chilean poet Pablo Neruda, who won the Nobel Prize for Literature in 1971), "Sweet Boy, Gimme Yr Ass," "Sad Dust Glories," "Ego Confessions," "Jaweh and Allah Battle," "Mugging," "We Rise on Sunbeams and Fall in the Night" (about the death of Ginsberg's mentor, William Carlos Williams, who wrote the introduction to *Howl and Other Poems*), "Hadda Be Playing on the Jukebox," "Rolling Thunder Stones," "Don't Grow Old," and "Contest of Bards."

Highly political rap metal band Rage Against the Machine (RATM) set "Hadda Be Playing on the Jukebox" to music and performed it live at a Detroit, Michigan, concert. The song appears on RATM's album *Live & Rare*, which was released only in Japan. The album also features such gems as "Bullet in the Head," "Bombtrack," "Take the Power Back," "Freedom," "Black Steel in the Hour of Chaos" (with Chuck D from Public Enemy), "Fuck the Police" (N.W.A. cover), and "The Ghost of Tom Joad" (Bruce Springsteen cover), among others.

White Shroud: Poems 1980–1985 (1986)

One of the best collections of poetry of Allen Ginsberg's later works, *White Shroud* contains such classics as "Going to the World of the Dead," "Happening Now? End of Earth? Apocalypse Days?," "I Love Old Whitman So," "I'm a Prisoner of Allen Ginsberg," "Moral Majority," "They're All Phantoms of My Imagining," and "World Karma," among others. The volume also contains an homage to Ginsberg's mentor, the acclaimed poet William Carlos Williams, in "Written in My Dream by W. C. Williams," as well as two haunting poems about Ginsberg's mother, Naomi: the dreamlike "White Shroud" and the nightmarish "Black Shroud" (an unflinching account of her lobotomy).

In her 1989 book, *The Music of What Happens: Poems, Poets, Critics*, literary critic Helen Vendler wrote, "[Ginsberg's] powerful mixture of Blake, Whitman, Pound, and Williams, to which he added his own volatile, grotesque, and tender humor, has assured him a memorable place in modern poetry." In a February 15, 1987, review for the *Los Angeles Times*, Ann Charters commented, "*White Shroud* is a mellow sampler of Ginsberg in his prime, autobiographical poems chronicling his travels, public appearances, emotions, dreams and reading over the last five years . . . The tender humor characterizing Ginsberg's best work permeates these poems, yet they are no soft sellout to the upbeat Muzak of Madison Avenue."

Death and Fame: Last Poems 1993–1997 (1999)

"If you've an ounce of strength, use it to look inside." Allen Ginsberg's poetry from the last years of his life has been collected into this impressive single volume, which *Publishers Weekly* called "a perfect capstone to a noble life." *Death and Fame* features a foreword by poet Robert Creeley. Many of the poems were written when Ginsberg's health was failing and he was faced to confront his own mortality. In fact, his last poem is the haunting "Things I'll Not Do (Nostalgias)," with the poet looking back on his life and listing the things he will never be able to do again. The cover photo features Ginsberg standing contemplatively in his apartment with a framed photo of his idol, Walt Whitman, in full view.

In a review of *Death and Fame* for *Jack* magazine, Adrien Begrand wrote, "While I love the poetry of Jack Kerouac, Lew Welch, and Charles Bukowski,

Opened in 1993, the Allen Ginsberg Library at Naropa University in Boulder, Colorado, features a collection of more than 30,000 books and approximately 130,000 e-books, periodicals, and audiovisual materials.   *Photo by David Shankbone/Wikimedia Commons*

no other poet ever touched me so deeply as Allen Ginsberg. His writing provided us with a complete glimpse of his soul, sparing us nothing in the process. From that fateful Blake vision in the forties, to his deathbed thoughts, and the myriad life events in between, Allen has left us with a collection of work that will forever go unparalleled. The circle may be complete, but that wheel will turn forever."

Deliberate Prose: Selected Essays 1952–1995 (2000)

Edited by Bill Morgan, *Deliberate Prose* presents Allen Ginsberg's thoughts on a wide range of subjects split into eight parts: "Politics and Prophecies," "Drug Culture," "Mindfulness and Spirituality," "Censorship and Sex Laws," "Autobiographical Fragments," "Literary Technique and the Beat Generation," "Writers," and "Further Appreciations." The diverse collection of essays features a foreword by Edward Sanders, who writes, "The 124 essays in *Deliberate Prose* read like the burning signposts of our age. In them we are amazed at the wide range of his mind, the evidence of his wild curiosity, his goodwill, his dedication to a better world, to good causes, to a new kind of openness and truth emblemized by his watch-sentence, 'Candor ends paranoia.'"

Highlights of *Deliberate Prose* include essays on Jean Genet, the Six Gallery Reading, Andy Warhol, John Cage, the 1968 Democratic National Convention, Ray Bremser, Hell's Angels, Anne Waldman, LSD, John Lennon and Yoko Ono, "Howl," "Kaddish," Gary Snyder, William S. Burroughs, Vietnam, Jack Kerouac, William Blake, and Walt Whitman. In his essay about Kerouac, "The Great Rememberer," Ginsberg commented, "Jack Kerouac didn't write [*Visions of Cody*] for money, he wrote it for love, he *gave* it away to the world; not even for fame, but as an explanation and prayer to his fellow mortals, and gods—with naked motive, and humble piety search—that's what makes *Visions of Cody* a work of primitive genius that grooks next to Douanier Rousseau's visions, and sits well-libraried beside Thomas Wolfe's *Time and River* (which Thos. Mann from his European eminence said was the great prose of America) and sits beside Tolstoi for its *prayers*. A La La Ho!"

Deliberate Prose also contains an unpublished recommendation (ca. 1995) for William S. Burroughs to be considered for the Nobel Prize for Literature, with Ginsberg concluding, "His continued influence, world wide from Europe thru China, on writing, music lyric, and politics on the latest pre-millennial generation perhaps surpasses that of any other literary figure of this last half century."

The Letters of Allen Ginsberg (2008)

In a 1956 letter to his father, Louis, Allen Ginsberg commented, "You have no idea what a storm of lunatic-fringe activity I have stirred up." In another letter to Bertand Russell in 1962, Allen Ginsberg wrote, "All I know is, I've lived in the midst of apparent worldly events and apparent transcendental insights, and it all adds up to I don't know what." These are just a couple of the many gems that can be found in *The Letters of Allen Ginsberg*, which was edited by Bill Morgan and culled from more than 3,700 of the author's letters (out of an estimated total of more than 7,500 letters the author wrote in his lifetime).

Indeed, Ginsberg was simply one of the most prolific American letter writers of the twentieth century. The 165 letters selected for this volume include some of his most legendary correspondence with the Beat inner circle of Jack Kerouac, William S. Burroughs, Neal Cassady, Gregory Corso, Peter Orlovsky, and Lawrence Ferlinghetti, as well as the likes of Lionel Trilling (Ginsberg's mentor at Columbia University), Ken Kesey, Arthur Miller, Charles Olson, Philip Glass, Robert Creeley, and friend/nemesis Norman Podhoretz. Much of Ginsberg's letter writing revolves around actively promoting the Beat Generation and/or the work of various Beat writers to others. The letters span from his earliest letter to the *New York Times* in 1941 to one of his last messages to President Bill Clinton requesting an arts prize shortly before his death in 1997.

10

Fast, Mad, Confessional

The Genesis of *On the Road*

I n Jack Kerouac's *On the Road*, which was published by Viking Press in September 1957, the wild-eyed maniacal "Dean Moriarty" (Neal Cassady) and the quiet, introspective "Sal Paradise" (Kerouac) embark on a reckless odyssey of self-discovery—fueled by alcohol, drugs, jazz, and prostitutes—across the cultural wasteland of post–World War II America. Moriarty represented one of the "mad ones, the ones who are mad to live, mad to talk, mad to be saved, desirous of everything at the same time, the ones who never yawn or say a commonplace thing, but burn, burn, burn, burn, like fabulous roman candles exploding like spiders across the stars and in the middle you see the blue centerlight pop and everybody goes 'Awww!'" The book contains many thinly disguised characters, including "Old Bull Lee" (William S. Burroughs) and "Carlo Marx" (Allen Ginsberg).

Arrival of Neal Cassady

A born hustler who had grown up along Larimer Street, the then–skid row district of Denver, Colorado, Neal Cassady claimed to have stolen five hundred cars by his twenty-first birthday. Cassady did receive mentoring from Justin Brierly, an English literature teacher and guidance counselor at East High School in Denver. Brierly, a graduate of Columbia University, was impressed by Cassady's intelligence and turned him on to literature. In 1945, Cassady was released from the Colorado State Reformatory after serving eleven months of a one-year sentence for possession of stolen goods, and married sixteen-year-old LuAnne Henderson ("Marylou" in *On the Road*).

The newlyweds made their way to New York City the following year in December 1946 to visit Cassady's friend Hal Chase, who was studying anthropology at Columbia University (Cassady had his own vague plans of entering Columbia that were never realized). It was through Chase that Cassady met

Jack Kerouac and Allen Ginsberg, as well as William S. Burroughs (who tended to keep his distance, immediately recognizing the con man in Cassady). Chase would later remark about the early Beat scene, "The key to the whole thing was boredom."

Chase, who had met Cassady at the Denver Public Library during the summer of 1945, later served as the model for "Chad King" in *On the Road* and "Val Hayes" in *Visions of Cody*. In anticipation of Cassady's arrival, Chase had told Kerouac and Ginsberg all about Cassady's frantic lifestyle and may have shown them Cassady's letters, which were full of misspellings but evinced an energetic, stream-of-consciousness style. Cassady desired to learn to write from Kerouac and got involved in a sexual relationship with Ginsberg. Cassady left New York City in March 1947 and began corresponding with Kerouac, who took his first cross-country road trip to visit Cassady in Denver later that year. Kerouac and Cassady eventually embarked on a series of travel adventures between 1947 and 1950 that would later provide the framework of Kerouac's 1957 novel, *On the Road*.

Cross-Country Trips (1947–50)

After meeting as kindred spirits in 1947, Kerouac and Cassady set about on a madcap series of cross-country trips over the next three years that provided the ingredients for *On the Road*. In his journal entry for December 28, 1947, Kerouac wrote, "That makes 12,000 miles of travelling for 1947 for me anyway, which isn't exactly a dull or lazy year—along with the 250,000 words of writing."

On the Road is divided into five parts, three of which detail road trips with "Sal Paradise" (Kerouac) and "Dean Moriarty" (Cassady). Part one highlights Paradise's first trip to San Francisco. He stops in Denver along the way and parties with Dean and "Carlo Marx" (Allen Ginsberg). Sal makes his way to San Francisco where he stays with his old friend "Remi Boncoeur" (Henri Cru) and briefly serves as a night watchman before hitting the road again. Sal meets "Terry" (Bea Franco) on a bus to Los Angeles, and the couple travels to the town of "Sabinal," where Terry's extended family works as migrant workers. Sal eventually leaves Terry and heads back to New York City.

In part two, Dean, along with "Marylou" (LuAnne Henderson) and "Ed Dunkel" (Al Hinkle), crashes the Paradise family Christmas celebration in "Testament," Virginia (actually Rocky Mount, North Carolina, which was also the birthplace of jazz great Thelonious Sphere Monk). Sal joins them to New York City and then down to Algiers, Louisiana (just outside New Orleans), to visit "Old Bull Lee" (William S. Burroughs) and his common-law wife, "Jane" (Joan Vollmer), along with unwanted houseguest "Galatea Dunkel" (Helen

Hinkle), who had been stranded there by her husband, "Ed." In due time, Sal, Dean, and Marylou continue on to San Francisco, where Dean abandons them and goes back to "Camille" (Carolyn Cassady). Marylou soon leaves Sal, and he takes a bus back to New York City.

In part three, Sal takes a bus to Denver, discovers that none of his old friends are there, and heads to San Francisco to stay with Dean and Camille, who soon throws both of them out. Sal and Dean decide to take another road trip back to New York City. In part four, Sal travels alone to Denver (Dean is working as a parking lot attendant in Manhattan) and hangs out with his friend "Stan Shephard" (Frank Jeffries). Dean soon quits his job and joins them in Denver, and the trio heads down to Mexico City and spends a couple of wild days in a whorehouse. Sal soon becomes violently ill, and Dean leaves him behind.

In part five, Sal returns to New York City and meets "Laura" (Joan Haverty, who would briefly become Kerouac's second wife). The couple plans to move

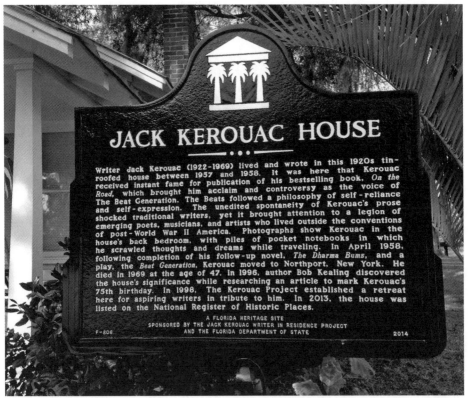

As *On the Road* quickly evolved into a national sensation in 1957–58, Jack Kerouac lived quietly in College Park, a neighborhood in Orlando, Florida, that is now home to the Kerouac Project, a writer-in-residence retreat. *Courtesy of Alternative Reel/alternativereel.com*

to San Francisco. Dean writes Sal that he will come to New York City and accompany Sal and Laura to San Francisco. However, Dean arrives more than five weeks early. Sal and Laura are heading out to a jazz concert with a group that includes Remi Boncoeur, who denies Sal's request to give Dean a lift. Sal last sees Dean wandering off into the night.

Interestingly, by the time *On the Road* was finally published in 1957, it had been a full decade since Kerouac had actually hit the road with Cassady for the first time. The world depicted in the novel had already begun to disappear with the advent of the Interstate Highway System, followed by a slew of hotel chains and fast food joints in its wake. In addition, the jazz music Kerouac had written so eloquently about in the novel was already making way for rock 'n' roll. As for Kerouac, he was thirty-five years old when *On the Road* was published, had long since left the road, was drinking heavily, and would soon be living rather reclusively with his mother in a series of modest suburban locales, including Orlando, Florida; Northport, Long Island; Lowell, Massachusetts; and ultimately St. Petersburg, Florida, where he died at the age of forty-seven in 1969.

Joan Anderson Letter

According to Jack Kerouac, "I got the idea for the spontaneous style of *On the Road* from seeing how good old Neal Cassady wrote letters to me, all first-person, mad, confessional." Specifically, Kerouac was inspired to write in the "spontaneous" style of *On the Road* after receiving the legendary "Joan Anderson Letter," one of the most important documents in Beat lore, from Cassady in December 1950. Although Kerouac had been planning a "road novel" for several years before this time, he had not discovered the appropriate style to explore the cross-country trips he took with Cassady between the years 1947 and 1950. Kerouac's first published novel, *The Town and the City* (1950), had been written in imitation of Thomas Wolfe (*Look Homeward, Angel*) in linear style with third-person narrative and long descriptive passages of prose.

The sixteen-thousand-word, eighteen-page "Joan Anderson Letter" detailed one of Cassady's teenage sexual conquests back in Denver. After reading Cassady's letter, Kerouac wrote him back, exclaiming, "I have renounced fiction and fear. There is nothing to do but write the truth." Kerouac later called the "Joan Anderson Letter" "the greatest piece of writing I ever saw, better'n anybody in America, or at least enough to make Melville, Twain, Dreiser, Wolfe, I dunno who, spin in their graves."

The "Joan Anderson Letter" had been missing for years, and according to rumor, Allen Ginsberg lent the letter to poet Gerd Stern, a former literary agent for Ace Books, who reportedly threw it into the San Francisco Bay or accidentally dropped it from a houseboat (Stern always denied the accusation, claiming that it was Ginsberg who lost the letter). However, in a near-miraculous discovery, the "Joan Anderson Letter" actually turned up in the fall of 2014. Apparently Ginsberg had forgotten he had sent the letter to publisher Richard Emerson at Golden Goose Press in Sausalito, California. The letter ended up unread in Emerson's archives, which were turned over to one of his business associates, the daughter of whom found the letter when she was cleaning out her father's house after his death. The letter was supposed to go up for auction in December 2014 and was expected to command up to $500,000. However, both the Cassady and Kerouac estates got involved, delaying the auction indefinitely.

Vintage Cassady, the "Joan Anderson Letter" is full of such classic lines as "To hell with all the dirty lousy shit, I've had enough horseshit. I got my own pure little bangtail mind and the confines of its binding please me yet. I wake to more horrors than Celine, not a vain statement for now I've passed thru just repetitious shudderings and nightmare twitches." The "Joan Anderson Letter" inspired the little-known (and deservedly so!) 1997 drama, *The Last Time I Committed Suicide*, which was directed by Stephen T. Kay and starred Thomas Jane, Keanu Reeves, Adrien Brody, Gretchen Mol, and Claire Forlani.

Creative Process

According to popular legend, Kerouac wrote *On the Road* during a three-week period on one long roll of teletype paper with no margins, single spacing, and no paragraph breaks. In fact, Kerouac had an obsessive habit of keeping journals and notebooks, and had conceived his "road novel" as early as 1948 when he had recently embarked on the legendary cross-country trips with Neal Cassady. According to Lucien Carr, "Whatever else Jack was doing, he had to write. It's like you gotta breathe, or shit, or eat."

According to Beat historian Douglas Brinkley (in a 2007 *Library of America* interview):

> There is such a thing as the scroll which is Kerouac's original version of *On the Road* that he typed up on Japanese tracing paper in long sessions while he listened to a late-night New York jazz station. That's the reality. What it belies though is that Kerouac took many trips around the country and he kept detailed journals. What he was doing when he was engaged in that marathon typing bout was sitting with his journals. Like anyone keeping a road or travel journal he took those

journals and turned them into a novel. It wasn't just coming from the head in a burst of inspiration.

In his August 23, 1948, journal entry, Kerouac wrote, "I have another novel in mind—On the Road—which I keep thinking about: about two guys hitch-hiking to California in search of something they don't really find, and losing themselves on the road, and coming all the way back hopeful of something else. Also, I'm finding a new principle of writing. More later." In a November 3, 1948, journal entry, Kerouac exclaims that he has written six thousand words of *On the Road*—"roughly, swiftly, experimentally"—followed by an entry less than two weeks later that says, "Thinking up mad new ideas for 'On the Road.'" The novel's title changed several times as well, and was at one point going to be called "Hip Generation."

Looking back on his creative process, Kerouac remarked in a 1968 *Paris Review* interview, "You think out what actually happened, you tell friends long stories about it, you mull it over in your mind, you connect it together at leisure, then when the time comes to pay the rent again you force yourself to sit at the typewriter, at the writing notebook, and get it over with as fast as you can . . . and there's no harm in that because you've got the whole story lined up." The fascinating evolution of *On the Road* from Kerouc's early journals to the frantic typewritten manuscript can be studied in *Windblown World: The Journals of Jack Kerouac 1947–1954*, which was published in 2006.

The Original Scroll

According to legend, Jack Kerouac typed his first draft of *On the Road* during a whirlwind three-week session on a 120-foot scroll of tracing paper in April 1951. Kerouac had told John Clellon Holmes (*Nothing to Declare*), "I'm going to get me a roll of shelf-paper, feed it into the typewriter, and just write it down as fast as I can, exactly like it happened, all in a rush." Kerouac was living with his second wife, Joan Haverty, at her apartment at 454 West Twentieth Street in Manhattan at the time. Although Kerouac did indeed pound out the manuscript in one long, single-spaced paragraph and taped together eight long sheets of tracing paper to form the scroll, it is evident through his journals and notebooks that he had been meticulously planning his "road novel" for several years.

Unfortunately, Lucien Carr's cocker spaniel, Potchky, evidently chewed up the last few feet of the manuscript. Kerouac even wrote a note in the margin: "DOG ATE [Potchky-a dog]." Carr later confirmed that Potchky had indeed devoured a portion of the scroll, remarking that the pooch "had an appetite for literature" ("The Beat Goes On," *Eagle-Tribune*, August 26, 2007). The original scroll was purchased by Indianapolis Colts owner Jim Irsay in 2001 for $2.43 million and was donated to the Lilly Library at Indiana University Bloomington. The scroll is occasionally made available for public viewing in museums and libraries. Irsay commented, "I look at it as a stewardship. I don't believe you own anything in this world. It's a great thing and for Jack, wherever his spiritual vibes are floating around, he can feel good about it."

Described as "rougher, wilder, and more provocative" than the official work that appeared, heavily edited, in 1957, the original scroll was published as *On the Road: The Original Scroll* in 2007 to correspond with the fiftieth anniversary of the publication of *On the Road.* The scroll features all of the real names of Kerouac's friends and acquaintances (Viking Press made him use pseudonyms in the first edition in order to avoid lawsuits), as well as many lines censored from the final draft, such as "She spread her little legs and I made love to her in the sweetness of the weary morning." The scroll is slightly longer than the published version.

Minor Characters

In addition to the legendary characters of *On the Road*—"Sal Paradise" (Kerouac), "Dean Moriarty" (Neal Cassady), "Marylou" (LuAnne Henderson), "Carlo Marx" (Allen Ginsberg), and "Old Bull Lee" (William S. Burroughs)—a host of thinly disguised but essential characters appears in the novel. For instance, Hal Chase, who introduced Neal Cassady to Kerouac, appears as "Chad King," while Lucien Carr, who introduced Kerouac, Allen Ginsberg, and William S. Burroughs to each other, served as the model for "Damion." Chase also turns up as "Val Hayes" in *Visions of Cody.*

Kerouac's own mother, Gabrielle, has been transformed into Paradise's unnamed aunt. His sister's house in Rocky Mount, North Carolina, was changed to the fictional "Testament," Virginia. Kerouac's brother-in-law Paul Blake appears as "Rocco." Kerouac's second wife, Joan Haverty, appears briefly in part five as Sal's new love interest, "Laura," depicted as "the girl with the pure and innocent dear eyes that I had always searched for so long. We agreed to love each other madly."

Times Square hustler Herbert Huncke was the model for the character "Elmer Hassel," whom Sal constantly searches for whenever he hits the streets of New York City. Expatriate writer Alan Ansen, who visited William S. Burroughs in Tangier in 1957 and helped type *Naked Lunch*, served as the inspiration for the character of "Rollo Greb." A famous photo exists of Burroughs on a beach in Tangier "hanging" Ansen, who also appears in *The Subterraneans* as "Austin Bromberg." In addition, Burroughs's common-law wife, Joan Vollmer, appears as "Jane," and their troubled son, Billy Jr., appears

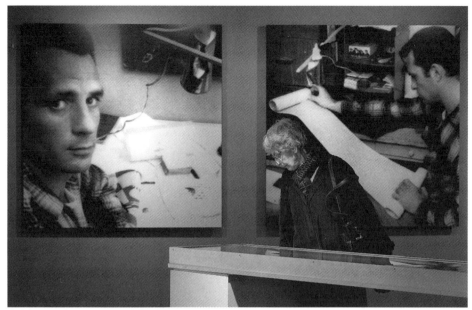

A thirty-six-foot section of the famous *On the Road* scroll toured the United States in 2006. The scroll was on loan from the private collection of Indianapolis Colts owner James Irsay.

Photo by Justin Sullivan/Getty Images

as the rambunctious toddler "Ray Lee" in the famous section of the novel where the travelers descend on Old Bull Lee's spread in Algiers, Louisiana. Other characters include "Inez" (Cassady's third wife, Diana Hansen), "Ed and Galatea Dunkel" (Al and Helen Hinkle), "Tom Saybrook" (John Clellon Holmes), and "Roland Major" (architecture critic Allen Temko), among others.

Cultural References

On the Road is full of allusions to jazz musicians, authors, philosophers, actors and films, historical figures, and pop culture. In addition, some of the more indirect references involved the pseudonyms Jack Kerouac uses for his thinly disguised characterizations. For example, "Dean Moriarty" (Neal Cassady) suggests both *Rebel Without a Cause* actor James Dean and "Professor Moriarty," the criminal mastermind in the Sherlock Holmes series of stories by Sir Arthur Conan Doyle. In addition, "Carlo Marx" (Allen Ginsberg) brings to mind both Karl and Groucho Marx (who is mentioned several times throughout the text).

A jazz enthusiast, Kerouac name-drops several of his favorite musicians throughout *On the Road*, such as Charlie "Bird" Parker, Duke Ellington, Count

Basie, Roy Eldridge, Dizzy Gillespie, Louis Armstrong, Lucky Millinder, Lester Young, Billie Holiday, Miles Davis, Dexter Gordon, George Shearing, Benny Moten, Wardell Gray, Lionel Hampton, Wynonie Harris, and Stan Getz. In one such memorable jazz-fueled passage, Kerouac provides a brief history of the art form, writing, "Once there was Louis Armstrong blowing his beautiful top in the muds of New Orleans; before him the mad musicians who had paraded on official days and broke up their Sousa marches into ragtime. Then there was swing, and Roy Eldridge, vigorous and virile, leaning into it with glittering eyes and a lovely smile and sending it out broadcast to rock the jazz world . . . Charlie Parker leaving home and coming to Harlem, and meeting mad Thelonius Monk and madder Gillespie."

Movie references in *On the Road* include *Of Mice and Men* (1939), which was based on the John Steinbeck novel, directed by Lewis Milestone, and starred Lon Chaney Jr. and Burgess Meredith; and *Sullivan's Travels* (1942), which was directed by Preston Sturges, and starred Joel McCrea and Veronica Lake. Works of literature cited include Eugene Sue's *Mysteries of Paris*, Herman Melville's *Moby Dick*, Henri Alain-Fournier's *Le Grand Meaulnes*, and Ernest Hemingway's *The Sun Also Rises* and *Green Hills of Africa*.

Publishing History

Although Jack Kerouac wrote the first draft of *On the Road* in April 1951, the novel was not published until more than six years later by Viking Press on September 5, 1957. Harcourt Brace, which had published Kerouac's *The Town and the City* in 1950, rejected all of Kerouac's subsequent novels, including *On the Road*. Although Kerouac had dedicated *The Town and the City* to Robert Giroux, "Friend and Editor," Giroux's rejection of *On the Road* ended both their personal and professional relationships.

Sterling Lord became Kerouac's literary agent in 1952 and set about trying to find a publisher for the work, facing rejection after rejection over the years from editors who felt the manuscript was simply "unpublishable." According to Lord, "I felt that Jack's was a very important new voice and ought to be heard . . . And I was totally convinced of that." One of the publishers to reject *On the Road* was Knopf—with one editor there remarking, "This is a badly misdirected talent and . . . this huge sprawling and inconclusive novel would probably have small sales and sardonic indignant reviews from every side."

During the years that the unpublished manuscript languished, Kerouac stayed busy writing several novels and novellas, including *Doctor Sax*, *Book of Dreams*, *Maggie Cassidy*, *The Subterraneans*, *Tristessa*, and *Visions of Cody*. None of these were published until after *On the Road* hit the bookstores and there became a sudden demand for his work. However, excerpts from *On the Road*

A jacket worn by Jack Kerouac during the early 1950s is currently on display at the Beat Museum, a must-visit for Beat fans that lies in North Beach, San Francisco.   *Author's collection*

were printed in the *Paris Review* during the mid-1950s to enthusiastic response from the readership. It was the legendary Malcolm Cowley, an editorial consultant for Viking, who championed the publication of *On the Road.*

Reception

In his landmark review for the *New York Times* (September 4, 1957), Gilbert Millstein raved that *On the Road* was "a major novel" and "its publication is a historic occasion in so far as the exposure of an authentic work of art is of any great moment in an age in which the attention is fragmented and the sensibilities are blunted by the superlatives of fashion." Millstein continued, "There are sections of *On the Road* in which the writing is of a beauty almost breathtaking . . . there is some writing on jazz that has never been equaled in American fiction, either for insight, style, or technical virtuosity."

Thirty-five-year-old Jack Kerouac and his girlfriend, Joyce Johnson, picked up the review shortly after midnight at a newsstand, hurried into a neighborhood bar, and read the review over and over. In *Minor Characters*, Johnson recalls, "Jack kept shaking his head as if he couldn't figure out why he wasn't happier than he was." Kerouac's life truly changed overnight, for

Johnson remembers that the "ringing phone woke him the next morning, and he was famous."

As fate would have it, Millstein was simply filling in for the regular daily book reviewer, Orville Prescott, who was on vacation. Prescott was outraged by the review since he hated the novel. Just a few days later, critic David Dempsey wrote another, much more critical, review of *On the Road* in the *New York Times Review of Books*, writing, "As a portrait of a disjointed segment of society acting out of its own neurotic necessity, *On the Road* is a stunning achievement. But it is a road, as far as the characters are concerned, that leads to nowhere." Interestingly, when Millstein passed away in 1999 at the age of eighty-three, the title of his *New York Times* obituary was "Reviewer Who Gave Early Boost to Kerouac."

Other reviewers piled on the criticism, most treating the book in cultural terms rather than focusing on the actual writing itself. *Time* called *On the Road* a "barbaric yawp of a book" with Kerouac commanding "attention as a kind of literary James Dean." In a letter to Allen Ginsberg, Kerouac wrote, "I hitchhiked and starved, for art, and that makes me the Fool of the Beatniks with a crown of shit. Thanks, America."

Legacy

According to William S. Burroughs, "Kerouac opened a million coffee bars and sold a million pairs of Levis to both sexes. Woodstock rises from his pages." Indeed, *On the Road* has influenced everyone from legendary singer-songwriter Bob Dylan and Jim Morrison of the Doors to photographer Robert Frank and postmodern writer Thomas Pynchon. Author Thomas McGuane remarked, "[Kerouac] trained us in the epic idea that . . . you didn't necessarily have to take it in Dipstick, Ohio, forever . . . Kerouac set me out there with my own key to the highway."

Other artists to proclaim the influence of *On the Road* at one time or another include singer-songwriter Tom Waits, actors Jack Nicholson and Johnny Depp, Merry Prankster Ken Kesey, Jerry Garcia of the Grateful Dead, director Francis Ford Coppola, actor and playwright Sam Shepard, Ben Gibbard of Death Cab for Cutie, and rock critic Lester Bangs, among many others. In addition, classic road films such as *Easy Rider* (1969), *The Rain People* (1969), *Two-Lane Blacktop* (1971), *Vanishing Point* (1971), *Badlands* (1973), *The Last Detail* (1973), *Kings of the Road* (1976), *Lost in America* (1985), *The Sure Thing* (1985), *Drugstore Cowboy* (1989), *Powwow Highway* (1989), *My Own Private Idaho* (1991), *Thelma and Louise* (1991), *Fear and Loathing in Las Vegas* (1998), *Sideways* (2004), and others all owe a debt to *On the Road*.

In 1982, the twenty-fifth anniversary national celebration of *On the Road* was held at the Naropa Institute (now known as Naropa University) in Boulder, Colorado. Naropa is home to the Jack Kerouac School of Disembodied Poetics. In 2007, the original scroll of *On the Road* was displayed throughout the United States to celebrate the fiftieth anniversary of the book's publication. The scroll itself was published in book form that same year.

According to Douglas Brinkley in a 2007 Library of America interview, "*On the Road* is still the premier coming-of-age book for people who have a travel bug, who want a sense of adventure, who want to discover themselves. And that's the key. At its heart, like all road odysseys, it's about finding oneself. You're going on these journeys to find your authentic self. *On the Road* is filled with the possibilities you can have today and the fun you will have tomorrow. It's clearly one of the four or five most significant novels of twentieth-century literature."

In 2012, a film version of *On the Road* was released to mixed reviews. Directed by Walter Salles, the film starred Sam Riley as "Sal Paradise," Garrett Hedlund as "Dean Moriarty," Kristen Stewart as "Marylou," Amy Adams as "Jane," Kirsten Dunst as "Camille Moriarty," and Viggo Mortensen as "Old Bull Lee."

Somewhere Along the Line

To say that Jack Kerouac was a prolific writer would be a gross understatement—his vast body of work comprises what he labeled the "Duluoz Legend" (the word "duluoz" being derived from the French-Canadian slang word for "louse"). As Kerouac often remarked, "My work comprises one vast book like Proust's . . . seen through the eyes of poor Ti Jean (me), otherwise known as Jack Duluoz." According to Sterling Lord, Kerouac's literary agent, in *Lord of Publishing: A Memoir* (2013), "I was impressed with [Kerouac's] commitment to serious writing at the expense of everything else in his life. At a time when the middle class was burgeoning with new homes, two-tone American cars, and black-and-white TVs, when American happiness was defined by upwardly mobile consumerism, Kerouac etched a different existence and he wrote in an original language."

The Dharma Bums (1958)

Dedicated to the fabled Chinese poet Hanshan, *The Dharma Bums* served as Jack Kerouac's follow-up to *On the Road*. According to John Clellon Holmes (*Jack's Book*, 1978), Kerouac "wrote *The Dharma Bums* in three weeks, or maybe a month. They wouldn't publish *The Subterraneans*. They wouldn't publish any of the other books that he'd written, so he wrote *The Dharma Bums*."

In *The Dharma Bums*, Kerouac assumes the role of first-person narrator "Ray Smith," while Beat poet and Buddhist scholar Gary Snyder takes on the inspirational sidekick role as "Japhy Ryder," a "kid from eastern Oregon brought up in a log cabin deep in the woods," who went on to become "an Oriental scholar and discovered the greatest Dharma Bums of them all, the Zen lunatics of China and Japan." Ryder represents one of the "rucksack wanderers," who refuse "to subscribe to the general demand that they consume production and therefore have to work for the privilege of consuming, all that crap they don't really want anyway . . . all of them imprisoned in a system of work, produce, consume, work, produce, consume."

Significantly, Neal Cassady appears only as a minor character, "Cody Pomeray," in *The Dharma Bums.* Cody's girlfriend, "Rosie Buchanan," is based on Cassady's real-life girlfriend Natalie Jackson, who committed suicide. Meanwhile, Kenneth Rexroth was satirized as "Rheinhold Cacoethes," the "father of the Frisco poetry scene." Other characters that appear in *The Dharma Bums* include "Alvah Goldbook" (Allen Ginsberg), "Warren Coughlin" (Philip Whalen), "Francis DaPavia" (Philip Lamantia), "Ike O'Shay" (Michael McClure), "Sean Monahan" (Locke McCorkle), "Arthur Whane" (Alan Watts), and "George" (Peter Orlovsky).

In *The Dharma Bums,* Kerouac provides a lively account of the legendary Six Gallery Reading in 1955: "I followed the whole gang of howling poets to the reading at Gallery Six that night, which was, among other important things, the night of the birth of the San Francisco Poetry Renaissance." In addition, Kerouac highlights his stint as a fire lookout at Desolation Peak in Washington during the summer of 1956: "I was alone on Desolation Peak for all I knew for eternity, I was sure I wasn't going to come out of there alive anyway." *The Dharma Bums* also details Smith, Ryder, and "Henry Morley" (John Montgomery) hiking 12,285-foot Matterhorn Peak, which lies at the northern boundary of Yosemite National Park. Smith makes the astute observation, "You can't fall off a mountain."

Malcolm Cowley (*Jack's Book*, 1978) remarked that "I never liked *The Dharma Bums* very much, because it had no people in it except Jack—and oh, yes, Gary Snyder's in there, too; he's the only other one." Interestingly, the seventh printing of *The Dharma Bums* featured a hippie couple on the cover and a tagline that reads "by the man who launched the hippie world, the daddy of the swinging psychedelic generation."

The Subterraneans (1958)

"No girl had ever moved me with a story of spiritual suffering and so beautifully her soul showing out radiant as an angel wandering in hell and the hell the selfsame streets I'd roamed in watching, watching for someone just like her." A fast-paced, semi-autobiographical novella written by Jack Kerouac in just three days, *The Subterraneans* details the brief romance between Kerouac's alter ego, "Leo Percepied," and "Mardou Fox" (based on Alene Lee, who was half African American and half Cherokee) amid the smoky jazz clubs and bustling nightclubs of San Francisco.

Other thinly disguised characters in *The Subterraneans* include "Frank Carmody" (William S. Burroughs), "Jane" (Joan Vollmer), "Sam Vedder"

Jack Kerouac's fast-paced, semi-autobiographical 1958 novella, *The Subterraneans*, was transformed into a watered-down, poorly reviewed Hollywood movie that starred Leslie Caron, George Peppard, Roddy McDowell, and *Laugh-In* regular Arte Johnson.   *Author's collection*

(Lucien Carr), "Adam Moorad" (Allen Ginsberg), "Julian Alexander" (Anton Rosenberg), "Roxanne" (Iris Brodie), and "Arial Lavalina" (Gore Vidal). *The Subterraneans* ends with the lines "And I go home having lost her love. And write this book." Censored from the book was the alleged one-night stand Kerouac and Vidal had at the Chelsea Hotel.

In his *New York Times* review (February 22, 1956) of *The Subterraneans,* David Dempsey commented, "It is written less for laughs ('kicks') and more as an attempt to put down every recollected fact about an affair between two psychologically 'sick' people . . . You appreciate Kerouac (if you do at all) on his own terms. The story is nothing—the sorrows of young Werther without the formality of the marriage or the tragedy of the suicide—while the unraveling is everything. The most notable feature of *The Subterraneans* is the complete, almost schizophrenic disintegration of syntax."

An ad for *The Subterraneans* that appeared in the March 22, 1958, edition of the *Saturday Review* exclaimed, "His newest! His greatest! A sharp, beautifully written novel of love, lust and despair among the young writers, poets and artists of San Francisco today." *The Subterraneans* was turned into a

Hollywoodized MGM film of the same name in 1960 with two-dimensional characters and the dubious casting decision of Leslie Caron as "Mardou Fox" and George Peppard as "Leo Percepied," as well as comedian Arte Johnson as the Gore Vidal character, in this case known as "Arial Lavalerra."

Lee (1931–91) also served as the model for the character "Irene May" in Kerouac's 1962 novel, *Big Sur*, while Rosenberg, an artist, musician, and all-around hipster, became known as "the angel of the subterraneans." When he died of cancer in 1998 at the age of seventy-one, the *New York Times* noted in its obituary (February 22, 1998) that Rosenberg "embodied the Greenwich Village hipster ideal of 1950's cool to such a laid-back degree and with such determined detachment that he never amounted to much of anything."

Doctor Sax (1959)

Although *Doctor Sax* (subtitled *Faust Part Three*) was published in 1959, Jack Kerouac actually wrote the novel while living with William S. Burroughs in Mexico City in 1952. Along with *Mary Cassidy* and *Visions of Gerard*, it is one of the Lowell novels featuring Kerouac's alter ego, "Jackie Duluoz." According to William S. Burroughs (*Rolling Stone*, 1980), "Jack said once that he wrote *Doctor Sax* in *my* toilet in Mexico City. I recall that, on occasion, he would retire to the toilet to write if there were too many people in the apartment and too much talk. At other times he wrote at the kitchen table or in the front room or sitting on a bench somewhere." However, as evidenced in a November 1948 journal entry, Kerouac was working up the idea of *Doctor Sax* years earlier: "I must do this 'Doctor Sax' in 2 months; only a short novel, 50,000-wds. or so, in order to present it possibly in a contest by that time, or simply to have another work besides T & C [*The Town and the City*] on the market by New Year's."

Doctor Sax is divided into six books: "Ghosts of the Pawtucketville Night," "A Gloomy Bookmovie," "More Ghosts," "The Night the Man with the Watermelon Died," "The Flood," and "The Castle." The book highlights Kerouac's dream of his early childhood, hanging out with his buddies, and reading pulp magazines like *The Shadow*, *Doc Savage*, and *Phantom Detective*, while inventing superheroes like Doctor Sax roaming throughout Lowell: "Doctor Sax I first saw in his earlier lineaments in the early Catholic childhood of Centralville—deaths, funerals, the shroud of that, the dark figure in the corner when you look at the dead man coffin in the dolorous parlor of the open house with a horrible purple wreath on the door."

The thinly disguised characters in *Doctor Sax* include several of Kerouac's childhood friends, including "Rigopoulos" (George "G. J." Apostolos), "Paul 'Scotty' Boldieu" (Henry "Scotty" Beaulieu), "Lucky Bergerac" ("Happy"

Bertrand), "Vinny Bergerac" (Fred Bertrand), and "Albert 'Lousy' Lauzon" (Roland Salvas). Kerouac also wrote a screenplay adaptation of the novel that was never filmed, titled *Doctor Sax and the Great World Snake*. John Clellon Holmes called *Doctor Sax* "one of the most extraordinary, influential, maddening, and ultimately prodigious achievements in recent literature." However, in a scathing *New York Times* review of *Doctor Sax*, titled "Beatnik Bogeyman on the Prowl" (May 3, 1959), David Dempsey wrote, "Dr. Sax is not only bad Kerouac; it is a bad book. Much of it is in bad taste, and much more is meaningless. It runs the gamut from the incoherent to the incredible, a mishmash of avant-gardism (unreadable), autobiography (seemingly Kerouac's) and fantasy (largely psychopathic)."

Maggie Cassidy (1959)

"I saw her, standing in the crowd, forlorn, dissatisfied, dark, unpleasantly strange." Published by Avon Books in 1959 and considered one of Jack Kerouac's most accessible works, *Maggie Cassidy* is a straightforward, coming-of-age story that focuses on Kerouac's awkward, adolescent relationship with high school sweetheart "Maggie Cassidy" (based on his real-life romance with Mary Carney) in Lowell, Massachusetts, and featured the tagline "The Bard of the Beat Generation reveals a startling new dimension to his personality in this brilliant and profoundly moving novel of adolescence and first love."

Kerouac had actually written the novel in 1953, but it was not even considered for publication until the success of *On the Road* in 1957. *Maggie Cassidy* is one of Kerouac's Lowell novels, which also include *The Town and the City* (1950), *Doctor Sax* (1959), *Visions of Gerard* (1963), and *Vanity of Duluoz* (1968).

In *Maggie Cassidy*, high school football star "Jack Duluoz" (Kerouac's alter ego) meets the Irish beauty at a New Year's Eve dance, and they embark on a brief, torrid, and ultimately doomed adolescent romance. The cast of characters includes "Emil 'Pop' Duluoz" (Leo Kerouac), "G. J. Rigopoulos" (George "G. J." Apostolos), and "Pauline 'Moe' Cole" (Margaret "Petty" Coffey), as well as "Lu Libble" (legendary Columbia University football coach Lou Little).

Maggie Cassidy contains some of Kerouac's best descriptive passages about his Lowell hometown, such as "I walked home in the dead of Lowell night— three miles, no buses—the dark ground, roads, cemeteries, streets, construction ditches, millyards—The billion winter stars hugeing overhead like frozen beads frozen suns all packed and inter-allied in one rich united universe of showery light, beating, beating, like great hearts in the non-understandable bowl void black."

A somewhat lurid cover design by Mitchell Hooks was featured for a British edition of *Maggie Cassidy* in 1960 to capture the beatnik crowd that included the improbable tagline "The vibrant, demanding, woman-bodied girl who fascinated and confused the man she yearned for—a brilliant and profoundly moving novel." In a June 15, 1961, letter to Bernice Lemire, a scholar inquiring about his boyhood for a biographical study of his work, Kerouac wrote, "Maggie Cassidy herself is Mary Carney, and still lives in the same house (with her mother) (or did, in 1954). (Has 2 daughters now.) (Her husband abandoned her.) . . . The mistake you've made is that you failed to realize that my totally 100% true biography is right there in my writings about Lowell: in Doctor Sax, Maggie Cassidy. Only the names were changed." The Maggie Cassidy character appears again in both *Desolation Angels* and *Vanity of Duluoz.*

In an illuminating essay titled "Kerouac's Lowell: A Life on the Concord and Merrimack Rivers" by John Suiter (published at www.jackkerouac.com/photo-essay), Carney is quoted as hardly recognizing herself in Kerouac's portrayal. According to Carney, "There was never any sex . . . We were good kids . . . And I never kissed anybody that way, not like he wrote it."

Tristessa (1960)

"How frail, beat, final, is Tristessa as we load her into the quiet hostile bar." Jack Kerouac spent the summer of 1955 in Mexico City, where he holed himself up in a small room above the house of Bill Garver (an old junkie friend of William S. Burroughs) and started writing the 242 choruses that would eventually make up his landmark poem, *Mexico City Blues*, which was not published until 1959. A frequently drunk and disheveled Kerouac also embarked on a doomed relationship with an impoverished, drug-addicted Mexican prostitute named Esperanza Villanueva, who inspired his work *Tristessa*, which was first published by Avon Books in 1960.

A fast-paced novella rather sensationally billed as "a new and hauntingly different novel about a morphine-racked prostitute," *Tristessa* depicts Kerouac's alter ego, "Jack Duluoz," as he attempts to reconcile the title character's exotic beauty and her intense Catholic faith with her "junk-racked body" and self-destructive nature. Garver appears in the novel as "Old Bull Gaines"—"a sweet and tender person, though just a little of the con man."

Tristessa is full of religious imagery—blending elements of both Buddhism and Catholicism. It is interesting and quite relevant that Kerouac gave Esperanza (Spanish for "hope") the name Tristessa (Spanish for "sadness"). Indeed, an overall feeling of sadness and despair engulfs each of the characters, with Kerouac regularly commenting about the "dreariness of the world" and how every one of us is "born to die." *Tristessa* is divided into two sections: "Trembling and Chaste" and "A Year Later . . . " In the second section, Duluoz returns to Mexico City after spending more than a year away (during which he spent the summer as a fire lookout on Desolation Peak) but realizes quickly that he "waited too long." Tristessa's addiction has worsened, and she treats Duluoz with disdain as he refers to her as "the sad mutilated blue Madonna." The novel ends famously with the line "I'll write long sad tales about people in the legend of my life—This part is my part of the movie, let's hear yours."

In a blurb used to promote the book, Allen Ginsberg described *Tristessa* as a "narrative meditation studying a hen, a rooster, a dove, a cat, a chihuahua dog, family meat, and a ravishing, ravished junky lady, first in their crowded bedroom, then out to drunken streets, taco stands, & pads at dawn in Mexico slums." In a *New York Times* review of the book, critic Daniel Talbot wrote, "In the end, *Tristessa* will seem like so much more of the same to those who never did care for Kerouac's work—but read it out of boredom or to be 'with it' cocktail party-wise. For those who do care about his work, it swings."

Mexican novelist and critic Jorge Garcia-Robles translated *Tristessa* into Spanish in 1997. Garcia-Robles also wrote a colorful account of Burroughs's time in Mexico City between 1949 and 1952, titled *The Stray Bullet: William S. Burroughs in Mexico* (2013), as well as *At the End of the Road: Jack Kerouac in Mexico* (2014).

Visions of Cody (1972)

Allen Ginsberg called Jack Kerouac's experimental novel *Visions of Cody* "the most sincere and holy writing I know of our age" (although his initial reaction upon reading the finished manuscript was to call it "a holy mess"). Written in the early 1950s, *Visions of Cody* wasn't published until three years after Kerouac's death in 1972. The book focuses on the relationship between "Jack Duluoz" (Kerouac) and "Cody Pomeray" (Neal Cassady) with a supporting cast of characters that includes "Evelyn," (Carolyn Cassady), "Bull Hubbard" (William S. Burroughs), "Irwin Garden" (Ginsberg), "Julien Love" (Lucien Carr), "Val Hayes" (Hal Chase), "Huck" (Herbert Huncke), and "Finistra" (Bill Cannastra), among others.

Kerouac, who always thought of *Visions of Cody* as his masterwork, referred to the book's structure as a "vertical" study of Cassady and his relationship to America. The first section of *Visions of Cody* consists of descriptive "sketches" of the post–World War II scene as Duluoz prepares to visit Pomeray in San Francisco. The second section features a transcript of taped conversations between Duluoz and Pomeray over a five-night period as they drink heavily and smoke marijuana. The final sections include "Imitation of the Tape," along with a recap of Duluoz's travels with Pomeray.

During his appearance on *The Steve Allen Show* in 1959, Kerouac read selections from both *Visions of Cody* and *On the Road*. In a 1968 interview with the *Paris Review*, Kerouac remarked, "I typed up a segment of taped conversations with Neal Cassady, or Cody, talking about his early adventures in L.A." Portions of the book were published by New Directions in 1960 as the limited-edition *Excerpts from Visions of Cody*. Ginsberg wrote an introduction to the first edition of *Visions of Cody* called "The Visions of the Great Rememberer."

Not everyone was as enthusiastic as Ginsberg in praising the merits of *Visions of Cody*. For example, in his 1981 memoir, *Those Drinking Days: Myself and Other Writers*, Donald Newlove wrote, "*Visions of Cody* is a mess that begins enticingly, fades, and picks up after page 275. It's the least revised of all his big books and has the largest ballast of sheer bilge—and a few intense passages he never surpassed. He liked it the best of all his books, just as Faulkner thought one of his feeblest novels, *A Fable*, was his masterpiece." In the *New York Times* review of *Visions of Cody* (January 28, 1973), Aaron Latham wrote, "The book may, at first, seem like a raft that has broken up—no order, no plan, everything afloat in the stream of Jack Kerouac's consciousness. But if you can stand some disorder, you will find some of Kerouac's very best writing in this book. It is funny, it is serious. It is eloquent. To read *On the Road* but not *Visions of Cody* is to take a nice sightseeing tour but to forgo the spectacular rapids of Jack Kerouac's wildest writing." According to critic Michael Rogers in his review of *Visions of Cody* for *Rolling Stone* (April 12, 1973), "Kerouac's posthumously published paean to Neal Cassady . . . manages in the course of its four hundred pages to run the gamut from absolutely impenetrable pseudo-Joycean incoherence to passages of crystal-clear observation and lyric emotion."

Big Sur (1962)

"I wake up all woebegone and goopy, groaning from another drinking bout." In *Big Sur*, Jack Kerouac's alter ego, "Jack Duluoz," a worn-out alcoholic, seems light years away from the freewheeling "Sal Paradise" from *On the Road*. Allen Ginsberg called *Big Sur* "a humane, precise account of the extraordinary ravages of alcohol delirium tremens on Kerouac." Published in 1962, *Big Sur* documents Duluoz's struggles with alcoholism, insecurity, and unwanted fame as he resides on and off at a cabin in Bixby Canyon owned by his friend Lawrence Ferlinghetti (who appears as "Lorenzo Monsanto" in the novel).

Upon his arrival in San Francisco after being away several years, Duluoz makes a spectacular entrance in North Beach: "I've bounced drunk into City Lights bookshop at the height of Saturday night business, everyone recognized me . . . and 't'all ends up a roaring drunk in all the famous bars the bloody 'King of the Beatniks' is back in town buying drinks for everyone." Duluoz describes the negative aspects of fame after his book was published as being "driven mad for three years by endless telegrams, phonecalls, requests, mail, visitors, reporters, snoopers . . . Drunken visitors puking in my study, stealing books and even pencils." Feeling "surrounded and outnumbered," Duluoz gets "drunk practically all the time" and then realizes he has "to get away to solitude or die."

In *Big Sur*, Neal Cassady served as the model for "Cody Pomeray," who introduces Duluoz to his mistress "Billie" (Jackie Gibson Mercer). Duluoz and Billie soon embark on a brief relationship. Other characters in the novel include Pomeray's long-suffering wife, "Evelyn" (Carolyn Cassady), "Pat McLear" (Michael McClure), "Dave Wain" (Lew Welch), "Arthur Ma" (Victor Wong), "Ben Fagan" (Philip Whalen), "George Baso" (Alberg Saijo), "Jarry Wagner" (Gary Snyder), "Irwin Garden" (Allen Ginsberg), "Romana Swartz" (Lenore Kandel), "Arthur Wain" (Alan Watts), and "Robert Browning the beatnik painter" (Robert LaVigne). In the final line of *Big Sur*, Kerouac wrote, "Something good will come out of all things yet—And it will be golden and eternal just like that—There's no need to say another word." The novel also features an addendum containing Kerouac's poem "Sea: Sounds of the Pacific Ocean at Big Sur."

Time panned *Big Sur*: "A child's first touch of cold mortality—even when it occurs in a man of 41—may seem ridiculous, and is certainly pathetic." A documentary, *One Fast Move or I'm Gone: Kerouac's Big Sur*, was directed by Curt Worden and released on DVD by Kerouac Films in 2008 with an accompanying soundtrack album featuring songs by Jay Farrar and Benjamin Gibbard. The documentary revisits settings in the novel and recollections from the likes of Ferlinghetti, Carolyn Cassady, and Joyce Johnson, among others. Directed by Michael Polish, *Big Sur*, a compelling film adaptation of the novel, was released in 2013 and stars Jean-Marc Barr, Josh Lucas, Radha Mitchell, Henry Thomas, Anthony Edwards, Balthazar Getty, Patrick Fischler, and Stana Katic.

Visions of Gerard (1963)

"All is well, practice Kindness, Heaven is Nigh." Written in 1956 but not published until 1963, *Visions of Gerard* focuses on the author's older brother, the saintly nine-year-old Gerard, whose life was tragically cut short from rheumatic heart disease, an inflammatory disorder affecting the heart, on June 2, 1926 (Kerouac was just four years old at the time). *Visions of Gerard* serves as the first novel chronologically in the series of novels that makes up Kerouac's "Duluoz Legend." It is also one of Kerouac's Lowell novels, along with *Doctor Sax* (1959) and *Maggie Cassidy* (1959). Narrated by "Jack Duluoz" (Kerouac), the novel focuses on his brother, "Gerard Duluoz" (Gerard Kerouac), and parents, "Ange Duluoz" (Gabrielle Kerouac) and "Emil Duluoz" (Leo Kerouac). The Kerouac family was living at a house on Beaulieu

Street at the time, and the novel expertly weaves Kerouac's earliest recollections of his childhood in Lowell, Massachusetts, with the "brief, tragic-happy life" of Gerard intermixed with a strong Catholic sensibility.

Kerouac, who reportedly wrote the book on Benzedrine in just fifteen days, concludes, "I believe my brother was a saint, and that explains all." In a letter to Gary Snyder on January 15, 1956, Kerouac called *Visions of Gerard* his "best most serious sad and true book yet." Kerouac sold *Visions of Gerard* to Farrar, Straus and Cudahy in 1962 for a $10,000 advance, and in a December 1962 letter to Philip Whalen remarked, "I'm proofreading *Visions of Gerard* . . . [it] will be published by Fall 1963 and will be ignored I guess, or called pretentious, but who cares."

In a *New York Times* review (September 8, 1963) of *Visions of Gerard* titled "A Yawping at the Grave," Saul Maloff wrote,

THREE ROOMS PRESS & RWM PLAYWRIGHTS LAB PRESENT

The Jack Kerouac Literary Group

Inside Jack Kerouac
with special guest
Andrew Blackman

PLUS

A Reading of Larry Myers'
"Jack Kerouac, Catholic"

AND

Original Works Written & Acted by
Dr. Myers' Independent Studies Students in Playwriting

SATURDAY, APRIL 25, 2009

The Jack Kerouac Literary Group in New York City was organized by award-winning off-Broadway playwright Larry Myers, who wrote several critically acclaimed Beat-related plays, including *Jack Kerouac: Catholic.*   *Author's collection*

"Kerouac's familiar rhapsodic prose, persistently inflated beyond the requirements of the occasion, is interrupted only infrequently by dramatic scene and action; and finally it is that—the author's relentless voice—which asserts itself and prevails, erasing all else. This is a pity, for in this book Kerouac writes of what might have been a deeply moving event in this ongoing attempt to make a legend of his life."

In an October 1963 letter to John Clellon Holmes in regard to the negative reviews for *Visions of Gerard*, Kerouac remarked, "Everybody's become so mean, so sinister, so hypocritical I can't believe it. So I turn to drink like a lost maniac . . . They make me feel like never writing another work again." The novel's title connects it to Kerouac's experimental work *Visions of Cody*, which serves as a celebration of Neal Cassady ("Cody Pomeray"). In addition, the novel reportedly inspired the title of Bob Dylan's song "Visions of Johanna" from his 1966 *Blonde on Blonde* album.

Desolation Angels (1965)

"And I will die, and you will die, and we all will die, and even the stars will fade out one after another in time." Author Nelson Algren commented, "Kerouac . . . defines the sensibilities of members of his own subgeneration: we knew them as wearing such guises as the Beat Generation, the Subterraneans, the Dharma Bums; now we see them as Desolation Angels, sadly pursuing their empty futilities." The book is divided into two main sections: "Desolation Angels," which covers Kerouac's stint as a fire lookout on Desolation Peak in the Pacific Northwest, and "Passing Through," which focuses on his life just before the 1957 publication of *On the Road*. The novel's main cast of characters include "Jack Duluoz" (Kerouac), "Bull Hubbard" (William S. Burroughs), "Cody Pomeray" (Neal Cassady), "Evelyn" (Carolyn Cassady), "Irwin Garden" (Allen Ginsberg), "Raphael Urso" (Gregory Corso), "Deni Bleu" (Henri Cru), "Geoffrey Donald" (Robert Duncan), "Old Bull Gaines" (Bill Garver), "Jarry Wagner" (Gary Snyder), "David D'Angeli (Philip Lamantia), "Simon Darlovsky" (Peter Orlovsky), and "Alyce Newman" (Joyce Glassman). In addition, Norman Mailer (as "Harvey Marker") and William Carlos Williams (as "Dr. Williams') make appearances.

In a scathing review of *Desolation Angels* for the *New York Times* (May 2, 1965), titled "A Line Must Be Drawn," Saul Maloff wrote, "With remorseless exuberance, Kerouac continues the vast, inconsequential epic of himself and his friends, no longer even attempting to disguise memoir with the trappings of fiction, and offering this as the sacred book of the Movement, the canonical work . . . Aging, Kerouac grows younger. The prose still leaps up and down, overjoyed to be itself; the boys and girls arrive and depart with inexhaustible energy; everything dissolves in the everlasting sea of confusion." Bruce Cook in *The Beat Generation* (1971) wrote that "while it contains some fine episodes," *Desolation Angels* "ranges far too wide—New York, Europe, Mexico City, and back to San Francisco—and attempts too much."

According to legend, Bob Dylan got the title for his song "Desolation Row" off the 1965 *Highway 61 Revisited* album from Kerouac's novel. In addition, Bad Company named their 1979 album *Desolation Angels* after the novel. In his review of the album for *Rolling Stone*, Ken Tucker wrote, "Fully half of the new album consists of medium-tempo ballads, songs as garrulously melancholy as the Jack Kerouac novel from which the LP's title is taken. Kerouac's book was an exhausted excoriation of the aging writer's themes of betrayed friendship and unbalanced love affairs, and that's also what Paul Rodgers is singing about in such numbers as 'Early in the Morning' and 'Lonely for Your Love.' Rodgers' vocals and Ralphs' guitar playing are every bit as ragged and repetitious as Kerouac's prose—song for song, there's a lot of sincere, mediocre work earnestly being committed to vinyl."

Vanity of Duluoz (1968)

"Did I come into this world through the womb of my mother the earth just so I could talk and write just like everybody else?" Jack Kerouac's last published novel while he was alive, *Vanity of Duluoz* (originally subtitled *An Adventurous Education, 1935–46*) focuses on the author's recollections of his life as a high school student in Lowell, Massachusetts, during the late 1930s, along with his experiences at Columbia University in the early 1940s, and the emerging Beat scene in New York City.

In addition to Kerouac's alter ego, "Jack Duluoz," the thinly disguised characters in *Vanity of Duluoz* include "Emil Duluoz" (Kerouac's father, Leo), "Ange Duluoz" (Kerouac's mother, Gabrielle), "G. J. Rigolopoulos" (George "G. J." Apostolos), "Maggie Cassidy" (Mary Carney), "Sabby Savakis" (Sebastian "Sammy" Sampas), "Stavroula Savakis" (Kerouac's third wife, Stella Sampas), "Will Hubbard" (William S. Burroughs), "June" (Joan Vollmer), "Irwin Garden" (Allen Ginsberg), "Claude de Maubris" (Lucien Carr), "Franz Mueller" (David Kammerer), "Deni Bleu" (Henri Cru), "Edna 'Johnnie' Palmer" (Edie Parker), and "Lu Libble" (Columbia University football coach Lou Little).

The wild gatherings of the early Beat scene at June and Johnnie's 119th Street apartment in New York City are vividly re-created by Kerouac, especially when June's husband, "Harry Evans," returns unexpectedly "from the German front, around September 1945" and is "appalled to see us, six fullgrown people, all high on Benny sprawled and sitting and cat-legged on that vast double-doublebed of 'skepticism' and 'decadence,' discussing the nothingness of values, pale-faced, weak bodies, Gad the poor guy said: 'This is what I fought for?'"

In a Summer 1968 *Paris Review* interview, Kerouac remarked, "And finally I decided in my tired middle age to slow down and did *Vanity of Duluoz* in a more moderate style so that, having been so esoteric all these years, some earlier readers would come back and see what ten years had done to my life and thinking . . . which is after all the only thing I've got to offer, the true story of what I saw and how I saw it."

12

Outside Any Social Contract

Naked Lunch and the Nightmare of Addiction

T he Planet drifts to random insect doom . . ." Saturated with a dark, paranoid vision, *Naked Lunch* by William S. Burroughs was originally published by Olympia Press in Paris in 1959 and later arrived in the United States via Grove Press in 1962. Full of surreal, nightmarish, frequently darkly comic, and existential imagery, *Naked Lunch* features fragmented text and random, often grotesque episodes that one critic labeled "a savage cry from hell," as well as a cast of bizarre characters, such as Clem Snide the Private Asshole, the Paregoric Kid, the Gimp, and, of course, the notorious Dr. Benway, "a manipulator and coordinator of symbol systems, an expert on all phases of interrogation, brainwashing and control."

Early Writing Attempts

Even though William S. Burroughs studied English literature at Harvard University during the 1930s, he never considered himself a writer or had inclinations toward a literary career (although he did write his first work of fiction, "The Autobiography of a Wolf," at the tender age of eight). Burroughs did collaborate on a short story, "Twilight's Last Gleamings," with his childhood friend Kells Elvins in 1938. According to Burroughs, he had a "special abhorrence" for writing, for putting his thoughts and feelings down on a piece of paper. Occasionally he would write a passage and then stop, "overwhelmed with disgust and a sort of horror." Featuring an early appearance by "Dr. Benway," "Twlight's Last Gleamings" was included in a 1989 collection of Burroughs's short stories called *Interzone*, which also contained such classic Burroughs tales as "The Junky's Christmas" and "Spare Ass Annie." Burroughs read from "Twilight's Last Gleamings" during a legendary appearance on

The cult-like nature of William S. Burroughs's classic 1959 novel, *Naked Lunch*, has taken many forms—including a popular sandwich shop of the same name located in North Beach, San Francisco.   *Author's collection*

Saturday Night Live in 1981 (he was introduced by actress Lauren Hutton as "the greatest living American writer").

According to Burroughs in *With William Burroughs* (1981), "In the 1940s, it was Kerouac who kept telling me I should write and call the book I would write *Naked Lunch* . . . Jack insisted quietly that I did have talent for writing and that I should write a book called *Naked Lunch*." In 1945, Burroughs and Kerouac collaborated on a novel called *And the Hippos Were Boiled in Their Tanks*, a highly fictionalized account of Lucien Carr's killing of David Kammerer that wasn't published until 2008. In the 1986 documentary *What Happened to Kerouac?* Burroughs describes *Hippos* as "not a very distinguished work."

Accidental Killing of Joan Vollmer Burroughs

William S. Burroughs accidentally shot and killed his common-law wife, Joan Vollmer, in a drunken William Tell act in Mexico City on September 6, 1951. Right before the tragedy, Vollmer allegedly remarked, "I can't watch this—you know I can't stand the sight of blood." According to Burroughs in *With William Burroughs* (1981), "I was very drunk. I suddenly said, 'It's about time for our William Tell act. Put the glass on your head.' I aimed at the top of the glass, and then there was a great sort of flash . . . I was aiming for the very tip of the glass. This gun was a very inaccurate gun, however." Burroughs told a different version of events during a 1965 *Paris Review* interview: "I had a revolver that I was planning to sell to a friend. I was checking it over and it went off—killing her. A rumor started that I was trying to shoot a glass of champagne from her head William Tell–style. Absurd and false."

A headline about the tragedy that appeared in the September 8, 1951, edition of the *New York Daily News* read, "Heir's Pistol Kills His Wife; He Denies Playing Wm. Tell." Burroughs spent thirteen days in jail before his older brother, Mortimer, arrived to bail him out. Burroughs was represented by a sleazy lawyer named Bernabe Jurado. Vollmer's daughter from a previous marriage, Julie Adams, was sent to live with her grandmother, while William S. Burroughs Jr. went to live with his paternal grandparents in St. Louis, Missouri, and then Palm Beach, Florida. In the preface to his novel *Queer*, which was not published until 1985, Burroughs wrote, "I am forced to the appalling conclusion that I would have never become a writer but for Joan's death . . . The death of Joan brought me in contact with the invader, the Ugly Spirit, and maneuvered me into a lifelong struggle, in which I have had no choice except to write my way out."

Writing Habits

After spending time in London, Burroughs returned to Tangier in 1957 where he took the apomorphine cure with Dr. Yerbury Dent. Various friends visited Burroughs that year and helped type and assemble the *Naked Lunch* manuscript, such as Jack Kerouac, Allen Ginsberg, and Allen Ansen. According to author Ted Morgan in *Literary Outlaw* (1988):

> Back in Tangier that September of 1957, Burroughs found that his own novel seemed to be taking a form of its own. All he had to do was transcribe. It came in great hunks, faster than he could get it down . . . It was developing into a saga of lost innocence, the fall, with some kind of redemption through knowledge of basic life processes. If anyone found the form confusing it was because they were accustomed to the conventional novel form, which was always a chronology of events that had already happened. Whereas this novel was concerned with events that were still happening at the writing, or had not yet happened.

In a 1965 *Paris Review* interview, Burroughs remarked, "I don't make myself work. It's just the thing I want to do. To be completely alone in a room, to know that there'll be no interruptions and I've got eight hours is just exactly what I want—yeah, just paradise."

Title Origin

According to William S. Burroughs, it was Jack Kerouac who suggested the title *Naked Lunch*: "a frozen moment when everyone sees what is on the end of every fork." Interestingly, in a June 1960 letter to Allen Ginsberg, Kerouac discussed the title's origin, writing, "Didn't hear from Burroughs but was pleased he mentioned I named *Naked Lunch* (remember, it was you, reading the manuscript, mis-read 'naked lust' and I only noticed it) (interesting little bit of litry history tho)." The novel was first published as *The Naked Lunch* in Paris in 1959 by Olympia Press but was changed to *Naked Lunch* when published in the United States by Grove Press in 1962.

In his 1965 novel, *Desolation Angels*, Kerouac refers to *Naked Lunch* as *Nude Supper*: "All about shirts turning blue at hangings, castration, and lime—Great horrific scenes with imaginary doctors of the future tending machine cataton- ics with negative drugs so they can wipe the world out of people but when that's accomplished the Mad Doctor is alone with a self operated self tape recordings he can change or edit at will . . . so horrible that when I undertook to start typing it neatly doublespace for his publishers the following week I had horrible nightmares in my roof room—like of pulling out endless bolo- gnas from my mouth, from my very entrails, feet of it, pulling and pulling out all the horror of what Bull saw, and wrote."

Themes and Structure

Naked Lunch was caught between the straightforward narrative style of Burroughs's early works like *Junkie* and the highly experimental cut-up style of his subsequent Nova Trilogy. In an August 18, 1954, letter to Jack Kerouac, Burroughs wrote, "I am having serious difficulties with my novel. I tell you the novel form is completely inadequate to express what I have to say. I don't know if I can find a form. I am very gloomy as to prospects of publication."

Naked Lunch is structured in a series of loosely connected routines that can be read in any order. In his "Atrophied Preface" to *Naked Lunch*, Burroughs noted, "You can cut into *The Naked Lunch* at any intersection point . . . I have written many prefaces." Open one page and you may discover Dr. Benway performing an appendectomy "with a rusty sardine can"; turn to another and you might read about "Rock and roll adolescent hoodlums" storming "the streets of all nations. They rush into the Louvre and throw acid in the Mona

Lisa's face . . . they shit on the floor of the United Nations and wipe their ass with treaties, pacts, alliances."

In "Recollections of Burroughs Letters" (*Deliberate Prose*), Allen Ginsberg recounts the nightmare of being faced with assembling the manuscript. When Ginsberg arrived in Tangier in 1957, Burroughs "had begun retyping the preliminary assemblage of texts and letters which compose Naked Lunch. I was to bring my entire manuscript—hundreds of pages, in chronological order of invention, to Tangier. There all of us were to sit together and assemble a final manuscript. The difficulty was that Dr. Benway and other characters introduced from 1953 on were refined and developed from letter to letter with new adventures and routines and additional skits and episodes. How to weave it all together?" The final editing arrangement of the novel "was a dramatic accident," according to Ginsberg: "[Olympia Press publisher Maurice] Girodias' message was that the manuscript had to be ready for printer in two weeks . . . The way it came off the typewriter was the way it worked."

According to Michael J. Dittman in *Masterpieces of Beat Literature* (2006), "Much of [*Naked Lunch*'s] structure was planned by Allen Ginsberg, who gathered the scraps of paper that he found scattered around in Burroughs's room. The book consists of 21 satirical pieces that purport to lay bare the horrors of reality; hence the title, a naked lunch allows the diners to 'see what they eat.' The book also tries to find from its use of drugs and homosexuality a philosophical statement—addiction as metaphor for the human condition."

Publishing History

According to Maurice Girodias, the founder of Olympia Press, "Allen Ginsberg brought me the first manuscript of *Naked Lunch* in 1957. He was acting as Burroughs' friendly agent. It was such a mess, that manuscript! You couldn't physically read the stuff, but whatever caught the eye was extraordinary and dazzling. So I returned it to Allen saying, 'Listen, the whole thing has to be reshaped.' The ends of the pages were all eaten away, by the rats or something."

On the recommendation of Ginsberg, Burroughs moved to Paris in 1958 and took up residence at no. 9, rue Git-le-Coeur (a.k.a. the "Beat Hotel"), bringing a suitcase full of manuscripts with him. In "The Name Is Burroughs" (*The Adding Machine*, 1986), Burroughs wrote, "Maurice Girodias of Olympia Press had rejected the first version of *Naked Lunch*. Other rejections from American publishers, including Lawrence Ferlinghetti [at City Lights Publishing], followed, and I was again losing interest in writing. It was Allen Ginsberg who insisted I send some short extracts to *The Chicago Review* which was edited by Irving Rosenthal. The *Big Table* issue followed."

Olympia Press finally published *Naked Lunch* in July 1959 (according the legend, the manuscript was sent to the publisher in pieces and was prepared that way in no particular order). However, the novel did not appear in the United States until Grove Press published it in 1962. Burroughs reportedly spent his entire $3,000 advance from Grove Press on heroin.

Reception

There was nothing lukewarm about the various responses to *Naked Lunch*. For instance, British poet and critic Dame Edith Sitwell denounced the novel as "psychopathological filth." However, author (and friend of Burroughs) Terry Southern called *Naked Lunch* "an absolutely devastating ridicule of all that is false, primitive, and vicious in current American life: the abuses of power, hero worship, aimless violence, materialistic obsession, intolerance, and every form of hypocrisy." John Wain of the *New Republic* (December 1, 1962) wryly remarked, "No lover of medical textbooks on deformity should miss it."

Newsweek called *Naked Lunch* "a masterpiece. A cry from hell, a brutal, terrifying, and savagely funny book," while journalist Dorothy Kilgallen, in court testimony defending Lenny Bruce in 1964, remarked, "There's another book called *The Naked Lunch* which I couldn't even finish reading, but it's published, and I think the author should be in jail." John Ciardi of the *Saturday Review* (June 27, 1959) called *Naked Lunch* "a monumentally moral descent into the hell of narcotic addiction" and referred to Burroughs as "a writer of great power and artistic integrity engaged in a profoundly meaningful search for true values." Author Norman Mailer referred to it as "a book of great beauty, great difficulty, and maniacally exquisite insight."

In the *Nation*, Marshall McLuhan remarked, "It is amusing to read reviews of Burroughs that try to classify his books as non-books or as failed science fiction. It is a little like trying to criticize the sartorial and verbal manifestations of a man who is knocking on the door to explain the flames are leaping from the roof of our home." Interestingly, Herbert Huncke in *Guilty of Everything* wrote that he found Burroughs's satire "a little too biting, a little too cold. I think he has an incredible style . . . But there is that coldness—he's forgotten the human element somehow it seems to me." Allen Ginsberg stated, "This novel will drive everyone mad," while author J. G. Ballard called *Naked Lunch* "a rollercoaster ride through hell."

Naked Lunch on Trial

After finally getting published in the United States by Grove Press in 1962, *Naked Lunch* was banned for obscenity by the Superior Court of Boston the

Carl Solomon, Patti Smith, Allen Ginsberg, and William S. Burroughs appeared together at the Gotham Book Mart in New York City in 1977 for a reissue of Burroughs's first published novel, *Junky*.   *Photo by Marcelo Noah/Wikimedia Commons*

following year (one of the judges declaring the novel to be "trash" written by a "mentally sick" individual). The attorney appearing on behalf of the book and its publisher was Edward de Grazia, assisted by Daniel Klubock. Noted authors such as Allen Ginsberg, Norman Mailer, and John Ciardi testified in favor of the work. Mailer testified that Burroughs "has extraordinary talent. Possibly he is the most talented writer in America . . . The man has extraordinary style . . . he also has an exquisite poetic sense. His poetic images are intense. They are often disgusting; but at the same time there is a sense of collision in them, of montage that is quite unusual . . . This man might have been one of the greatest geniuses of the English language if he had never been an addict. Through this there is a feeling of great torture in the composition of the book." In addition, literary critic and then-professor at MIT Norman Holland testified, "If Saint Augustine were writing today he might well write something like *Naked Lunch*."

Regardless of the testimony, the Superior Court of Boston ultimately found that *Naked Lunch* was obscene, stating, "'Naked Lunch' may appeal to the prurient interest of deviants and those curious about deviants. To us, it is grossly offensive and is what the author himself says, 'brutal, obscene and disgusting.'" Ironically, on a positive note for Grove Press and Burroughs, the widely publicized trial served to spur sales of *Naked Lunch* in other parts of the country. However, on July 7, 1966, the Supreme Court of Massachusetts ended up reversing the earlier decision of the Superior Court of Boston by declaring *Naked Lunch* not obscene, thereby closing a chapter on the last significant obscenity trial in American literature.

In the only other censorship action taken against *Naked Lunch* outside of Massachusetts since its publication in the United States in 1962, a Los Angeles judge remarked in a ruling declaring the novel not obscene, "It appears to me too abundantly clear that [the] book, in almost every page goes substantially beyond the customary limits of candor in its description and representation of nudity, sex and excretion . . . I cannot say that its predominant appeal is such or that it is matter which is utterly without redeeming social importance . . . as a whole."

References in Popular Culture

As much as any work of cult fiction in the latter half of the twentieth century, *Naked Lunch* has weaved itself into the fabric of popular culture over the years. Perhaps most notoriously, the band Steely Dan took its name from a steam-powered dildo that appears in the novel. In addition, there was a short-lived 1960s rock band named the Mugwumps composed of Cass Elliot and Dennis Doherty (later of the Mamas and the Papas), as well as John Sebastian and Zal Yanovsky (later of the Lovin' Spoonful), and Jim Hendricks. Another 1960s rock band, the Insect Trust, took its name from *Naked Lunch* (via the poetry journal *Insect Trust Gazette*). The 1980s rock band Thin White Rope also took its name from the novel.

Last but not least, in the 1984 cult film *Repo Man*, both a "Dr. Benway" and a "Mr. Lee" are paged in a hospital scene (an indirect tribute that was emulated in the 1998 science fiction film *Dark City*). An outrageous endeavor that combines the seedy world of automobile repossession with science fiction (there's an anti–nuclear war subtext thrown in there as well!), *Repo Man* stars Harry Dean Stanton as "Bud," a seasoned repo veteran, and Emilio Estevez as the young upstart, a punk rocker and former stock clerk at a supermarket. The duo has run-ins with ruthless government agents, UFO cultists, hired killers, a lobotomized nuclear scientist, and the infamous Rodriguez Brothers—all in search of a mysterious '64 Chevy Malibu. Everyone drinks generic beer. Directed by Alex Cox (*Sid and Nancy*), *Repo Man* perfectly captures the nihilism of the 1980s. Iggy Pop supplies the title tune. The stellar soundtrack also includes Black Flag's "TV Party" and the Circle Jerks' "When the Shit Hits the Fan."

Legacy

Even though *Naked Lunch* was first published in 1959, the novel has lost none of its power to shock, offend, disgust, and/or amuse. Love it or loathe it, *Naked Lunch* leaves an indelible impression on first-time readers and remains among the landmark works of American literature. In 2005, *Time* magazine included *Naked Lunch* among its "100 Best English-language Novels from 1923 to 2005." According to director John Waters, "Sure, [Burroughs] romanticized drug use as joyous, and terrible, and wonderful. Did anybody read *Naked Lunch* and try heroin? Probably. So what? That doesn't mean that that book shouldn't be read. I'm for anybody that writes about their obsession."

Naked Lunch @50: Anniversary Essays was published in 2009 and features contributions from the likes of Anne Waldman, John Giorno, Barry Miles, Harold Chapman, James Grauerholz, Peter Weller, Penny Lane, Michael McClure, Genesis P-ORRIDGE, Barney Rosset, Hal Willner, DJ Spooky, Jennie Skerl, and others. Burroughs himself summed it up nicely: "'Disgusting,' they said . . . 'Pornographic' . . . 'Un-American trash' . . . 'Unpublishable' . . . Well, it came out in 1959, and it found an audience . . . Town meetings . . . Book burnings . . . And an Inquiry by the State Supreme Court . . . That book made quite a little impression."

13

Unlock My Word Horde

Language as a Virus in the Works of William Burroughs

Fellow author Norman Mailer once declared William S. Burroughs "the only American writer who may be conceivably possessed by genius." After *Naked Lunch*, Burroughs continued to experiment with forms, most notably the "cut-up technique" (inspired by Brion Gysin with a tradition leading back to Dadaism) evident in his Nova Trilogy of *The Soft Machine* (1961), *The Ticket That Exploded* (1962), and *Nova Express* (1964). Burroughs's diverse body of work extends from straightforward narratives such as *Junkie* (1953) to film scripts like *The Last Words of Dutch Schultz* (1969), and collected short stories and essays, including *Exterminator!* (1973) and *The Adding Machine* (1986). Burroughs's later work did have its critics, such as Andy Warhol, who claimed in his March 1, 1980, diary entry, "I don't think he's a good writer. I mean, he wrote that one good book, *Naked Lunch*, but now it's like he lives in the past."

Junkie (1953)

"I have learned the junk equation. Junk is not, like alcohol or weed, a means to increased enjoyment of life. Junk is not a kick. It is a way of life." Subtitled *Confessions of an Unredeemed Drug Addict*, William S. Burroughs's first published novel follows the protagonist, "William Lee," as he dabbles in petty crime, wanders aimlessly, and makes a gradual descent into the hell of drug addiction. In *Junkie* (a.k.a. *Junky*, although Burroughs's preferred title was simply *Junk*), which was originally published under the pen name of William Lee (his mother's maiden name), Burroughs sticks to a classic, straightforward narrative that details his early life. However, the deadpan style does reveal flashes of the genius to come in his later writing, such as *Naked Lunch*, in such

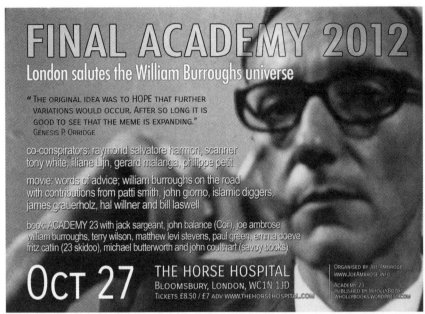

FINAL ACADEMY 2012

London salutes the William Burroughs universe

" THE ORIGINAL IDEA WAS TO HOPE THAT FURTHER
VARIATIONS WOULD OCCUR. AFTER SO LONG IT IS
GOOD TO SEE THAT THE MEME IS EXPANDING."
GENESIS P. ORRIDGE

co-conspirators: raymond salvatore harmon, scanner
tony white, liliane Lijn, gerard malanga, phillipe petit

movie: words of advice; william burroughs on the road
with contributions from patti smith, john giorno, islamic diggers,
james grauerholz, hal willner and bill laswell

book: ACADEMY 23 with jack sargeant, john balance (Coil), joe ambrose
william burroughs, terry wilson, matthew levi stevens, paul green, emma doeve
fritz catlin (23 skidoo), michael butterworth and john coulthart (savoy books)

OCT 27   THE HORSE HOSPITAL
BLOOMSBURY, LONDON, WC1N 1JD
TICKETS £8.50 / £7 ADV WWW.THEHORSEHOSPITAL.COM

ORGANISED BY JOE AMBROSE
WWW.JOEAMBROSE.INFO
ACADEMY 23
PUBLISHED BY WHOLLYBOOKS
WHOLLYBOOKS.WORDPRESS.COM

Billed as an "unofficial" celebration of William S. Burroughs, Final Academy / 2012 served as a tribute to the original event, which took place thirty years earlier in 1982 and featured Burroughs, Brion Gysin, 23 Skidoo, and Psychic TV.   *Author's collection*

passages as "There was something boneless about her, like a deep-sea creature . . . I could see those eyes in a shapeless, protoplasmic mass undulating over the dark sea floor."

One of the most memorable characters Lee befriends is "Herman" (Herbert Huncke), hustler, thief, and strong early influence on the Beat Generation. Huncke would later depict the same period in his 1990 autobiography, *Guilty of Everything*. In addition, Bill Garver, Burroughs's drug addict buddy in Mexico City, appears as "Bill Gains" in *Junkie*. Interestingly, Burroughs, who would later be dubbed the "Godfather of Punk," actually used the word "punk" in his description of two young thugs in the subway in *Junkie*.

Burroughs started writing *Junkie* around 1950 when he was thirty-five years old. In a 1965 *Paris Review* interview, he admitted that "there didn't seem to be any strong motivation. I simply was endeavoring to put down in more or less straightforward journalistic style about my experiences with addiction and addicts . . . I had nothing else to do. Writing gave me something to do every day. I don't feel the results were at all spectacular . . . I knew very little about writing at that time." *Junkie* was published by Ace Books as a "Double Book" bound back-to-back with Maurice Helbrant's *Narcotic Agent*, the "Gripping

True Adventures of a T-Man's War Against the Dope Menace." Billed as "Two Books in One," it sold for thirty-five cents. Ace Books was founded in 1952 by A. A. Wyn, the uncle of Carl Solomon, who had befriended Allen Ginsberg in a New Jersey psychiatric hospital. Solomon worked for Ace and wrote the publisher's note for the first printing of *Junkie*, as well as the introduction to the 1964 edition. The fiftieth anniversary definitive edition of *Junky* was published by Penguin Books in 2003 and features a re-creation of the author's original text from archival typescripts, Burroughs's original unpublished introduction, an entire omitted chapter, several "lost passages," and auxiliary texts by Ginsberg and others.

The Nova Trilogy (1963–67)

After *Naked Lunch*, William S. Burroughs continued to experiment with forms, most notably the "cut-up technique" evident in his Nova Trilogy (a.k.a. Cut-Up Trilogy), which consisted of *The Soft Machine* (1961), *The Ticket That Exploded* (1962), and *Nova Express* (1964). *The Soft Machine* includes an expansion of Burroughs's South American experiences in 1953 with "surreal extensions" that feature routines involving "Dr. Benway" and "The Sailor." Burroughs claimed a lot of the content featured in *The Ticket That Exploded* also came from his travels throughout Columbia, Peru, and Ecuador as he searched for the hallucinogen yage (*Bannisteria caapi*).

Burroughs learned the cut-up technique from his good friend, the artist Brion Gysin, while both were residing at the "Beat Hotel" at 9 rue Git-le-Coeur in Paris in the late 1950s and early 1960s. According to Burroughs, in a 1965 *Paris Review* interview, "Brion Gysin . . . was, as far as I know, the first to create cut-ups . . . Of course, when you think of it, 'The Waste Land' was the first great cut-up collage, and [Dadaist] Tristan Tzara had done a bit along the same lines. Dos Passos used the same idea in 'The Camera Eye' sequence in *U.S.A.*" In fact, Tzara (1896–1963) had gone so far as to pull words out of a hat to create poems during a Dadaist rally in the 1920s. The whole point of Dadaism, according to fellow artist George Grosz, was the "organized use of insanity to express contempt for a bankrupt world."

Burroughs shared his enthusiasm for the cut-up technique with whomever would listen—including other "Beat Hotel" residents such as Allen Ginsberg and Gregory Corso. According to Corso, in a September 18, 1997, *Rolling Stone* interview, "We would cut up these speeches by Eisenhower and works by Rimbaud and Shakespeare, and we'd combine them. [Burroughs] taught me it would work if the eye catches something. It was pure magic." Not every writer Burroughs encountered was enamored with the cut-up technique. For instance, when Burroughs described the method to Samuel Beckett, the

Irish writer of *Waiting for Godot* reportedly responded, "That's not writing, that's plumbing."

According to Paul Bowles in his 1972 autobiography *Without Stopping*, "Once when I expressed doubts about the advisability of using the cut-up method in fiction, [Burroughs] replied that 'in the hands of a master' it became a viable technique." The cut-up technique received cinematic treatment in 1963 when Burroughs collaborated with director Anthony Balch on the short experimental film *Towers Open Fire*. Balch had bought the British rights to Tod Browning's 1932 horror classic, *Freaks*, which had been banned in England since 1932. Balch eventually released *Freaks* and *Towers Open Fire* as part of a double-bill.

Freaks delves into the world of the sideshow and features an eclectic cast that includes Prince Randian ("The Living Torso"), Daisy and Violet Hilton ("Siamese Twins"), Josephine Joseph ("Half Woman–Half Man"), Frances O'Connor ("Armless Girl"), Peter Robinson ("Human Skeleton"), Olga Roderick ("Bearded Lady"), Schlitzie ("Pinhead"), and Johnny Eck ("The Half Boy"). Eck (real name: Johnny Eckhardt) was born without a body below the waist and had a normal twin named Robert. He joined the freak show circuit at the tender age of twelve and soon earned the title "King of the Freaks." Eck and his brother toured the country as part of a famous magic show, performing a routine where Eck was "sawed in half," much to the horror of many theatergoers. Eck once famously remarked, "If I want to see freaks, I can just look out the window."

The Yage Letters (1963)

William S. Burroughs's first published novel, *Junkie* (1953), ended with the lines "Maybe I will find in yage what I was looking for in junk and weed and coke. Yage may be the final fix." Published by City Lights in 1963, *The Yage Letters* features the correspondence between Allen Ginsberg and Burroughs as the latter journeyed to the Amazon rainforest in 1953 in a seven-month search for the hallucinogenic yage (ayahuasca). Burroughs's travels took him through the remote village and jungles of Columbia, Ecuador, and Peru. The correspondence included in the epistolary narrative runs up to 1960 and concludes with Ginsberg detailing his own experiences with yage. The book's epilogue contains a poetic cut-up by Burroughs called "I Am Dying Meester?"

In addition, various "routines" interspersed throughout the narrative foreshadow Burroughs's masterwork, *Naked Lunch*. For instance, in a letter to Ginsberg dated February 28, 1953, Burroughs wrote, "On my way back to Bogota with nothing accomplished. I have been conned by medicine men (the most inveterate drunk, liar and loafer in the village is invariably the medicine man), incarcerated by the law, rolled by a local hustler." Burroughs and Ginsberg began putting the work into shape as early as 1953, and portions appeared in literary journals such as *Black Mountain Review*, *Big Table*, and *The Floating Bear* over the next ten years. Burroughs's bitter satire, "Roosevelt After Inauguration," was omitted from the first edition of *The Yage Letters* but was later restored in a subsequent reprinting of the book. The anarchic story involves a "purple-assed baboon" appointed to the Supreme Court.

In 2006, City Lights Books published a new edition of the *The Yage Letters* called *Yage Letters Redux*, which was edited by Oliver Harris and contains previously unpublished material by Ginsberg and Burroughs, along with an extensive introduction by Harris that details the fascinating history of the book. According to *The Independent UK* (May 24, 2006), "*The Yage Letters* marks the point when Burroughs moved full-time into his own fully realized universe."

The Last Words of Dutch Schultz (1969)

"A boy has never wept . . . or dashed a thousand Kim." Subtitled *A Fiction in the Form of a Film Script*, *The Last Words of Dutch Schultz* was based on the surreal final hours of the legendary mobster (born Arthur Flegenheimer, 1901–35) who was famously gunned down in the men's room at the Palace Chop House in Newark, New Jersey, on October 23, 1935. Two of Schultz's bodyguards, Abe "Misfit" Landau and Bernard "Lulu" Rosencranz, and his accountant, Otto "Abbadabba" Berman, were also shot and eventually died in the hospital.

Schultz survived for the next two days and was placed under guard around the clock at Newark City Hospital, where he proceeded to spout a nonstop

After residing abroad for more than twenty-six years, the "Godfather of Punk" himself, William S. Burroughs, returned to New York City and resided in "The Bunker" at 222 Bowery in the heart of the Lower East Side and just around the block from the legendary CBGB music club. *Author's collection*

People often ask me if I have any

WORDS OF ADVICE FOR YOUNG PEOPLE

Well, here are a few simple admonitions for young and old.

Never interfere in a boy-and-girl fight.
Beware of whores who say they don't want money. The hell they don't. What they mean is they want more money. *Much* more.

If you're doing business with a religious son-of-a-bitch, get it in writing. His word isn't worth shit. Not with the good lord telling him how to fuck you on the deal.

If, after having been exposed to someone's presence, you feel as though you've lost a quart of plasma, *avoid* **that presence.** You need it like you need pernicious anemia. By the inexorable logistics of the vampiric process, they always take more than they need.

Avoid fuck-ups. We all know the type. Anything they have anything to do with, no matter how good it sounds, turns into a disaster.

Do not offer sympathy to the mentally ill. Tell them firmly: "*I am not paid to listen to this drivel. You are a terminal boob!*". Now some of you may encounter **the Devil's Bargain,** if you get that far.

Any old soul is worth saving, at least to a priest, but **not every soul is worth buying.** So you can take the offer as a compliment.
He tries the easy ones first. You know like money, all the money there is. *But who wants to be the richest guy in some cemetery?* Money won't buy. *Not much left to spend it on, eh gramps?* Getting too old to cut the mustard. Well, **time hits the hardest blows, especially below the belt.** How's a young body grab you? Like three card monte, like pea under the shell, now you see it, now you don't. *Haven't you forgotten something, gramps? In order to FEEL something, You've got to BE there. You have to BE eighteen. You're not eighteen. You are seventy-eight. Old fool sold his soul for a strap-on.*

There are no honorable bargains involving exchange Of qualitative merchandise like souls for quantitative merchandise like time and money.
So piss off Satan and don't take me for dumber than I look.
An old junk pusher told me: **Watch whose money you pick up.**

WILLIAM S. BURROUGHS
Writer • Theoretician • Exterminator

@ɐⱦWꬰɐ$ 2011 • artworks66@gmail.com

The classic "Words of Advice" bit from William S. Burroughs can be found on the cult author's 1993 spoken word collaboration album, *Spare Ass Annie and Other Tales.*

Author's collection

barrage of surreal, nonsensical, stream-of-consciousness rants, all of which were recorded by a police stenographer. In *With William Burroughs: A Report from the Bunker* (1996) by Victor Bockris, Burroughs commented, "[It] went on for 24 hours . . . Gertrude Stein said that [Schultz] outdid her. Gertrude really liked Dutch Schultz." Schultz's actual last words were "Shut up, you got a big mouth! Please help me up, Henry. Max, come over here. French-Canadian bean soup. I want to pay. Let them leave me alone." Burroughs's screenplay itself consists of a series of flashbacks from the dying Schultz as he looks back on his childhood and rise to power (Burroughs plays very loosely with the actual facts of the mobster's life). Intermixed with the script are an eclectic collage of images, including the crowd milling outside the Palace Chop House after the shooting, mugshots, and the deathbed scene, among others.

In the *New York Times* review of *The Last Words of Dutch Schultz* (June 22, 1975), Alan Friedman wrote, "The genuinely amazing fact is not that the script is a fiction, but that Burroughs has composed a work in the Hollywood vein—relentlessly stereotyped, virtually a parody—that is at the same time congruent with the rest of his unique work."

The two hitmen who killed Schultz were later identified as Charles "The Bug" Workman and Emanuel "Mendy" Weiss, associates of notorious gangster and racketeer Louis "Lepke" Buchalter, head of Murder, Inc. Workman was eventually arrested and convicted for the crime. He served twenty-three years in Trenton State Prison before being paroled in 1964. Weiss, who was convicted of another murder, died in the electric chair at Sing Sing Prison in 1944. The building that housed the Palace Chop House at 12 East Park Street was demolished in 2008 to make room for a parking lot. Despite several attempts, *The Last Words of Dutch Schultz* has yet to be made into a feature-length film (Dennis Hopper actually owned the rights to the film at one point). Burroughs's 1993 spoken-word album, *Spare Ass Annie and Other Tales*, a collaboration with hip-hop band the Disposable Heroes of Hiphoprisy, includes the track "The Last Words of Dutch Schultz (This Is Insane)."

The Wild Boys (1971)

"I am not a person and I am not an animal. There is something I am here for something I must do before I can go." Subtitled *A Book of the Dead*, *The Wild Boys* was billed as "a futuristic tale of global warfare" that depicts "a guerrilla gang of boys dedicated to freedom" battling "the organized armies of repressive police states." *The Wild Boys* features one of Burroughs's recurring characters, "Audrey Carsons," and refers to his hometown of St. Louis, Missouri, as "the old broken point of origin."

According to author Ted Morgan in *Literary Outlaw: The Life and Times of William S. Burroughs* (1988), *The Wild Boys* "was Burroughs' Utopian vision of an alternative society, and, like all his writing, a search for a way to escape social conditioning, time, and his own body." David Bowie reportedly based the look of his "Ziggy Stardust" on a character from *The Wild Boys*, and Malcolm McDowell's "Alex" character in Stanley Kubrick's 1971 film *A Clockwork Orange* reveals the novel's influence as well. Bowie's landmark album *The Rise and Fall of Ziggy Stardust and the Spiders from Mars* was released in 1972.

In addition, Ian Curtis, the lead singer of Joy Division who committed suicide in 1980, often cited *The Wild Boys* and *Naked Lunch* as two of his favorite books ("Controlled Chaos," *The Guardian*, May 9, 2008).

Burroughs wrote a screenplay based on *The Wild Boys* in 1972, but the film project never got off the ground. English post-punk/neo-psychedelic band the Soft Boys (originally known as Dennis and the Experts), which formed in 1976, took their name from a hybrid of *The Wild Boys* and *The Soft Machine.* A sample of the band's songs include "The Pig Worker," "The Return of the Sacred Crab," "Sandra's Having Her Brain Out," "Old Pervert," "Fatman's Son," and "I Wanna Destroy You." *The Wild Boys* also inspired English rock band Duran Duran's hit song "The Wild Boys," which reached No. 2 on the Billboard charts in 1984.

Exterminator! (1973)

During World War II, William S. Burroughs briefly resided in Chicago and got a job working for "A. J. Cohen Exterminators ground floor office dead-end street by the river," as detailed in his short story "Exterminator!" Burroughs lasted just eight months at the profession, going door to door and announcing, "Exterminator! You got any bugs, lady?" Several aspects of the story were used in David Cronenberg's 1991 film adaptation of *Naked Lunch.*

"Exterminator!" is one of thirty fascinating short stories included in the collection of the same name published by Viking Press in 1973. Highlights of *Exterminator!* include "The Lemon Kid," "Short Trip Home," "Wind Die. You Die. We Die.," "The Discipline of DE," "Ali's Smile," "Twilight's Last Gleaming," "The Coming of the Purple Better One," and "The 'Priest' They Called Him." Some of the pieces had been previously published in *Evergreen Review, Esquire, Village Voice, Rolling Stone,* and other publications. In "The Lemon Kid," Burroughs utilizes one of his recurring characters, Audrey Carsons, who wanted to be a writer "because writers were rich and famous. They lounged around Singapore and Rangoon smoking opium in a yellow pongee silk suit. They sniffed cocaine in Mayfair and they penetrated forbidden swamps with a faithful native boy and lived in the native quarter of Tangier smoking hashish and languidly caressing a pet gazelle."

Actor Ed Asner reportedly recorded a spoken-word adaptation of "Wind Die. You Die. We Die." in the 1980s. "The 'Priest' They Called Him" was later recorded by Burroughs accompanied by Kurt Cobain from Nirvana on guitar for a 1993 album. "Ali's Smile" was also featured in Burroughs's 1971 work *Ali's Smile/ Naked Scientology.* In one of the strangest pieces included in the collection, "The Discipline of DE," the DE standing for "Do Easy," Burroughs outlined the correct techniques for daily activities, such as "Guide a dustpan lightly to the floor as if you were landing a plane."

The Red Night Trilogy (1981–87)

By the time the novels that make up William S. Burroughs's Red Night Trilogy were published in the 1980s, the author had moved from bustling New York City to the sedate climes of Lawrence, Kansas, where he would reside for the rest of his life. Burroughs's final trilogy of novels consists of *Cities of the Red Night* (1981), *The Place of Dead Roads* (1983), and *The Western Lands* (1987).

Cities of the Red Night features two parallel plots: one involving a group of freedom-loving pirates in the eighteenth century under the leadership of a Captain James Mission who set out to establish a utopia, and the other featuring detective Clem Snide (the "Private Asshole" from *Naked Lunch*) seeking an abducted child. The novel concludes with the haunting last lines "I remember a dream of my childhood. I am in a beautiful garden. As I reach out to touch the flowers they wither under my hands. A nightmare feeling of foreboding and desolation comes over me as a great mushroom-shaped cloud darkens the earth. A few may get through the gate of time. Like Spain, I am bound to the past."

According to Allen Ginsberg in a *Paris Review* interview, *Cities of the Red Night* is Burroughs's "magnum opus—big work . . . maybe his greatest work . . . about a world plague . . . And the only people exempt from the plague are the ex-junkies, the junkies, and heroin addicts—because perhaps the heroin has subdued their sexual appetite and made them disillusioned." The *Los Angeles Times Book Review* called *Cities of the Red Night* "Burroughs's masterpiece," while author Ken Kesey remarked that the novel was "not only Burroughs's best work, but a logical and ripening extension of all of Burroughs's great work." The second novel in the Red Night Trilogy, *The Place of Dead Roads*, takes place in the American West and tells the story of gunfighter "Kim Carsons." Burroughs writes, "There is nothing more provocative than minding your own business."

The final novel in the Red Night Trilogy, *The Western Lands*, was inspired by the Egyptian Book of the Dead, and explores the afterlife. Dedicated to Brion Gysin and billed as "a Book of the Dead for the nuclear age," the novel contains an acknowledgment by Burroughs to "Norman Mailer and his *Ancient Evenings*, for inspiration." The last lines of the novel are truly unforgettable, foreshadowing death and featuring a line from "The Waste Land" by T. S. Eliot: "The old writer couldn't write anymore because he had reached the end of words, the end of what can be done with words . . . In

Tangier the Parade Bar is closed. Shadows are falling on the Mountain. 'Hurry up, please. It's time.'"

In a review of *The Western Lands* for the *Los Angeles Times*, John Rechy wrote, "*The Western Lands* illuminates and puts into perspective the whole body of work of the Grand Iconoclast, who has altered the concept of the novel more powerfully—some would say 'violently'—than any other writer of his time."

Queer (1985)

"Like many people who have nothing to do, he was very resentful of any claims on his time." William S. Burroughs once remarked, "I consider [*Queer*] a rather amateurish book and I did not want to republish it." Although Burroughs wrote *Queer* in the early 1950s, the book was not published until 1985. *Queer* was written as a straightforward narrative (although in the third person) like his first published novel, *Junkie* (1953), in contrast to the collage-style episodes of *Naked Lunch*. Partially a sequel to *Junkie*, *Queer* continues the story of protagonist "William Lee," during his "hallucinated month of acute withdrawal," as he roams from bar to bar as an expatriate in Mexico City and South America in a rather pathetic search of sexual fulfillment. The insecure Lee soon sets his sights on an indifferent American drifter, "Eugene Allerton" (based on Adelbert Lewis Marker). Lee eventually embarks on an excursion to South America in a futile search for the hallucinogen yage.

Jack Kerouac admired the manuscript and believed that it would appeal to "east coast homosexual literary critics." In the introduction to *Queer*, Burroughs remarked, "While it was I who wrote *Junky*, I feel that I was being written in *Queer*." According to Allen Ginsberg, "*Queer* is a major work, Burroughs' heart laid bare, the origin of his writing genius, honest, embarrassing, humorously brilliant, naked—the secret of the invisible man."

An Erling World opera version of *Queer* premiered in 2001. Several years ago, it was reported widely that Steve Buscemi was set to direct a film version of *Queer* from a script by Oren Moverman (*Jesus' Son*), but nothing has yet come of it. According to Moverman, "*Queer* was written with *Junkie*, which was the first Burroughs book, but it was never published because the publisher said, you know, 'I've got *Junkie*, you want to put *Queer* in there? How far can I push this thing? . . . And once it was published, it was really the story of William S. Burroughs kind of discovering himself as a writer by being obsessed with this boy. And there's very little in it about the wife, but what's happening at the same time is it's the time where [Burroughs] killed his wife, you know, during the whole famous William Tell routine. So that's sort of the incident that we started working with and built this whole movie around."

The Adding Machine (1986)

In *The Adding Machine*, William S. Burroughs presents a scintillating array of forty-three essays (covering thirty years of writing) on an eclectic range of topics ranging from Jack Kerouac and Samuel Beckett to the "Johnson family" depicted in Jack Black's 1926 classic of hobo literature, *You Can't Win*, and even Austrian psychoanalyst Wilhelm Reich's orgone box. The book's title refers to the adding machine, which was perfected by Burroughs's grandfather, William Seward Burroughs I (1857–1898), the founder of the American Arithmometer Company, which morphed into the Burroughs Adding Machine Company and later the Burroughs Corporation.

In Burroughs's superb essay "Remembering Jack Kerouac," he comments that "a whole migrant generation rose from Kerouac's *On the Road* to Mexico, Tangier, Afghanistan, India . . . Writers are, in a way, very powerful indeed. They write the script for the reality film. Kerouac opened a million coffee bars and sold a million pairs of Levis to both sexes . . . Kerouac may have felt that I did not include him in my cast of characters but he is of course the anonymous William Lee as defined in our collaboration—a spy in someone else's body where nobody knows who is spying on whom." In his "Hemingway" essay, Burroughs discusses how "Hemingway had such a distinctive style that he was trapped in it forever." Burroughs singles out Hemingway's short story "The Snows of Kilimanjaro" as "one of the greatest stories about death ever written."

In "Beckett and Proust," Burroughs recalls a meeting with playwright Samuel Beckett in Berlin along with Allen Ginsberg and Susan Sontag: "Beckett was polite and articulate. It was, however, apparent to me at least that he had not the slightest interest in any of us, nor the slightest desire ever to see any of us again." In one of his most political essays, "Bugger the Queen," Burroughs sides with the Sex Pistols over the controversial song "God Save the Queen (It's a Fascist Regime)" and later remarks, "I don't think of Reagan as OUR President, do you? He's just the one we happen to be stuck with at the moment." In "It Is Necessary to Travel . . .," Burroughs discusses space as the "new frontier" where it will be necessary to "leave the old verbal garbage behind: God talk, country talk, mother talk, love talk, party talk. You must learn to exist with no religion, no country, no allies. You must learn to live alone in silence. Anyone who prays in space is not *there*." Last and certainly least, Burroughs's notorious misogyny rears its ugly head in his essay "Women: A Biological Mistake?"

Other standout essays in *The Adding Machine* include "The Great Gatsby," "On Coincidence," "In the Interest of National Security," "Immortality," "Who Did What Where and When?," "Notes from Class Transcript," "My

Own Business," and "My Experiences with Wilhelm Reich's Orgone Box," among others.

My Education: A Book of Dreams (1995)

"Freud says that the only happy men are those whose boyhood dreams are realized. The danger is to walk through life without seeing anything." An eclectic collection of William S. Burroughs's dreams dating back to 1959, *My Education: A Book of Dreams* is notable as the last work published before the author's death in 1997. The dreams recounted are a mixed bag ranging from the mundane to the truly bizarre, with Burroughs pushing "into new territory" and "once again committing the unspeakable crime of questioning the reality structure," according to promotional material for the book.

During an interview with *The Independent* (September 23, 1995), Burroughs was asked what he thought of a reviewer of *Book of Dreams* calling him a "dirty old man." Burrroughs responded, "I wish I was a dirtier old man . . . I'm ashamed to go 24 hours without thinking about sex. It's alarming. It really is." The book's title comes from the very first dream dating from 1959 where Burroughs attempts to board a plane but the employee at the ticket counter who has "the cold waxen face of an intergalactic bureaucrat" refuses to let him past, remarking, "You haven't had your education yet." *Book of Dreams* was dedicated to one of Burroughs's assistants, Michael Emerton, who committed suicide in 1994, a tragedy that reportedly devastated the writer.

Regarding *Book of Dreams*, the *New York Times* (January 15, 1995) commented, "Dreams, guns, sea disasters, fringe science, conspiratorial struggles for control—the familiar obsessions are still around. One of this book's more touching suggestions is that everything is still around: the things we've seen, the places we've lived, the lovers we've had, the friends we've lost, the books we've written. All exist in a kind of eternal Interzone, in which the line between the dead and the living is as indistinguishable as that between dream and waking, autobiography and fiction, past and present." *Library Journal* called *Book of Dreams* "a simple dream diary, interspersed with brief interpretive comments and presented in clear, accessible prose. Most of the dreams involve visits to the Land of the Dead, where nearly all of Burroughs's friends and enemies have long since vanished."

14

Swimming the River of Hardship

Women of the Beat Generation

asual readers of the Beat Generation may not realize the extent that women writers such as Diane di Prima, Joyce Johnson, Hettie Jones, Joanne Kyger, Elise Cowen, and others have helped shape the literary movement. In addition, several fascinating Beat memoirs have been published over the years by the likes of Carolyn Cassady (*Off the Road: My Years with Cassady, Kerouac and Ginsberg*, 1996), Joan Haverty (*Nobody's Wife*, 2000), and Edie Parker (*You'll Be Okay: My Life with Jack Kerouac*, 2007). Last but not least, the tragic life and death of Joan Vollmer should never obscure her role as an invigorating and inquisitive force among the early Beat scene in the 1940s.

Edie Parker (1922–93)

A young socialite from Grosse Pointe, Michigan, with a relatively sheltered upbringing, Edie Parker headed to New York City in 1940 to study art. Parker shared an apartment with Joan Vollmer (who later became William S. Burroughs's common-law wife). Folk singer Burl Ives lived next door and "dropped in with his banjo and we sang his 'Shoo Fly' number," according to Parker (*You'll Be Okay*, 2007). Parker became Kerouac's first wife briefly in 1944. Kerouac was being held in jail as an accessory after the fact in his friend Lucien Carr's killing of David Kammerer, and he desperately needed bail money (which Parker allegedly provided on the condition that Kerouac agree to marry her). Kerouac moved to Grosse Pointe to live with Parker's family, but he quickly grew tired of the lifestyle there and headed back to New York City without her. The marriage was annulled in 1948. Interestingly, not one photo exists of Parker and Kerouac together.

Parker was fictionalized as "Judie Smith" in Kerouac's first published novel, *The Town and the City* (1950), as well as "Elly" in *Visions of Cody* and

"Edna 'Johnnie' Palmer" in *Vanity of Duluoz*. Allen Ginsberg referred to Parker as "sort of bird-brained and strong as an ox and funnier than anybody, and at the same time more incisive in a funny way. Awkward and brilliant at once." Parker remained in Grosse Pointe for the rest of her life and was married two more times (to a golf pro and a used car salesman). Kerouac would often call Parker late at night in a drunken stupor and talk for hours. She was one of the few members of the early Beat circle (besides Ginsberg) to attend Kerouac's funeral in 1969 in Lowell, Massachusetts. In 1982, Ginsberg invited Parker to lecture at the Naropa Institute in Boulder, Colorado, on the subject of her life with Kerouac in honor of the twenty-fifth anniversary of *On the Road*.

Parker wrote a memoir titled *You'll Be Okay: My Life with Jack Kerouac*, which was published posthumously by City Lights in 2007, in which she remarks, "Jack Kerouac was the fulfillment and nemesis of my youth. He was not a rebel by nature, but was curious and fascinated by those unlike himself, and could not resist the lure of those temptations." The memoir's title comes from a letter Kerouac wrote Parker just before he died that ends with the phrase "You'll be okay." In a review of the memoir for the *San Francisco Chronicle*, Jonah Raskin wrote, "Sad and funny, full of pathos and the lost dreams of youth, *You'll Be Okay* will find its way to the short list of exceptional books by women of the Beat Generation that includes Carolyn Cassady's *Off the Road* and Joyce Johnson's *Minor Characters*."

Carolyn Cassady (1923–2013)

According to Jerry Cimino, founder of the Beat Museum in North Beach, San Francisco, Carolyn Cassady was "the grande dame of the Beat Generation." Born in East Lansing, Michigan, on April 28, 1923, Carolyn Robinson grew up in Nashville, Tennessee, and graduated from Bennington College in Vermont in 1944 with a bachelor of arts degree in drama. At Bennington, Carolyn took courses with Martha Graham, Theodore Roethke, Francis Ferguson, Peter Drucker, and Erich Fromm. Carolyn met Neal Cassady in Denver in the spring of 1947 while attending a graduate program in theater design at the University of Denver. Soon after, Carolyn was shocked when she walked in on Neal, his first wife, LuAnne, and Allen Ginsberg in bed together. Neal quickly divorced LuAnne, and Carolyn became his second wife in April 1948.

While Neal was on the road, carousing and raising hell, Carolyn stayed home and raised the couple's three children: Cathy, John Allen, and Jami. At the insistence of Neal, Carolyn had an affair with Jack Kerouac that started in the early 1950s. Carolyn appeared as "Marilyn" in John Clellon Holmes's 1952 novel *Go* and "Camille" in Jack Kerouac's *On the Road* (1957), as well as "Evelyn Pomeray" in Kerouac's *Big Sur* (1962), *Desolation Angels* (1965), and *Visions of Cody* (1972). During the 1950s, both Carolyn and Neal became followers of the American mystic Edgar Cayce. The couple divorced in 1963; Neal went off and joined the Merry Pranksters, and died in Mexico in 1968.

Carolyn authored *Heart Beat: My Life with Jack and Neal* (1976) and *Off the Road: My Years with Cassady, Kerouac and Ginsberg* (1990). *Heart Beat* was turned (rather unsuccessfully) into a 1980 film of the same name directed by John Byrum and starring Sissy Spacek as Carolyn, Nick Nolte as Neal, and John Heard as Jack. Carolyn reportedly hated the script, as well as the finished product, but enjoyed Spacek's performance. Carolyn also wrote the foreword to *As Ever: The Collected Correspondence of Allen Ginsberg and Neal Cassady* (1977), as well as the introduction to *Neal Cassady: Collected Letters, 1944–1967* (2005).

Carolyn never watched the 2012 film version of *On the Road*, but she met with actor Garrett Hedlund who played "Dean Moriarty" and later remarked in an interview (quoted on www.vice.com), "I think he was the most boring person I have ever met . . . He didn't ask me a single question about Neal, but instead told me how his turkeys in Minnesota bobbed their heads to Johnny Cash music." In a 2008 interview with *Notes from the Underground*, Carolyn remarked, "As far as I'm concerned, the Beat Generation was something made up by the media and Allen Ginsberg." Carolyn died on September 20, 2013, at the age of ninety after lapsing into a coma during an emergency appendectomy in Bracknell, England (she had relocated to the United Kingdom in 1983).

Joan Vollmer (1923–51)

According to Herbert Huncke in his 1990 memoir, *Guilty of Everything*, Joan Vollmer "particularly fascinated me. I have never met a girl quite like Joan, and to this day I remember her as one of the most interesting people I have ever known . . . Joan was a quiet woman. She was an observer, but invariably her remarks never failed to start action of some kind. And she took to the underworld types like a natural, too." Vollmer was born on February 4, 1923, in Loudonville, New York, to an upper-middle-class family. While attending Barnard College in New York City, Vollmer lived a bohemian life and shared an apartment near Columbia with Jack Kerouac's future wife Edie Parker. The apartment soon became a bustling gathering place for Jack Kerouac, Allen Ginsberg, William S. Burroughs, Lucien Carr, Hal Chase, Huncke, and other members of the early Beat scene. Vollmer was drawn deeper into the sordid world of Benzedrine addiction and at one point in 1946 was sent to the mental ward at Bellevue Hospital. In his 1968 novel, *Vanity of Duluoz*,

Kerouac described the scene at the apartment in 1944 as "a year of low, evil decadence."

Vollmer and Burroughs, who was a homosexual, related to each other on an intellectual plane, and they started a relationship in 1946. She later became his common-law wife. The couple had a son, William Jr. (1947–81), and Vollmer had a daughter, Julie, from a previous relationship to Paul Adams, a GI serving overseas during World War II. The family moved to New Waverly, Texas, then just outside New Orleans, Louisiana (famously depicted in *On the Road*), and eventually Mexico City. Tragically, Vollmer was accidentally shot and killed by Burroughs during a drunken game of "William Tell" in Mexico City on September 6, 1951. She was just twenty-eight years old. Vollmer's grave is located at the Panteon Americano cemetery in Mexico City. In the introduction to his novel *Queer* (which was written in 1953 but not published until 1985), Burroughs wrote, "I am forced to the appalling conclusion that I would have never become a writer but for Joan's death."

Vollmer served as the model for "Mary Dennison" in Kerouac's first published novel, *The Town and the City* (1950), and "Jane" in *On the Road* (1957). The 2000 film *Beat*, which was written and directed by Gary Walkow, covers the events leading up to Vollmer's accidental murder. *Beat* suffers from not only a poor script, but also the miscasting of Kiefer Sutherland as Burroughs and Courtney Love as Vollmer. Norman Reedus as Carr, Daniel Martinez as Kerouac, and Ron Livingston as Ginsberg round out the cast. *Beat* premiered at the Sundance Film Festival in January 2000 and can now be found in the bargain bin at your local flea market.

LuAnne Henderson (1930–2008)

LuAnne Henderson has gained immortality as the model for "Marylou," the beautiful teenage bride of "Dean Moriarty" (Neal Cassady) AND the love interest of "Sal Paradise" in Jack Kerouac's 1957 novel, *On the Road*. Kerouac once described Henderson as a "nymph with waist-length dirty blond hair" (*Women of the Beat Generation*, 1998).

Henderson met Neal Cassady in Denver, Colorado, in 1945, and the couple got married the following year when she was just sixteen years old. The Cassadys headed to New York City in December 1946 to visit old friend Hal Chase at Columbia University. Chase introduced them to the early Beat circle that included Kerouac and Allen Ginsberg. Henderson played a central role in the subsequent cross-country trips that she made with Cassady and Kerouac between 1947 and 1950 as highlighted in *On the Road*. Even after Cassady got an annulment from Henderson and married Carolyn Robinson in the spring of 1948, he continued to see Henderson for years after. Henderson was married two more times and later became a heroin addict.

Henderson, who died in 2008, was the subject of the book *One and Only: The Untold Story of On the Road and LuAnne Henderson, the Woman Who Started Jack Kerouac and Neal Cassady on Their Journey* by Gerald Nicosia and Henderson's daughter, Anne Marie Santos. Published in 2013, *One and Only* contains Nicosia's exclusive interviews with Henderson. According to promotional material for the book, "LuAnne became the secret link between Kerouac and Cassady, helping to ignite the Beat Generation, and giving Kerouac material for one of the seminal novels of the twentieth century, *On the Road*." Critically acclaimed poet Anne Waldman, who cofounded with Ginsberg the Jack Kerouac School of Disembodied Poetics at the Naropa Institute, called Henderson "an unsung teen-heroine of the time." In the 2012 film version of *On the Road*, Kristen Stewart (*Twilight* series) portrays "Marylou."

Elise Cowen (1933–62)

The tragic story of Elise Nada Cowen tends to overshadow her genuine poetic talents. Cowen grew up in a wealthy Jewish family in Washington Heights, New York, and attended Barnard College in the 1950s where she befriended Joyce Glassman (Johnson). Her early influences included Ezra Pound and T. S. Eliot. Cowen met Allen Ginsberg through a philosophy professor at Barnard College, and the unlikely couple became romantically involved briefly during the spring and summer of 1953 (they even looked like each other). They had a mutual acquaintance, Carl Solomon, who had met them both separately during stays at a psychiatric hospital. However, Ginsberg soon met and quickly fell in love with Peter Orlovsky. Cowen took a lover named Sheila, and for a time both couples shared an apartment.

In his 1990 memoir, *Guilty of Everything*, Herbert Huncke remarks, "On the floor above Allen's there lived an interesting girl named Elise Cowen, who, it seemed, had developed a crush on Allen . . . Allen had already acquired followers, or disciples, that would invariably run up to him when he walked down the street. It was quite amazing how rapidly he'd come into his own." Cowen suffered with various mental issues throughout her brief life, resulting in a stay at Bellevue Hospital. Against her doctor's orders, Cowen checked herself out of the hospital and returned to her parents' apartment, where she committed suicide by jumping through a closed living room window and falling seven stories to the ground. Cowen was killed instantly. She was just twenty-eight years old.

None of Cowen's poetry was published during her lifetime, and little of Cowen's work actually survives—having been destroyed either by her or at the behest of her parents (who reportedly were aghast by the "objectionable" content of the poems) after her death. However, some of her work found its way to various periodicals such as *Evergreen Review, City Lights Journal, Fuck You: A Magazine of the Arts*, and others. Fourteen of Cowen's shorter poems are included in the "Short Poem Dossier" of the 2012 issue of *Court Green*. In addition, a volume of work from Cowen's only surviving notebook, titled *Elise Cowen: Poems and Fragments* (edited by Tony Trigilio, an English professor at Columbia College Chicago), was published by Ahsahta Press in 2014. Cowen also appears prominently in Joyce Johnson's *Minor Characters: A Beat Memoir* (1999).

Diane di Prima (1934–)

Allen Ginsberg referred to Diane di Prima as a "revolutionary activist of the 1960s Beat literary renaissance, heroic in life and poetics: a learned humorous bohemian, classically educated and twentieth-century radical, her writing, informed by Buddhist equanimity, is exemplary in imagist, political and mystical modes. A great woman poet in second half of American century, she broke barriers of race-class identity, delivered a major body of verse brilliant in its particularity" (www.citylights.com). A highly influential feminist Beat poet, Diane di Prima was born in Brooklyn, New York, on August 6, 1934. Her maternal grandfather, Domenico Mallozzi, was an active anarchist and associate of Carlo Tresca and Emma Goldman. Di Prima's earliest influences were the English Romantic poets, including Percy Bysshe Shelley and John Keats.

Totem Press (owned by LeRoi and Hettie Jones) published di Prima's first book of poetry, *This Kind of Bird Flies Backward*, in 1958. Di Prima started the Poets Press in 1961 and edited the literary newsletter *The Floating Bear* (1961–71) with LeRoi Jones. She also cofounded the New York Poets Theatre in 1961 along with Jones, James Waring, Alan Marlowe, and Fred Herko. In 1961, di Prima was arrested by the FBI for publishing two "obscene" works in *The Floating Bear*. Di Prima spent some time in the mid-1960s living at Timothy Leary's Millbrook Estate and then relocated to San Francisco where she got involved with the Diggers, a radical activist group, and later started Eidolon Editions. In 1969, she published the semi-fictional *Memoirs of a Beatnik*, which was quite controversial for the time due to its graphic sexual depictions (including a memorably disturbing account of her participation in an orgy with Allen Ginsberg and Jack Kerouac).

Di Prima taught poetry at the Jack Kerouac School of Disembodied Poetics at the Naropa Institute in Boulder, Colorado, from 1974 to 1997. She appeared in *The Last Waltz*, Martin Scorsese's 1978 documentary about the Band, during which she read two of her poems, "Get Yer Cut Throat off My

Allen Ginsberg referred to highly influential Beat poet Diane di Prima as a "revolutionary activist of the 1960s Beat literary renaissance."   *Photo by Fred W. McDarrah/Getty Images*

Knife" and "Revolutionary Letter #4." In 2001, di Prima published a memoir titled *Recollections of My Life as a Woman: The New York Years*. She was named the Poet Laureate of San Francisco in 2009. Di Prima, who has five children, was married to Alan Marlowe during 1962–69 and Grant Fisher during 1972–75. In 2011, di Prima collaborated with filmmaker Melanie La Rosa on the impressionistic documentary *The Poetry Deal: A Film with Diane di Prima*.

Hettie Jones (1934–)

Born Hettie Cohen in 1934 into a middle-class Jewish family in Brooklyn, New York, Hettie Jones earned her bachelor of arts in drama from the University of Virginia. In 1958, Jones married African American writer LeRoi Jones (later known as Amiri Baraka), after which her family disowned her. The couple eventually had two children, Kellie and Lisa, before divorcing in 1965. By then, Baraka had embraced a militant form of Black nationalism. Hettie and LeRoi established an influential literary journal called *Yugen* between 1957 and 1963 that published the works of Jack Kerouac, Allen Ginsberg, William S. Burroughs, Philip Whalen, and other writers. The couple also founded Totem Press.

In 1974, Jones published *Big Star Fallin' Mama: Five Women in Black Music*, which profiled the lives of legendary talents Ma Rainey, Bessie Smith, Mahalia Jackson, Billie Holiday, and Aretha Franklin. In 1990, Jones published a critically acclaimed memoir, *How I Became Hettie Jones*, which highlights the Beat scene in New York City during the 1950s and 1960s. Concerning *How I Became Hettie Jones*, Lawrence Ferlinghetti remarked, "A feminist scrutiny such as this is just what those lost decades needed, as the Beats themselves needed it" (www.groveatlantic.com). In 1997, Jones's first collection of poetry, *Drive*, won the Norma Farber Award from the Poetry Society of America. In its review of *Drive*, *Booklist* called Jones "a potent and fearless poet." In addition, Jones assisted Rita Marley with the 2005 autobiography *No Woman No Cry: My Life with Bob Marley*.

Jones currently lives in New York City where she writes and teaches at the 92nd Street Y Poetry Center and in the Graduate Writing Program of the New School. She has also been heavily involved with the PEN American Center's Prison Writing Committee and operated a writing workshop at the New York State Correctional Facility for Women at Bedford Hills between 1989 and 2002. Jones's daughter Lisa is a writer and journalist, and her daughter Kellie is an associate professor in the Department of Art History and Archaeology at Columbia University. In a May 22, 2014, interview with *PRISM International*, Jones remarked, "Writing is very important to me and makes me feel like I've done what I've set out do in this life. I would rather write than see a bad movie, for example, or watch a stupid television show. The act of writing, it's good. It keeps you involved with words and that will take you far."

Joanne Kyger (1934–)

Poet David Meltzer has called Joanne Kyger "a poet of transparently easy and immediate wisdom that, in its dispatch, is gracefully disarming and ultimately immensely profound." Kyger is known for her ties not only to the Beat Generation but also to the Black Mountain poets and San Francisco Renaissance. Kyger was born on November 19, 1934, in Vallejo, California, to Anne and Jacob Kyger. She studied philosophy and literature at the University of California, Santa Barbara, before moving to San Francisco in

With strong ties to not only the Beat Generation but also to the Black Mountain poets and the poets of the San Francisco Renaissance, Joanne Kyger has published more than twenty books of poetry and occasionally teaches at the Jack Kerouac School of Disembodied Poetics.   *Photo by Gloria Graham/Wikimedia Commons*

1957, where she worked at Brentano's Bookstore, and was mentored by Jack Spicer and Robert Duncan. She also befriended other area writers, including John Wieners, Richard Brautigan, Gary Snyder, and Philip Whalen.

Kyger joined Snyder in Kyoto, Japan, and the couple was married there in 1960. Kyger traveled to India with Snyder, Allen Ginsberg, and Peter Orlovsky in 1963 and returned by herself to San Francisco the following year, while Snyder stayed overseas in his continued search for enlightenment. Kyger's *Strange Big Moon: The Japan and India Journals, 1960–1964* (2000) presents a colorful memoir of her travels during this period. Kyger's first book of poetry, *The Tapestry and the Web*, was published in 1965. Her poetry is heavily infused with Zen Buddhism. According to *The Beat Book* (1996, edited by

Anne Waldman), "Of all the Beat poets, Kyger, with her wide-open, daily accountings of her observations and readings, seems the most directly to point to a younger generation of poets, hence her inclusion in magazines by the experimentalists known as the Language poets." Kyger married the painter Jack Boyce in 1966.

Kyger has published more than twenty books, including *Joanne, Places to Go* (1970), *Desecheo Notebook* (1971), *Trip Out and Fall Back* (1974), *All This Every Day* (1975), *The Wonderful Focus of You* (1980), *Mexico Blonde* (1981), *Going On: Selected Poems, 1958–1980* (1983), and *Just Space: Poems, 1979–1989* (1991). In 2000, a collection of Kyger's autobiographical writings was published as *Strange Big Moon: The Japan and India Journals, 1960–1964*, which Anne Waldman referred to as "one of the finest books ever in the genre of 'journal writing.'" Kyger's *About Now: Collected Poems* (2007) won the 2008 PEN Oakland Josephine Miles National Award for Poetry. Kyger also appeared in the 2010 documentary *The Practice of the Wild: A Conversation with Gary Snyder and Jim Harrison.* Kyger currently resides in Bolinas, California, and occasionally teaches at the Jack Kerouac School of Disembodied Poetics at Naropa University in Boulder, Colorado.

Joyce Johnson (1935–)

Quoted in *Jack's Book*, Joyce Johnson remarked, "The whole Beat scene had very little to do with the participation of women as artists themselves. The real communication was going on between the men, and the women were there as onlookers. Their old ladies. You kept you mouth shut, and if you were intelligent and interested in things you might pick up what you could. It was a very masculine aesthetic." Johnson was born Joyce Glassman in 1935 in Brooklyn, New York, and attended Barnard College. She dated Kerouac briefly during 1957–58 during the pivotal period just before and after *On the Road* was published. She was married briefly to abstract expressionist painter James Johnson, who was killed in a motorcycle accident in 1963. Johnson's first novel, *Come and Join the Dance*, was published in 1962.

Johnson received the National Book Critics Circle Award for her 1983 Beat memoir, *Minor Characters*, the title referring to the women of the Beat Generation. In *Minor Characters*, Johnson writes, "Those of us who flew out the door had no usable models for what we were doing . . . Though no warning would have stopped us, so hungry were we to embrace life and all of reality. Even hardship was something to be savored." Other works by Johnson include *Door Wide Open: A Beat Love Affair in Letters, 1957–1958* (2000), detailing her correspondence with Kerouac; *Missing Men: A Memoir* (2005); and *The Voice Is All: The Lonely Victory of Jack Kerouac* (2012).

In a 2007 interview with the *Guardian*, Johnson commented, "What has been frustrating to me is that the people who know my work seem to remember it only in the context of my writing about Jack . . . But I have other books . . . And all of my books have been very well reviewed. I'd like to establish my reputation as a writer, apart from all that . . . It's getting a little late. But I'd like it to happen at some point."

Jan Kerouac (1952–96)

Jack Kerouac had already left his second wife, Joan Haverty (who appeared as "Laura" in *On the Road*), when she gave birth to Janet Michelle "Jan" Kerouac on February 16, 1952. The marriage had lasted just eight months. Kerouac

The daughter of Jack Kerouac and his second wife, Joan Haverty, Jan Kerouac published two autobiographical novels: *Baby Driver* (1981) and *Trainsong* (1988).   *Photo by Chris Felver/Getty Images*

refused to acknowledge that the child was his (he had reportedly tried to pressure Joan into getting an abortion) and refused to pay child support. For years, Joan fought tirelessly and unsuccessfully to get Kerouac to pay child support and even wrote an article in *Confidential* magazine titled "My Ex-Husband, Jack Kerouac, Is an Ingrate."

Jan only met her father on two occasions, as she detailed in the 1986 documentary *What Happened to Kerouac?* In the first instance, at the age of nine, she accompanied Kerouac to a liquor store so he could buy a bottle of Harvey's Bristol Cream. The second and last time Jan saw her father was during a stop through Lowell, Massachusetts, on her way to Mexico with a boyfriend at the age of fifteen. Kerouac was drinking whisky and watching *The Beverly Hillbillies*. During the brief encounter, Kerouac encouraged Jan to write—telling her, "Yeah, you go to Mexico, write a book, you can use my name"—and wished her well on her travels. When Kerouac died in 1969, he left no provisions for Jan in his will.

Jan published two semiautobiographical novels, *Baby Driver* (1981), which details her turbulent childhood growing up in New York City during the 1960s, and *Trainsong* (1988), which highlights her extensive travels. In *Baby Driver*, Jan writes, "Everything fascinated me and I wanted to do everything and go everywhere." Jan was working on a third novel, *Parrot Fever*, when she died in Albuquerque, New Mexico, on June 5, 1996, at the age of forty-four, a day after her spleen was removed (she had suffered kidney failure five years earlier and had been on dialysis). She is buried in the Kerouac family plot at Saint Louis de Gonzague Cemetery in Nashua, New Hampshire.

Joan Haverty died of breast cancer in 1990, and her memoir, *Nobody's Wife*, was published posthumously in 2000. A straightforward narrative, *Nobody's Wife* details her life in New York City during the late 1940s and early 1950s as she lived with Bill Cannastra, a member of the early Beat circle who died in a freak subway accident, as well as her impulsive marriage to Kerouac. The memoir features a preface by Jan Kerouac, as well as a foreword by Kerouac biographer Ann Charters. Edited by Beat Generation historian and Jack Kerouac biographer Gerald Nicosia, *Jan Kerouac: A Life in Memory* was published in 2009. The book features a collection of memoirs and photos, as well as an extensive interview with Jan Kerouac.

15

A Ghost in Daylight

The Beats on Drugs

In regard to drug and alcohol usage (and abuse) among members of the Beat Generation, poet Gary Snyder remarked in a 1974 interview (*The Beat Vision*, 1987), "[Jack] Kerouac was a casualty too. And there were many other casualties that most people never hear of, but were genuine casualties. Just as, in the '60s, when Allen [Ginsberg] and I for a period there were almost publicly recommending people to take acid. When I look back on that now I realize there were many casualties, responsibilities to bear." According to author Ken Kesey (*Beat Writers at Work*, 1999), "I think most artists who, as the saying goes now, 'push the envelope,' wind up as casualties. If you think about the history of writers and artists, the best often don't end up with pleasant, comfortable lives; sometimes they go over the edge and lose it." William S. Burroughs had a different take on the drug issue in the prologue to *Junkie* (1958): "I have never regretted my experience with drugs . . . When you stop growing you start dying. An addict never stops growing."

Alcohol

After literally becoming a celebrity overnight with the 1957 publication of *On the Road*, Jack Kerouac increasingly turned toward the bottle in a misguided attempt to cope with the repercussions of fame. The model for "Marylou" in *On the Road*, LuAnne Henderson in *One and Only* (2013) claimed that when she saw Kerouac in 1957, she "was shocked by how changed he was . . . That was when I first became aware that Jack was drinking. Before that, I had never seen Jack drunk—never . . . That's why I was concerned and surprised to see him drinking steadily, just one after another." In a futile attempt to dry out just three years after the publication of *On the Road*, Kerouac headed to Lawrence Ferlinghetti's secluded Bixby Canyon cabin as depicted in his 1962 novel, *Big Sur*—one of the most disturbing literary portraits of alcoholism. According to Lawrence Ferlinghetti in *Beat Writers at Work* (1999), "When [Kerouac] became famous overnight after the publication of *On the Road*, he immediately started cutting out. He didn't want to be around. He couldn't handle the fame. The way he handled it was to drink more and more."

One of Jack Kerouac's favorite hangouts during the twilight of his St. Petersburg years, the Flamingo Bar pays tribute to the beloved author twice a year with a "Jack Kerouac Night," as well as a "Jack Kerouac Special"—a shot and a wash for just $2.25.

Courtesy of Alternative Reel/alternativereel.com

Benzedrine

Introduced by the Smith, Kline & French pharmaceutical company in 1928 and available only as an inhaler for dilating nasal and bronchial passages, Benzedrine proved to be both a short-term blessing and long-term curse for several members of the Beat Generation. It was reportedly Vicki Russell, a prostitute and friend of Herbert Huncke, who introduced the early Beat scene to the Benzedrine technique (Russell would later appear as "Mary" in *Junkie*), which involved cracking open a Benzedrine inhaler and swallowing the paper strips inside.

William S. Burroughs's common-law wife, Joan Vollmer, quickly descended into the nightmare of Benzedrine addiction. According to an interview with LuAnne Henderson (*Jack's Book*, 1978), "I never saw [Joan] sleep. I don't care what time I got up or came home or anything. Joan was up, either with the broom or rake, scraping lizards off of the tree, in the kitchen washing walls, continuously scrubbing."

Kerouac biographer Ann Charters wrote, "Each of Kerouac's books was written on something and each of the books has some of the feel of what he was on most as he wrote it. *On the Road* has a nervous, tense and Benzedrine feel." However, other biographers have insisted that Kerouac simply subsisted on coffee when he frantically typed up his notes for the novel in a three-week period during April 1951. Kerouac completed his novella *The Subterraneans* in just three frantic days, reportedly with the help of Benzedrine.

In his "Letter from a Master Addict to Dangerous Drugs," which was first published in the *British Journal of Addiction* (January 1957), Burroughs wrote, "The period of euphoria" of Benzedrine was "followed by a horrible depression. The drug tends to increase anxiety. It causes indigestion and loss of appetite." According to Mikal Gilmore in *Stories Done* (2009), "In 1959, after a night of taking Benzedrine, listening to the rhythm & blues of Ray Charles, and walking New York's streets, Ginsberg sat down to write 'Kaddish.' It was his tribute to his mother Naomi."

Dilaudid

Hyromorphone, a derivative of morphine, was first synthesized in Germany in 1924 and introduced by the brand name Dilaudid in 1926. In 1946, Burroughs was arrested over a forged prescription for Dilaudid (the brand name had been misspelled on the prescription) and briefly imprisoned in the Tombs before getting bailed out by his parents. In his 1959 novel, *Naked Lunch*, Burroughs writes, "Delaudid deliver poor me (Delaudid is souped up dehydrate morphine)." In one of the last scenes of *Drugstore Cowboy* (1989), the eyes of "Old Tom the Junkie Priest" (Burroughs) light up when "Bob" (Matt Dillon) gifts him some Dilaudid, and he exclaims, "This should earn you an indulgence."

Heroin

The *New York Times* obituary for William S. Burroughs on August 3, 1997, noted that the author had "spent so much of his younger days engulfed in narcotics addiction, an imperative so demanding that . . . he sold his typewriter to buy heroin, although he kept working in longhand." During a 1977 TV interview, Burroughs was asked if he had any regrets using heroin, and he replied, "A writer can profit from things that may be just unpleasant or boring to someone else, because he uses those subsequently for material in writing. And I would say that the experience I had, that's described in *Junkie*, later led to my subsequent books like *Naked Lunch*. So I don't regret it. Incidentally, the damage to health is minimal—no matter what the American Narcotics Department may say." With his on-again-off-again heroin addiction, Burroughs followed in the footsteps of his uncle Horace, a morphine addict who committed suicide in 1915. Other books about heroin include Aleister Crowley's *Diary of a Drug Fiend* (1922) and *Trainspotting* (1993) by Irvine Welsh.

LSD

Lysergic acid diethylamide (LSD) was first synthesized by Swiss scientist Albert Hofmann (1906–2008) in 1938. However, Hofman did not ingest LSD until five years later when he had the first "acid trip," feeling the full effects of the drug as he rode his bike home on April 19, 1943 (now commemorated by psychedelic enthusiasts as "Bicycle Day"). In his 1980 book, *LSD: My Problem*

Beat poets such as Allen Ginsberg and Gary Snyder advocated for the use of LSD in the 1960s (with Snyder later regretting his role as an advocate for the drug). With a nice dose (no pun intended!) of cynicism and paranoia, the 1978 film *Blue Sunshine* effectively slammed the door on the counterculture's love affair with LSD. *Author's collection*

Child, Hofmann writes, "Of greatest significance to me has been the insight that I attained as a fundamental understanding from all of my LSD experiments: what one commonly takes as 'the reality,' including the reality of one's own individual person, by no means signifies something fixed, but rather something that is ambiguous—that there is not only one, but that there are many realities, each comprising also a different consciousness of the ego."

In the early 1960s, the use of LSD was popularized by Timothy Leary's psychedelic experiments at Harvard University, as well as the anarchic activities of Ken Kesey and the Merry Pranksters—ultimately leading to the heyday of the counterculture that culminated with the "Summer of Love" in San Francisco in 1967. According to Kesey in the 1987 BBC documentary *The Beyond Within: The Rise and Fall of LSD*, "I believe that with the advent of acid, we discovered a new way to think, and it has to do with piecing together new thoughts in your mind. Why is it that people think it's so evil? What is it about it that scares people so deeply, even the guy that invented it, what is it? Because they're afraid that there's more to reality than they have confronted. That there are doors that they're afraid to go in, and they don't want us to go in there either, because if we go in we might learn something that they don't know. And that makes us a little out of their control."

During his infamous "Public Solitude" speech at the Arlington Street Church in Boston, Massachusetts, in November 1966, Allen Ginsberg shocked the audience by suggesting that everyone in the United States take LSD at least once in their lives. As a guest on William F. Buckley's *Firing Line* TV show in 1968, Ginsberg read a poem, "Wales Visitation," written under the influence of LSD. In the foreword to *The Beat Book* (1996), Ginsberg wrote, "Our interest in psychedelic substances as educational tools, particularly marijuana, mushrooms and LSD, led to a more realistic approach to drug laws, recognizing that tobacco and alcohol are physically more destructive than all other drugs except cocaine."

Marijuana

According to Allen Ginsberg (*Beat Writers at Work*), Jack Kerouac's novel *Doctor Sax* "was written on marijuana, so it has an elaborate marijuana openness." Ginsberg himself was one of the first people to address marijuana's legal status on TV in a February 12, 1961, appearance on a talk show, where he discussed "Hips and Beats" with Norman Mailer. A famous photo shows Allen Ginsberg holding a protest sign proclaiming "POT IS A REALITY KICK" at a 1963 rally for the legalization of marijuana in New York City (in another he is holding a sign that reads "POT IS FUN").

In his "Letter from a Master Addict to Dangerous Drugs" (*British Journal of Addiction*, January 1957), Burroughs wrote, "The ill effects of marijuana have been grossly exaggerated in the U.S. Our national drug is alcohol. We tend to regard the use of any other drug with special horror." In a 1974 interview included in *Conversations with William S. Burroughs* (2000), the author stated, "I wrote nearly the whole of *Naked Lunch* on cannabis. I think it stimulates the associational process, and vizualization."

The dangers of marijuana use were famously sensationalized in such camp classic films as *Reefer Madness* (1936). The use of marijuana was widespread among Beat writers, who steadfastly refused to heed the warnings.   *Author's collection*

Morphine

The main psychoactive chemical in opium, morphine was discovered in 1804 by German pharmacist Friedrich Serturner. William S. Burroughs's uncle Horace was reportedly a morphine addict who committed suicide in 1915. Burroughs himself became addicted to morphine in the mid-1940s and wrote about his sordid experiences in *Junkie* (1953), including the depiction of a morphine fix: "Morphine hits the back of the legs first, then the back of the neck, a spreading wave of relaxation slackening the muscles away from the bones so that you seem to float without outlines, like lying in warm salt water."

In "Deposition: Testimony Concerning a Sickness" (the introduction to the 1960 edition of *Naked Lunch*), Burroughs wrote, "I have used junk in many forms: morphine, heroin, delaudid, eukodal, pantopon, diocodid, diosane, opium, Demerol, dolophine, palfium. I have smoked junk, eaten it, sniffed it, injected it in vein-skin-muscle, inserted it in rectal suppositories. The needle is not important. Whether you sniff it smoke it eat it or shove it up your ass the result is the same: addiction."

Paregoric

"The Paregoric Kid" serves as one of the memorable characters in William S. Burroughs's *Naked Lunch* (1959). A weak tincture of opium, paregoric was commonly used as a household remedy in the eighteenth and nineteenth centuries. According to Herbert Huncke (*Guilty of Everything*, 1990), "When Burroughs settled in Texas, he'd cased every town for miles around for paregoric, a mixture with a tincture of laudanum sold over the counter. He had succeeded in getting a paregoric habit. He would chill it overnight, skim the surface off, burn the alcohol out of it, and end up with a fairly clean texture of opium mixture, and shoot it mainline. It gives a nice lift, but he didn't really like that. He was very anxious to get his hands on something closer to the real thing—preferably morphine."

Peyote

A small, spineless cactus native to southwestern Texas and Mexico, peyote (*Lophophora williamsii*) has been used as a physical and spiritual medicine by Native Americans for thousands of years. As the principal active ingredient in peyote, mescaline is responsible for creating hallucinations and "extraordinary visions." William S. Burroughs describes a peyote high in *Junkie* (1953): "My whole body contracted in convulsive spasms, but the peyote wouldn't come up. It wouldn't stay down either. Finally the peyote came up solid like a ball of hair, solid all the way up, clogging my throat. As horrible a sensation as I ever stood for. After that, the high came on slow."

Allen Ginsberg wrote Part II of "Howl" on peyote in 1954 at his apartment in North Beach, San Francisco, and had his vision of "Moloch" that appears so prominently in the poem after looking out the window and viewing the lit-up Sir Francis Drake Hotel. One of Michael McClure's most prominent works, "Peyote Poem," was written in 1959 after his experience with the hallucinogen and depicts an overwhelming sense of alienation in a barren universe. Ken Kesey famously wrote the opening of his 1962 novel *One Flew Over the Cuckoo's Nest* under the influence of peyote. In *Beat Writers at Work* (1999), Kesey remarks, "I did write the first several pages of *Cuckoo's Nest* on peyote, and I changed very little of it. It had little effect on the plot, but the mood and particularly the voice in those first few pages remained throughout the book."

In his essay "Letter from a Master Addict to Dangerous Drugs" (*British Journal of Addiction*, January 1957), Burroughs wrote, "Peyote intoxication causes a peculiar vegetable consciousness or identification with the plant. Everything looks like a peyote plant. It is easy to understand why Indians believe there is a resident spirit in the peyote cactus."

Yage

In 1953, William S. Burroughs traveled throughout South America—primarily Columbia, Peru, and Ecuador—in search of the powerful hallucinogen yage (*Bannisteria caapi*). Burroughs had become interested in the drug after reading an article on the hallucinogen by noted biologist Richard Evans Schultes, who has been called "the Father of Modern Ethnobotany."

A lot of his bizarre experiences in South America were transformed into "routines" in his subsequent novels such as *Naked Lunch* (1959), *The Soft Machine* (1961), and *The Ticket That Exploded* (1962). At the end of *Junkie* (1953), "William Lee" decides to embark on his quest for yage, remarking, "Kick is momentary freedom from the claims of the aging, cautious, nagging, frightened flesh. Maybe I will find in yage what I was looking for in junk and weed and coke." In *Naked Lunch*, Burroughs writes, "Yage is space-time travel."

The correspondence between Burroughs and Allen Ginsberg revolving around the discussion of yage (a.k.a. ayahuasca) was published by City Lights in 1963 as *The Yage Letters*. In 2006, City Lights published a new edition of the book edited by Oliver Harris and titled *Yage Letters Redux*. In "Letter from a Master Addict to Dangerous Drugs" (*British Journal of Addiction*, January 1957), Burroughs called yage "a hallucinating narcotic that produces a profound derangement of the senses."

16

Every Face You See

The Rise of the Beatniks

The word "beatnik" was initially coined rather disparagingly by columnist Herb Caen of the *San Francisco Chronicle* in 1958 and quickly became a media stereotype, turning the Beat writers and their spiritual quest into the cartoonish stereotype of a ridiculous-looking freak playing bongo drums while sporting a goatee and beret. A "Rent-A-Beatnik" service actually emerged in New York City, while Bob Denver brought beatnik to primetime with "Maynard G. Krebs" in *The Many Lives of Dobie Gillis*. In September 1960, even *Mad* magazine got in on the act, publishing the satiric "Beatnik: The Magazine for Hipsters." Let's not forget the flippant remark of "Lily Munster" (Yvonne De Carlo) on *The Munsters* ("Grandpa Leaves Home," 1964): "Well, let's hope it'll be nicer inside and not one of those beatnik joints. If there's anything I can't stand, it's weird people."

Beatnik Origins

San Francisco Chronicle columnist Herb Caen (1916–97) coined the word "beatnik" in an April 2, 1958, article by simply coming up with a play on words based on the Russian satellite Sputnik. Ironically, Caen's beatnik comment was just an aside: "*Look* magazine, preparing a picture spread on S.F.'s Beat Generation (oh, no, not AGAIN!), hosted a party in a No. Beach house for 50 Beatniks, and by the time word got around the sour grapevine, over 250 bearded cats and kits were on hand, slopping up Mike Cowles' free booze. They're only Beat, y'know." Caen stated that he ran into Jack Kerouac that night at El Matador, a North Beach saloon. According to Caen, "He was mad. He said, 'You're putting us down and making us sound like jerks. I hate it. Stop using it.' And onward into the night."

Use of the term "beatnik" quickly spread across the country. In a scathing letter to the *New York Times*, Allen Ginsberg condemned the use of "the foul word beatnik," writing, "If beatniks and not illuminated Beat poets overrun this country, they will have been created not by Kerouac but by industries of mass communication which continue to brainwash man." The

Beats eventually got a semblance of revenge by hanging up a poster in the Co-Existence Bagel Shop that read, "We feature separate toilet facilities for HERB CAEN." In addition, a footnote to "beatnik" in Norman Mailer's 1959 collection of essays, *Advertisements for Myself*, reads, "A word coined by an idiot columnist in San Francisco." Caen (a.k.a. "Mr. San Francisco") later remarked, "I coined the word 'beatnik' simply because Russia's Sputnik satellite was aloft at the time and the word popped out."

Beatnik Fashion and Slang

The stereotypical beatnik male dressed in a turtleneck, with a beret, scarf, and dark sunglasses, while the beatnik female wore black Capri pants or leotards, along with a turtleneck or sweater and minimal jewelry. Bongos were common accessories as well. Ironically, NONE of the Beat writers dressed this way (with the possible exception of Ted Joans, who briefly joined a Rent-A-Beatnik service in New York City). Beatnik women wore their hair straight, while men sported pointed goatees.

According to Joyce Johnson in *Minor Characters* (1983), "'Beat Generation' sold books, sold black turtleneck sweaters and bongos, berets and dark glasses, sold a way of life that seemed like dangerous fun—thus to be either condemned or imitated. Suburban couples could have beatnik parties on Saturday nights and drink too much and fondle each other's wives."

Beatniks also developed their own slang with commonly used words such as "bread," "daddy-o," "chick," 'kicks," "pad," "cat," "square," and "gas." In *The Holy Barbarians* (1959), author Lawrence Lipton even included a "Beat Glossary" with such beatnik terms as "crazy" ("anything from mild to wild that meets with a cat's approval"), "get with it" ("comprehend, understand, participate, dig?"), "hipster" ("one who is in the know"), "joint" ("a place, a penis, a marijuana cigarette, preferably a combination of all three"), "shack up" ("to cohabit, in every sense and sex of the word"), and "work" ("sexual intercourse").

Legendary Beatnik Hangouts

In his 1990 autobiography, *Guilty of Everything*, Herbert Huncke related how he had seen a photo of Allen Ginsberg in *Life* magazine reading poetry at the Gaslight Café in Greenwich Village. So he decided to visit the Gaslight one night to look for Ginsberg: "I sat at a table and a chick in a black leotard and black turtleneck, with heavily shadowed eyes, came over . . . Obviously . . . I appeared like the law to them. I was dressed in a suit and tie, and my hair was cut short. I did not fit into the scene at all, and felt it instantly."

Venice Beach poet Lawrence Lipton appeared in the low-budget horror flick *The Hypnotic Eye* (1960) as the "King of the Beatniks."
Author's collection

Also in Greenwich Village, Café Wha?, which opened in 1959, hosted a variety of musicians and comedians such as Lenny Bruce, Bob Dylan, Woody Allen, Jimi Hendrix, Cat Mother and the All Night Newsboys, and the Velvet Underground. Another beatnik hotspot was the Five Spot Café in the Bowery, where Thelonious Monk's quartet—featuring John Coltrane, Wilbur Ware, and Shadow Wilson—performed a six-month stay in 1957. The Five Spot Café drew the likes of Jack Kerouac, Ginsberg, Frank O'Hara, Ted Joans, Gregory Corso, Franz Kline, Willem de Kooning, Larry Rivers, and others. Beatniks, including many up-and-coming folk musicians, also descended upon Washington Square Park, which was the site of the infamous "Beatnik Riot" on April 9, 1961, when the New York Police Department decided to crack down on all the "undesirables" hanging out at the park.

On the West Coast, the place to be for beatniks in the late 1950s and early 1960s was Vesuvio Café in North Beach, San Francisco, next to City Lights Bookstore. At one point, Vesuvio even hired artist Wally Hedrick to sit in the window dressed like a beatnik and create his improvisational paintings.

Maynard G. Krebs

Perhaps the most famous beatnik of all was the TV character "Maynard G. Krebs" as portrayed by Bob Denver (1935–2005) in the half-hour sitcom *The Many Loves of Dobie Gillis*, which aired on CBS from 1959 to 1963 (running for 142 episodes). It was the first TV sitcom to focus entirely on the lives of teenagers, as well as the only show at the time to feature a beatnik character. The show was based on a series of short stories published by writer Max Shulman as *The Many Loves of Dobie Gillis* (1951) that evolved into a 1953 movie called *The Affairs of Dobie Gillis* (a.k.a. *Casanova Junior*), which starred Bobby Van, Debbie Reynolds, and Bob Fosse, as well as Hans Conried (*The 5,000 Fingers of Dr. T*) as "Professor Pomfritt." Interestingly, there was no Krebs character in either the book or the film.

The Many Loves of Dobie Gillis starred Dwayne Hickman as "Dobie Gillis," a high school student in "Central City." The cast included Tuesday Weld as Dobie's dream girl, "Thalia Menninger"; Sheila Gilroy as his bookish classmate, "Zelda Gilroy"; Florida Friebus as Dobie's mother, "Winnie Gillis"; and Frank Faylen as his father, "Herbert T. Gillis." In addition, a young Warren Beatty had a brief recurring role as spoiled rich kid "Milton Armitage." However, it was Dobie's beatnik buddy Maynard G. Krebs (the "G" stood for "Walter"!) who often stole the show with his goatee, unkempt bohemian attire, beatnik slang, bongo playing, and tendency to freak out whenever he heard the word "work." Since Denver was a fan of jazz in real life, Krebs idolized jazz legends such as Thelonious Monk and Dizzy Gillespie. A rumor even started up during the series that Denver had actually recorded an album as Krebs called *Like What?* (which turned out to be a total myth). Krebs was also a fan of a cheesy horror film called *The Monster That Devoured Cleveland*, which enjoyed a perpetual run at the local movie theater.

Denver, who was working as a school teacher and moonlighting at the post office when he auditioned for the role, went on to appear as "Gilligan" in the CBS sitcom *Gilligan's Island*, which ran from 1964 to 1967. Hickman later starred in several movies during the 1960s, such as *Cat Ballou* (1965), before becoming a production executive. Two TV movie reunion specials aired featuring the original cast: *Whatever Happened to Dobie Gillis?* (1977) and *Bring Me the Head of Dobie Gillis* (1988). The character of "Shaggy Rogers" on *Scooby-Doo* was reportedly modeled after Maynard G. Krebs, who was named No. 23 on TV Guide's "50 Greatest TV Characters of All Time" list in 2011 (between "Mary Richards" from *Mary Tyler Moore* at No. 22 and "Sgt. Andy Sipowicz" from *NYPD Blue* at No. 24).

Beatnik Exploitation Books

A variety of lurid paperbacks were published in the late 1950s and early 1960s to cash in on the beatnik craze. For example, a twenty-five-cent edition of *The Beat Generation* by Albert Zugsmith was published in conjunction with the 1959 film of the same name that starred Mamie Van Doren and Steve Cochran. It was billed as "the shocking and revealing novel of a generation gone wild based on the sensational MGM motion picture release." Zugsmith was no stranger to exploitation, having produced the film version of *The Beat Generation*, as well as such classics as *The Incredible Shrinking Man* (1957), *High School Confidential!* (1958), *The Private Lives of Adam and Eve* (1960), *Sex Kittens Go to College* (1960), *Confessions of an Opium Eater* (1962), and *The Incredible Sex Revolution* (1965), among many others.

Other examples of beatnik exploitation books include *Beatnik Wanton* by Don Elliott, which featured the tagline "She lusted in sin orgies and reefer brawls!"; *The Beatniks* by Richard E. Geis, which offered "the erotic and exotic—a lost world where naked sex flaunts its message to the sensuous beat of a dream"; and *Beatnik Party* by John Schulyer, which promised "the truth about the wild orgies of San Francisco's beat generation!" In addition, *Epitaph for a Dead Beat* by David Markson featured the tagline "She was out for kicks at a Greenwich Village tea party—so was her killer." *Sin Hipster* by Don Holliday claimed, "Life was an orgy for these passion bums!"

Some of the beatnik "literature" was actually nonfiction works such as *Beatville U.S.A.* by George Mandel ("a hilarious, opinionated and uncensored view of the Beat Generation by a noted author who saw it coming—and ducked!"); *The Cool Book* by Art Unger ("a book that swings for real!"); *Beat, Beat, Beat* by William F. Brown ("a hip collection of cool cartoons about life and love among the beatniks"); and *Beat Generation Cook-Book*, which featured the following introduction: "Most of the recipes are inexpensive (who has bread for steaks?), quick to prepare, and a gas to gobble, compiled over a period of three years spent On the Road and two years Up the Creek . . . A Loft is not a Pad without a Beat Generation Cook Book—Eat Beat! It's the way out, Man."

Rent-A-Beatnik

The entire beatnik phenomenon reached its pinnacle (or nadir, depending on your point of view) with the creation of a "Rent-A-Beatnik" service that first appeared in ads within the *Village Voice* in 1959. Rent-A-Beatnik was the brainchild of Fred W. McDarrah (1926–2007), a longtime photographer for the *Village Voice*, skilled self-promoter, and self-described "square" who placed the following (albeit tongue-in-cheek) newspaper ad: "RENT genuine BEATNIKS. Badly groomed but brilliant (male and female)." The ad suggested beatniks could be rented for "Fund Raising & Private Parties," "To Lecture at Your Club," "Model for Photographs," "Entertain or Read Poetry," and/or "Play Bongo Drums." It all started out as a joke, but when McDarrah got flooded with calls, he promptly turned Rent-A-Beatnik into a functioning business. The rental price was $40 nightly. *Mad* magazine soon countered with "Rent a SQUARE for your next Beatnik Party."

Jazz poet, trumpeter, artist, former roommate of jazz great Charlie Parker, and all-around hipster Ted Joans (1928–2003) was the highest-profile Beat writer to actually charge for his beatnik services, which involved appearing at parties, reading poetry, and playing bongo drums. During the waning days of the Rent-A-Beatnik era, Joans published a book called *The Hipsters* (1961), which was billed as "the funny, wild, hilarious and witty world of the hipsters from Greenwich Village to Paris. A mixture of Dali, Ernst and Kerouac stirred up in a surrealist stew by America's only true 'insider' and 'outsider.'"

McDarrah, who first joined the *Village Voice* in the mid-1950s and served as the newspaper's staff photographer, soon became a fixture of the Greenwich Village scene. In addition to coming up with "Rent-A-Beatnik," McDarrah was one of the foremost chroniclers of Beat activity in New York City. In fact, McDarrah took a famous image of Kerouac with arms outstretched during a public reading (*Jack Kerouac Reading Beatnik Poetry in Lower East Side Loft*, February 15, 1959).

In addition, McDarrah took one of the first portraits of Bob Dylan in 1965 (*Dylan Salutes in Sheridan Square*) and captured images of the historic Stonewall uprising in 1969. Some of McDarrah's other famous images include *Warhol with Cow Wallpaper at Castelli* (1966), *The Velvet Underground, Big Eye of Nico, April 1, 1966* (1966), *Robert Kennedy in Slum Apartment, May 8, 1967* (1967), and *Martin Scorsese, Robert De Niro, Jodie Foster Filming of Taxi Driver, July 25, 1975* (1975). McDarrah once confessed, "I was a groupie at heart . . . and my camera was my ticket to admission" (quoted in "Fred's Hungry Eye" by Helen A. Harrison, February 27, 2014). McDarrah was also the author of *The Beat Scene* (1960), *New York, NY* (1964), and *Beat Generation: Glory Days in Greenwich Village* (1996), among others.

A Bucket of Blood (1959)

"Life is an obscure hobo bumming a ride on the omnibus of art." An amusing, low-budget dark comedy/horror flick that expertly pokes fun at beatnik culture, *A Bucket of Blood* was directed by B-movie king Roger Corman, written by Charles B. Griffith, and released by American International Pictures. Reportedly shot in just five days with a budget of $35,000, the film clocks in at just 66 minutes.

Dick Miller portrays "Walter Paisley," a slightly unhinged artist wannabe who works as a busboy at the Yellow Door coffee house/art gallery, a smoky Bohemian den full of colorful characters such as the absurdly pretentious beatnik poet "Maxwell Brock" (Julian Burton), who spouts off such gems as "Creation is graham crackers . . . let it all crumble to feed the creator." After he accidentally kills his landlady's cat with a knife, covers it with clay, and passes it off as art ("Dead Cat"), Walter improbably becomes the toast of the café. He then is forced to find other "subjects" for his disturbingly realistic brand of artistic creation.

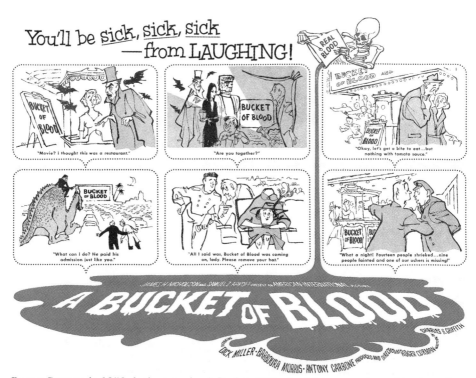

Roger Corman's 1959 dark comedy, *A Bucket of Blood*, which was released by American International Pictures and starred Dick Miller, effectively satirized beatnik culture.

Author's collection

The plot for *A Bucket of Blood* was partially based on the 1933 horror film *Mystery of the Wax Museum*, which was directed by Michael Curtiz (*Casablanca*) and starred Lionel Atwill, Fay Wray, and Glenda Farrell, as well as its 1953 remake, *House of Wax*, which starred Vincent Price. The great supporting cast for *A Bucket of Blood* included Anthony Carbone, Barboura Morris, Bert Convy, Ed Nelson, John Brinkley, and Myrtle Vail. American cellist and composer Fred Katz provided the comical jazz score, while the tagline screamed, *"You'll be sick, sick, sick—from LAUGHING!"*

In his 1998 memoir, *How I Made a Hundred Movies in Hollywood and Never Lost a Dime*, Corman remarks, "I was, as I believed at the time, virtually creating a new genre—the black-comedy horror film. Whereas I had mixed a little humor and science fiction in films like *Not of This Earth*, now I was out to create a different kind of film—more cynical, darker, more wickedly funny."

However, Miller was later quoted in *Roger Corman: Blood-Sucking Vampires, Flesh-Eating Cockroaches, and Driller Killers* (2004) by Beverly Gray Miller that "if they'd had more money to put into the production . . . this could have been a very classic little film." Miller went on to portray a character named "Walter Paisley" in six additional movies: *Hollywood Boulevard* (1976), *The Howling* (1981), *Heartbeeps* (1981), *The Twilight Zone: The Movie* (1983), *Chopping Mall* (1986), and *Shake, Rattle and Rock!* (1994). A much less successful and uninteresting remake of *A Bucket of Blood* was produced by Corman for Showtime in 1995 and starred ex–Brat Packer Anthony Michael Hall as "Walter" (also look for Will Ferrell as "Young Man" in his film debut).

Corman and Griffith also collaborated on 1960's *The Little Shop of Horrors* (which used the same sets as *A Bucket of Blood*), *Creature from the Haunted Sea* (1961), and *Death Race 2000* (1975), among other films. For the definitive guide to Corman's life and career, look no further than *Crab Monsters, Teenage Cavemen, and Candy Stripe Nurses: Roger Corman: King of the B Movie* (2013) by Chris Nashawaty. The 2014 documentary *That Guy Dick Miller* serves as a mildly entertaining profile of the legendary character actor. Directed by Elijah Drenner (*American Grindhouse*), the film features the tagline "After This Movie, You'll Know Dick."

The Nervous Set (1959)

Based on an unpublished novel by Jay Landesman, *The Nervous Set* was the first (and only!) Beat musical. It premiered on March 10, 1959, in a three-hundred-seat club called the Crystal Palace in the heart of Gaslight Square in St. Louis, Missouri. Landesman, who ran an art gallery in the Little Bohemia district of St. Louis, founded the quarterly literary magazine *Neurotica* in New York City in 1948. *Neurotica* published the early writings of Allen Ginsberg,

John Clellon Holmes, Carl Solomon (under the pseudonym "Carl Goy"), Judith Malina, and Larry Rivers. Landesman and his brother, Fred, opened the Crystal Palace in 1952. Lenny Bruce, Woody Allen, and Barbra Streisand were among the early performers at the saloon-style Crystal Palace, which was formerly a bar called Dante's Inferno.

The basis for the play, Landesman's novel focuses on his relationships with Beat icons such as Jack Kerouac, Ginsberg, and others in Greenwich Village during the late 1940s and early 1950s—particularly highlighting the "life and death" of an avant-garde literary magazine based on *Neurotica* (*Nerves* in the musical). According to Landesman, "My story was a very small canvas, an insider's view of the flotsam and jetsam of the intellectual life that I was a part of. All I had in the beginning was the opening line, 'You can't stay married if you want to make it in New York,' the title *The Nervous Set*, and a regular schedule" (www.newlinetheatre.com). One of the characters was based on eccentric *Neurotica* editor Gershon Legman.

Ted Flicker directed the musical, which featured the original cast of Don Heller, Arlene Corwin, Tom Aldredge, Del Close, Janice Meshkoff, and Barry Primus. In the spring of 1959, producer Robert Lantz saw the show and decided to bring it to Broadway. Lantz also wanted to change the show's title to *Like Tomorrow*. The New York cast included Larry Hagman (later to star in *I Dream of Jeannie* and *Dallas*), Richard Hayes, Tani Seitz, Gerald Hiken, David Sallade, Del Close, Janice Meshkoff, and Tom Aldredge. Heller, Corwin, and Primus, from St. Louis, were demoted to the chorus.

The upbeat musical numbers included "Ballad of the Sad Young Men," "Spring Can Really Hang You Up the Most," "Man, We're Beat," and "Laugh, I Thought I'd Die." One of the unused songs for the Broadway version, "Pitch for Pot," featured the controversial lyrics "I've got the finest grade of pot you've ever seen / I guarantee it'll get you high." The Broadway show met with mixed reviews, with the *New York Daily News* calling it "the most brilliant, sophisticated, witty and completely novel production of the past decade," while the *World-Telegram & Sun* referred to it as "a weird experience. Something exclusively for the beat, bop, and beret brigade." The musical lasted for just twenty-three performances on Broadway. Fran Landesman later remarked in the *Riverfront Times* (2004), "It turned out that the New Yorkers were much squarer than the people of St. Louis."

Mad Magazine Beat Satire Issue (1960)

The true indication that the beatnik craze had gone mainstream was in September 1960 when *Mad* magazine got in on the act, publishing the satiric "Beatnik: The Magazine for Hipsters." The special issue featured an introduction announcing, "There have been many magazine articles written about the Beat Generation in an attempt to defend the movement. Now MAD presents its version of a magazine written *by* the Beat Generation which really *defends* the movement . . . the movement to *abolish* it!"

Billed as "All the Jazz that's Cool to Print," "Beatnik" promised articles on "How to Get High on Espresso," "What to Do If the Landlord Shows Up," and "The Night We Slept Twelve in a Bed." Other features included "The Inquiring Hipster," which quoted "Free-Lance Philosopher" Sidney Sfortz stating, "I became a Beatnik because I hadda get out of the 'rat-race', Man! I mean, I got fed up with the way things are these days . . . with everybody running around, trying to out-do everybody else. Like, a 'competitive society' is a drag! You dig me?" "Beatnik" also featured satiric advertisements such as "Oversize Sweaters for Beatnik Chicks" and "Rent a SQUARE for your Next Beatnik Party."

Founded by William Gaines and Harvey Kurtzman in August 1952, *Mad* began as a comic book published by EC Comics. After *Mad* converted to magazine form in 1955 and soon hired a new editor, Al Feldstein, the magazine's creative staff added a slew of legendary artists such as Dave Berg, Antonio Prohias, Frank Jacobs, Mort Drucker, and Don Martin. With its groundbreaking parodies and gap-toothed mascot, Alfred E. Neuman ("What, me worry?"), *Mad* skewered everything sacred in mainstream culture.

Beatnik Cartoon Characters

The beatnik phenomenon was so pervasive that it even infiltrated the world of cartoons, such as the Looney Tunes character Cool Cat, who wore a beret, spoke in beatnik slang, and was voiced by Larry Storch ("Corporal Randolph Agarn" from the TV show *F Troop*). Created by Bob Clampett, the *Beany and Cecil* cartoon series featured the beatnik "wild man" Go Man Van Gogh, who lived in the jungles of Wildsville and played the bongo drums. He was originally voiced by Lord Buckley in 1959's "The Wildman of Wildsville," followed by Scatman Crothers (who later voiced the cartoon character Hong Kong Phooey).

Hanna-Barbera's *Top Cat* featured a beatnik character voiced by Leo De Lyon named Spook—"The Original Hep Cat." A pool shark and skilled poker player with green fur, Spook hung out with T. C., Benny the Ball, Choo-Cho, Brain, and Fancy-Fancy, much to the chagrin of Officer Dibble. Spook had a tendency to use the word "like" before every sentence. In addition, the beatnik Banty Rooster appeared in the classic 1963 Warner Brothers/Merry Melodies Foghorn Leghorn short *Banty Raids* with a beret, sunglasses, and a guitar, while spouting off lines such as "Man, you're the sickest" and "I dig you, daddy-o!"

Last but certainly not least, Shaggy Rogers (voiced by disc jockey Casey Kasem for many years) in *Scooby-Doo* was part beatnik (the character was reportedly inspired by Maynard G. Krebs in *The Many Loves of Dobie Gillis*) and part hippie with his slovenly appearance, goatee, wild hair, slacker attitude, and trademark exclamations such as "Zoinks!"

17

Only the Most Bitter

Notorious Beat Generation Critics

n general, the academic community of the 1950s derided the Beats as unrefined and anti-intellectual. Critics of Jack Kerouac called him a "know-nothing Bohemian," "the latrine laureate of Hobohemia," and "a slob running a temperature." Truman Capote famously stated, "That isn't writing at all; it's typing," in reference to *On the Road*. Dame Edith Sitwell denounced *Naked Lunch* as "psychopathological filth." Former President Herbert Hoover, speaking at the 1960 GOP convention in Chicago, jumped in on the act, blaming the "communist front, and the beatniks and the eggheads" for destroying the social fabric of the nation.

Life Magazine

When it came to its opinion of the Beat Generation during the late 1950s, *Life* magazine clearly represented a mainstream, if not totally reactionary, viewpoint, the basic gist of which was that the Beats were a threat to the American way of life. Most telling, *Life* focused primarily on the negative aspects of the Beat lifestyle while paying scant attention to their actual literary output. For example, in September 1959, *Life* published a condescending article aimed at the Beat Generation titled "Squaresville vs. Beatsville," which highlighted the story of three teenagers from Hutchinson, Kansas, who invited a beatnik in Venice, California, to their small town, which caused a major uproar.

In another scathing article, "Sad but Noisy Rebels" (subtitled "The Only Rebellion Around"), published just two months after "Squaresville vs. Beatsville" (November 30, 1959), *Life* staff writer Paul O'Neill described the Beat individual as someone who "finds society too hideous to contemplate and so withdraws from it." However, "he does not go quietly," according to O'Neill, "nor so far that his voice is inaudible, and his route of retreat is littered with old beer cans and marijuana butts." O'Neill also described the Beats as "some of the hairiest, scrawniest and most discontented specimens of all time: the improbable rebels of the Beat Generation, who not only refuse to sample the seeping juices of American plenty and American social advance but scrape their feelers in discordant scorn of any and all who do."

O'Neill's article reserved special scorn for William S. Burroughs, whom he described as "a pale, cadaverous and bespectacled being who has devoted most of his adult life to a lonely pursuit of drugs and debauchery [and] has rubbed shoulders with the dregs of a half-dozen races." Burroughs's mother read the account of her son in *Life* and wrote him a letter reportedly stating how horrified she was with his lifestyle based on the contents of the article.

In order to calm the waters, Burroughs sent a letter to his mother (ca. December 1959): "Yes I have read the article in Life and after all . . . a bit silly perhaps . . . but it is a mass medium . . . and sensational factors must be played up at the expense often of fact . . . I hope I am not ludicrously miscast as The Wickedest Man Alive, a title vacated by the late Aleister Crowley . . . And remember the others who have held the title before . . . Byron Baudelaire Poe people are very glad to claim kinship now . . . But really anyone in the public eye that is anyone who enjoys any measure of success in his field is open to sensational publicity."

Herbert Gold

Even though prolific novelist Herbert Gold cultivated a lifelong friendship with Allen Ginsberg (they met as students at Columbia University in the 1940s), he was no fan of the Beat Generation, particularly Jack Kerouac. In fact, he once remarked, "When you take dehydrated Hipster and add watery words to make Instant Beatnik, the flavor is gone but the lack of taste lingers on."

Reviewing *On the Road* for the *Nation* on November 16, 1957, Gold wrote, "Where Thomas Wolfe broke his head butting against the world of intellectual highlife, Jack Kerouac is butting but unbroken against the world of hipsters . . . Despite its drag race of words and gestures, *On the Road* does nothing, thinks nothing, acts nothing, but yet manages to be a book after all—a loving portrait of Dean Moriarty and his beat, cool friends as they run a hundred and ten miles an hour in order to stand still. It's a frantic book, and for that reason there is hope for Jack Kerouac."

Gold referred to Kerouac as a "bullshitter" and would frequently call him out on his anti-Semitism and reactionary viewpoints, although he did give Kerouac a favorable review for his 1962 novel, *Big Sur*. In a 2008 *Jewish Journal* interview, Gold remarked about Kerouac, "I crossed the street to avoid him." In his November 25, 1962, review of William S. Burroughs's *Naked Lunch* for the *New York Times*, Gold stated that the book was "less a novel than a series of essays, puns, epigrams—all hovering about the explicit subject matter of making out on drugs while not making out in either work or love." In his 1993 book, *Bohemia: Digging the Roots of Cool*, Gold described Gregory Corso as an "orphan street kid adopted by the Beats . . . Most of the Beats were middle-aged college kids, but Corso came out of real poverty. That made him different."

Gold was born on March 9, 1924, in Cleveland, Ohio, to Russian Jewish immigrants and published his first novel, *Birth of a Hero*, in 1951. His works include *The Prospect Before Us* (1954), *The Optimist* (1959), *Therefore Be Bold* (1960), *The Great American Jackpot* (1969), *Slave Trade* (1979), and *True Love* (1982), among others. In 2008, he published a memoir titled *Still Alive!: A Temporary Condition*.

Diana Trilling

Although cultural and social critic Diana Trilling (1905–96) was married to literary critic, author, and teacher Lionel Trilling, Allen Ginsberg's mentor at Columbia University, she did not have many kind words for the Beat Generation. For example, she wondered why her husband always bailed Ginsberg out whenever he got into trouble, such as the time he scrawled an obscenity on a dusty dormitory window, and also referred disparagingly to the "infantile camaraderie" of Jack Kerouac's *On the Road*. Ginsberg kept in touch with Lionel Trilling but was devastated when he sent him a copy of *Howl and Other Poems* and his former mentor wrote back that he thought the poem was "dull."

After attending a poetry reading by Ginsberg at Columbia in 1959, Diana Trilling wrote a sarcastic review called "The Other Night at Columbia: A Report from the Academy" in which she commented, "It is no accident that today in the fifties our single overt manifestation of protest takes the wholly nonpolitical form of a group of panic-stricken kids in blue jeans, many of them publicly homosexual, talking about or taking drugs, assuring us that they are out of their minds, not responsible . . . Is it any wonder, then, that *Time* and *Life* write as they do about the 'beats'—with such a conspicuous show of superiority, and no hint of fear? These periodicals know what genuine, dangerous protest looks like, and it doesn't look like Ginsberg and Kerouac. Clearly, there is no more menace in 'Howl' or *On the Road* than there is in the Scarsdale PTA."

It was said that, as a critic for the *Nation*, Diana Trilling read a novel a day for six-and-a-half years. Both of the Trillings were members of the New York Intellectuals, a group of writers and literary critics that included Dwight Macdonald, Irving Howe, Hannah Arendt, Saul Bellow, Richard Hofstadter, Paul Goodman, Alfred Kazin, Mary McCarthy, Irving Kristol, Harold Rosenberg, Delmore Schwartz, and Norman Podhoretz (another notorious Beat critic!), among others.

Charles Bukowski

Charles Bukowski occasionally gets lumped in with Beat Generation writers, but "Hank" was a true loner, an outsider all the way, and vehemently rejected labels of any kind. Asked in a 1975 interview if he felt "akin at all to the Beat Generation writers," Bukowski responded, "Oh no . . . I find a certain type of phoniness about them . . . I don't like the whole gang of them. They gathered together and they'd do this and they'd do that, but I guess the artists have done that for a long time. Just gather and read some poems and all that; but this has always irritated me. I like a man who makes it on his own, without having to join, sitting around . . . I stopped writing for ten years and just got drunk. While the Beats were beating, I was drinking."

In a 1962 letter to Jon Webb (reprinted in *Screams from the Balcony*, Black Sparrow Press, 1993), Charles Bukowski wrote, "Now, the original Beats, as much as they were knocked, had the Idea. But they were flanked and over-whelmed by fakes, guys with nicely clipped beards, lonely-hearts looking for free ass, limelighters, rhyming poets, homosexuals, bums, sightseers—the same thing that killed the Village. Art can't operate in Crowds. Art does not belong at parties, nor does it belong at Inauguration Speeches."

However, Bukowski did have a beer with Neal Cassady just weeks before the hero of *On the Road* died in Mexico of a suspected drug overdose in 1968. The two writers shared an obsession with horse racing. Bukowski wrote a very memorable article about the brief encounter in *Notes of a Dirty Old Man*: "I met Kerouac's boy Neal C. shortly before he went down to lay along those Mexican railroad tracks to die." According to Bukowski, "You liked [Cassady] even though you didn't want to because Kerouac had set him up for the sucker punch and Neal had bit, kept biting, but you know Neal was o.k. and another way of looking at it, Jack had only

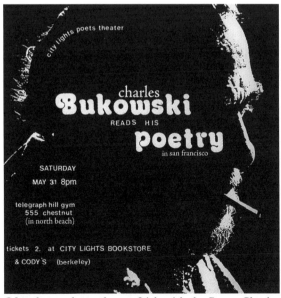

Often lumped together unfairly with the Beats, Charles Bukowski was a true outsider who disliked what he saw as the "phoniness" of many of the Beat writers.

Author's collection

written the book, he wasn't Neal's mother. just his destructor, deliberate or otherwise."

In a 1967 interview, Bukowski remarked, "This is where the Dylans and the Ginsbergs and the Beatles fail—they spend so much time talking about living that they don't have time to live." Bukowski once confronted Allen Ginsberg at a poetry reading in the early 1970s and told him, "Everybody knows that after 'Howl' you never wrote anything worth a shit." In his 1989 novel, *Hollywood*, a thinly disguised depiction of the making of the film *Barfly* (1987), Bukowski refers to Jack Kerouac as "Mack Derouac"—"a writer who couldn't write but who got famous because he looked like a rodeo rider."

Several Beat writers admitted their fondness for Bukowski's down-to-earth, gritty poetry style. For example, Kenneth Rexroth wrote a review of Bukowski's *It Catches My Heart in Its Hands* for the *New York Times* (July 5, 1964): "No Establishment is likely ever to recruit Bukowski . . . He belongs in the small company of poets of real, not literary, alienation, that includes Herman Spector, Kenneth Fearing, Kenneth Patchen and a large number of Bohemian fugitives unknown to fame. His special virtue is that he is so much less sentimental than most of his colleagues. Yet there is nothing outrageous about his poetry. It is simple, casual, honest, uncooked." In addition, Gary Snyder, in *The Real Work*, remarks, "I love Charles's poems. Bukowski is a big animal . . . on the toilet. I love Charles's poems. He manifests a kind of human biology right there. You know, eating, drinking, farting. What could be more natural?"

In his 1978 novel, *Women*, Bukowski describes going to a poetry reading and staying at the same hotel as Burroughs. They did not meet. Bukowski walked by Burroughs room and noticed the writer sitting in a chair by the window, looking at him indifferently. According to Bukowski, "When we left Burroughs was sitting in his chair by the window. He gave no indication of having seen me."

James Dickey

Although James Dickey (1923–97) is remembered in academic circles as one of the greatest poets of his generation (he received the prestigious National Book Award in 1966 for his collection of poetry *Buckdancer's Choice*), his fame today rests almost entirely on his poetic novel, *Deliverance*, published in 1970, which was made into a critically acclaimed film in 1972. Dickey himself had a small role in the film as the cynical "Sheriff Bullard."

However, Dickey was no fan of the Beat Generation, particularly Allen Ginsberg's poetry, which he detested passionately. In a 1976 *Paris Review* interview, Dickey remarked, "I think Ginsberg has done more harm to the craft that I honor and live by than anybody else by reducing it to a kind of mean that enables the most dubious practitioners to claim that they are poets because they think, If the kind of thing Ginsberg does is poetry, I can do that. They damn themselves to a life of inconsequentiality when they could have been doing something more useful. They could have been garbage collectors, or grocery-store managers." In addition, Dickey, in his 1971 book, *Babel to Byzantium: Poets and Poetry Now*, declared poet Robert Duncan "unpityingly pretentious."

As his reputation grew, Dickey started to live out the myth of the hard-drinking, foul-mouthed, womanizing poet—an attitude that only intensified after the astronomical success of *Deliverance*, which was his first novel. Only Erich Segal's melodramatic *Love Story* kept *Deliverance* from reaching No. 1 on the bestseller list. Dickey had his own share of critics, however. For instance, fellow poet Robert Bly in his essay "The Collapse of James Dickey" (*The Sixties*, Winter 1964) called Dickey a "huge blubbery poet, pulling out Southern language in long strings, like taffy . . . a sort of Georgia cracker Kipling." In his revealing 1998 memoir, *Summer of Deliverance*, Dickey's son, Christopher, stated: "My father was a great poet, a powerful intellect and a son of a bitch I hated."

After his first wife, Maxine, died in 1976, Dickey waited just two months before marrying Deborah Dodson, one of his students at the University of South Carolina. Indeed, the quality of Dickey's work declined substantially after the early 1970s. "I blamed *Deliverance* for what happened to my father and our family," said Christopher Dickey in *Summer of Deliverance*. "It seemed to me then and for a long time afterward that forces of self-indulgence and self-destruction, which were always there in my father but held in check, were now cut loose." Dickey died at the age of seventy-three in 1997 and is buried in the All Saints Waccamaw Episcopal Church cemetery on Pawley's Island, South Carolina.

Truman Capote

Appearing on David Susskind's TV show *Open End* in 1959, Truman Capote famously stated, "That isn't writing at all; it's typing" in reference to Jack Kerouac's *On the Road*. He went on to elaborate that "none of [the Beat writers] have anything interesting to say." Kerouac and Capote finally met face-to-face in a Manhattan TV studio nearly a decade later in the late 1960s (Kerouac was in town to appear on William F. Buckley's *Firing Line* TV show). "Hello, you queer bastard," Kerouac reportedly said, shaking Capote's hand. "You've been saying bad things about me, but I have nothing against you."

Capote was also critical of the work of William S. Burroughs, once remarking that the *Naked Lunch* author didn't have an ounce of talent. In 1970,

Burroughs fired off a scathing letter to Capote, writing, "I have in line of duty read all your published work. The early work was in some respects promising—I refer particularly to the short stories. You were granted an area for psychic development. It seemed for a while as if you would make good use of this grant. You choose instead to sell out a talent that *is not yours to sell* . . . You will never write another sentence above the level of *In Cold Blood.*"

Capote (real name: Truman Streckfus Persons) grew up in Monroeville, Alabama, and was a childhood friend of author Harper Lee, who reportedly based the character of "Dill" in her 1960 novel, *To Kill a Mockingbird*, on Capote. In 1948, Capote's debut novel, *Other Voices, Other Rooms*, was published when the author was just twenty-three years old. His popular novella, *Breakfast at Tiffany's*, was published in 1958 and became an award-winning film in 1961 starring Aubrey Hepburn. However, Capote's talents peaked (as predicted by Burroughs!) upon publication of his 1965 "nonfiction novel," *In Cold Blood*, based on the notorious 1959 murder of a Kansas farm family that was turned into a critically acclaimed film starring Robert Blake in 1967.

Never at a loss for words, Capote once remarked, "I had to be successful, and I had to be successful early . . . I was a very special person, and I had to have a very special life. I was not meant to work in an office or something, though I would have been successful at whatever I did. But I always knew that I wanted to be a writer and that I wanted to be rich and famous" (*New York Times*, August 28, 1984).

Capote had his share of critics as well and carried on a longstanding feud with several writers, including Gore Vidal, who called him "a full-fledged housewife from Kansas with all the prejudices." On hearing of Capote's death from liver cancer in 1984 just a month shy of his sixtieth birthday, Vidal simply responded, "Good career move."

Jack Spicer

Although he was a fixture on the San Francisco poetry scene, Jack Spicer despised the Beat Generation (as well as any other movement or school for that matter!). According to author Bill Morgan in the *Beat Atlas* (2011), "Spicer loathed the idea of the Beat Generation so much that he refused to allow Lawrence Ferlinghetti to sell his books at City Lights." Poet David Meltzer stated that Spicer "had it in for City Lights and had it in for Beat anything. He thought it was preposterous." Born John Lester Spicer in Los Angeles, California, on January 30, 1925, Spicer, along with fellow poets Robin Blaser and Robert Duncan, formed the so-called "Berkeley Renaissance." He was also a cofounder of the Six Gallery in 1954 and served as emcee for a Dadaist-style poetry event called "Blabbermouth Night" at the Place, a bohemian hangout on Grant Street in North Beach.

Lew Welch once remarked, "The only person I ever met that reminded me of Charles Parker was Jack Spicer. They were the same man. They were just hell-bent on self-destruction. They were both six feet plus and heavy. They were big and strong." Spicer, who had a history of depression and alcoholism, died in the poverty ward of San Francisco General Hospital in 1965. In 2009, *My Vocabulary Did This to Me: The Collected Poetry of Jack Spicer*, won the American Book Award for Poetry.

Norman Podhoretz

Arguably the most notorious Beat critic of them all, Norman Podhoretz wrote an infamous article titled "The Know Nothing Bohemians" in the Spring 1958 *Partisan Review* in which he proclaimed that "the Bohemianism of the 1950s is hostile to civilization; it worships primitivism, instinct, energy, 'blood.'" In response to Podhoretz's devastating critique of the Beat Generation, poet LeRoi Jones wrote a letter to the editor of *Partisan Review* that appeared in the Summer 1958 issue: "Violence is just fine. I don't mean that someone ought to walk up to Mr. Podhoretz and smack him down, but that this generation of writers must resort to violence in literature, a kind of violence that has in such as short time begun to shake us out of the woeful literary sterility which characterized the '40s."

Interestingly, Podhoretz had actually been an acquaintance of Allen Ginsberg when they were both undergraduates at Columbia University in 1943. Podhoretz had submitted a poem about the prophet Jeremiah to the college literary magazine of which Ginsberg was the editor, and he had accepted it for publication. Podhoretz served as editor-in-chief of *Commentary* for thirty-five years until he retired in 1995 to devote himself mainly to writing. In 1998, Podhoretz published *Ex-Friends: Falling Out with Allen Ginsberg, Lionel and Diana Trilling, Lillian Hellman, Hannah Arendt, and Norman Mailer*, with the first chapter titled "At War with Allen Ginsberg." In *Ex-Friends*, Podhoretz outlined his commitment to challenging the left: "I shouldered the burden of challenging the regnant leftist culture that pollutes the spiritual and cultural air we breathe, and to do so with all my heart and all my soul and all my might."

According to Podhoretz in *Ex-Friends*, Ginsberg at Columbia had unfortunately "[fallen] in with an assortment of hustlers, junkies, and other shady or disreputable characters who were always getting themselves and him into trouble." Although Podhoretz lost touch with Ginsberg, he was surprised to receive an advance copy of *Howl and Other Poems* from the poet in 1956.

John Updike

Best known for his "Rabbit" series of novels starting with *Rabbit, Run* (1960), author John Updike (1932–2009) disdained the works of the Beat Generation but held special contempt for Jack Kerouac, especially in his early years. "On the Sidewalk," a satire Updike wrote after reading *On the Road*, appeared in the February 21, 1959, issue of the *New Yorker*. In "On the Sidewalk," a little boy named Lee and his friend Gogi take an adventure around the neighborhood (Lee on his tricycle and Gogi on his scooter). Gogi ditches Lee for a pretty girl and leaves him stranded on the corner. Lee isn't allowed to cross the street until he grows up but says to himself: "But what do they mean grown up? I'm thirty-nine now."

Updike once claimed that he wrote *Rabbit, Run* in response to *On the Road* in order to depict "what happens when a young American family man goes on the road—the people left behind get hurt." In a 1967 *Paris Review* interview, Updike commented sarcastically, "Somebody like Kerouac who writes on teletype paper as rapidly as he can once slightly alarmed me. Now I can look upon this more kindly. There may be some reason to question the whole idea of fineness and care in writing. Maybe something can get into sloppy writing that would elude careful writing."

Author and historian Douglas Brinkley fired back at Updike in his 1993 book, *The Majic Bus: An American Odyssey*, calling *Rabbit at Rest* a "classic American downer . . . an anti–*On the Road* . . . Updike fancies he has put his finger on our national pulse in his Rabbit quartet. Our problem, he says, is that Americans don't know the word enough, which is probably true, but to my mind this disregard of limits is the core of our national genius."

Hunter S. Thompson

Legendary gonzo journalist Hunter S. Thompson (1937–2005), who wrote *Fear and Loathing in Las Vegas: A Savage Journey to the Heart of the American Dream* (1971), had a love-hate relationship with the Beats. For example, Thompson once wrote a letter to a friend, deriding the works of Jack Kerouac: "Certainly I've read [*The Subterraneans*] . . . all his crap for that matter. The man is an ass, a mystic boob with intellectual myopia. The *Dharma* thing was not quite as bad as *The Subterraneans* and they're both withered appendages to *On the Road*—which isn't even a novel in the first place." In a 1962 letter to Paul Semonin, Thompson wrote, "I have tonight begun reading a shitty, shitty book by Kerouac called *Big Sur*."

Douglas Brinkley, who served as Thompson's literary executor and edited his letters, stated that Thompson "told me he thought Kerouac was a genius for two things: discovering Neal Cassady, whom Hunter thought was flat-out amazing, and using the literary construct of 'looking for the lost dad I never had.'" Thompson also shared a love of guns with Burroughs, and they spent time on a shooting range together on at least one occasion. Thompson claimed that Burroughs "shot like he wrote—with extreme precision and no fear."

In addition, Thompson and Allen Ginsberg shared a mutual respect for each other. In a 1968 letter to William J. Kennedy, Thompson called Ginsberg "one of the few honest people I've ever met, for good or ill." Thompson even wrote an offbeat eulogy for Ginsberg's memorial service that was read by Johnny Depp that described the poet as "a dangerous bull-fruit with the brain of an open sore and the conscience of a virus . . . crazy, queer, and small."

Although Hunter S. Thompson and Allen Ginsberg shared a mutual respect for one another, the legendary gonzo journalist once called Jack Kerouac "an ass, a mystic boob with intellectual myopia." *Photo by Michael Ochs Archives/Getty Images*

18

The Mad Ones

Other Key Figures in the Beat Generation

A variety of eclectic personalities orbited in the Beat circle at various times and made solid contributions to the literary movement, such as Brion Gysin, who introduced the cut-up technique to William S. Burroughs at the "Beat Hotel" in Paris during the late 1950s. Other key figures include Bill Cannastra, the "wild man" of the early Beat scene in New York City who died in a freak subway accident; Tuli Kupferberg, poet, anarchist, and cofounder of the influential 1960s rock band the Fugs; Robert Frank, award-winning photographer and filmmaker who directed the landmark Beat short film *Pull My Daisy* (1959); Carl Solomon, who befriended Allen Ginsberg at a psychiatric hospital in the late 1940s and helped get Burroughs's first book, *Junkie*, published (through his uncle A. A. Wyn, the founder of Ace Books); influential jazz poet Ted Joans; outlaw poet Jack Micheline; Peter Orlovsky, longtime companion of Ginsberg and a poet in his own right; Amiri Baraka, acclaimed and highly controversial writer and critic; and jazz poet (and ex-con) Ray Bremser.

Brion Gysin (1916–86)

A true Renaissance man, Brion Gysin wore many hats during his eclectic life and career, such as artist, writer, calligrapher, entrepreneur, world traveler, and mystic. In a 1997 interview with the *Guardian*, William S. Burroughs praised Gysin as "the only man that I've respected in my life. I've admired people, I've liked them, but he's the only man I've ever respected."

John Clifford Brian Gysin was born on January 19, 1916, at Taplow House, England, a Canadian military hospital, to Stella Margaret Martina and Leonard Gysin, a captain in the Canadian Expeditionary Force who was killed in action during World War I, just eight months after his son was born. Gysin grew up with his mother in Edmonton, Alberta. In 1934, Gysin moved to Paris to study art and soon joined the Surrealist Group. However, the day before he was supposed to have his first exhibition at the Galerie Quatre Chemins in Paris, nineteen-year-old Gysin was expelled from the group for no apparent reason by Andre Breton, who ordered the poet Paul Éluard to remove all of his paintings.

Gysin moved to Tangier, Morocco, in 1950. Between 1954 and 1958, he operated a restaurant/nightclub in Tangier called the 1001 Nights with his friend Mohamed Hamri. In Tangier, Gysin met Burroughs through mutual friend Paul Bowles. In 1959, Gysin returned to Paris and moved into the legendary "Beat Hotel" at 9 rue Git-le-Coeur, basically a flophouse where other artists and writers resided, such as Burroughs, Gregory Corso, and Allen Ginsberg. It was here that Gysin discovered the cut-up technique by accident: "While cutting a mount for a drawing in room No. 15, I sliced through a pile of newspapers with my Stanley blade and thought of what I had said to Burroughs some six months earlier about the necessity of turning painters' techniques directly into writing. I picked up the raw words and began to piece together texts that later appeared as 'First Cut-Ups' in *Minutes to Go*" (*A William Burroughs Reader*, 1982).

Burroughs soon latched onto Gysin's discovery and became a leading proponent of the cut-up technique as evidenced in his Nova Trilogy, which consisted of *The Soft Machine* (1961), *The Ticket That Exploded* (1962), and *Nova Express* (1964). Burroughs and Gysin collaborated on *The Third Mind* (1978), which served to showcase the cut-up technique. In his essay "It Belongs to the Cucumbers" (*The Adding Machine*, 1986), Burroughs remarks, "In 1959 Brion Gysin said 'Writing is fifty years behind painting' and applied the montage technique to words on a page. These cut-up experiments appeared in *Minutes to Go*, in 1959. Subsequently we cut up the Bible, Shakespeare, Rimbaud, our own writing, anything in sight. We made thousands of cut-ups. When you cut and rearrange words on a page, new words emerge. And words change meaning."

With electronic technician Ian Sommerville, Gysin built the Dreamachine in 1961—"the first art object to be seen with the eyes closed." According to Gysin, the Dreamachine "gives an extended vision of one's own interior capacities." Gysin's critically acclaimed novel, *The Process*, was published in 1969. Critic Robert Palmer called the book "a classic of 20th century modernism." Gysin died of lung cancer at the age of seventy on July 13, 1986. Throughout his life, Gysin held true to his philosophy: "I enjoy inventing things out of fun. After all, life is a game, not a career" (*Brion Gysin: Tuning In to the Multimedia Age*, 2003).

Bill Cannastra (1922–50)

Once described by Jack Kerouac as "the fabulous mad star," William "Bill" Cannastra was a member of the early Beat scene in New York City known for hosting legendary all-night parties in his Chelsea loft (125 West Twenty-First Street, now a Sherwin-Williams paint store). Cannastra, who came from a wealthy family and graduated from Harvard Law School, lived with Joan Haverty, who would (briefly) become Kerouac's second wife in 1952. Tragically, Cannastra was killed at the age of twenty-eight on October 12, 1950, after reportedly trying to climb out the window of a subway train just as it was pulling out of the station (reportedly at the Bleecker Street stop) during a drunken stunt and getting decapitated. According to John Clellon Holmes, the girl Cannastra was with claimed that he told her, "I'm going to go get a drink."

Cannastra was fictionalized as "Agatson" in Holmes's novel *Go* and as "Finistra" in Kerouac's *Visions of Cody*. Allen Ginsberg also described him in "Howl" as the guy who "fell out of the subway window" and "danced on broken wineglasses barefoot." In a 1974 interview, Holmes described Cannastra as a "self-destructive," embittered alcoholic who gave "raunchy" parties that went on for days. According to Holmes, "Cannastra would do anything: humiliate people, usually himself first, you know, take off all his clothes and fart, scream and yell. He seemed to be somebody playing on the edge." In *Go*, Holmes has a disheveled "Agatson" bursting into a party and shouting, "Is everyone drunk here?" In addition to "Howl," several poems have memorialized Cannastra over the years, such as Alan Ansen's "Dead Drunk: In Memoriam William Cannastra, 1924–1950" (*Partisan Review*, 1959), Ginsberg's "In Memoriam: William Cannastra, 1922–1950," and Robert Creeley's "N. Truro Light—1946."

Tuli Kupferberg (1923–2010)

Cofounder of the influential 1960s band the Fugs, a "literary folk-rock group," Naphtali "Tuli" Kupferberg was a Beat poet, author, satirist, songwriter, and publisher. Kupferberg graduated from Brooklyn College in 1944 and got a job as a medical librarian. In 1944, a despondent Kupferberg tried to commit suicide by jumping off the Manhattan Bridge. After getting picked up by a passing tugboat, Kupferberg was taken to Gouverneur Hospital and treated for severe injuries to his spine. In the prose poem "Memorial Day 1971," written by Ted Berrigan and Anne Waldman, a fictional "Kupferberg" (he later denied that the exchange ever took place) describes the incident as "nothing happened. I landed in the water, & I wasn't dead. So I swam ashore,

& went home, & took a bath, & went to bed. Nobody even noticed." Kupferberg appeared in Allen Ginsberg's "Howl" as the individual "who jumped off the Brooklyn Bridge" and "walked away unknown and forgotten" into the "ghostly daze of Chinatown."

In 1958, Kupferberg founded *Birth* magazine, which ran for only three issues but published the works of Allen Ginsberg, Diane di Prima, LeRoi Jones, and Ted Joans. In 1961, Kupferberg self-published the book *Beatniks; or, The War Against the Beats.* Other popular works followed, such as *1001 Ways to Live Without Working* (1961) and *1001 Ways to Beat the Draft* (1966). Kupferberg founded the absurdist, antiwar rock group the Fugs with poet Ed Sanders in 1964. Just as irreverent as Kupferberg, Sanders was the owner of the Peace Eye Bookstore, a former kosher meat store on East Tenth Street in Manhattan, and had begun *Fuck You: A Magazine of the Arts* in 1962 with the motto "I'll print anything." The band also included Ken Weaver, who would later write *Texas Crude* (1983), a collection of Texan slang that featured illustrations by R. Crumb. Already in his forties at

Cofounded by poets Tuli Kupferberg and Ed Sanders (along with drummer Ken Weaver), the underground band known as the Fugs played a critical role in the anti-war movement of the 1960s and released several eclectic albums, including *It Crawled into My Hand, Honest* (1968), which featured such gems as "Marijuana," "Johnny Pissoff Meets the Red Angel," and "Whimpers from the Jello." *Author's collection*

the time, Kupferberg described himself as "The world's oldest rock star." According to Kupferberg in a June 1997 interview with *Perfect Sound Forever*, "Our goal was to make the revolution. That would have been a complete revolution, not just an economic or political one. We had utopian ideals and those are the best ideals."

Acknowledged by *Village Voice* critic Robert Christgau as "the Lower East Side's first true underground band," the Fugs took their name from Norman Mailer's censored word for "fuck" in his 1948 novel, *The Naked and the Dead.* The group released its first album, *The Village Fugs Sing Ballads of Contemporary*

Protest, Points of View and General Dissatisfaction, in 1965. Kupferberg wrote many of the band's most memorable songs, such as "Morning, Morning," "Kill for Peace," "CIA Man," and others. The Fugs appeared at numerous antiwar rallies, including the legendary "exorcism" of the Pentagon in 1967.

The Fugs broke up in 1969 but reunited in 1984 for several concerts, and periodically reunited over the years. In 2003, the group released *The Fugs Final CD (Part 1)*, followed by *Be Free: The Fugs Final CD (Part 2)*. In addition, Kupferberg released two solo albums: *No Deposit, No Return* (1966) and *Tuli & Friends* (1989). Kupferberg remained a nonconformist throughout his life. In one of his last interviews (*Mojo* magazine, 2008), Kupferberg remarked, "Nobody who lived through the '50s thought the '60s could've existed. So there's always hope." Kupferberg died of kidney failure and sepsis in 2010 at the age of eighty-six.

Robert Frank (1924–)

New York Times film critic Manohla Dargis has called Robert Frank "one of the most important and influential American independent filmmakers of the last half-century." Born in Zurich, Switzerland, on November 9, 1924, Frank immigrated to the United States in 1947, settled in New York City, and worked as a fashion photographer for several magazines, including *Harper's Bazaar*, before moving to freelance journalism. After receiving a Guggenheim Fellowship in 1955, Frank embarked on a two-year trip across the country and took more than twenty-eight thousand photographs, eighty-three of which were published in his seminal (and at the time highly controversial) photography book, *The Americans*, which was published in 1958 and featured an introduction by Jack Kerouac. Frank had met Kerouac at a party in New York City and showed him the photos. Kerouac was impressed and remarked, "Sure I can write something about these pictures."

According to Kerouac in the introduction, Frank's "tremendous photographs" captured "THAT CRAZY FEELING IN AMERICA when the sun is hot on the streets and music comes out of the jukebox or from a nearby funeral" and "with the agility, mystery, genius, sadness and strange secrecy of a shadow photographed scenes that have never been seen before on film." Kerouac also foreshadowed the still unpublished *On the Road* with the line "Madroad driving men ahead—the mad road, lonely, leading around the bend into the openings of space towards the horizon Wasatch snows promised us in the vision of the west." Kerouac concluded that Frank "sucked a sad poem right out of America onto film, taking rank among the tragic poets of the world."

In addition, Kerouac called attention to one of the images that featured a "little ole lonely elevator girl" and asked, "What's her name & address?"

In 2009, NPR interviewed the "elevator girl," Sharon Collins, who remarked that Kerouac "saw in me something that most people don't see. I have a big smile and a big laugh, and I'm usually pretty funny. So people see one thing in me. And I suspect Robert Frank and Jack Kerouac saw something that was deeper. That only people who were really close to me can see. It's not necessarily loneliness, it's . . . dreaminess."

During his odyssey across the country, Frank tried to be as unobtrusive as possible, taking photos of unsuspecting subjects but often placing himself in precarious situations. As a foreign-looking individual with an accent taking photos during the height of the Cold War, Frank definitely stuck out, especially in the South, where he was actually jailed briefly in Arkansas for being a suspicious character.

The striking images captured by Frank reveal Americans who were living a world away from post–World War II prosperity, with greasy diners, jukeboxes, wide open desolate spaces, park benches, lonely stretches of endless highway, barber shops, drive-ins, tenement houses, crosses on the sides of roads, TV sets, extremes of wealth and poverty, faces of desperation and loneliness, homelessness, cars, and American flags flying everywhere. Frank admitted that he "always had a cold eye" and "saw things realistically . . . But, it's also easier to show the darkness than the joy of life. Life is not beautiful all the time. Life can be good, then you lie down, and stare up at the ceiling, and the sadness falls on you. Things move on, time passes, people go away, and sometimes they don't come back" (*Guardian*, October 20, 2004). In fact, the book was generally not well received by the corporate media, with established publications such as *Popular Photography* referring to it as "a sad poem for sick people."

In 1959, Frank turned to filmmaking when he codirected the landmark short film *Pull My Daisy* with American artist and filmmaker Alfred Leslie. A critically acclaimed short film, *Pull My Daisy* boasted a Beat cast of Allen Ginsberg, Gregory Corso, and Peter Orlovsky, along with narration by Kerouac. The film has an overall improvisational feel in the spontaneous style of the Beats, although it was later revealed by Leslie to be carefully scripted and rehearsed.

Frank's first feature-length film, *Me and My Brother* (1965–68), also features Ginsberg, Corso, and Orlovsky, as well as Orlovsky's brother, Julius. The film was reedited in 1997 to mark the passing of Ginsberg. In 1983, Frank directed *This Song for Jack*, based on footage he shot at "On the Road: The Jack Kerouac Conference" held at the Naropa Institute in Boulder, Colorado, in 1982. The film boasted appearances by Ginsberg, William S. Burroughs, John Clellon Holmes, Corso, Herbert Huncke, Michael McClure, Edie Parker (Kerouac's first wife), Ken Kesey, Carl Solomon, Ken Babbs, Abbie

Hoffman, David Amram, Kerouac biographer Ann Charters, Jack Micheline, and Joyce Johnson.

Other films directed by Frank include *The Sin of Jesus* (1961), *O.K. End Here* (1963), *Conversations in Vermont* (1969), *Life-Raft Earth* (1969, featuring Wavy Gravy and *Whole Earth Catalog* editor Stewart Brand), *About Me: A Musical* (1971), *Cocksucker Blues* (1972), *Keep Busy* (1975), and *Life Dances On* (1980), among others. *Cocksucker Blues*, his best-known and most controversial film, documents the Rolling Stones on tour and features some images so shocking that the band itself successfully squelched its release. The short documentary *Fire in the East: A Portrait of Robert Frank* was released in 1986 and features interviews with Ginsberg, Emile de Antonio, Jonas Mekas, and Rudy Wurlitzer. A new edition of *The Americans* was released in 2008 to mark the fiftieth anniversary of the book's first publication. In reference to his extensive body of work, Frank once remarked, "I'm always looking outside, trying to look inside. Trying to tell something that's true. But maybe nothing is really true. Except what's out there—and what's out there is always changing" ("5 Films by Robert Frank," *Spot*, Fall 2002).

Carl Solomon (1928–93)

No matter what, Carl Solomon will always be known as the guy to whom Allen Ginsberg dedicated "Howl." Born in the Bronx, New York City, on March 30, 1928, Carl Solomon was proclaimed a "child prodigy' at the age of seven for his ability to memorize the batting averages of all baseball players in the National and American leagues, which won him stories in many New York newspapers. Solomon was devastated by his father's untimely death in 1939 and later commented, "I drifted into indiscipline and intellectual adventure that eventually became complete confusion." He graduated high school at the age of fifteen and enrolled at City College of New York but dropped out to join the merchant marine in 1943.

During his travels overseas as a seaman, Solomon became interested in Dadaism and Surrealism, and even witnessed a rather intense poetry reading by French playwright, poet, actor, and theater director Antonin Artaud. Just after his twenty-first birthday, Solomon had himself voluntarily committed into the Greystone Park Psychiatric Institute, where he later received shock treatments. Solomon's article "Report from the Asylum: Afterthoughts of a Shock Patient" was published in *Neurotica* 6 (Spring 1950) and features a disturbing personal account of shock-therapy treatment. In addition, the piece details Solomon's first encounter with Allen Ginsberg, who was visiting his mother in the waiting room at the time: "I mumbled amicably, 'I'm Kirillov.' He mumbled in reply, 'I'm Myshkin.' The cadence of the superreal was never challenged; not one of us would dare assume responsibility for a breach of the unity which each hallucination required."

Through the persistence of Ginsberg, Solomon was able to convince his uncle, A. A. Wyn (1898–1967), the publisher of Ace Books and a notorious tightwad, to publish William S. Burroughs's first novel, *Junkie*, in 1953 (paired with *Narcotic Agent* by Maurice Helbrant and billed as "Two Books in One"). Ace Books was among many publishers to later reject Jack Kerouac's novel *On the Road*. Ginsberg dedicated "Howl" to Solomon and name-dropped his friend directly within the poem itself, as well as referring to him as an "intuitive Bronx Dadaist and prose-poet" on the book's back cover. Another passage from "Howl" related to an incident where Solomon "threw potato salad" at a college lecture in a Dadaist-type stunt.

Solomon's own writing output was extremely limited and includes such works as *Mishap, Perhaps* (1966), *More Mishaps* (1968), and *Emergency Messages* (1989). A collection of essays, *Mishap, Perhaps* includes "Pilgrim State Hospital" and "Suggestions to Improve the Public Image of the Beatnik," among others.

Ted Joans (1928–2003)

Ted Joans's motto was "Jazz is my religion and Surrealism is my point of view." A true American original, jazz poet, surrealist, musician, and painter, Theodore "Ted" Jones (he changed the spelling of his last name as an adult) was born in Cairo, Illinois, on July 4, 1928. His parents worked on riverboats that cruised along the Ohio and Mississippi rivers (a long-since disproven myth held that Joans was actually born on a riverboat). Joans's father was murdered during the 1943 Detroit Race Riot.

Joans took up the trumpet at a young age and went on to receive his BFA degree from Indiana University. He moved to Greenwich Village, New York City, in 1951. Joans's poems were strongly influenced by American poet, novelist, and playwright Langston Hughes, a leading figure in the Harlem Renaissance known for his insightful poems such as "I, Too, Sing America" and "Harlem." Joans created a personal style called "Jazz Poetry" and frequented Greenwich Village, where he befriended other writers and jazz musicians (jazz great Dexter Gordon later referred to Joans as "the last of the great hipsters").

Joans eventually authored more than thirty books, including *Funky Jazz Poems* (1959), *The Hipsters* (1960), *A Black Pow-Wow of Jazz Poems* (1969), *Afrodisia* (1970), *A Black Manifesto in Jazz Poetry and Prose* (1971), *Double Trouble* (1991), and *Teducation: Selected Poems 1949–1999* (1999). For a brief period in the early 1950s, Joans actually roomed with jazz legend Charlie Parker. After

Parker died of a heart attack at the age of thirty-four in 1955, Joans organized a "BIRD LIVES" graffiti movement throughout New York City. Joans's famous painting *Bird Lives* hangs in the de Young Museum in San Francisco.

A close friend of Allen Ginsberg, Jack Kerouac, and other leading Beat writers, Joans even participated in a "Rent-A-Beatnik" service during the late 1950s, earning good money for making appearances at parties where he would read poetry and play the bongo drums.

During the 1960s, Joans traveled extensively around the world using Timbuktu, Mali, as his home base, initially as "self-imposed exile because of America's racism." Renowned French surrealist Andre Breton reportedly acknowledged Joans as the only African American surrealist he ever met. In 1968, Joans released his "Black Flower" statement, a surrealist manifesto that envisioned the defeat of American imperialism using poetic imagery as a weapon. A committed surrealist, Joans even named one of his daughters Daline, after Salvador Dali. In addition to poetry, Joans dabbled in the visual arts and even created a new photography technique called "outagraphy," where the subject of a photograph is cut out of an image. In addition, Joans reportedly got William S. Burroughs interested in painting (Burroughs would later specialize in "shotgun art").

A totally penniless Joans died from complications of diabetes on April 25, 2003, at the age of seventy-four in an apartment in Vancouver, British Columbia. He was survived by ten children. Shortly before his death, he had written (according to his May 20, 2003, *Village Voice* obituary) that "I find myself filled to the beautiful brim with love and with this shared love I continue to live my poem-life."

Jack Micheline (1929–98)

"I am fifty-two, live alone, considered some mad freak genius / In reality I am a fucked up poet who will never come to terms with the world . . ." A largely unheralded but supremely talented outlaw poet and artist, Jack Micheline was active in the New York City poetry scene (he received the Revolt in Literature Award in 1957) before relocating to San Francisco in the 1960s. Micheline was born Harold Martin Silver on November 6, 1929, in the East Bronx, New York City. He took his pen name from Jack London and his mother's maiden name. Micheline's early literary influences were Walt Whitman, Carl Sandburg, Vachel Lindsay, Charles Baudelaire, Langston Hughes, James T. Farrell, and Sherwood Anderson.

Micheline's first book of poetry, *River of Red Wine*, which was published in 1957, featured an introduction by Jack Kerouac, who said that he had "the swinging free style I like and his sweet lines revive the poetry of open hope in

Diane di Prima once referred to outlaw poet and artist Jack Micheline as "a wandering poet singing timeless songs for our own sad, desperate time." *Photo by Mark Christal/Wikimedia Commons*

America." None other than legendary critic Dorothy Parker gave the book a favorable review in the September 1958 issue of *Esquire* magazine. Although Micheline was friends with Kerouac, Gregory Corso, Bob Kaufman, and other Beat writers, he hated being lumped into the Beat Generation, which he regarded as a "media hustle." According to fellow poet and friend A. D. Winans, Micheline "refused to bow down to anyone, choosing to write poetry for the people; Hookers, drug addicts, blue-collar workers, the dispossessed, and he did it from deep inside the heart." Indeed, Micheline often referred to himself as one of the last American troubadours. Micheline considered his poetry "erotic in a sense. It must scare some of these fucking academics to death."

Beat historian John Tytell called Micheline "a poet of urgency and exhortation in the tradition of Jack London and Vachel Lindsay." In an interview with Winans, Micheline remarked, "I never wanted to be a poet. I still don't want to be a poet. I just want to live my life. The thing is people don't understand poetry. All they have is their football, baseball, and television. They've never had a chance to see a real poet that relates to them. What they need are poems that relate to their own way of life. In America, everything is profit motivation. It's the spirit that I relate to. The church doesn't do the job. Television doesn't do the job. Everything in America is based on greed, money and mediocrity."

After one of Micheline's short stories, "Skinny Dynamite," was published in *Renaissance* 2 in September 1968 (Charles Bukowski served as guest editor), he got arrested for obscenity but was not convicted. Bukowski once wrote, "Micheline is all right—he's one-third bull shit, but he's got a special divinity and a special strength . . . I like the way his poems roll and flow. His poems are total feelings beating their heads on barroom floors."

Micheline's other works include *I Kiss Angels, Letter to Jack Kerouac in Heaven,* and *A Man Obsessed Who Does Not Sleep Who Wanders About the Night Mumbling to Himself Counting Empty Beer Cans.* In 1994, he even appeared on *Late Night with Conan O'Brien* and read his poetry accompanied by a jazz trumpet. Micheline, who had suffered from diabetes for years and was living in near-poverty in a cheap San Francisco hotel, died of a heart attack aboard a BART commuter train in 1998 at the age of sixty-eight. According to Diane di Prima, Micheline was "a wandering poet singing timeless songs for our own sad, desperate time."

Peter Orlovsky (1933–2010)

The longtime companion of Allen Ginsberg, Peter Orlovsky was a talented poet in his own right. In his 1990 autobiography, *Guilty of Everything,* Herbert Huncke remarked, "I think Peter is probably what one would call a natural poet, if there is such a thing. His whole life is poetic in a way." Orlovsky was born on the Lower East Side of New York City on July 8, 1933, to Katherine and Oleg Orlovsky, a Russian immigrant. Orlovsky first met Ginsberg while working as a model for painter Robert LaVigne in San Francisco in 1954. Orlovsky appears in several of Jack Kerouac's novels, including *The Dharma Bums* ("George") and *Desolation Angels* ("Simon Darlovsky").

Orlovsky began writing in the late 1950s while living with Ginsberg in the "Beat Hotel" in Paris. He appeared with Ginsberg in the landmark 1959 short film *Pull My Daisy,* which was directed by Robert Frank. He also appeared in Andy Warhol's underground film *Couch* (1965), as well as *Me and My Brother* (1969), which was directed by Frank and documented his brother Julius's struggles with mental illness. Orlovsky's books include *Lepers Cry* (1972), *Clean Asshole Poems & Smiling Vegetable Songs* (1978), and *Straight Hearts' Delight: Love Poems and Selected Letters* (with Ginsberg, 1980). According to Philip Whalen in an interview with *Jacket* magazine (www.jacketmagazine.com), Ginsberg's "long relationship with Peter was sometimes very hard for him because Peter had periods of total insanity and had to be taken care of and was a mess.

Allen Ginsberg's longtime companion, Peter Orlovsky, was a talented poet in his own right who published several collections of poetry, such as *Clean Asshole Poems & Smiling Vegetable Songs* (1978).
Photo by Cynthia Macadams/Courtesy of the LIFE Images Collection/Getty Images

Later on . . . Peter just got totally crackers, and Allen paid to put him in some expensive sanitarium in Wisconsin. When Peter got out he was just fine until he'd get a drink of liquor, and then he would go bananas. It was terrible."

Orlovsky joined the faculty of the Jack Kerouac School of Disembodied Poetics at the Naropa Institute in Boulder, Colorado, in 1974. He died of lung cancer on May 30, 2010, at the age of seventy-six, and his ashes are interred at the Shambhala Mountain Center in Red Feather Lakes, Colorado.

Amiri Baraka (LeRoi Jones) (1934–2014)

"The so-called Beat Generation was a whole bunch of people, of all different nationalities, who came to the conclusion that society sucked." A controversial poet, playwright, and novelist, Amiri Baraka was born Everett LeRoi Jones on October 7, 1934, in Newark, New Jersey, to Anna Lois and Colt LeRoy Jones. He studied at Rutgers, Columbia, and Howard universities, and also served three years as a gunner in the US Air Force. With his wife, Hettie, Jones founded a literary magazine, *Yugen*, along with Totem Press in 1958. The couple had two children. He also established the Black Arts Repertory Theater in Harlem. Jones published his first book of poetry, *Preface to a Twenty Volume Suicide Note*, in 1961. In a review in the *Reporter* (January 3, 1963), M. L. Rosenthal remarked, "*Preface to a Twenty Volume Suicide Note* is close to the spirit of modern jazz . . . [Jones] has a natural gift for quick, vivid imagery and spontaneous humor."

From 1961 to 1963 Jones was coeditor, with Diane di Prima, of *The Floating Bear*, a literary newsletter. His controversial play, *Dutchman*, received the Off Broadway Award for the best American play of 1963–64. It was made into a film in 1966 that starred Shirley Knight and Al Freeman Jr. Jones's first novel, *The System of Dante's Hell*, was published in 1965. Jones became deeply involved in the Black nationalism movement during the mid-1960s and eventually changed his name to Imamu Amiri Baraka.

When later asked about the Beat Generation's impact, Baraka responded, "That's all media stuff . . . as far as some sustained philosophical approach to whatever, that's not there." However, Baraka had his critics, such as fellow poet Kenneth

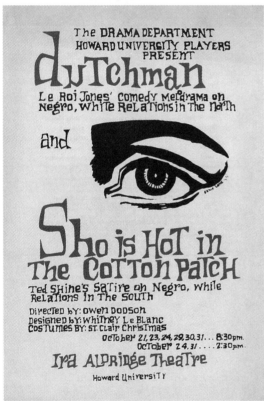

Supremely talented and often controversial poet, playwright, and novelist Amiri Baraka (LeRoi Jones) received the Off Broadway Award for the Best American Play of 1963–64 for *Dutchman*.   *Author's collection*

Rexroth, who remarked that "the people that came up after the war are now also locked into the establishment. Like LeRoi Jones. What is LeRoi Jones? Is he a genuine motherfucker? He is a college professor! How does he make his living? He has never been anything else but a college professor . . . He is a professional bureaucrat. Roi's a college professor. He has never in his life been anything else."

Ray Bremser (1934–98)

Almost entirely forgotten today, Ray Bremser was a gritty creature of the streets who always considered himself a jazz poet rather than a Beat poet (he was "beat" in the same way as Herbert Huncke, beaten down by a combination of hard luck and bad decisions). Bremser's life was punctuated by prison sentences, alcoholism, drug addiction, and homelessness. According to fellow poet Charles Plymell, Bremser's poetry "had the same jazz, surrealist, existential, hip tones as did his 'street-beat' contemporaries, Jack Micheline and Bob Kaufman" (www.evergreenreview.com).

Bremser was born on February 22, 1934, in Jersey City, New Jersey. After going AWOL from the US Air Force at the age of seventeen, Bremser was briefly imprisoned. The next year he was arrested for armed robbery and spent six years in the Bordentown Reformatory. During his prison stint, Bremser started to write poetry, which he sent to Ginsberg, Gregory Corso, and LeRoi Jones (later known as Amiri Baraka), who published some of the poems in his influential literary magazine *Yugen*. According to Baraka in the 1987 documentary *The Beat Generation: An American Dream*, "It was a lively poetry, and it seemed like he had that healthy disrespect, you know, for the powers that were, and are, and I guess that's how we got hooked up."

A year after his release from prison in 1958, Bremser married Bonnie Fraser after the couple had only known each other for three weeks. When Bremser violated his parole on a drug charge two years later, the couple (along with their baby, Rachel) fled to Mexico. Out of pure desperation, Bonnie was soon forced into a life of prostitution in order for the family to simply survive (and support Bremser's drug habit). Bonnie's account of her life on the run with Bremser was published as *Troia: Mexican Memoirs* in 1969.

Bremser's first book of poetry, *Poems of Madness*, was published in 1965, followed by *Angel* in 1967. Ginsberg wrote the introduction to *Poems of Madness*, referring to Bremser's "powerful curious Hoboken language, crank-blat phrasing, [and] rhythmic motion that moves forward in sections to climaxes of feeling." Bremser was name-dropped (along with Ginsberg) in the liner notes of Bob Dylan's 1964 album *The Times They Are A-Changin'*: "an' jail songs of Ray Bremser."

Bremser briefly appeared in the 1987 documentary *The Beat Generation: An American Dream*, and one of his poems can be found in *The Portable Beat Reader* (2003), which was edited by Ann Charters. He died of lung cancer on November 3, 1998, in Utica, New York. Bremser's friends reportedly scattered his ashes at Ginsberg's Cherry Valley farm.

19

Forlorn Rags of Growing Old

The Demise of the Beat Generation

The advent and commodification of "beatnik" culture in the late 1950s, along with the onset of the hippie counterculture in the mid-1960s, signaled the end of the Beat Generation. During the 1960s, Allen Ginsberg embraced the counterculture, while William S. Burroughs continued to reside overseas, and Jack Kerouac retreated to his living room with a bottle of booze. According to John Clellon Holmes in the 1986 documentary *What Happened to Kerouac?*, "Jack Kerouac was never taken seriously while he lived . . . They weren't looking in the right place. They weren't looking at the work, they were looking at their image of the man . . . They kept mixing Jack up with Dean Moriarty . . . and he wasn't."

Neal Cassady Busted

In 1958, Neal Cassady was arrested at a San Francisco nightclub for allegedly offering to share some marijuana with an undercover cop. He ended up serving a two-year sentence in San Quentin State Prison. A rather bitter Cassady wrote to a journalist from prison, "I'm not interested in Jack's book or all that phony beat stuff or kicks . . . Jack and I, we drifted apart over the years. He became a Buddhist and I became a Cayceite [follower of mystic Edgar Cayce]. Yeah, he was impressed with me. Let's see if he was impressed enough to send me a typewriter" (*Jack's Book*, 1978).

According to Carolyn Cassady in her article "Debunking the Myths" (posted at www.nealcassadyestate.com), "Two pillars supported [Cassady's] self-respect: his railroad job, at which he was the best they ever had, and his family. After he was falsely accused and imprisoned for two years he lost them both. First, the railroad wouldn't hire him back, and I, mistakenly thinking I was freeing him to live as he liked without the burden of a family to support, divorced him [in 1963]. In five years he was dead."

Opened in 1852, San Quentin is California's oldest prison and houses the largest death row population in the United States. Convicted rapist Caryl Chessman was executed here in 1960, leading to widespread outrage and a reevaluation of the death penalty in California. Future outlaw country music star Merle Haggard ("Okie from Muskogee") was imprisoned for armed robbery at San Quentin during the same time as Cassady.

"Is There a Beat Generation?"

Sponsored by Brandeis University in Waltham, Massschusetts, the "Is There a Beat Generation?" forum took place at the Hunter College Playhouse on November 6, 1958. Moderated by Joseph Kauffman, dean of students at Brandeis, the forum featured a panel consisting of an inebriated Jack Kerouac; English author and critic Kingsley Amis (*Lucky Jim*), who was loosely associated with the "Angry Young Men" movement; James Wechsler, *New York Post* editor; and Dr. Ashley Montagu, a British anthropologist.

Kerouac rambled on during the symposium, obviously making a mockery of the serious nature of the analysis and the overall preposterous nature of the gathering in general. For instance, Kerouac singled out the whole purpose of the symposium at the outset as "very silly because we should be wondering tonight, 'Is there a world?' . . . But I could go and talk for five, ten, twenty minutes about 'Is there a world?' . . . because there is, really, no world, because sometimes I'm walking on the ground and I can see right through the ground, and there is no world."

Then Kerouac embarked on a rather rambling, humorous discourse that was met with several incidences of nervous laughter from the audience. For instance, at one point he name-dropped W. C. Fields, mentioned "the senseless babbles of the Three Stooges" and "the ravings of the Marx Brothers," and then launched into a zany poem about Harpo Marx ("Harpo, I'll always love you . . ."). Kerouac then remarked, "Anyway, you're all out of your minds. And I'm out of my mind . . . and doesn't that make it like void?" He concluded his Zen-like "presentation" with an energetic reading of chorus 230 from *Mexico City Blues*.

None of the remaining speakers could even come close to matching Kerouac's intensity or originality. Amis commented, "There may conceivably be a Beat Generation, but I very much doubt it," while Wechsler remarked, "The issue is not whether there is a Beat Generation but whether there is a civilization that will survive the next decade." Montagu stated, "It is not condemnation or contempt that is called for but compassion and understanding."

Lost in Big Sur

Three years after his phenomenal literary breakthrough with *On the Road*, Jack Kerouac was a shell of his former self—a burnt-out alcoholic totally disillusioned with "fame" (he was known more for his media-generated notoriety as "King of the Beatniks" rather than any appreciation for his literary talents). Realizing he needed to dry out, Kerouac accepted poet Lawrence Ferlinghetti's invitation to retreat to his secluded cabin in Bixby Canyon near Big Sur in 1960. Although Kerouac's stint in Big Sur didn't turn out as planned—he went on a drunken binge in North Beach, San Francisco, as soon as he arrived in town, brought old friends to the cabin, and later suffered a nervous breakdown—he did churn out one of his most memorable, truly haunting novels (*Big Sur*, 1962) from the experience.

A fascinating documentary and accompanying CD, both titled *One Fast Move or I'm Gone: Kerouac's Big Sur*, were released in 2008. Directed by Curt Worden, *One Fast Move or I'm Gone* includes interviews with Lawrence Ferlinghetti, Carolyn Cassady, David Amram, Michael McClure, Jack Hirschman, Joyce Johnson, Herbert Gold, Tom Waits, and others. The equally impressive companion CD features a unique collaboration between Jay Farrar (Uncle Tupelo, Son Volt) and Ben Gibbard of Death Cab for Cutie. According to Farrar in the CD's liner notes, "The novel *Big Sur* is like Kerouac's version of *Heart of Darkness*—waking up in a place where you start to lose your grip and are not sure if you can make it out of that descent into a reality where the lows get lower and the highs are harder to artificially recreate. In the spirit of Kerouac—the bulk of these songs were written over a five-day span with minimal revisions. I hope Jack would be OK joining in on these campfire songs." In addition, a haunting film adaptation of the novel directed by Michael Polish and starring Jean-Marc Barr appeared in 2013 with the tagline "Some souls never stop searching."

Another famous author associated with Big Sur was Henry Miller (*Tropic of Cancer*), who resided there between 1944 and 1962. Miller's 1957 memoir, *Big Sur and the Oranges of Hieronymus Bosch*, describes his life in Big Sur; in it he suggests, "One's destination is never a place, but rather a new way of looking at things." Miller was the subject of an insightful 1969 documentary, *The Henry Miller Odyssey*. Today, Big Sur is home to the Henry Miller Memorial Library, a nonprofit organization "championing the artistic contributions of Henry Miller, while serving as a cultural resource center for artists, writers, and musicians."

Route 66 (1960–64)

In a 1999 *Salon* interview, *Slaughterhouse-Five* author Kurt Vonnegut stated, "I knew Jack Kerouac at the very end . . . It was accidentally. He'd moved to Cape Cod for a short time, and I was living there. So somebody brought him around . . . He was furious because he had been screwed out of a fortune, which was *Route 66*. It was a huge television hit, and it was an obvious rip-off of *On the Road*."

Aired on CBS between 1960 and 1964, *Route 66* depicted the adventures of two restless wanderers—"Tod Stiles" (Martin Milner, who would later star in the TV show *Adam-12*) and "Buz Murdock" (George Maharis, later replaced by Glenn Corbett as "Lincoln Case")—traveling across the United States in a Chevy Corvette convertible. Maharis bore a strong resemblance to a young Kerouac. The series presented a very watered-down version of *On the Road* fit for the consumption of mass television audiences.

In a June 21, 1993, *Hartford Courant* article, "*66* Producer Denies Link to *On the Road*," Herbert B. Leonard, who created and coproduced *Route 66*, commented, "I don't think [*On the Road*] was what I had in mind . . . I visualized these guys as positive, young—little knights in shining armor. They weren't beatniks, in the sense that they had some kind of sense of feeling of

Jack Kerouac once complained to none other than fellow author Kurt Vonnegut that the hit TV series *Route 66* was "an obvious rip-off" of *On the Road*.   *Author's collection*

social injustice." However, Leonard also quipped, "Two guys in a car—you can't exactly copyright that."

Last Gathering of Beats

The famous "Last Gathering of North Beach Poets and Artists" photo captured a historic moment in time in front of City Lights Bookstore in North Beach, San Francisco, in 1965 and featured Robert LaVigne, Shig Murao, Larry Fagin, Leland Meyezove, Lew Welch, Peter Orlovsky, David Meltzer, Michael McClure, Allen Ginsberg, Daniel Langton, Richard Brautigan, Gary Goodrow, Nemi Frost, Stella Levy, Lawrence Ferlinghetti, and others.

The iconic image was taken by photographer Larry Keenan (1943–2012), who had just earlier completed a Bob Dylan photo shoot in front of City Lights for the singer-songwriter's seventh studio album, *Blonde on Blonde* (the photos never made the album). All of the artists in the "Last Gathering" photo had reportedly dropped by simply to witness the Dylan photo shoot. According to Keenan (as quoted in the *Encyclopedia of Beat Literature*, 2006), "Ferlinghetti wanted to document the 1965 Beat scene in San Francisco in the spirit of the early twentieth-century classic photographs of the Bohemian artists and writers in Paris." Keenan also took the famous photo of Dylan, Ginsberg, and McClure hanging out in the alley (now known as Jack Kerouac Alley) between City Lights Bookstore and Vesuvio Café. Dylan had been hiding out in the basement of the bookstore, while his fans were attempting to break down the door of the establishment. Dylan, Ginsberg, McClure, and Keenan escaped through a window and ran down the alley where Keenan took the photo.

The "Last Gathering" photo came to represent the end of an era for the Beat Generation. Most of the counterculture activity had moved from North Beach to Haight-Ashbury during the mid-1960s. North Beach itself had become overrun with sleazy strip clubs such as the Condor Club, which featured legendary dancer Carol Doda and "the new twin peaks of San Francisco." Today, a plaque outside the Condor Club acknowledges its history as "The Birthplace of the World's First Topless & Bottomless Entertainment." However, City Lights Bookstore would remain open as a lasting Beat Generation landmark in North Beach.

Exile in St. Petersburg

In his 1966 novella *Satori in Paris*, Jack Kerouac writes, "As I grew older I became a drunk. Why? Because I like ecstasy of the mind." Kerouac spent the last few years of his life in a modest ranch house in St. Petersburg, Florida,

Jack Kerouac's bar stool at one of his favorite hangouts, the Flamingo Bar in St. Petersburg, Florida. The Flamingo hosts a Jack Kerouac Night featuring poetry readings and live music twice a year in March and October.   *Courtesy of Alternative Reel/alternativereel.com*

with his third wife, Stella, and his mother, Gabrielle, who suffered a stroke in 1966 that made her an invalid for the rest of her life. According to John Clellon Holmes, Kerouac "was pathetically lonely, tragically lonely, down there [in St. Petersburg], and got into all kinds of messes as a result." A drunken Kerouac would often call Holmes, as well as Carolyn Cassady and Lucien Carr, in the middle of the night and talk for hours.

Kerouac initially moved to 5155 Tenth Avenue North and then to his final home at 5169 Tenth Avenue North. He usually spent his time at home drinking in a chair with the TV set on with no sound and loud classical music blaring from speakers in the other room. When he did leave the house, Kerouac could usually be found at area dive bars, such as the Wild Boar across from the University of South Florida in Tampa or the Flamingo Bar, which today honors the author with a Jack Kerouac Night of poetry and live music twice a year in March and October.

In addition, Kerouac frequented Haslam's Book Store, which was founded in 1933 at 2025 Central Avenue in St. Petersburg. The author reportedly would rearrange his own books in the best positions on the shelves, while obscuring Ken Kesey's novels from view. Today, Haslam's remains Florida's largest new and used bookstore with approximately three hundred thousand books. According to legend, the ghost of Kerouac haunts the bookstore (still rearranging books on the shelves in his favor!). John Montgomery's 1986 book *Kerouac at the Wild Boar & Other Skirmishes* (good luck finding it!) provides interesting anecdotes about the author's life in St. Petersburg during his last years.

Interestingly, most Beat Generation biographers describe Kerouac's mother, Gabrielle, as overbearing, overprotective, and generally unbearable to be around. However, poet Philip Whalen offered an entirely different perspective (in a *Jacket* magazine interview, www.jacketmagazine.com): "[Kerouac] had this wonderful relationship with his mother. Which people seem to have misconstrued or misunderstood. His mother was this wonderfully lively Canadian, and she was a great cook and a great storyteller. He says that's where he learned to tell stories. She was a bouncy, lively lady, and she was very devout."

Death of Neal Cassady

In 1968, totally burnt out and exhausted, Neal Cassady died just four days short of his forty-second birthday in San Miguel de Allende, a beautiful colonial town in the state of Guanajuato in central Mexico. Although much of his final hours are shrouded in mystery, a drug-fueled Cassady had attended a wedding party in San Miguel de Allende and reportedly drank the potent alcoholic drink pulque after taking barbiturates earlier in the day.

Wearing just a T-shirt and jeans on a cold and rainy night, Cassady then decided to count the nails in the railroad ties between towns (a more likely story was that he forgot his traveling bag at the railroad station and was walking back alongside the tracks to retrieve it). According to legend, his last words were "sixty-four thousand nine hundred and twenty-eight." He was found in a coma by the railroad tracks and taken to a local hospital in San Miguel de Allende where he died a couple of hours later. Cassady's death certificate indicates that he was pronounced dead in San Miguel de Allende, Guanajauata, Mexico, at one p.m. on February 5, 1968. The cause of death was listed as "general congestion." His ashes were sent to Carolyn, and they remain with the Cassady family today. Ken Kesey's short story "The Day After Superman Died," which was originally published in *Esquire* magazine in October 1979, features a vivid, albeit heavily fictionalized, depiction of Cassady's final hours.

When Jack Kerouac heard of Cassady's death, he refused to believe the news and often commented that Neal was bound to show up sooner or later. Kerouac's novel *Vanity of Duluoz* was published just two days after Cassady's death. In a July 7, 1969, letter to Ferlinghetti, Kerouac joked, "Hope Neal is really wearing a beard with changed name in Spain." Allen Ginsberg penned several poetic tributes to Cassady, such as "On Neal's Ashes," "Elegy for Neal Cassady," and "The Green Automobile."

Author Robert Stone, who hung out with Ken Kesey and the Merry Pranksters while attending graduate school at Stanford University in the

1960s, based the character of "Ray Hicks" in his 1974 novel, *Dog Soldiers*, on Cassady. The novel was turned into a 1978 movie, *Who'll Stop the Rain*, which starred Nick Nolte as Hicks, whose death scene alongside railroad tracks mirrors Cassady's demise. Nolte would go on to portray Cassady in the mediocre 1980 film *Heart Beat*, which was based on the Carolyn Cassady autobiography.

Firing Line

Just a little over a year before his death, Jack Kerouac made an ill-advised, drunken, and ultimately disastrous appearance on William F. Buckley's conservative *Firing Line* TV show, which was taped on September 3, 1968. The topic of the day was "The Hippies" and panel members also included poet, singer, and social activist Ed Sanders of the Fugs, as well as sociologist Lewis Yablonsky, a professor of sociology and criminology at Cal State Northridge and author of *The Hippie Trip* (1968).

Kerouac was reportedly traveling with a small entourage that included two of his brothers-in-law. William S. Burroughs, who also happened to be in New York City (he had just returned from covering the turbulent Democratic National Convention in Chicago for *Esquire* magazine), met with an extremely inebriated Kerouac shortly before the show's taping and urged him not to go: "I told him, 'No, Jack, don't go, you're not in any condition to go.' But he did go that night . . . It was, of course, a disaster . . . That was the last time I ever saw him" (*With William Burroughs*, 1981).

At one point during the interview, Buckley asked Kerouac to what extent he believed the Beat Generation was related to the hippies. Kerouac responded, "I'm forty-six years old, these kids are eighteen, but it's the same movement, which is apparently some kind of Dionysian movement, in later civilization, which I did not intend, any more than, I suppose, Dionysus did, or whatever his name was." At times, Kerouac slumped in his chair and appeared totally uninterested in the discussion, and at other times he would throw out surreal comments in order to diffuse the seriousness of the arguments, as when he answered one of Buckley's earnest questions about the Vietnam War by claiming the "Vietnamese just want to get hold of our jeeps!" Several times, Kerouac mispronounced Yablonsky's name, leading the sociologist to accuse him of anti-Semitism. Kerouac also frequently amused the audience, as when he turned to Sanders and remarked, "Hey Ed, I was arrested two weeks ago and the arresting policeman said, 'I'm arresting you for decay.'"

Allen Ginsberg made the mistake of sitting in the audience during the taping. At one point, Kerouac launched into a diatribe, remarking, "A lot of hoods, hoodlums, communists, jumped on our backs, well on my back, not his [pointing to Ginsberg]. Ferlinghetti jumped on my back. And turned the idea that I had, the Beat Generation was a generation of beatitude and pleasure in life and tenderness . . . but they called it in the papers, 'beat mutiny,' 'beat insurrection,' words I never used . . . being a Catholic, I believe in order, tenderness, and piety."

According to Ginsberg in the 1986 documentary *What Happened to Kerouac?*, "Jack thought he was going to have this big intelligent conversation with Buckley . . . Kerouac wasn't paying attention, he wouldn't relate to Sanders . . . and he wouldn't relate to the sociologist . . . And Kerouac was so uncooperative, and at times spaced out . . . So Buckley I think got upset, because Kerouac was no inconsiderable figure, and Kerouac had spoken nicely to Buckley, and Buckley had invited him in, and here was this great hunk of drunken meat, making witty remarks (and completely irreverent remarks), like destroying the format, by being completely honest and clear."

Ginsberg himself had appeared earlier as a *Firing Line* guest during a May 7, 1968, taping titled "The Avant Garde," where he read a poem and then chanted "Hare Krishna" repeatedly while playing a harmonium to a somewhat bemused Buckley. The founder and publisher of *National Review* magazine, Buckley hosted 1,504 episodes of *Firing Line* over a 33-year period from 1966 to 1999. The popular public affairs show won an Emmy Award in 1969.

"After Me, the Deluge"

In one of Jack Kerouac's last published works, the essay "After Me, the Deluge," which was published in the *Chicago Tribune* Sunday magazine section on September 28, 1969 (less than one month before he died), the alienated, bitter author attacked the counterculture figures—"the Hippie Flower Children out in the park with their peanut butter sandwiches"—who claimed to be carrying on in his name. Kerouac received $1,500 for the article. An "Editor's Memo" introducing the piece stated, "The Great White Father of the Beat Movement looks back on the progeny he spawned. What does the author of *On the Road* and *The Subterraneans* think of the hippie, the dropout, the war protestor, the alienated radical? Does he have anything in common with them? Does he disown them? Does he qualify as an intellectual forbear of any sort? What is Jack Kerouac thinking about these days?"

In the essay, an incredulous Kerouac remarked, "I've got to figure out . . . how I could possibly spawn Jerry Rubin, Mitchell Goodman, Abbie Hoffman, Allen Ginsberg and other warm human beings from the ghettoes who say they suffered no less than the Puerto Ricans in their Barrios and the blacks in their Big and Little Harlems, and all because I wrote a matter-of-fact account of a true adventure on the road (hardly an agitational propaganda account) featuring an ex-cowhand and an ex-footballer driving across the continent north, northwest, Midwest and southland looking for lost fathers, odd jobs, good times, and girls and winding up on the railroad. Yup, I'd better convince myself that these thinkers were not on an entirely different road."

Considered the first major counterculture celebration, the Human Be-In drew approximately twenty-thousand revelers at Golden Gate Park in San Francisco and featured special appearances by Timothy Leary, Allen Ginsberg, and Gary Snyder, among others.   *Courtesy of the Estate of Allen Cohen and Regent Press*

Death of Jack Kerouac

St. Petersburg Times reporter Jack McClintock visited Jack Kerouac in the unassuming St. Petersburg, Florida, house he shared with his third wife, Stella, and paralyzed mother, Gabrielle, several times for a story that was published on October 12, 1969. The reporter noticed that the TV was on without the sound, while Handel's *Messiah* was "blaring from speakers in the next room." Kerouac admitted to McClintock that "I don't go out much anymore . . . I don't really go out at all." When asked about Ken Kesey, Kerouac remarked, "I don't like Ken Kesey . . . He ruined [Neal] Cassady." Kerouac also said he didn't believe Cassady was really dead. During the entire interview, Kerouac sipped regularly from a vial of whisky.

On October 21, 1969, Kerouac died at the age of forty-seven at St. Anthony's Hospital in St. Petersburg, Florida, of a severe hemorrhage brought on by a mixture of Johnny Walker Red and Dexedrine pills. Kerouac was at home watching TV (not *The Galloping Gourmet* as originally reported, since it was not on that day). At the time of Kerouac's death, only three of his novels were still in print. The *New York Times* obituary for Kerouac by Joseph Lelyveld quoted Stella as saying, "He had been drinking heavily for the past few days . . . He was a very lonely man." Kerouac had been beaten badly outside a Tampa bar just a week or so before his death.

William S. Burroughs later remarked, "All writers lose contact. I wouldn't say he was particularly miserable. He had an alcohol problem. It killed him." According to Burroughs, Kerouac didn't change that much over the years: "He was always like that. First there was a young guy sitting in front of the television in a tee shirt drinking beer with his mother, then there was an older fatter person sitting in front of the television in a tee shirt drinking beer with his mother" (*The Beat Generation*, 1971).

Kerouac is one of the alcoholic authors profiled by Donald Newlove in *Those Drinking Days*: "Twenty thousand in the bank, downing two fifths of scotch daily, and gone to his golden eternity with a ruptured stomach bleeding massively. Genius is no excuse for self-destruction."

20

All Went Their Own Way

During the 1960s, Jack Kerouac, who was a political conservative, sought to distance himself from the beatniks and hippies who cropped up everywhere proclaiming his influenced. Interviewed by Bruce Cook in *The Beat Generation* (1971), Kerouac remarked, "I want to make this very clear. I mean, here I am, a guy who was a railroad brakeman, and a cowboy, and a football player—just a lot of things ordinary guys do. And I wasn't trying to create any kind of consciousness or anything like that. We didn't have a whole lot of abstract thoughts. We were just a bunch of guys who were out trying to get laid." However, Allen Ginsberg easily embraced the counterculture and seemingly showed up everywhere, such as the Human Be-In in 1967, the Democratic National Convention in 1968 (with William S. Burroughs), and even the Chicago Seven Trial in 1969.

Timothy Leary

A noted lecturer in clinical psychology at Harvard University, Dr. Timothy Leary oversaw the Harvard Psilocybin Project with Dr. Richard Alpert (a.k.a. Ram Dass), which ran between 1960 and 1962. LSD was still legal in the United States at the time. Leary eventually distributed thirty-five hundred doses of acid to more than four hundred people, including poets Robert Lowell and Charles Olson, as well as jazz greats Charles Mingus and Thelonious Monk. After many concerns were raised by the school's administration about the nature of the experiments, Leary and Alpert were eventually both fired from the university (the reason given for Leary's dismissal was that he "failed to keep his classroom appointments").

Leary moved his psychedelic experiments to the Millbrook Estate, a giant sixty-three-room Victorian gothic stone mansion in upstate New York. Leary later remarked, "We saw ourselves as anthropologists from the twenty-first century inhabiting a time module set somewhere in the dark ages of the 1960s. On this space colony we were attempting to create a new paganism and a new dedication to life as art" (*Storming Heaven: LSD and the American Dream*, 1998).

Allen Ginsberg enthusiastically participated in Leary's LSD experiments and enlisted William S. Burroughs and Jack Kerouac as well. Burroughs later commented to Paul Bowles that Leary was the most "unscientific" man he'd ever met. In a February 16, 1994, *Los Angeles Times* interview, Ginsberg remarked, "Once when Kerouac was high on psychedelics with Timothy Leary, he looked out the window and said, 'Walking on water wasn't built in a day.' Our goal was to save the planet and alter human consciousness. That will take a long time, if it happens at all."

Ken Kesey and the Merry Pranksters

A true hero of the counterculture and the celebrated author of *One Flew Over the Cuckoo's Nest* (1962), Ken Kesey was called "a great new American novelist"

The celebrated author of *One Flew Over the Cuckoo's Nest* (1962), Ken Kesey founded the Merry Pranksters, who famously headed across the country in the summer of 1964 aboard a psychedelic bus nicknamed "Further."   *Courtesy of Miami-Dade College Archives*

by none other than Jack Kerouac. In a 1999 interview, Kesey remarked, "I was too young to be a beatnik, and too old to be a hippie." Kesey, who was born on September 17, 1935, in La Junta, Colorado, attended the University of Oregon, where he was a champion wrestler and graduated with a bachelor of arts degree in journalism in 1957. He then attended Stanford University's creative writing program under the tutelage of Wallace Stegner, who was known as the "Dean of Western Writers." During his time at Stanford, Kesey participated in a series of US Army experiments involving lysergic acid diethylamide (LSD), mescaline, and other drugs.

In 1964, Kesey founded the Merry Pranksters, an anarchistic group of like-minded individuals dedicated to the promotion of psychedelic drugs. The group included Kesey's best friend, Ken Babbs (an ex-Marine helicopter pilot who had served in one of the earliest American advisory units in Vietnam in 1962–63), as well as Neal Cassady, Stewart Brand (who later published the *Whole Earth Catalog*), Wavy Gravy (a.k.a. Hugh Romney), and others. During the summer of 1964, the Merry Pranksters headed across the country (ostensibly to attend the New York World's Fair) aboard a 1939 International Harvester school bus, painted in psychedelic Day-Glo patterns, nicknamed "Further," and driven by Cassady (a.k.a. "Speed Limit").

According to Kesey in *Beat Writers at Work* (1999), "Cassady was a hustler, a wheeler-dealer, a conniver. He was a scuffler . . . He was literally and figuratively behind the wheel of our bus, driving it the way Charlie Parker worked the saxophone. When he was driving he was improvising an endless monologue about what he was seeing and thinking, what we were seeing and thinking, and what we had seen, thought, and remembered."

When the Further bus rolled up to Timothy Leary's Millbrook Estate in upstate New York with the Merry Pranksters tossing smoke bombs and rock 'n' roll blaring from speakers, the group was greeted with a chilly welcome to say the least. When all was said and done, the Pranksters had compiled more than forty hours of raw footage from their trip. A group of Pranksters would gather at Kesey's house, party, watch the footage, and listen to live music from the Warlocks (later the Grateful Dead)—eventually leading to the evolution of the so-called "Acid Tests."

In 1965, Kesey was arrested for marijuana possession, faked his death, and fled to Mexico for eight months. When he returned to the United States, Kesey was arrested and spent five months in jail. Books devoted to chronicling the Merry Pranksters' journey include Tom Wolfe's *The Electric Kool-Aid Acid Test* (1968), Paul Perry's *On the Bus* (1990), and Kesey's own *The Further Inquiry* (1990). In addition, the 2011 documentary *Magic Trip* features some great original footage from the Merry Pranksters' cross-country adventure.

Acid Tests

The Acid Tests were initially simply just an outgrowth of the huge parties Ken Kesey and the Merry Pranksters held after they returned home from their legendary "Further" cross-country trip during the summer of 1964. They had captured approximately forty hours of filmed footage from the adventure (some of which can be viewed in the 2011 documentary *Magic Trip*) and played the movie for hours on end during parties that would sometimes last for days.

The first Acid Test was held on November 27, 1965, at Ken Babbs's place near Santa Cruz, a chicken ranch known as "The Spread." Allen Ginsberg was in attendance chanting Hindu and Buddhist mantras during the event. Live music was provided by the Warlocks, which later morphed into the Grateful Dead. According to Jerry Garcia of the Dead in a 1989 *Rolling Stone* interview, "What the Acid Test was was formlessness. It's like the study of chaos . . . If you go into a situation with nothing planned, sometimes wonderful stuff happens." By 1966, the Acid Tests had been moved to larger venues such as the Fillmore in San Francisco. Posters were created for the event that asked, "Can

The original Further bus used by the Merry Pranksters was a 1939 International Harvester school bus painted in psychedelic Day-Glo patterns and driven by Neal Cassady (a.k.a. "Speed Limit"). A restored Further bus toured the country in 2014.   *Photo by Joe Mabel/Wikimedia Commons*

You Pass the Acid Test?" Of course, author Tom Wolfe brought the term "acid test" into the mainstream with his 1968 book, *The Electric Kool-Aid Acid Test.*

Haight-Ashbury

The September 6, 1965, edition of the *San Francisco Chronicle* referred to Haight-Ashbury as "the City's new bohemian quarter for serious writers, painters and musicians, civil rights workers, crusaders for all kinds of causes, homosexuals, lesbians, marijuana users, young working couples of artistic bent and the outer fringe of the bohemian fringe—the 'hippies,' the 'heads,' the 'beatniks.'" One of the main reasons for the hippie influx into the Haight-Ashbury (a.k.a. "The Haight") was simply that the rent was cheap. Brothers Ron and Jay Thelin opened the Psychedelic Shop at 1535 Haight Street in January 1966. The Grateful Dead moved into an 1890 Queen Anne–style house at 710 Ashbury in September of 1966. The Human Be-In, which drew approximately twenty thousand people, was held in nearby Golden Gate Park in January 1967. It was at the Human Be-In that Timothy Leary famously declared, "Turn on, tune in, and drop out."

As many as one hundred thousand hippies descended upon the Haight during the "Summer of Love." According to Mikal Gilmore in *Stories Done* (2009), "In the heart of the summer of 1967 in Haight-Ashbury, there were bad drugs—drugs that weren't what they were purported to be—being sold and consumed, there were street beatings, and there were confrontations with the police . . . The Haight was like a tinderbox, but instead of blowing up, the neighborhood steadily burned itself down." On October 6, 1967, the Diggers, a radical activist group, staged a mock funeral known as "Death of the Hippie."

Comic artist R. Crumb stated, "The Haight-Ashbury was appealing . . . It was much more open than any other place. But the air was so thick with bullshit you could cut it with a knife. Guys were running around saying, 'I'm you and you are me and everything is beautiful, so get down and suck my dick.' These young, middle-class kids were just too dumb about it. It was just too silly. It had to be killed." According to Ed Sanders of the Fugs, "The Haight attracted vicious criminals who grew long hair. Bikers tried to take over the LSD market with crude sadistic tactics. Bad dope was sold by acne-faced Methedrine punks. Satanists and satanist-rapist death-freaks flooded the whirling crash pads. People began getting ripped off in the parks. There was racial trouble. Puke was sold as salvation. Ugliness was."

In a 1971 *EVO* interview, film director Paul Morrissey remarked, "This hippie nonsense about the virtues of poverty has had it as a trend . . . Money will be the next big youth kick, with cash, clothes, and jewelry replacing peace, love, and poverty."

The Human Be-In (1967)

Billed as "A Gathering of the Tribes," the Human Be-In, which drew approximately twenty thousand revelers to the Polo Fields at Golden Gate Park in San Francisco on January 14, 1967, was the first major counterculture celebration and served as the prelude to the "Summer of Love." The event was primarily organized by artist Michael Bowen (1937– 2009), who had cofounded with poet Allen Cohen the *San Francisco Oracle*, an underground newspaper in Haight-Ashbury. Bowen and Cohen had previously organized a Love Pageant Rally that featured free performances by Big Brother and the Holding Company and the Grateful Dead on October 6, 1966, the same day that LSD became illegal due to a new California law. Ken Kesey and the Merry Pranksters were also on hand for the acid-fueled gathering.

Word spread rapidly about the Human Be-In via a press release that read, "Berkeley political activists and the love

A counterculture music event later known as the "ultimate high," Mantra-Rock Dance took place at the Avalon Ballroom in San Francisco on January 29, 1967, and featured performances by the Grateful Dead, Big Brother and the Holding Company, and Moby Grape. In addition, Allen Ginsberg led the singing of the Hare Krishna mantra onstage.

Courtesy of Harvey W. Cohen/harveywallacecohen.com

generation of the Haight-Ashbury will join together with members of the new nation who will be coming from every state in the nation, every tribe of the young (the emerging soul of the nation) to pow-wow, celebrate, and prophesy the epoch of liberation, love, peace, compassion and unity of mankind." The star-studded lineup of attendees at the Human Be-In included a mix of old school Beat writers and emerging counterculture figures such as Timothy Leary, Allen Ginsberg, Lawrence Ferlinghetti, Gary Snyder, Michael McClure, Richard Alpert (later known as Ram Dass), Dick Gregory, Jerry Rubin, and Lenore Kandel, as well as free performances by Jefferson Airplane, the Grateful Dead, Country Joe and the Fish, Big Brother and the Holding Company, and Quicksilver Messenger Service. The Doors were in attendance and dropped some acid but did not perform at the event.

The Diggers, an anarchist guerilla street theater group that included future actor Peter Coyote in their midst, provided free food, while legendary LSD "cook" and sound engineer for the Grateful Dead Augustus Owsley Stanley III supplied the acid (dubbed "White Lightning" and specially produced for the Human Be-In). The Hell's Angels provided security with Angel Freewheelin Frank Reynolds guarding the sound truck (he later claimed he had burnt his eyes staring at the sun on acid). It was at the Human Be-In that Leary famously declared, "Turn on, tune in, drop out." In addition, Ginsberg and Snyder chanted mantras, while Kandel, who was celebrating her thirty-fifth birthday, read from her controversial book of poetry, *The Love Book* (one of the poems was titled "To Fuck with Love"). Meanwhile, Rubin announced, "Our smiles are our political banners and our nakedness is our picket sign."

The Human Be-In drew national media attention to the burgeoning Haight-Ashbury scene (a.k.a. "Hashbury," as dubbed by Hunter S. Thompson), setting the stage for the huge influx of hippies from all over the country during the "Summer of Love." Soon every significant gathering would have an "in" attached to it, such as Rowan and Martin's *Laugh-In* sketch comedy TV show, which made its debut just over a year later on January 22, 1968.

The Electric Kool-Aid Acid Test

A highly innovative "nonfiction novel" by Tom Wolfe published in 1968, *The Electric Kool-Aid Acid Test* chronicles the antics of Ken Kesey and the Merry Pranksters as they journey across the United States in the psychedelic school bus "Further," meet rather disastrously with Timothy Leary and his cohorts, host the legendary Acid Tests, interact with the Grateful Dead, and help inaugurate the hippie counterculture. In addition, Wolfe chronicles how once-bustling North Beach, the hive of Beat activity, "was dying" and "nothing but tit shows" and "the action was all over Haight-Ashbury . . . Everything was Haight-Ashbury and the acid heads."

The Electric Kool-Aid Acid Test is full of great Kesey quotes such as "I'd rather be a lightning rod than a seismograph" and "You're either on the bus or off the bus." In an interview published in *Beat Writers at Work*, Kesey remarked, "I had no major problems with [*The Electric Kool-Aid Acid Test*] then, though I haven't looked at it since. When he was around us, he took no notes. I suppose he prides himself on his good memory. His memory may be good, but it's *his* memory and not mine."

As a leading advocate of the "New Journalism," Wolfe utilized unconventional techniques, including subjectivity, a strong point of view, narrative that unfolds in "scenes," and extensive use of dialogue. In an interview with the *Paris Review* (Spring 1991), Wolfe remarked, "I felt the novel had taken a lot of wrong turns since 1950 in the United States and that its future would be highly detailed realism, a kind of hypernaturalism." Wolfe's other works include *The Kandy-Kolored Tangerine-Flake Streamline Baby* (1965), *The Pump House Gang* (1968), *Radical Chic & Mau-Mauing the Flak Catchers* (1970), *The Right Stuff* (1979), *The Bonfire of the Vanities* (1987), *A Man in Full* (1998), *I Am Charlotte Simmons* (2004), and *Back to Blood* (2012).

Wolfe's unique writing style definitely has had its critics over the years. In a 1999 interview, author John Irving remarked, "[Wolfe's] a journalist, man, he's a journalist. He doesn't know how to write fiction, he can't create a character, he can't create a situation . . . he can't write . . . his sentences are bad . . . It's like reading a bad newspaper or a bad piece in a magazine. It makes you wince, it makes you wince. You know, if you were a good skater, could you watch someone just fall down all the time? Could you do that? I can't do that."

Richard Brautigan: A True Outsider

Best known today for his 1967 cult novel, *Trout Fishing in America*, author Richard Brautigan (1935–84) was caught chronologically between the Beat Generation and the counterculture—while not fitting easily into *any* such movements. In addition to *Trout Fishing in America*, Brautigan's eclectic novels include *A Confederate General from Big Sur* (1964), *In Watermelon Sugar* (1968), *The Hawkline Monster: A Gothic Western* (1974), *Willard and His Bowling Trophies: A Perverse Mystery* (1975), *Sombrero Fallout: A Japanese Novel* (1976), *The Tokyo-Montana Express* (1980), *So the Wind Won't Blow It All Away* (1982), and *An Unfortunate Woman: A Journey* (1994).

Brautigan's 1971 work *The Abortion: An Historical Romance 1966* was described as a "novel about the romantic possibilities of a public library in California." In the novel, Brautigan describes his own "anachronistic appearance," looking "as if he would be more at home in another era." He concludes, "I think we have the power to transform our lives into brand-new instantaneous rituals that we calmly act out when something hard comes up that we must do. We become like theaters."

In an article in the *New Republic* (March 20, 1971), Jonathan Yardley remarked, "Right now Brautigan is riding high. He is the Love Generation's answer to Charlie Schulz. Happiness is a warm hippie . . . He is the literary embodiment of Woodstock . . . His exceedingly casual, off-hand style is wholly vogue." In addition to his novels, Brautigan published ten volumes of poetry, including *The Return of the Rivers* (1958), *The Galilee Hitchhiker* (1958), *The Octopus Frontier* (1960), *All Watched Over by Machines of Loving Grace* (1967), *Please Plant This Book* (1968), *The Pill Versus the Springhill Mine Disaster* (1969), *Rommel Drives On Deep into Egypt* (1970), and *Loading Mercury with a Pitchfork* (1971).

In 1984, Brautigan committed suicide with a shot to the head at the age of forty-nine. In a *Vanity Fair* article published after Brautigan's death, Michael McClure remarked, "His wasn't a dangerous voice so much as a voice of diversity, potentially liberating in that it showed the possibilities of dreaming, of beauty and the playfulness of the imagination."

1968 Democratic National Convention

Set amid a year of turbulence that included the assassination of Martin Luther King Jr. on April 4 (followed by riots in more than 100 cities), the assassination of presidential hopeful Senator Robert F. Kennedy on June 5 and the ongoing Vietnam War, the 1968 Democratic National Convention from August 26 to August 29, 1968, quickly devolved into an eruption of violence on August 28 as Chicago police assisted by the Illinois National Guard brutally clashed with antiwar demonstrators. The unlikely crew of Allen Ginsberg, William S. Burroughs, Jean Genet, and Terry Southern wandered amid the chaos—all four being commissioned by *Esquire* magazine to write a story on the convention.

Yippie activists had scheduled a "Festival of Life" and approximately ten thousand protestors descended upon Grant Park for a rally. Police used tear gas to quell the crowd. According to poet John Sinclair who was manager of the Detroit rock band MC5 (quoted in *Please Kill Me*, 2006), "We insisted we play at the Festival of Life outside the 1968 Democratic Convention in Chicago. We were this hungry band from Detroit . . . Abbie Hoffman came up onstage, grabbed the microphone, and started rapping about 'the pigs' and 'the siege of Chicago.' I said, 'Oh dear, this does not bode well for us.' So I kind of signaled to the guys, 'Let's get the fuck outta here . . .'"

MC5 drummer Dennis Thompson remarked, "Chicago was supposed to be the show of solidarity, goddamn it. This is the alternative culture? Come on. Where were all the other bands? No one showed up but us. That's what pissed me off. I knew the revolution was over at that moment—I looked over my shoulder, and no one else was there" (*Please Kill Me*, 2006).

At some point during the "police riot," Genet turned to Burroughs and stated, "I can't wait for this city to rot. I can't wait to see weeds growing through empty streets." According to Burroughs in *With William Burroughs* (1981), Genet "was being chased by a cop, and he turned around and shrugged as the cop was about to hit him with his club, and the cop veered away. But more cops were coming, so Genet took refuge in the nearest apartment building. Then he just knocked on the first door he came to. It turned out to be a student's apartment. This guy with a beard opened the door and Genet said. 'Je suis Monsieur Genet.' And the guy said. 'Oh, great. Come on in. I'm doing my thesis on you'." In addition, Venice Beach Beat poet Lawrence Lipton, who was covering the convention for the *Los Angeles Free Press*, was reportedly badly beaten by police.

After Chicago, the so-called "Chicago Eight"—Abbie Hoffman, Tom Hayden, David Dellinger, Rennie Davis, John Froines, Jerry Rubin, Lee Weiner, and Bobby Seale—were charged with conspiracy and incitement to riot charges by the Justice Department. Ginsberg testified for the defense at the ensuing trial, which was presided over by Judge Julius Hoffman.

The Majic Bus: An American Odyssey (1993)

In the summer of 1992, Hofstra University Professor Douglas Brinkley of Hofstra, at the urging of his students, decided to take them out of the sometimes stifling confines of the classroom for a six-week educational adventure across the United States—visiting a total of thirty states and ten national parks, while reading fourteen classic books by great American writers— aboard a fully equipped sleeper "Majic Bus."

Along the way the seventeen students toured Thomas Jefferson's Monticello in Charlottesville, Virginia; paid their respects to the one and only "King," Elvis Presley, at Graceland in Memphis Tennessee; visited William Faulkner's Rowan Oak in Oxford, Mississippi; strolled along Bourbon Street in New Orleans, Louisiana; chatted with William S. Burroughs in his unassuming house in Lawrence, Kansas; gambled in a Las Vegas, Nevada, casino; explored Jack Kerouac Alley in North Beach, San Francisco; took a spin with Ken Kesey on the psychedelic bus Further II (complete with Day-Glo jumpsuits!) in Eugene, Oregon; caught a Bob Dylan concert in Seattle, Washington; and marveled at Theodore Roosevelt's North Dakota Badlands; among other intrepid adventures.

During their visit with Burroughs, the elderly author announced he was voting for the Libertarian Party in the upcoming Presidential election since he "opposes foreign aid, government subsidies of business, censorship, and laws restricting private sexual conduct between consenting adults or the recreational use of drugs." Burroughs also got "genuinely animated" when one of the students brought up the subject of guns and [he was] proud to talk about his big Smith & Wesson .45 and his beloved Colt .45 with a fellow enthusiast." When asked about writers he admired, Burroughs named T. S. Eliot, Louis-Ferdinand Celine, Franz Kafka, Raymond Chandler, and Dashiell Hammett.

The official reading list for the Majic Bus odyssey included such classic works as *On the Road*, *Mexico City Blues*, and *The Dharma Bums* by Kerouac; *Leaves of Grass* by Walt Whitman; *The Adventures of Huckleberry Finn* by Mark Twain; *O, Pioneers!* by Willa Cather; *The Ballad of the Sad Café* by Willa Cather; *Selected Poems of Langston Hughes*; *The Last Picture Show* by Larry McMurtry; *Black Elk Speaks* (edited by John Neihardt); *Fear and Loathing in Las Vegas* by Hunter S. Thompson; *The Call of the Wild* and *Black Fang* by Jack London; and *The Wayward Bus* by John Steinbeck.

Inspiration for the Majic Bus experience was in large part due to the example of discovery and self-expression set forth by Jack Kerouac's *On the Road*, which according to Brinkley is "the best-known highway book of the century, which is both a protest against Eisenhower-era conformity and a self-celebration of Whitmanesque proportions. The prose is high-octane wanderlust." Prior to the Majic Bus experience, Brinkley had devised a course called "The Beat Generation and Counterculture in America," which included a visit by guest lecturer Allen Ginsberg, who "performed poetry, accompanying himself on his harmonium," according to Brinkley. The success of that course led to an upper-level seminar called simply "Jack Kerouac," which featured guest speaker Stanley Twardowicz, an abstract painter and drinking buddy of Kerouac's at Gunther's Bar when the author lived in Northport, Long Island, between 1961 and 1964. Through Twardowicz's colorful anecdotes, the students "got to know the Kerouac who never drove a car, who shopped at the Walt Whitman Mall, and who was an admirer of William F. Buckley Jr."

Published in 1993, *The Majic Bus: An American Odyssey* is a lively travelogue that highlights the unique and rewarding experience of students in the traveling course titled "An American Odyssey: Art and Culture Across America." Brinkley dedicated *The Majic Bus* "to the Memories of: Jack Kerouac, Thomas Wolfe, Stephen Forster, Miles Davis and Robert Kennedy." Brinkley currently is a professor of history at Rice University and a fellow at the James Baker Institute of Public Policy. He served as the editor of *Windblown World: The Journals of Jack Kerouac, 1947–1954* (2004) and *Jack Kerouac: Road Novels 1957–1960* (2007).

Magic Trip (2011)

In 1964, *One Flew Over the Cuckoo's Nest* author Ken Kesey (1935–2001) and his Merry Pranksters took a legendary trip across the United States aboard a psychedelic bus (a 1939 International Harvester) nicknamed "Further" with none other than speed freak Neal Cassady (the real-life model of "Dean Moriarty" from Jack Kerouac's classic 1957 novel *On the Road*) behind the wheel.

Billed as "Ken Kesey's Search for a Kool Place," this fascinating documentary directed by Alison Ellwood and Alex Gibney, which uses restored 16 mm color footage shot by Kesey and the Pranksters, follows the motley crew on their amazing, LSD-fueled journey to visit the New York World's Fair during a pre-hippie era that definitely served as a harbinger of things to come. In addition to Kesey (a.k.a. "Swashbuckler") and Cassady ("Speed Limit"), the fearless group of psychedelic explorers included Ken Babbs ("Intrepid Traveler"), Kathy Casamo ("Stark Naked"), George Walker ("Hardly Visible"), Jane Burton ("Generally Famished"), and John Babbs ("Sometimes Missing"),

A fascinating documentary released in 2011, *Magic Trip* features restored footage shot by Ken Kesey and the Merry Pranksters during their epic adventure across the country in the summer of 1964.

Author's collection

among others. Actor Stanley Tucci (*The Lovely Bones*) provides the rather sparse narration.

A true artifact from the 1960s, the documentary includes some rare footage of Jack Kerouac and Allen Ginsberg hanging out with the Pranksters in New York City, as well as the Pranksters' notorious visit to Timothy Leary's Millbrook Estate in upstate New York. According to Gibney in a 2011 interview with www.gothamist.com, "The [Leary] encounter is kind of a bust . . . It was supposed to be the West Coast acid heads meet the East Coast acid heads. Well, the East Coast acid heads basically ran and hid when they saw the pranksters coming full of smoke bombs and tootling instruments."

Magic Trip received generally positive reviews. Critic Shawn Levy at the *Oregonian* (August 11, 2011) wrote that the film was filled with "amazing glimpses of ordinary and extraordinary life in the America of 1964 . . . It's genuinely mindblowing to see things you've only ever read or heard about actually unfolding." Critic Mark Feeney of the *Boston Globe* (September 1, 2011) commented that "It's the movie Yellow Submarine should have been but didn't know how to be."

Gibney has directed several critically acclaimed documentaries, including *Enron: The Smartest Guys in the Room* (2005), *Taxi to the Dark Side* (winner of the 2007 Academy Award for Best Documentary Feature), *Gonzo: The Life and Work of Dr. Hunter S. Thompson* (2008), and *Client 9: The Rise and Fall of Eliot Spitzer* (2010). For more information about *Magic Trip*, visit www.magictripmovie.com.

Safe in Heaven Dead

Final Beat Resting Places

A lthough Jack Kerouac died in St. Petersburg, Florida, he is buried at the Edson Cemetery in his hometown of Lowell, Massachusetts, with the simple epitaph "He Honored Life." Similarly, William S. Burroughs is buried at the Bellefontaine Cemetery in his hometown of St. Louis, Missouri, while Allen Ginsberg rests in peace in the family plot at Gomel Chesed Cemetery near Newark, New Jersey. Perhaps the most exotic final resting place among the Beat writers is Gregory Corso, whose ashes are buried at the foot of his idol Percy Bysshe Shelley's grave in the Cimitero Acattolico (Protestant Cemetery) in Rome, Italy.

Harleigh Cemetery, Camden, New Jersey

Opened in 1885 and listed on the New Jersey Register of Historic Places, Harleigh Cemetery is one of the oldest cemeteries in New Jersey and serves as the final resting place for poet Walt Whitman (1819–92), a major influence on many Beat writers such as Jack Kerouac and Allen Ginsberg. Whitman himself commissioned the construction of the impressive granite mausoleum, which cost the hefty sum of $4,000 and stands fifteen feet tall, fifteen feet wide, and twenty feet deep.

Adjacent to the mausoleum lies a stone plaque inscribed with a famous excerpt from Whitman's "Song of Myself" from *Leaves of Grass*: "I bequeath myself to the dirt to grow from the grass I love, If you want me again look for me under your bootsoles." The mausoleum also holds the remains of Whitman's parents, as well as two of his brothers and their families. Whitman, who first published his most famous work, *Leaves of Grass*, on July 4, 1855, continued to revise the book throughout his life. In 1891, he published the final edition of the poetry collection (known as the "Deathbed Edition"). Near the end of his life, Whitman often visited the mausoleum under construction that he had commissioned.

Whitman died on March 26, 1892, in Camden, New Jersey, at the age of seventy-two. The official cause of death was listed as "pleurisy of the left side,

consumption of the right lung, general miliary tuberculosis and prenchyma-
tous nephritis." More than a thousand mourners visited Whitman's Camden
home for a public viewing of his body. Four days after his death, Whitman was
buried in Harleigh Cemetery during a public ceremony. Noted orator Robert
Ingersoll, known as "The Great Agnostic," delivered the eulogy.

One of Whitman's brothers, Colonel George Washington Whitman
(1829–1901) was a Civil War Union Army officer who fought in many notable
battles, including New Bern, Antietam, Fredericksburg, Second Bull Run, the
Wilderness, and Petersburg. However, he was not too fond of his brother's
poetry, once remarking about *Leaves of Grass*, "I saw the book—didn't read it
all—didn't think it worth reading" (*In Re Walt Whitman*, 1893).

Harleigh Cemetery covers more than 130 acres and also serves as the
final resting place for radical labor organizer Ella Reeve "Mother" Bloor
(1862–1951), whose 1940 autobiography, *We Are Many*, served as the basis
for the Woody Guthrie song "1913 Massacre." In addition, internationally
recognized haiku poet Nick Virgilio (1928–89) is buried here. Virgilio helped
popularize the haiku style of poetry in the United States. A native of Camden,
Virgilio was also instrumental in the founding of the Walt Whitman Center
for the Arts and Humanities (today known as the Walt Whitman Arts Center).
Virgilio's popular "Lilly" haiku is engraved on his grave: "lily: out of water . . .
out of itself."

Camden is also home to the Walt Whitman House, a New Jersey State
Historic Site and National Historic Landmark at 330 Mickle Boulevard. In
Whitman's Wild Children (1989), author Neeli Cherkovski related an anecdote
about his visit to the Walt Whitman House in 1975. When he told the attendant he wrote poetry, she asked, "Do you know Allen Ginsberg? I like him a
lot. He's a nice man. But when he comes here, he acts like he owns the place.
One time he told me that the living room needed cleaning."

Riverside Cemetery, Asheville, North Carolina

The final resting place of Thomas Wolfe, one of Jack Kerouac's early and
strongest influences (especially evident in his first published novel, *The
Town and the City*), can be found at Riverside Cemetery in his hometown of
Asheville, North Carolina. Wolfe's grave states "A Beloved American Author"
and features quotes from two of his novels: "The Last Voyage, The Longest,
The Best," from *Look Homeward, Angel* (1929) and "Death Bent to Touch His
Chosen Son with Mercy, Love and Pity and Put the Seal of Honor on Him
When He Died" from *The Web and the Rock* (published posthumously in 1939).

Originally called the Asheville Cemetery and established in 1885, the
Riverside Cemetery contains the graves of more than thirteen thousand

people, including Wolfe's brother, Ben (who died during the 1918 Flu Pandemic), noted short story author William Sydney Porter (a.k.a. O. Henry), North Carolina Governor Zebulon Vance, Union Colonel and Congressional Medal of Honor recipient Andrew Jackson McGonnigle, and James H. Posey, one of President Abraham Lincoln's bodyguards, as well as Confederate generals Thomas Clingman (Clingman's Dome, the highest mountain in the Smokies at 6,643 feet, was named in his honor), Robert B. Vance, and James Martin. Listed on the National Register of Historic Places, the Riverside Cemetery is located within the Montford Area Historic District along Birch Street off Pearson Drive.

Downtown Asheville is home to the Thomas Wolfe Memorial (52 North Market Street), where visitors can visit the historic Old Kentucky Home depicted in *Look Homeward, Angel* as "Dixieland." Guided tours are offered and the onsite visitor center offers exhibits on Wolfe and his family, as well as an audiovisual presentation on his life and writing.

Known as "Wolfe's Angel," the famous angel statue referenced in *Look Homeward, Angel* can be found at Oakdale Cemetery on Highway 64 West just a short drive from downtown Hendersonville, North Carolina (about twenty-five miles from Asheville). A historical marker located on the highway marks the location of the statue, which is protected by a wrought iron fence.

Edson Cemetery, Lowell Massachusetts

After Jack Kerouac passed away on October 21, 1969, in St. Petersburg, Florida, his casket was shipped to his hometown of Lowell, Massachusetts, for burial. A wake was held at Archambault Funeral Home. Kerouac's old friend, Father "Spike" Morrisette, presided over the funeral service at Saint Jean de Baptiste Church on Merrimack Street. Among those in attendance were Allen Ginsberg (who served as one of the pallbearers), John Clellon Holmes, Gregory Corso, Robert Creeley, and Edie Parker (Kerouac's first wife). Kerouac's old buddy, Lucien Carr, was too upset to attend, while William S. Burroughs was conspicuously absent. According to Corso (quoted in *Jack's Book*, 1978), "When I saw Jack in the funeral parlor, where everybody was paying a last visit to him, I had this idea of picking up his body and throwing it across the room. I thought it might have been a Zen thing that he would have dug."

Parker provided her own recollections of the funeral service in her memoir, *You'll Be Okay: My Life with Jack Kerouac* (which was published posthumously in 2007): "Allen was all hair with sandals, no socks, and a lute . . . Of all the people Jack and I knew back at Columbia and his friends I had met in Lowell, no one, with the exception of Allen, showed up. There were only

Jack Kerouac's final resting place can be found at the Edson Cemetery in his hometown of Lowell, Massachusetts. His epitaph simply reads "He Honored Life."

Courtesy of Daniel Penfield/ Wikimedia Commons

profiteers and media . . . The Kerouacs were from nearby Nashua, New Hampshire. That made me wonder. Why wasn't Jack being buried with his family, in Nashua? . . . My, I was upset. I kept thinking of Jack saying, 'Life slips away, as does the time of day.'"

Kerouac is buried in the Edson Cemetery on Gorham Street in South Lowell with a modest plaque and the straightforward epitaph "He Honored Life." Kerouac's third wife, Stella Sampas, who died on February 10, 1990, was later buried with him in the Sampas family plot next to the grave of Kerouac's childhood friend, Sebastian (Stella's brother), who was killed in 1944 during World War II. Visitors often leave mementos on Kerouac's grave such as bottles of whisky or wine, stones, books, coins, photos, flags, and handwritten notes. In 2014, a new, three-thousand-pound granite monument measuring six feet wide and three feet tall was erected at Edson Cemetery to mark Kerouac's gravesite, featuring his signature and the words "The road is life" from *On the Road*.

Gomel Chesel Cemetery, Elizabeth, New Jersey

An ailing Allen Ginsberg had made a special guest appearance at the NYU Poetry Slam on February 20, 1997. However, his last poetry reading is believed to have been at The Booksmith in San Francisco on December 16, 1996. Ginsberg continued writing up until the end of his life, completing his last poem, "Things I'll Not Do (Nostalgias)," on March 30, 1997. Ginsberg had been diagnosed with liver cancer just days before his death. After returning home from the hospital for the last time, Ginsberg reportedly called everyone in his address book to say goodbye. The day before he died, Ginsberg told William S. Burroughs, "I thought I'd be terrified, but I'm not! I'm exhilarated." Upon hearing about Ginsberg's condition, Lawrence Ferlinghetti composed a poem called "Allen Ginsberg Dying," which celebrated the fact that his poetic voice had spread throughout the land and would never die.

Surrounded by family and friends in his East Village apartment in New York City, Ginsberg died on April 5, 1997, at the age of seventy. Quoted in the *New York Times* obituary for Ginsberg published on April 6, 1997, Burroughs remarked, "Allen was a great person with worldwide influence. He was a pioneer of openness and a lifelong model of candor. He stood for freedom of expression and for coming out of all the closets long before others did. He has influence because he said what he believed."

Ginsberg is buried in his family plot in Gomel Chesed Cemetery in Newark, New Jersey, with the poignant epitaph: "Father Breath Once More Farewell / Birth You Gave Was No Thing Ill / My Heart Is Still, As Time Will Tell." Gomel Chesed Cemetery is located at the corner of McClellan Street and Mt. Olivet Avenue near the city lines of Newark and Elizabeth, New Jersey. The Ginsberg family plot can found toward the western edge of the cemetery. Visitors sometimes leave stones or personal items such as books on the grave in tribute to Ginsberg.

Bellefontaine Cemetery, St. Louis, Missouri

In William S. Burroughs's final journal entry, he scrawled, "Love? What is it?" The following day, August 2, 1997, Burroughs died of a heart attack in Lawrence, Kansas, at the age of eighty-three. A funeral service was held at Liberty Hall in Lawrence, Kansas. Among the casket bearers were poet and performance artist John Giorno, Burroughs's longtime assistant James Grauerholz, and literary agent Andrew Wylie. Music selections included "Paris, Texas" by Ry Cooder, "Down-Hearted Blues" by Bessie Smith, and "Ain't Misbehavin'" by Louis Armstrong.

Burroughs is buried in the family plot at the Bellefontaine Cemetery in St. Louis, Missouri, with a simple marker bearing his name, dates of birth and death, and with the simple epitaph "American Writer." His grave lies just to the right of the grave of his grandfather, William Seward Burroughs I (1857–98), of adding machine fame, whose marker (a massive white granite

The simple epitaph "American Writer" marks the grave of William S. Burroughs at the Bellefontaine Cemetery in St. Louis, Missouri.   *Photo by Christina Rutz/Wikimedia Commons*

obelisk) reads "Erected by his Associates as a Tribute to His Genius." Burroughs's grandfather perfected the adding machine and received a patent in 1888, leading to the formation of what became to be known as the Burroughs Corporation. In his epilogue to *Word Virus: The William S. Burroughs Reader* (2000), James Grauerholz wrote, "According to Burroughs' express wishes, he was laid to rest in the Burroughs family plot at Bellefontaine Cemetery in St. Louis, alongside his grandfather, the inventor; his uncle Horace, the drug addict; his father, Mote; and his mother, Laura."

Other famous people buried at Bellefontaine Cemetery include General William Clark (1770–1838) of the famous Lewis and Clark Expedition; Adolphus Busch (1839–1913), cofounder of Anheuser-Busch brewing company; poet Sara Teasdale (1884–1933), who died by suicide, overdosing on sleeping pills; and David Kammerer (1911–44), a friend of Burroughs who was killed by Lucien Carr, a pivotal member of the early Beat circle at Columbia University. In addition, Bellefontaine Cemetery serves as the final resting place of several Civil War generals, including Stephen Watts Kearney, Sterling Price, and Don Carlos Buell. The Lemp family tomb is the largest tomb at Bellefontaine Cemetery. Successful St. Louis beer brewers (Falstaff Beer was one of their brands), the Lemps were marred by tragedy (three family members committed suicide at the purportedly haunted Lemp Mansion, which today serves as a restaurant and inn).

Founded in 1849, Bellefontaine Cemetery encompasses 314 acres and features several other architecturally significant monuments and mausoleums, including the Wainwright tomb, which was designed by acclaimed architect Louis Henry Sullivan—the "Father of Modernism" and mentor to Frank Lloyd Wright. Listed on the National Register of Historic Places, the Wainwright tomb became a St. Louis Landmark in 1971.

Cimitero Acattolico, Rome, Italy

Gregory Corso died of prostate cancer at the age of seventy on January 17, 2001, in Robbinsdale, Minnesota, where he was residing with his daughter, Sheri Langerman. In a tribute to Corso in the *Village Voice* (January 24–30, 2001), Patti Smith wrote, "He was part Pete Rose, part Percy Bysshe Shelley. He could be explosively rebellious, belligerent, and testing, yet in turn, boyishly pure, humble and compassionate. He was always willing to say he was sorry, share his knowledge, and was open to learn." Corso's ashes were placed near the foot of Perce Bysshe Shelley's grave and not far from the marker of John Keats in the Cimitero Acattolico (Non-Catholic Cemetery, a.k.a. Protestant Cemetery or English Cemetery) in Rome, Italy. An exception was made to allow Corso, a Catholic, to be buried there. Corso had composed

Gregory Corso's ashes were placed near the foot of his idol Percy Bysshe Shelley's grave at the Cimitero Acattolico in Rome, Italy.   *Photo by Giovanni Dall'Orto/Wikimedia Commons*

his own epitaph: "Spirit / is Life / It flows / thru / the death of me / endlessly / like a river / unafraid / of becoming / the sea."

Shelley (1792–1822), who drowned while sailing off the Italian coast, was cremated on the beach near Viareggio, Italy, and his ashes were sent to the Protestant Cemetery for burial. His epitaph reads "Cor Cordium" ("Heart of Hearts"), along with several lines from "Ariel's Song" from Shakespeare's play *The Tempest*: "Nothing of him that doth fade / But doth suffer a sea-change / Into something rich and strange." Shelley had earlier wrote about the cemetery in lines from *Adonaïs* his 1821 pastoral elegy written for John Keats: "It might make one in love with death, to think that one should be buried in so sweet a place." According to legend, Shelley's heart survived cremation and was given to Shelley's widow, Mary (best known for her Gothic novel, *Frankenstein*). Shelley's heart was reportedly buried with the couple's child, Sir Percy Florence Shelley, in 1889.

Keats (1795–1821) died of tuberculosis at the age of twenty-five, and his epitaph reads, "This grave contains all that was Mortal, of a YOUNG ENGLISH POET, Who on his Death Bed, in the Bitterness of his Heart, at the Malicious Power of his Enemies, Desired these Words to be engraven on his Tomb Stone: Here lies One whose Name was writ in Water." Other notable graves in the cemetery include Russian painter Karl Pavlovich Brullov (*The Last Day of Pompeii*), fashion designer Irene Galitzine, Norwegian sculptor Hendrik Andersen, German/Dutch painter Jacob Asmus Carstens, American sculptor William Wetmore Story, Italian novelist Carlo Emilio Gadda, Welsh sculptor John Gibson, American writer Constance Fenimore Woolson, English author Edward John Trelawny, Italian philosopher Antonio Gramsci, American explorer Thomas Jefferson Page, Dutch sculptor Pier Pander, English film actress Belinda Lee, English painter Joseph Severn, and August von Goethe, the son of Johann Wolfgang von Goethe, among others.

Santa Barbara Cemetery, Santa Barbara, California

Kenneth Rexroth died on June 6, 1982, at the age of seventy-six and was buried at the Santa Barbara Cemetery in Santa Barbara, California. He had moved to Santa Barbara in 1968 to take a job as a lecturer at the University of California, Santa Barbara. Rexroth's epitaph reads, "As the full moon rises / The swan sings / In sleep / On the lake of the mind." The lines are taken from Rexroth's 1976 collection of poetry, *The Silver Swan: Poems written in Kyoto, 1974–75*. Rexroth's grave is the only one that faces the Pacific Ocean. In 2006, author David Petry published *The Best Last Place: A History of the Santa Barbara Cemetery*. According to Petry, "the Santa Barbara Cemetery is a fascinating place to visit, offering us a wealth of information about our community, history, and culture and a wealth of information about ourselves. It is truly the best last place."

Other notable gravesites at the Santa Barbara Cemetery, which was founded in 1867, include those of actress Virginia Cherrill, who made her film debut as the blind flower girl in Charlie Chaplin's *City Lights* (1931); English actor Ronald Colman, who won a Best Actor Oscar for *A Double Life*; actor Leslie Fenton, who portrayed gangster "Nails Nathan" in *The Public Enemy* (1931); Domino Harvey, model, bounty hunter, and daughter of actor Laurence Harvey, who is also buried here; actress Jeanne Crain (*Pinky*); actress Evelyn Keyes, who portrayed Scarlet O'Hara's sister "Sue Ellen" in *Gone with the Wind* (1939); English actor Murray Kinnell, who portrayed gangster "Putty Nose" in *The Public Enemy*; Hall of Fame Major League baseball player Eddie Mathews; TV actor Fess Parker, who portrayed both Davy Crockett and Daniel Boone; and business magnate Sam Battistone, founder of the Sambo's restaurant chain.

St. Louis de Gonzague Cemetery, Nashua, New Hampshire

Although Jack Kerouac is buried in Edson Cemetery in his hometown of Lowell, Massachusetts, several of his family members—including his "saintly" brother, Gerard (who died of rheumatic fever in 1926 at the age of nine); father, Leo (who died of stomach cancer in 1946); and mother, Gabrielle (who died in 1973)—are buried in the Old Saint Louis de Gonzague Cemetery (a.k.a. St. Aloysius Cemetery) in Nashua, New Hampshire (the city where his parents first met and got married). In addition, the cremated ashes of Kerouac's daughter, Jan (who died of kidney failure in 1996 at the age of forty-four), were interred here in 1997.

Several months before her death, Jan Kerouac attempted to have her father's remains moved from Edson Cemetery to the Kerouac family plot in Nashua. She appeared on a radio talk show in Lowell, commenting that "it was in Nashua that [Kerouac's] Franco-American beginnings were and which got him started thinking about life." Executor of the Kerouac estate John Sampas (Stella's brother) informed a local newspaper, the *Lowell Sun*, "He is not going to be moved and that's it." The Lowell City Cemetery Commission quickly informed Jan that she did not have the right to move the body, and she withdrew her request within weeks of making it. The St. Louis de Gonzague Cemetery was opened in 1880 by the St. Louis Church. Kerouac's grandfather, Jean Baptiste Kerouac, had purchased space in the cemetery shortly after his family had immigrated to the United States from Quebec in 1890. The cemetery, which lies less than twenty miles from Lowell, is depicted in three of Kerouac's novels: *The Town and the City* (1950), *Visions of Gerard* (1963), and *Vanity of Duluoz* (1968).

Kerouac's older sister, Carolina (nicknamed "Nin"), died of a heart attack on September 19, 1964, at the age of forty-five and is buried in Greenwood Cemetery in Orlando, Florida. For years the grave remained unmarked until the Kerouac Project of Orlando raised funds to provide her with a proper marker. Founded in 1880, Greenwood is Orlando's oldest cemetery and also serves as the final resting place of Francis Wayles Eppes (1801–81), President Thomas Jefferson's grandson.

Mt. Olivet Cemetery, Wheat Ridge, Colorado

At the end of *On the Road*, Jack Kerouac laments, "I even think of Old Dean Moriarty the father we never found." However, the model for "Old Dean Moriarty," Neal Cassady Sr., is actually resting quite peacefully at the Mt. Olivet Cemetery in Wheat Ridge, Colorado (which lies just over twelve miles from Larimer Street in Denver). More than 120,000 people have been buried at Mt. Olivet Cemetery, which was opened in 1892 as sacred burial space for the Archdiocese of Denver. Mt. Olivet is located at 12801 West Forty-Fourth Avenue.

A barber by trade, Neal Cassady Sr. was born in 1893 and drifted to Denver, Colorado, in 1925, where he married Maude Schuer Daly. Neal Cassady Jr. was born a year later. After Maude left because of Neal Sr.'s alcoholism, he lived with Neal Jr. in a series of Denver flophouses (he is referred to as "one of the most tottering bums of Larimer Street" in *On the Road*) and passed away in 1963. Cassady Sr. lies in an unmarked grave (section 26, block 5, lot 6, grave 9). Neal's wife, Maude, and her first husband, James Daly, are also buried in the cemetery. Cassady Jr., who died in Mexico in 1968, was cremated, and his ashes are still reportedly in the possession of his family.

Mt. Olivet Cemetery also serves as the final resting place for astronaut John Leonard "Jack" Swigert Jr. (1931–82). Assigned to the Apollo 13 backup crew, Swigert replaced crewman Thomas K. Mattingly, who had been exposed to German measles, as command module pilot. Apollo 13 launched on April 11, 1970, as the third manned mission intended to land on the Moon, but the lunar landing was aborted after an oxygen tank exploded onboard. After several tense days, the Apollo 13 crew returned safely on April 17. The 1995 feature film *Apollo 13* was directed by Ron Howard and features Kevin Bacon as Swigert.

Panteón Americano, Mexico City, Mexico

After William S. Burroughs accidentally killed his common-law wife, Joan Vollmer, in Mexico City on September 6, 1951, he was imprisoned for thirteen days before being granted bail. Burroughs's initial version of events involved Joan getting accidentally shot during a drunken William Tell act, but Burroughs later changed his story to a claim that he had accidentally misfired his gun.

Burroughs later remarked, "Of course I was drunk. It was an utterly and completely insane thing to do. I mean quite apart from the fact, if I'd hit the glass, it would have been terribly dangerous for the two people sitting there! Glass splinters would have been flying everywhere. So it was literally an insane thing to do" (*The Death of Joan Vollmer Burroughs*, 2002, by James Grauerholz). Burroughs was eventually convicted of negligent homicide and given a two-year suspended sentence in absentia.

Joan's parents arrived from New York and later agreed to raise her daughter from a previous marriage, Julie, while Billy Jr. would be sent to St. Louis to be taken care of by Burroughs's parents. Burroughs's brother, Mortimer, handled Joan's funeral arrangements. Joan was buried in Mexico City at Panteón Americano ("American Cemetery") near the Tacuba Metro station. The grave is inscribed simply "Joan Vollmer Burroughs, Loudonville, New York, 1923, Mexico D.F. Sept. 1951." Founded in 1898, Panteón Americano encompasses seventeen acres and today is considered one of the many historical sites in Mexico City.

Panteón Americano also serves as the final resting place of actress Pituka de Foronda (1918–99), the daughter of author Mercedes Pinto. She made her film debut in Cuba's first "talkie," *La Serpiente Roja*, in 1937. Foronda headed to Hollywood and screen tested for the 1943 film *For Whom the Bell Tolls*, but lost the part to Ingrid Bergman. She then appeared in director Indio Fernandez's *La Isla de la Pasión*, which was filmed in Mexico, and remained there the rest of her life.

In Ginsberg's haunting poem "A Dream Record: June 8, 1955," the poet imagines a conversation with the ghost of Vollmer. The poem concludes with Vollmer fading away and then the poet having a vision of her "rain-stained tombstone" in an "unvisited garden" in Mexico. In one of his journal entries published in *Cursed from Birth* (2006), William S. Burroughs Jr. wrote, "One of my pipe dreams is to return to Mexico, find where Joan is buried, and, regardless of the red tape, bring her remains back to the U.S. for a decent Christian burial. Should I appeal for funds for such a 'silly' project? I think not." James Grauerholz's 2002 essay "The Death of Joan Vollmer Burroughs: What Really Happened" serves as the definitive account of Joan's tragic death and its aftermath.

22

Visions of Eternal Freedom

Beat-Related Literary Magazines

A variety of key publications sprouted up in the 1950s and early 1960s to publish the work of the Beat Generation, such as the famous last issue of *Black Mountain Review* that focused on the San Francisco Renaissance and Beat Generation writers. In addition, Allen Ginsberg was one of the founders of the short-lived but influential *Beatitude* poetry magazine. The No. 1 edition of *Big Table* in 1959 featured excerpts from *Naked Lunch*, giving the novel the exposure it needed to get published by Olympia Press later that year.

Neurotica (1948–51)

"Written by neurotics, for neurotics," the quarterly magazine *Neurotica* was founded by Jay Landesman in 1948 and provided an early outlet for aspiring authors such as Allen Ginsberg, John Clellon Holmes, Carl Solomon, Kenneth Patchen, Lawrence Durrell, Anatole Broyard, Larry Rivers (the "Godfather of Pop Art"), Marshall McLuhan (the "High Priest of Pop-Culture"), and Judith Malina (cofounder of the Living Theatre).

In the first issue of *Neurotica*, Landesman (1919–2011) introduced the magazine as "a literary exposition, defense, and correlation of the problems and personalities that in our culture are defined as 'neurotic' . . . We are interested in exploring the creativeness of this man who has been forced to live underground." Landesman, who had previously owned an art gallery in St. Louis, Missouri, operated *Neurotica* out of New York City. A frequent denizen of the San Remo in Greenwich Village, which drew a young, hip crowd, Landesman reportedly used the influential and avant-garde literary journal in his efforts to pick up women.

Holmes's first published work, "Tea for Two," appeared in *Neurotica* in 1948, while Ginsberg's first published poem, "Song: Fie My Fum," appeared in *Neurotica* 6 (Spring 1950). Solomon's two essays published in *Neurotica* (under the pseudonym "Carl Goy") dealt with his experiences (including being subjected to electroshock therapy) at the New York Psychiatric Institute. Controversial cultural critic and folklorist Gershon Legman (1917–99) was also a frequent contributor to *Neurotica*, his first published article being "The Psychopathology of the Comics," and eventually took over briefly as editor of the publication. As might be expected, *Neurotica* ran afoul of censorship issues, primarily after the word "fuck" appeared in *Neurotica* 5 (Autumn 1949), which led the issue to be banned by the Post Office, followed by Legman's lengthy essay about "the Castration Complex." *Neurotica* folded after just nine issues in 1951.

In his book *Representative Men: The Biographical Essays* (1988), Holmes referred to *Neurotica* contributors as "a strange bunch . . . as they wandered in and out of Landesman's eccentric living-room-cum-office on Fifty-Third Street in New York. Surfacing out of different worlds, most of them probably would not have met another if not for the magazine . . . Marshall McLuhan chatted about Elizabethan literature as pot was smoked in the kitchen . . . Legman scowled on the couch, indomitable and fatalistic as a ticking time bomb." Landesman ended up turning the story of *Neurotica* into the first Beat musical, *The Nervous Set*, in 1959. The show did fairly well in St. Louis but bombed miserably on Broadway. Landesman edited *Neurotica: Authentic Voice of the Beat Generation*, which was published in 1981. In addition, Landesman's "irreverent" memoir, *Rebel Without Applause* (1987), features some colorful anecdotes about his days as *Neurotica* publisher.

In Jack Kerouac's *Visions of Cody*, which was written during 1951–52, "Jack Duluoz" (Kerouac) and "Cody Pomeray" (Neal Cassady) have a brief discussion about *Neurotica*, with Pomeray remarking, "I felt a great deal of envy, just like in this *Neurotica* that I just read here, castration complex, see . . . the whole thing is devoted to that and this and that." Duluoz replies that "they wanted me to write a whole issue" but they have "no money."

Black Mountain Review (1954–57)

Black Mountain Review served as the art and literary journal of the progressive Black Mountain College, which was founded by John Andrew Rice in 1933 in Black Mountain, North Carolina, just a fifteen-minute drive from author Thomas Wolfe's hometown of Asheville. Rice was a former faculty member at Rollins College in Winter Park, Florida. A highly experimental and innovative institution, Black Mountain College attracted a diverse group of writers and artists such as composer John Cage (who staged the first "happening" here in 1952), artist Robert Rauschenberg, dancer and choreographer

Merce Cunningham, poet Charles Olson (who coined the term "projective verse" and authored *The Maximus Poems*), artists Franz Kline and Willem de Kooning, architect Buckminster Fuller (who developed the geodesic dome), and poets Robert Creeley and Robert Duncan. Black Mountain College served as a precursor for other progressive educational institutions such as the Buddhist-inspired Naropa University in Boulder, Colorado—founded in 1974 and home to the Jack Kerouac School of Disembodied Poetics.

Inspired by Olson, the so-called Black Mountain poets (a.k.a. projectivist poets) include Ed Dorn, Paul Blackburn, Joel Oppenheimer, Denise Levertov, John Wieners, Robert Duncan, and Creeley, who famously remarked, "Form is never more than an extension of content." *Black Mountain Review* was published in the mid-1950s in the waning days of Black Mountain College, which closed its doors for good in 1956. Creeley edited the *Black Mountain Review* for two years before moving to San Francisco. The highly influential seventh and final issue of *Black Mountain Review*—known as the "Beat issue" and published in the fall of 1957 long after the College had closed—was edited by Creeley and Allen Ginsberg. Issue No. 7 featured an excerpt from William S. Burroughs's *Naked Lunch*, "America" by Ginsberg, an excerpt from "October in the Railroad Earth" by Jack Kerouac, "Changes: 3" by Gary Snyder, and "Bottom: On Shakespeare (Part II)" by Louis Zukofsky, among other works.

The former site of Black Mountain College is now Camp Rockmount for Boys. Founded in 1993 by Mary Holden, the Black Mountain College Museum + Arts Center was created "to honor and pay tribute to the spirit and history of Black Mountain College and to acknowledge the College's role as a forerunner in progressive, interdisciplinary education with a focus on the arts," according to the official website at www.blackmountaincollege.org. The Center offers exhibitions, publications, lectures, films, seminars, and oral history interviews. In addition, a feature-length documentary on Black Mountain College, *Fully Awake*, was released in 2007. Directed by Cathryn Davis Zommer and Neeley House, *Fully Awake* features interviews with former Black Mountain College students, faculty, historians, and current artists.

Evergreen Review (1957–73)

Founded in 1957 by legendary Grove Press publisher Barney Rosset (1922–2012), *Evergreen Review* was hailed as an "outlaw bible for a generation of radicals and activists." From its very first issue—which featured an essay by Jean-Paul Sartre, a Samuel Beckett short story called "Dante and the Lobster," and an interview with jazz great Warren "Baby" Dodds—this innovative literary journal pushed the boundaries of cultural and political discourse in the United States.

However, it was the second issue of *Evergreen Review*, titled "San Francisco Scene," that made an immediate impact with its diverse collection of works from Beat writers such as Jack Kerouac ("October in the Railroad Earth"), Allen Ginsberg (the first separate printing of "Howl"), Gary Snyder ("The Berry Feast," which he read at the Six Gallery in 1955), Kenneth Rexroth, Brother Antoninus, Robert Duncan, Lawrence Ferlinghetti, Michael McClure, and Philip Whalen, as well as Henry Miller, Jack Spicer, Josephine Miles, and others. Edited by Rosset and influential editor/publisher Donald Allen, the landmark second issue was introduced as highlighting "the exciting

Hailed as an "outlaw bible for a generation of radicals and activists," the highly influential *Evergreen Review* featured the work of many Beat writers, including Jack Kerouac, William S. Burroughs, Allen Ginsberg, and many others.   *Courtesy of Evergreen Review/evergreenreview.com*

phenomenon of a young group in the process of creating a new American culture."

Subsequent issues of the *Evergreen Review* featured some of the most provocative literary writing from the likes of Edward Albee, John Rechy, Richard Brautigan, Hubert Selby Jr., Charles Bukowski, and Terry Southern. United States Supreme Court Justice William O. Douglas even wrote a rather controversial essay, "Redress in Revolution," that appeared in the April 1970 issue. The final issue of *Evergreen Review*, No. 96, was published in 1973. An online edition of *Evergreen Review* operated from 1998 to 2013 (the archives of which are still available at www.evergreenreview.com). In an ad in the back of the 1962 edition of Lawrence Lipton's *The Holy Barbarians, Evergreen Review* is billed as "America's liveliest magazine" with the tagline "Have you heard about Beckett, Ionesco, Robbe-Grillet, but never read their work? Have you meant to read Kerouac, Miller, Burroughs, but didn't know where to find them?"

Through Grove Press, Rosset went on to publish several controversial novels, including D. H. Lawrence's *Lady Chatterley's Lover* (1959), Henry Miller's *Tropic of Cancer* (1961), and William S. Burroughs's *Naked Lunch* (1962). The publication of these novels led to several high-profile trials. Rosset himself often referred to Grove Press as "a breach in the dam of American Puritanism." He often received death threats, and his office in Greenwich Village was even bombed on one occasion in the late 1960s. *Life* magazine even ran a 1969 article about Rosset titled "The Old Smut Peddler."

A riveting 2008 documentary about Rosset and Grove Press, *Obscene*, features archive footage of Burroughs and Ginsberg, as well as interviews with Ferlinghetti, McClure, Gore Vidal, Ed Sanders, Ray Manzarek, Jim Carroll, Al Goldstein, Erica Jong, John Waters, and others. That same year, Rosset was honored by the National Book Foundation as "a tenacious champion for writers who were struggling to be read in America."

Measure (1957–62)

In the late 1950s, eccentric American poet John Wieners (1934–2002) edited and published *Measure* magazine, which became a prime outlet for the work of many Beat writers, including Jack Kerouac, Gregory Corso, Philip Lamantia, and Michael McClure. Born in Boston, Wieners received his bachelor of arts degree in English from Boston College and then attended Black Mountain College in North Carolina during the mid-1950s, where he was mentored by Charles Olson and struck up a lifelong friendship with fellow poet Robert Creeley. The first issue of *Measure* was published in 1957. A benefit described by Allen Ginsberg as a "monster poetry reading" was held in San Francisco to raise money to put out a second edition of *Measure* that featured readings by Ginsberg, Robert Duncan, Lawrence Ferlinghetti, Gary Snyder, Michael McClure, Leonore Kandel, and others.

During the late 1950s, Wieners moved out west and joined the San Francisco Renaissance. Wieners published his first book of poetry, *The Hotel Wentley Poems*, in 1958 at the age of twenty-four. Editor and publisher Raymond Foye commented that the work read "like a resume of Beat poetry and of late romanticism as a whole: urban despair, poverty, madness, homosexual love, narcotics and drug addiction, the fraternity of thieves and loveless transients" (*Boston College Magazine*, Fall 2000). Wieners's poetry in general is characterized by its jazz-inspired improvisation, along with a straightforward depiction of sex and drug use. In fact, in an interview cited in *Cultural Affairs in Boston: Poetry & Prose 1956–1985* (1988), Wieners remarked, "I try to write the most embarrassing thing I can think of." Allen Ginsberg called Wieners the "most lyrical" of the Beat poets.

Often described as shy and aloof, Wieners experimented with drugs, suffered a series of nervous breakdowns over the years, and even lived with Times Square hustler and drug addict Herbert Huncke in New York City for a time during the early 1960s. In 1969, Wieners was institutionalized in Taunton State Hospital, a psychiatric institution (originally known as the State Lunatic Hospital of Taunton), where he wrote *Asylum Poems*. Existing on the very fringes of the Beat movement, Wieners commented (*Boston College Magazine*, Fall 2000), "I am living out the logical conclusion of my books, and those are out of print." In fact, Wieners's friend, the poet Jim Dunn, referred to him as "the poetic equivalent of the Velvet Underground" since "only a thousand people bought their albums, but they all started rock bands. It's the same with John" (*Boston College Magazine*, Fall 2000). Long active in both the antiwar and gay rights movements, Wieners, who was known as Boston's "Pure Poet," died in 2002.

Yugen (1958–62)

A groundbreaking literary journal published by LeRoi and Hettie Jones, *Yugen* sold for fifty cents, ran for eight issues between 1958 and 1962, and was subtitled *A New Consciousness in Arts and Letters*. According to LeRoi Jones (who later changed his name to Amiri Baraka), *Yugen* "was started because I didn't see publications coming out that carried poetry or writing that I was interested in. Therefore, I thought I should start one to try to gather that poetry that I thought was interesting . . . I just thought nothing was happening on the poetry scene as it should be so I started publishing" (*Conversations with Amiri Baraka*, 1994).

Issue No. 1 of *Yugen* appeared in 1958 and featured the work of Jones, Allen Ginsberg, Philip Whalen, Diane di Prima, Jack Micheline, Ernest Kean, Allen Polite, Stephen Tropp, Bob Hamilton, Judson Crews, and Tom Postell. Issue No. 6 contained Kerouac's poem "Rimbaud" (it was later published as a broadside by City Lights in 1960). The work of William S. Burroughs appeared in Issue No. 3 and Issue No. 8: "Have You Seen Pantapon Rose?" and "The Cut Up Method of Brion Gysin," respectively. *Yugen* offered a forum for not only Beat writers such as Gregory Corso, Ray Bremser, and John Wieners, but also poets of the New York School such as Frank O'Hara and Kenneth Koch, as well as Black Mountain poets, including Robert Creeley and Joel Oppenheimer, and San Francisco Renaissance poets like Robin Blaser.

Yugen also featured the early work of Hubert "Cubby" Selby Jr. (1928–2004), who was a good friend of LeRoi Jones. Best known for his critically acclaimed and controversial novels such as the gritty *Last Exit to Brooklyn* (1964) and *Requiem for a Dream* (1978), Selby, who dropped out of school at the age of fifteen and joined the merchant marine, managed to overcome significant obstacles throughout his life, such as advanced tuberculosis, drug addiction, alcoholism, major bouts of depression, and extreme financial difficulties. Ginsberg described *Last Exit to Brooklyn* as "a rusty hellish bombshell that should explode all over America and still be read in a hundred years." The fascinating and harrowing 2005 documentary *Hubert Selby Jr: It/ll Be Better Tomorrow* features insightful interviews with Selby himself, as well as Baraka, Lou Reed, Darren Aronofsky, Richard Price, Nick Tosches, Jerry Stahl, Ellen Burstyn, Jared Leto, James Remar, and others. The film's title was taken from Selby's 1976 novel, *The Demon*, and reflects his unconventional writing techniques.

Yugen magazine ceased publication after Issue No. 8 in 1962. According to Jones (quoted in *Conversations with Amiri Baraka*), the magazine had "outlived its usefulness as far as I was concerned. By the time *Yugen* stopped publishing there were innumerable magazines that were publishing poets and writers that I had some respect for." Hettie Jones would later document the early Beat scene in New York City, as well as the challenges of putting together a literary journal, in her 1990 memoir, *How I Became Hettie Jones*.

Beatitude (1959–60)

In 1959, Allen Ginsberg was one of the founders of the short-lived *Beatitude* poetry magazine, along with poets Bob Kaufman, A. D. Winans, William Margolis, and John Kelly. The title of the magazine referred to Jack Kerouac's more spiritual definition of the term "beat." The first issues of *Beatitude* contained the works of Ginsberg, Kaufman, Margolis, and Richard Brautigan, among others.

Beatitude was billed as "a weekly miscellany of poetry and other jazz designed to extol beauty and promote the beatific or poetic life among the various mendicants, neo existentialists, christs, poets, painters, musicians, and other inhabitants and observers of North Beach, San Francisco, California, United States of America." The first issues of *Beatitude* were published at the Bread and Wine Mission in San Francisco and sold for twenty-five cents per copy. In 1960, City Lights Books published the *Beatitude Anthology*, which contained work culled from the first sixteen issues, and took over the publication of *Beatitude* starting with Issue No. 17, which was edited by Lawrence Ferlinghetti.

In addition to being one of the cofounders of *Beatitude*, Winans was a native San Francisco poet, writer, and photographer who authored more than forty-five books and chapbooks of poetry and prose. His work has appeared internationally since the '60s and has been translated into eight languages. A song poem of his was set to music and performed at New York's Alice Tully Hall. He has won numerous awards, including a PEN Josephine Miles Award for excellence in literature.

In 1979, a twentieth-anniversary celebration of *Beatitude* magazine was held at Savoy Tivoli in San Francisco. Ginsberg performed William Blake's "The Tyger" with his harmonium, accompanied by Peter Orlovsky with vocals and banjo. The poetry reading included Joanne Kyger, Bob Kaufman, Howard Hart, Michael McClure, Gregory Corso, and Lawrence Ferlinghetti. The event was organized by Neeli Cherkovski (*Whitman's Wild Children*) and Raymond Foye, one of the cofounders of Hanuman Books.

Big Table (1959–60)

In the Autumn 1958 issue of the *Chicago Review*, the literary magazine of the University of Chicago, editors Paul Carroll and Irving Rosenthal caused much controversy by publishing excerpts from William S. Burroughs's yet-to-be published novel *Naked Lunch* (it was Allen Ginsberg who had called the editors' attention to the work). The same issue also featured the works of Philip Whalen, John Logan, Brother Antoninus, Hugh Kenner, and David Riesman—but it was the excerpts from Burroughs's "nightmarish satire," *Naked Lunch*, that created all the furor. A reporter from the *Chicago Daily News* named Jack Mabley fueled the flames with an October 25, 1958, article about the issue titled "Filthy Writing on the Midway."

Administrators at the University of Chicago decided to censor the subsequent issue of the *Chicago Review* (Winter 1958), which was supposed to feature another eight excerpts from *Naked Lunch* (as well as works by Jack Kerouac and Edward Dahlberg), leading all of the magazine's editors except one to resign and start a new magazine, *Big Table*, so they could freely publish the works of Beat writers.

As might be expected, the No. 1 edition of *Big Table* (March 1959) featured another excerpt from *Naked Lunch*, as well as Kerouac's long narrative poem "Old Angel Midnight." Because of "obscenity and filthy contents," the United State Post Office impounded more than four hundred copies of the issue and refused to deliver them. Although an initial court decision found *Big Table* obscene, Judge Julius Hoffman, who later presided over the infamous Chicago Seven Trial (1969–70), reversed the decision, thus freeing the magazine for distribution. Carroll edited four more issues of *Big Table* in 1959 and 1960. The final issue of *Big Table* included works by Ginsberg, LeRoi Jones, Denise Levertov, Robert Creeley, John Ashbury, Barbara Guest, and other writers.

Testifying on behalf of *Naked Lunch* after the book had been banned by the Boston courts, author Norman Mailer remarked, "I first encountered [*Naked Lunch*] in 1958, in the magazine *Big Table* . . . a magazine that was put out by some editors who had left the *Chicago Review*, which was a literary magazine of the University of Chicago."

The Floating Bear (1961–71)

An influential literary newsletter coedited by Diane di Prima and Leroi Jones (Amiri Baraka) in New York City, *The Floating Bear* ran from 1961 to 1971 and featured works from Allen Ginsberg, William S. Burroughs, Philip Whalen, Michael McClure, Robert Duncan, John Wieners, Jack Spicer, Robert Creeley, Denise Levertov, Charles Olson, Ed Dorn, Frank O'Hara, Joel Oppenheimer, Herbert Huncke, and others. Jack Kerouac's "How to Meditate" appeared in Issue No. 34 of *The Floating Bear*. According to di Prima, "Roi and I had gotten together as lovers about a year before we got together as editors."

A total of thirty-seven issues of *The Floating Bear* were printed and distributed rather sporadically for free via mailing list. The title was suggested by di Prima based on a boat Winnie-the-Pooh created out of a honey pot. The first fifteen issues of the mimeographed newsletter were printed in di Prima's apartment. *The Floating Bear*'s subscriber list included Kerouac, artist Jasper Johns, novelist Fielding Dawson, and Living Theatre cofounder Julian Beck. According to Jones in *The Autobiography of Leroi Jones* (1995), "[*The Floating Bear*] was coming out regularly and became the talk of our various interconnected literary circles. It was meant to be 'quick, fast, and in a hurry' . . . the publication had real impact and influence and was greatly talked about. And though it had a regular circulation of about 300, those 300 were sufficiently wired for sound to project the *Bear*'s presence and 'message' in all directions."

On October 18, 1961, di Prima and Jones were arrested for publishing Jones's "From the System of Dante's Hell" and Burroughs's "Roosevelt After Inauguration" in Issue No. 9 of *The Floating Bear* (June 1961). A copy of Issue No. 9 had been sent to poet Harold Carrington, who was incarcerated in Rahway Prison in New Jersey. The prison censors reported the newsletter for obscenity to US postal authorities. The charges were later dismissed by a grand jury, as celebrated in Issue No. 20 of the newsletter. Carrington, who earlier had shared a cell with poet Ray Bremser, frequently corresponded with Jones. He died of a drug overdose just three days after being released from prison on July 27, 1964. Bremser later wrote a poem for Carrington titled "blues for Harold . . ." that appeared in his 1978 book, *Blowing Mouth*.

As for Burroughs, in an October 25, 1961, letter to Brion Gysin, he wrote rather despairingly, "Editor of The Floating Bear arrested for sending obscene matter through the mails. Exhibit A—a piece of mine entitled 'The Routine' which I didn't know they had or who gave it to them or what it consists of."

Moody Street Irregulars (1978–92)

From 1978 to 1992, Joy Walsh edited and published twenty-eight issues of a literary magazine devoted to Jack Kerouac and the Beat Generation called *Moody Street Irregulars* (which was subtitled *A Jack Kerouac Newsletter*). Issue No. 1 of *Moody Street Irregulars* (Winter 1978) featured contributions from Walsh, Michael Basinski, John Montgomery, and George Dardess, among others. Subsequent issues included interviews with the likes of William S. Burroughs and Carolyn Cassady.

Several issues of *Moody Street Irregulars* were devoted to special topics, such as No. 9 (devoted to *Vanity of Duluoz*, Kerouac's last published novel before his death in 1969), No. 11 ("French Connection," highlighting Kerouac's French-Canadian ancestry), and No. 15 ("Music Issue"), which contained a diverse variety of articles, including "Jack and the Beatstalkers" by Warren Peace, "Van Morrison and Kerouac" by Alex Albright, and "Through a Swinging Looking Glass or Steps to Discovering Jack Kerouac" by Con Holland-Skinner.

The front cover of each issue of *Moody Street Irregulars* proved to be just as eclectic as the content, with such examples as No. 2 featuring a comic strip that Kerouac drew for Neal Cassady's children (ca. 1952), No. 3 showcasing 109 Liberty Street in San Francisco where the Cassadys lived during the first half of 1949, and No. 4 highlighting Kerouac in his Lowell High School football uniform in 1939. The magazine's title reportedly came from the "Baker

Street Irregulars," a gang of street urchins (led by a kid named "Wiggins") that appeared in several of Arthur Conan Doyle's Sherlock Holmes stories, including his first novel, *A Study in Scarlet* (1888). Textile Bridge Press published Walsh's *Jack Kerouac: Statement in Brown*, a collection of essays, in 1984. In 1990, Basinski's Index to *Moody Street Irregulars: A Jack Kerouac Newsletter* was also published by Textile Bridge Press. *Moody Street Irregulars* ceased publication in Fall 1992.

Beat Scene (1988–)

Founded in 1988 by editor and publisher Kevin Ring, *Beat Scene* is a popular United Kingdom–based magazine devoted to everything related to the Beat Generation. Over the years, *Beat Scene* has featured the work of Jack Kerouac, William S. Burroughs, Allen Ginsberg, Gary Snyder, Diane di Prima, Jack Micheline, Ken Kesey, Lew Welch, Richard Brautigan, Lawrence Ferlinghetti, Charles Plymell, Anne Waldman, David Meltzer, David Amram, Charles Bukowski (who became a regular contributor up until his death in 1994), and many other writers.

According to Ring on the *Beat Scene* website (www.beatscene.net), "I had been interested in the Beat Generation, in particular Jack Kerouac, since around 1971. News of the books, many were out of print in those far off days, and the writers in the English media were pitiful, sporadic and patchy. Finding out about Kerouac, Burroughs, Ginsberg, Ferlinghetti and the others was a difficult thing to do, they were not the media favourites they are today, relatively speaking."

Issue No. 1 of *Beat Scene* was published in 1988 with just two hundred copies that were "collated and stapled on my kitchen table," stated Ring, "and included stuff on Kerouac, Burroughs, Snyder, John Clellon Holmes, John Fante, Paul Bowles, Charles Bukowski, Nanao Sakaki, Patti Smith and more." Issue No. 2 featured Carolyn Cassady's sketch of a young Kerouac as the cover artwork, while No. 4 (Winter 1988) included an article on the newly created Kerouac monument park in Lowell, Massachusetts, and No. 5 had cartoonist R. Crumb on the cover. According to Ring, "Looking back these [first] issues were obviously primitive and basic things but full of enthusiasm for the Beats and all the associated writers, musicians and whomever that are forever linked with them." *Beat Scene* truly turned a corner with No. 6, the first full-sized edition that appeared in Spring 1989 and featured Kenneth Rexroth, Rickie Lee Jones, Kerouac, Burroughs, and Philip Whalen. For more information about *Beat Scene*, visit www.beatscene.net.

23

Don't Hide the Madness

Beat Live Performances and Recordings

A large part of the Beat mystique revolved around live poetry readings and later recordings such as Jack Kerouac's first spoken-word album, *Poetry for the Beat Generation* (1959), which featured piano accompaniment by Steve Allen. William S. Burroughs released some classic spoken-word albums full of "routines" from his works, such as *Dead City Radio* (1990) and *Spare Ass Annie and Other Tales* (1993), while Allen Ginsberg's *Holy Soul Jelly Roll* (1994) provides a comprehensive overview of the recordings of his work over the years.

San Francisco Poets (1958)

The landmark No. 2 issue of *Evergreen Review* covering the "San Francisco Scene" in 1957 featured the works of Allen Ginsberg, Jack Kerouac, Gary Snyder, Lawrence Ferlinghetti, Michael McClure, Philip Whalen, Robert Duncan, and Henry Miller. An exceedingly rare LP record, *San Francisco Poets*, was released by the short-lived Evergreen Records the following year and included readings by Ginsberg, Brother Antoninus (William Everson), Robert Duncan, Jack Spicer, McClure, Kenneth Rexroth, Whalen, and Ferlinghetti, as well as poet and experimental filmmaker James Broughton, and poet/literary critic Josephine Miles. *San Francisco Poets* features Ginsberg performing a lively reading of Part I of "Howl" in front of an audience. All of the rest of the poems are studio recordings.

Broughton (1913–99), whose favorite expression was "follow your own weird," was a pioneer of experimental filmmaking known for his 1968 film, *The Bed*, a "cinematic celebration of sexual liberation." Poet Neeli Cherkovski referred to Broughton as "the outsiders' outsider," while critic Amos Vogel called him the "great and wise master of the American avant-garde." Broughton served as the subject of the 2012 documentary *Big Joy:*

The Adventures of James Broughton, where he remarked, "I believe in ecstasy for everyone." Miles (1911–85), who was the first woman to receive tenure in the English Department at the University of California, Berkeley, wrote more than a dozen books of poetry. In 1974, Miles founded the *Berkeley Poetry Review*. Her *Collected Poems, 1930–1983* won the Lenore Marshall Poetry Prize from the *Nation* magazine in 1983. Miles suffered from a chronic case of rheumatoid arthritis, which she contracted at the age of two.

San Francisco Poets was reissued by Hanover Records in 1959. Hanover also released two of Jack Kerouac's early recordings, *Poetry for the Beat Generation* in 1958 and *Blues and Haikus* in 1959. In *Poetry for the Beat Generation*, Kerouac was accompanied by Steve Allen on the piano. In *Blues and Haikus*, he was accompanied by jazz saxophonists Al Cohn and Zoot Sims. Both albums are included on the 1990 CD box set *The Jack Kerouac Collection*. In addition, *San Francisco Poets* features iconic images of the poets on the back sleeve taken by celebrated photographer Harry Redl (1926–2011), who lived in San Francisco during the late 1950s and photographed the flourishing literary and art scenes there (in one of his most famous images, Ginsberg glares at the camera while pointing at San Francsico's Sir Francis Drake Hotel at night). Redl's work was also featured in *Evergreen Review* No. 2.

According to McClure (quoted on the *Beat Page*), "In the mid-fifties it was something special to have a brilliant photographer coming around to photograph the outlaw and outcast art scene. We didn't know yet that we were 'Beats' or the 'San Francisco Renaissance' but Harry Redl's photographs helped to delineate those movements, and helped us define ourselves."

Call Me Burroughs (1965)

The first spoken-word album from William S. Burroughs, *Call Me Burroughs* features readings from his novels *Naked Lunch* (1959), *The Soft Machine* (1961), and *Nova Express* (1964). Tracks include "Bradley the Buyer," "Meeting of International Conference of Technological Psychiatry," "The Fish Poison Con," "Thing Police Keep All Board Room Reports," "Mr. Bradley Mr. Martin Hear Us Through the Hole in Thin Air," "Where You Belong," "Inflexible Authority," and "Uranian Willy."

Produced by Ian Sommerville, the album was first released on LP by the English Bookshop, Paris, in 1965 and reissued on CD by Rhino Word Beat in 1995. According to Barry Miles in the album's liner notes, "The English Bookshop was the center of literary activity for the Beat Hotel writers and their crowd. The painter Guy Harloff, who first introduced Gregory Corso to the hotel (and through him caused Ginsberg and then Burroughs to move there), exhibited his work in the medieval *cave* beneath [English Bookshop proprietor Gait Froge's] shop."

Also in the album's liner notes, Barry Alfonso writes, "For some Burroughs is a notorious character more interesting for his scandalous past than anything else. Others dote on him as a king of futuristic vaudevillian, an apocalyptic Will Rogers cracking jokes before the sky falls down. And a few more consider him to be a visionary sage masquerading as a hipster antihero. *Call Me Burroughs* can be appreciated on all these levels and more. Meanwhile, Inspector Lee remains at large, ambiguous in his eminence, bringing back stolen reports from the front lines, for our entertainment and our enlightenment."

Dead City Radio (1990)

Released by Island Records, *Dead City Radio* consists of a classic collection of readings by William S. Burroughs accompanied by Sonic Youth, Donald Fagen of Steely Dan, John Cale of the Velvet Underground, Lenny Pickett of Tower of Power, Chris Stein of Blondie, and the NBC Symphony

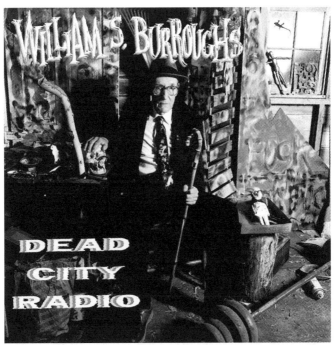

Some of William S. Burroughs's most memorable routines, such as "A Thanksgiving Prayer" and "Kill the Badger!," can be found on his 1990 spoken word album, *Dead City Radio*.   *Author's collection*

Orchestra, as well as composer/French hornist Tom Varner and drummer, composer, and bandleader Bobby Previte. Most of the recordings of Burroughs's readings were made at his Lawrence, Kansas, home in December 1988. Burroughs dedicated the album to "Keith Haring, at the Apocalypse."

Dead City Radio contains some of Burroughs's most memorable routines, such as "A Thanksgiving Prayer" ("Thanks for the wild turkey and the passenger pigeons, destined to be shit out through wholesome American guts"), "Scandal at the Jungle Hiltons" (from *The Western Lands*), "Ah Pook the Destroyer" (from *Ah Pook Is Here*), "No More Stalins, No More Hitlers" (from *Interzone*), and "Kill the Badger!" (from *The Cat Inside*, and featuring the classic line "Ask yourself, whose life is worth more? The badger, or this evil piece of white shit?"), as well as *Naked Lunch* excerpts ("Ever see a hot shot hit, kid? I saw the Gimp catch one in Philly."). A bonus track includes Burroughs's truly bizarre rendition of the German standard "Ich bin von Kopf bis Fuss auf Liebe eingestellt" ("Falling in Love Again").

In "A Nation of Finks" (*Unarmed But Dangerous*, 1995), award-winning essayist Hal Crowther writes, "My brother gave me a tape of William S. Burroughs reading a numbing epitaph for America ('The last and greatest betrayal of the last and greatest of human dreams') titled 'A Thanksgiving Prayer.' Burroughs may not be the single most reliable witness to our common experience. But I can't forget one of the lines in his prayer: 'Thanks for a nation of finks.'"

The Jack Kerouac Collection (1990)

A nicely packaged triple-disc box set that includes a lengthy companion booklet, *The Jack Kerouac Collection* contains the classic spoken-word albums *Poetry for the Beat Generation* (1959), *Blues and Haikus* (1959), and *Readings by Jack Kerouac on the Beat Generation* (1960).

Featuring Steve Allen on piano, *Poetry for the Beat Generation* includes "October in the Railroad Earth," "Deadbelly" (*Mexico City Blues*, chorus 221), "Charlie Parker" (*Mexico City Blues*, choruses 239–41), "The Sounds of the Universe Coming in My Window," "One Mother" (*Mexico City Blues*, chorus 149), "Goofing at the Table" (*Mexico City Blues*, choruses 80–83), "Bowery Blues," "Abraham," "Dave Brubeck," "I Had a Slouch Hat Too One Time," "The Wheel of the Quivering Meat Conception" (*Mexico City Blues*, chorus 211), "MacDougal Street Blues," "The Moon Her Majesty," and "I'd Rather be Thin than Famous" (*Mexico City Blues*, chorus 104). Showcasing the talents of saxophonists Al Cohn and Zoot Sims, *Blues and Haikus* includes "American Haikus," "Hard Hearted Old Farmer," "The Last Hotel," "Some of the Dharma," "Poems from the Unpublished 'Book of Blues,'" "Old Western Movies," and "Conclusion of the Railroad Earth."

Readings by Jack Kerouac on the Beat Generation features "The Beat Generation" (*Desolation Angels*, book 1, chapter 77), "Poems (Fragments)," "Lucien Midnight: The Sounds of the Universe, Part II," "Fantasy: The Early History of Bop," "Excerpts from *The Subterraneans*," "Visions of Neal: Neal and the Three Stooges, Part I," and "Visions of Neal: Neal and the Three Stooges, Part II." Bonus material includes "Is There a Beat Generation?" and "Readings from *On the Road* and *Visions of Cody.*"

The Jack Kerouac Collection includes more than thirty minutes of previously unreleased material, such as outtakes from the *Blues and Haikus* sessions, recitations from *On the Road* and *Visions of Cody* from the *Steve Allen Show*, and a recording from the "Is There a Beat Generation" symposium. The companion booklet to *The Jack Kerouac Collection* features an introduction by Jan Kerouac, who wrote, "Even people who can't get through his wild run-on prose on paper are instantly captured by his voice . . . A lullabye of this magnitude will be sorely needed in the mad decades to come." Other highlights include remembrances of Kerouac by the likes of Allen Ginsberg, William S. Burroughs, Michael C. Ford, Robert Frank, Edie Kerouac-Parker, Gerald Nicosia, Ann Charters, Steve Allen, Michael McClure, Harvey Robert Kubernik, Bob Thiele, Stephan Ronan, and David Perry. *The Jack Kerouac Collection* received a Grammy Award nomination for "Best Historical Album" (but lost out to *Robert Johnson—The Complete Recordings*).

Jack Kerouac's third and final spoken word album, *Readings by Jack Kerouac on the Beat Generation*, was recorded in 1958 and released in January 1960 on Verve Records.

Author's collection

The Beat Generation (1992)

A truly eclectic three-disc box set released by Rhino Records, *The Beat Generation* is saturated with the best of hipster culture and belongs in the collection of any true Beat aficionado. The box set features not only Jack Kerouac, William S. Burroughs, and Allen Ginsberg, but also the likes of

Tom Waits ("Jack & Neal"), Don Morrow ("Kerouazy"), Charlie Parker, Lord Buckley, Charles Mingus, Gerry Mulligan, Kenneth Patchen, Nelson Riddle, Kenny Clarke & His Fifty-Second Street Boys, David Amram Quintet, Lenny Bruce, Kenneth Rexroth, Charles Kuralt (" The Greenwich Village Poets"), Dizzy Gillespie, Carl Sandburg ("On Beatniks"), Oscar Brown Jr. ("But I Was Cool"), and others.

According to album producer James Austin in the liner notes, "The Beats were the ones who started the whole counterculture movement that led to the hippies, the punk rockers, and so on. *The Beat Generation* is a way of paying tribute to those people who have taken us away from the conventional and conformist in America." Highlights of *The Beat Generation* include Ben Hecht interviewing Kerouac, Burroughs reading an excerpt from *Naked Lunch*, Patchen reading "Murder of Two Men by a Young Kid with Colored Gloves" with jazz accompaniment, "Cosmic Rays" by the Charlie Parker Quartet, and Allen Ginsberg reading "America." The companion booklet to *The Beat Generation* features classic photos, cultural analysis, and great quotes about the Beats.

In a 1992 review of *The Beat Generation* for the *Fort Worth Star-Telegram*, Michael H. Price wrote, "In three compact discs and an accompanying book, the package captures the Beat spirit in spoken word, jazz, formal interviews and comedy. Even borderline hipsters will find plenty to admire in the boxed album."

The "Priest" They Called Him (1993)

A unique (although long-distance) collaboration between William S. Burroughs and Nirvana singer-guitarist Kurt Cobain, *The "Priest" They Called Him* features the Beat author's droll reading of a classic short story from his 1973 book *Exterminator!* backed by the grunge musician on dissonant guitar playing "Silent Night" and "To Anacreon in Heaven."

The bizarre story of *The "Priest" They Called Him* concerns a junkie known as the "Priest," who, desperate to score on Christmas Eve, steals an old leather suitcase, which he discovers in horror to contain a pair of severed legs. He ends up nonchalantly dumping the legs, selling the suitcase, and buying drugs from a sleazy doctor. The Priest then heads to his rooming house to shoot up but hears a groan from next door—a young Mexican kid in the throes of withdrawal. In an act of Christian charity, the Priest gives the kid a shot of his drugs. The Priest returns to his room and miraculously receives the "immaculate fix."

Nirvana bassist Krist Novoselic appears on the album's front cover as the priest. Interestingly, the inside cover image of Burroughs came from director Gus Van Sant's 1993 book, *108 Portraits*. Van Sant had directed the 1989 cult film *Drugstore Cowboy*, which featured Burroughs as "Old Tom the Junkie Priest." In addition, Van Sant directed *Last Days* (2005), a fictionalized account of the death of a musician named "Blake" (loosely based on Cobain) that received mixed reviews. *The Junky's Christmas* was also turned into a stop-motion animated short film in 1993.

Spare Ass Annie and Other Tales (1993)

Released by Island Records, William S. Burroughs's third spoken-word album features the musical accompaniment of the Disposable Heroes of Hiphoprisy, a short-lived but influential alternative hip-hop band that was formed in 1990 by Michael Franti and Rono Tse (guitarist Charlie Hunter soon joined the group). Produced by Hal Willner (who also worked on Burroughs's 1990 album, *Dead City Radio*), *Spare Ass Annie* contains some classic routines, including the title track, as well as "The Last Words of Dutch Schultz," "Mildred Pierce Reporting," "Dr. Benway Operates," "Warning to Young Couples," "Did I Ever Tell You About the Man Who Taught His Asshole to Talk?", and "The Junky's Christmas" (which was used for a stop-motion animation short of the same title released in 1993).

In a December 2, 1993, review for the *Chicago Tribune*, Rohan B. Preston wrote, "*Spare Ass Annie* features Burroughs' Vincent Price–like reading of original fiction over mid-paced hip-hop grooves. Even if the text seems quirky or bizarre, it's hard to resist nodding along to Burroughs' discourses on the human body and God drawn from such works as *Interzone* and *Nova Express*. But do not be distracted by the mixing of Christmas carols, TV theme music, live guitar and reggae instrumentation. This forward-looking release pairs figures who are supposed to be diametrically opposed (an older white with urban youth) for a seamless, interesting and original work."

In 1992, the Disposable Heroes of Hiphoprisy released their debut album, *Hypocrisy Is the Greatest Luxury*, which features such hard-hitting tracks as "Satanic Reverses," "Television, the Drug of the Nation," "Everyday Life Has Become a Health Risk," and "Financial Leprosy." Although well received critically, the album sold poorly and the group disbanded in 1993.

Holy Soul Jelly Roll: Poems & Songs 1949–1993 (1994)

A comprehensive four-disc box set that features the best of Allen Ginsberg, *Holy Soul Jelly Roll* is full of gems such as "Howl" (recorded at Town Hall Theater, Berkeley, March 18, 1956), "Kaddish" (Brandeis University, November 24, 1964), "The Green Automobile" (Neal Cassady's home, San

Jose, California, summer 1954), "America" (Berkeley, March 18, 1956), "Death to Van Gogh's Ear" (Library of Congress Recording Laboratory, February 27, 1959), and many others. The collection encompasses Vol. 1 ("Moloch!"), Vol. 2 ("Caw! Caw!"), Vol. 3 ("Ah!"), and Vol. 4 ("Ashes & Blues").

In the album's liner notes, producer Hal Willner comments, "Allen's ideas for the set were quite simple: He suggested that it comprise his *Howl* album (Fantasy Records); his William Blake interpretations (there are two completed LPs, one previously released on MGM, the second unissued); *First Blues* (a double album that was the very first release on John Hammond's Hammond Records); the recordings he made with Harry Smith in the Chelsea Hotel in 1971 (later released on Folkways); selections from *The Lion For Real*; and various other recordings that would surface during the process."

Holy Soul Jelly Roll includes a sixty-four-page booklet with Ginsberg's own recollections, as well as commentary from the likes of Lawrence Ferlinghetti, Michael McClure, Bob Rosenthal (Ginsberg's friend and secretary), and Bob Dylan, who calls Ginsberg "probably the single greatest influence on American poetical voice since Whitman."

Hotwalker (2005)

Subtitled *Charles Bukowski and a Ballad for Gone America*, singer-songwriter Tom Russell's 2005 conceptual album, *Hotwalker*, was described by critic Don McLeese as "an intensely personal travelogue through a bohemian America that no longer exists." Russell and his fictional cohort, circus midget "Little Jack Horton," take listeners on a nostalgic tour across the country in the '50s and '60s that cleverly blends songs, voiceover narration, excerpts from spoken-word pieces, field recordings, and background instrumentals.

Hotwalker features special appearances by Jack Kerouac reading "October in the Railroad Earth" accompanied by Steve Allen on the piano from the 1959 album *Poetry for the Beat Generation*; Charles Bukowski performing "On the Hustle" from the 1985 album *Hostage*; Lenny Bruce performing "Marriage, Divorce and Motels" from *Lenny Bruce Originals: Volume 2* (1992); Harry Partch excerpted from *Enclosures: Harry Partch*; and Edward Abbey, excerpted from the award-winning 1993 PBS documentary *Edward Abbey: A Voice in the Wilderness*. In addition, *Hotwalker* includes several eclectic tracks, including "96 Tears" by Rudy Martinez, "Cocaine Blues" by Gary Davis, "Sportin' Life Blues" by Dave Von Ronk, and "Pilgrim Land," "When We All Get to Heaven," and "Jesus Hold My Hand" performed by Reverend Baybie Hoover and Virginia Brown.

Russell first discovered the work of Bukowski through the column "Notes of a Dirty Old Man" in *Open City*, an underground newspaper in Los Angeles.

Conducted by Dub Spencer & Trance Hill and released in 2014, *William S. Burroughs in Dub* blends the Beat author with electronic dub beats from the four-piece live band from Switzerland.   *Author's collection*

Russell and Bukowski later struck up a correspondence. In an interview with the *Houston Chronicle* (August 4, 2005), Russell remarked, "I hit Bukowski at the right time. I was young; the beats were about done, and I was looking for something else. Bukowski said whatever was on his mind and young people dig that."

A native of Los Angeles, Russell has honed a reputation as a true outsider and iconoclast over the years. Poet Lawrence Ferlinghetti has acknowledged that he shares "a great affinity with Tom Russell's songs, for he is writing out of the wounded heart of America." Russell's songs have been covered by the likes of Johnny Cash, Guy Clark, Nanci Griffith, Jerry Jeff Walker, Dave Von Ronk, Joe Ely, Iris Dement, Ramblin' Jack Elliott, and Doug Sahm, among others.

Guilty of Everything (2012)

As a down-and-out drug addict, thief, and Times Square hustler, Herbert Huncke (1915–96) was truly the most "beat" character of all. He also gained a reputation as a great storyteller who held court in the all-night cafeterias and dive bars on Forty-Second Street. In fact, in a 1947 letter to Neal Cassady, Jack Kerouac remarked, "Huncke is the greatest storyteller I know."

Released by Unrequited Records, *Guilty of Everything* features a double CD of Huncke's 1987 live reading at Ins & Outs Press, Amsterdam, the Netherlands, and provides a great introduction to Huncke's consummate storytelling skills. It is the only recording ever made of a Huncke reading in Europe. Disc one consists of a brief introduction followed by three tracks: "Meeting Bill Burroughs," "Biographical Sketch," and "First Love Affair." Disc two features Huncke reading a selection from *Guilty of Everything*, his 1990 autobiography, along with his classic story "Whitey."

According to Jerome Poynton, Huncke's literary executor, in the liner notes, "For Herbert writing was a visceral release. He liked the sensation of putting pen to paper. He wrote in small notebooks, or on paper bags garnered at Greyhound Bus rest stops en route to a detox hospital in Lexington, Kentucky. Herbert's aim was to produce a 'living document.' To describe a scene as it happened, without adding his opinions . . . He was aided by an excellent memory and a great eye for detail."

24

Sullen Rebels, Defiant Chicks

The Beat Generation on Film

T he first Beat films could safely be labeled "beatnik exploitation flicks" with titles like *The Beat Generation* (1959), *Beat Girl* (1960), *The Beatniks* (1960), and the legendary 1959 Roger Corman cheapie, *A Bucket of Blood* (see review in chapter seventeen). Conversely, the short film *Pull My Daisy* (1959), which featured Allen Ginsberg, Peter Orlovsky, and Gregory Corso, along with narration by Jack Kerouac, is today considered a classic of American independent cinema. Feature films relating to the Beat Generation have included the rather sedate *Heart Beat* (1980), David Cronenberg's innovative take on *Naked Lunch* (1991), and the truly dismal *Beat* (2000) with Kiefer Sutherland totally miscast as William S. Burroughs. The recent resurgence of films based on the Beat Generation include *Howl* (2010), *Big Sur* (2013), *On the Road* (2013), and *Kill Your Darlings* (2013). In addition, William S. Burroughs has turned in memorable performances in both the truly bizarre *Twister* (1989) and the offbeat *Drugstore Cowboy* (1989) as "Old Tom the Junkie Priest," spouting such classic lines as "In the future, right wingers will use drug hysteria to set up an international police apparatus." Burroughs also provided narration for an abbreviated version of the classic 1922 silent film *Witchcraft Through the Ages* (a.k.a. *Haxan*).

Beat Exploitation Films (1959–63)

During the height of the beatnik frenzy in the late 1950s and early 1960s, Hollywood fed into the craze with a host of low-budget "Beat" films, many of which were of dubious quality, although the 1959 Roger Corman black comedy, *A Bucket of Blood*, towers above them all.

One of the earliest Beat exploitation films, *The Beat Generation* (1959), promised to capture the "wild, weird world of the Beatniks!" Produced by Albert Zugsmith for MGM, *The Beat Generation* featured an eclectic cast that

Produced by Albert Zugsmith for MGM, *The Beat Generation* (1959), which starred Mamie Van Doren, Ray Danton, Louis Armstrong, and Jackie "Uncle Fester" Coogan, was one of the earliest Beat exploitation films.   *Author's collection*

included sex symbol Mamie Van Doren, Ray Danton (*The George Raft Story*), jazz great Louis Armstrong, Jackie "Uncle Fester" Coogan, accordionist Dick Contino, Irish (Sheena, Queen of the Jungle) McCalla, Charles Chaplin Jr., and Maila "Vampira" Nurmi. In *The Psychotronic Encyclopedia of Film* (1983), author Michael Weldon describes *The Beat Generation* as "a lurid cop-after-a-rapist story with a beatnik-coffee-house background." Interestingly, the landmark 1959 Beat film *Pull My Daisy* was originally intended to be titled *The Beat Generation*, but the name had to be changed since this film was released first.

In the cheesy but eminently entertaining low-budget horror film *The Hypnotic Eye* (1959), the "King of the Beats" (portrayed by Venice Beach Beat denizen Lawrence Lipton) recites poetry accompanied by Ed "Big Daddy" Nord on bongos (several scenes were shot at Nord's beatnik café, the Gas House in Venice Beach, California). Filmed in "HypnoMagic," *The Hypnotic Eye* concerns a sleazy magician named "Desmond" (Jacques Bergerac), who uses his extraordinary powers of suggestion to hypnotize young women into grotesquely disfiguring themselves.

Other notable Beat exploitation films of this period include *Live Fast, Die Young* (1958), "The Sin-Steeped Story of Today's 'Beat' Generation!"; *Hot Car*

Girl (1958), "She's HELL-ON-WHEELS . . . fired up for any thrill!"; *The Rebel Set* (1959), "The Screen's Big Jolt About . . . The Beatnicks!"; *Daddy-O* (1959), "Meet the 'Beat'! Daring to Live . . . Daring to Love!"; and *The Beatniks* (1960), which exposed "the intimate secrets of the beat generation!"

In addition, the film noir thriller *D.O.A.* (1950), which was directed by Rudolph Mate and stars Edmond O'Brien, features a scene in a smoky jazz club that definitely exudes an early Beat vibe (with one of the characters even exclaiming, "Man, am I really hip!"). Also, in the enjoyable musical comedy *Funny Face* (1956), which was directed by Stanley Donen, Audrey Hepburn portrays the ultimate beatnik chick, "Jo Stockton."

Pull My Daisy (1959)

"Look at all those cars out there. There's nothing out there but a million screaming ninety-year-old men being run over by gasoline trucks. So throw the match on it." Directed by Robert Frank and Alfred Leslie, the short film *Pull My Daisy* (1959), which features Allen Ginsberg, Peter Orlovsky, Gregory Corso, artist Larry Rivers, and composer David Amram, along with narration by Jack Kerouac, is today considered a landmark avant-garde film and a true classic of American independent cinema.

The title *Pull My Daisy* was taken from an experimental poem that Ginsberg, Kerouac, and Neal Cassady collaborated on in the late 1940s. Although the thirty-minute film has a spontaneous, improvisatory quality, Leslie later revealed in a November 28, 1968, interview with the *Village Voice* that *Pull My Daisy* was actually carefully crafted, rehearsed, and directed. However, Kerouac improvised much of his narrative, resulting in such classic lines as "What is holy? Is baseball holy? Is a cockroach holy? Holy, holy!"

Based on Kerouac's unproduced play, *The Beat Generation* (an unrelated Beat exploitation flick of that name was released by MGM the same year starring Mamie Van Doren), *Pull My Daisy* tells the story of a bishop (Richard Bellamy) and his mother (Alice Neel) who are invited over to dinner by the wife of "Milo" (Rivers), a railroad brakeman (based on Cassady), who lives in a New York City apartment. All hell breaks loose when Milo's Beat buddies—Ginsberg, Orlovsky, and Corso—crash the dinner party.

Delphine Seyrig portrayed Milo's wife, while dancer Sally Gross played the bishop's sister, and Frank's son Pablo appeared as Milo's son. Amram, who starred as musician "Mezz McGillicuddy," also wrote the jazz score. Frank, who was then best known for his controversial, highly influential 1958 photobook, *The Americans* (which featured an introduction by Kerouac) also served as director of photography. Leslie was later quoted in the article "Jack Kerouac and the Beats, Off the Road and in a Film" (*New York Times*, July 12, 2000), saying, "It was a formal film, quiet in tone and movement . . . It had a strong subtext of subversiveness, a Samuel Beckett, Chehkovian kind of quality in which nothing happens. Like a *Seinfeld* incident of nothing."

In 1961, Grove Press published a sixty-four-page book, *Pull My Daisy*, which contains film stills accompanied by Kerouac's narration and an introduction by longtime *Village Voice* critic Jerry Tallmer (the book was republished in 2008). In 1996, *Pull My Daisy* was selected for preservation in the National Film Registry by the Library of Congress as being "culturally, historically, or aesthetically significant." Leslie and Frank discuss *Pull My Daisy* at length in the book *Naked Lens: Beat Cinema* by Jack Sargeant, which was originally published in 1997.

The Subterraneans (1960)

"TODAY'S Young Rebels—who live and love in a world of their own. This is their story told to the hot rhythms of fabulous jazz!" Leave it to Hollywood to take Jack Kerouac's raw, poetic 1958 novella, *The Subterraneans*, and turn it into a mainstream 1960 film (released by MGM no less!) fit for mass consumption. For instance, the film adaptation turned the African American character "Mardou Fox" into a fun-loving young French girl portrayed by Leslie Caron.

The Hollywoodized cast of two-dimensional characters includes George Peppard as "Leo Percepied," Janice Rule as "Roxanne," Roddy McDowell as "Yuri Gligoric," Anne Seymour as "Charlotte Percepied," Jim Hutton as "Adam Moorad," Scott Marlowe as "Julien Alexander," and none other than *Laugh-In* regular Arte Johnson as "Arial Lavalerra" (believe it or not, the Gore Vidal character "Arial Lavalina" from the novella!). The film's tagline read, "Love Among the New Bohemians!"

One of the final MGM films produced by Arthur Freed, *The Subterraneans* did feature an excellent jazz score by Andre Previn, as well as cameos by legendary singers and musicians such as Carmen McRae (who performs "Coffee Time" with the Andre Previn Trio), Gerry Mulligan, Shelly Manne, Buddy Clark, Dave Bailey, and Art Pepper, among others. *The Subterraneans* was directed by Ranald MacDougall, who had received an Oscar nomination for Best Adapted Screenplay for *Mildred Pierce* (1945), which was based on the 1941 novel of the same name by James M. Cain.

In a rather mixed review of *The Subterraneans* for the *New York Times* (July 7, 1960), critic A. H. Weiler called the film "a colorless pot-pourri of romance and disjointed drama that haltingly states a case for man's need of true love." Weiler did single out Caron's performance as "occasionally poignant and touching," while Peppard lent "a proper air of the confusion engendered by sudden love amid alien surroundings and people." In his two-and-a-half-star review of *The Subterraneans*, critic Leonard Maltin called the film a "glossy, superficial study of life and love among the beatniks, with pure cornball stereotype performances. MGM was not the studio for this one." When all was said and done, *The Subterraneans* turned out to be a box office bomb.

Kerouac had sold the rights to the novella to MGM in 1958 for $15,000 and bought a house in Northport, Long Island—the first house he ever owned. He lived in Northport with his mother off and on for the next six years before moving to St. Petersburg, Florida, in 1964. Remarkably, there wouldn't be another film adaptation of any of Kerouac's novels until *On the Road* (2012).

Heart Beat (1980)

"They shocked us. They outraged us. They didn't do anything wrong. They just did it first." Based on *Heart Beat: My Life with Jack and Neal*, Carolyn Cassady's rather sedate 1976 memoir, *Heart Beat* was directed by John Byrum (*Inserts*) and stars Sissy Spacek (*Badlands*) as Carolyn, Nick Nolte (*North Dallas Forty*) as Neal, and John Heard (*Cutter's Way*) as Jack, as well as Ray Sharkey as "Ira" (an amusing beatnik caricature of Allen Ginsberg, who didn't want his name attached to the project after he read the script) and Ann Dusenberry as "Stevie" (based on LuAnne Henderson).

In a June 3, 1979, interview with Roger Ebert (www.rogerebert.com), Nolte (who shares the same birthday with Cassady—February 8) remarked, "I was thinking of the comparisons between the Neal Cassady character and Hicks, the guy I play in *Who'll Stop the Rain*. At the end of *Rain*, Hicks walks down the railroad tracks . . . and that was lifted from a book about Cassady . . . and Cassady, the beatnik, and Hicks, the screwed-up war hero, were two sides of the same coin." According to Nolte, "To us, today, [the Beats] seem mild enough. What did they do? Write poetry, smoke dope, lead bohemian lives . . . they weren't really even political, they were more into an experiment about life."

Ebert, who gave the film two and a half stars, complained that the story from Carolyn's point of view "is not exactly the story we have in memory from the Kerouac legend, and there were long stretches of *Heart Beat* during which I found myself wishing instead for a film version of *On the Road*." Ebert concluded that the film "seems to exist almost entirely as a matter of style . . . What finally happens is that the whole period—the conformist '50s as well as the rebellious beats—gets frozen into the same flashback."

Two actual highlights of *Heart Beat* are the cool jazz score by Jack Nitzsche (who scored *One Flew Over the Cuckoo's Nest*) and the excellent cinematography by Lazlo Kovacs (*Five Easy Pieces*). Kerouac's only child, Jan, served as an extra in the film, which also features director David Lynch (*Eraserhead*) uncredited as a painter, John Larroquette ("Dan Fielding" on *Night Court*) as a TV talk show host, and Steve Allen (who had collaborated with Kerouac on a jazz poetry album) as himself. *Heart Beat* ended up receiving mixed reviews and totally bombed at the box office.

Burroughs visited the set of *Heart Beat* and wrote about his experience in an article titled "Heart Beat: Fifties Heroes as Soap Opera" in the January 24, 1980, issue of *Rolling Stone*, claiming that when he sat next to Nolte, he "felt Neal sitting there in his cheap 1950s suit with the sleeves pulled up."

Although Carolyn Cassady enjoyed Spacek's performance, she was overall disappointed with the film, remarking in a 2009 interview with editor Victoria Mixon (www.victoriamixon.com), "The script was absolutely horrible and the opposite of how we were . . . I met [director John] Byrum years later in New York and asked how he was doing. He said, 'Well, I did three TV pilots, all of which flopped, but Paramount has just given me two million and a studio.' Can anyone understand H'wood?" Spacek went on to win the Academy Award for Best Actress for her next film, *Coal Miner's Daughter*, a brilliant portrayal of legendary country music star Loretta Lynn.

Naked Lunch (1991)

"The book was banned. The film should never have been made. Too late." For years, William S. Burroughs's 1959 novel, *Naked Lunch*, was considered unfilmable. Believe it or not, at one point in the early seventies, *Gong Show* producer Chuck Barris was interested in the project and even flew Burroughs and Terry Southern (who had helped director Stanley Kubrick revise the screenplay for his 1964 film, *Dr. Strangelove*) out to Los Angeles but was "worried about all the sex and violence," according to Burroughs, in an interview with the *Michigan Quarterly Review* (Winter 1974), who added, "But what's Naked Lunch without sex and violence?" It gets even weirder—Burroughs and Southern had wanted James Taylor, Dennis Hopper, or Mick Jagger to portray "William Lee," as well as Groucho Marx for "Dr. Benway," but "[Barris] wouldn't hear of it."

However, filming the plotless novel proved to be the perfect challenge for Canadian film director David Cronenberg, who was known for his compelling, offbeat (and often quite disturbing!) films such as *Shivers* (1975), *Rabid* (1977), *The Brood* (1979), *Scanners* (1981), *Videodrome* (1983), *The Dead Zone* (1983), and *The Fly* (1986). Cronenberg decided to forgo a literal adaptation of the novel in favor of more of his own eclectic interpretation. The film features many of the novel's themes of control and addiction, blended with

In 1991, Canadian film director David Cronenberg brought his own eclectic vision to the film version of William S. Burroughs's 1959 novel, *Naked Lunch*, which was long considered unfilmable.

Courtesy of Photofest

musings about the creative process (specifically writer's block) and fictionalized scenarios taken from actual events in Burroughs's own life, such as the accidental shooting of his common-law wife, Joan Vollmer, in 1951; his friendships with Jack Kerouac and Allen Ginsberg ("Hank" and "Martin"); and his bizarre relationship with an expatriate couple in Tangier, Morocco, loosely modeled on Paul and Jane Bowles.

According to Cronenberg, "It's impossible to make a movie out of *Naked Lunch*. It would cost $400 million to make and would be banned in every country in the world . . . It was obvious, for both artistic and practical reasons, I was going to have to do my own version of *Naked Lunch*—a fusion of my own writing with Burroughs."

Naked Lunch opens in New York City in 1953 with exterminator "William Lee" (Peter Weller) discovering that somebody has been stealing his roach powder. When Lee arrives home, he catches his wife, "Joan" (Judy Davis), injecting herself with the powder. She exclaims, "It's a Kafka high . . . you feel like a bug." Lee is soon picked up by a couple of mysterious narcotics agents for "possession of a dangerous substance," taken into custody, and left alone where he views a huge bug in a box that informs him 'I am your case officer . . . Your wife is an agent of Interzone, Incorporated. You must kill her.'"

Film critic Jonathan Rosenbaum of the *Chicago Reader* wrote that *Naked Lunch* (1991) "may well be *the* most troubling and ravishing head movie since *Eraserhead.*"   *Author's collection*

A very confused Lee squashes the bug with his shoe and makes a quick exit. In an effort to kick his bug powder habit, Lee visits the mysterious "Dr. Benway" (Roy Scheider), who provides him with a vial of "aquatic Brazilian centipede." Lee returns home and tells Joan, "It's about time for our William Tell routine." After Joan places a glass on her head, Lee pulls out his revolver and fires but misses the glass, shooting her in the head and killing her instantly. Believe it or not, the plot starts to get even stranger after these opening scenes.

Concerning the inclusion of the true-to-life "William Tell" scene in the script, Burroughs commented in *Everything Is Permitted: The Making of Naked Lunch* (1992), "The whole film is so bizarre, so far out, so beyond the parameters of reality, so I didn't feel like it was an invasion of privacy. It is beyond the concept of privacy." In addition, the notorious "Talking Asshole" routine from the novel is included in the film. According to Scheider, "Dr. Benway is probably the sleaziest scumbag in the movie. He's a manipulator, a drug user, a drug seller, an autocrat, and a dreadful person" (*Everything Is Permitted: The Making of Naked Lunch*). The solid cast includes Ian Holm as "Tom Frost," Julian Sands as "Yves Cloquet," Robert A. Silverman as "Hans," John Friesen as "Hauser," Sean McCann as "O'Brien," Monique Mercure as "Fadela," Nicholas Campbell as "Hank," and Joseph Scorsiani as "Kiki."

In his two-and-a-half-star review of *Naked Lunch* on January 10, 1992 (www.rogerebert.com), critic Roger Ebert wrote, "While I admired it in an abstract way, I felt repelled by the material on a visceral level. There is so much dryness, death and despair here, in a life spinning itself out with no joy." In *Newsweek* (January 12, 1992), critic David Ansen commented, "Obviously this is not everybody's cup of weird tea: you must have a taste for the esthetics of disgust. For those up to the dare, it's one clammily compelling movie." Critic Jonathan Rosenbaum of the *Chicago Reader* (January 16, 1992) remarked that the film "may well be *the* most troubling and ravishing head movie since *Eraserhead.*"

The Last Time I Committed Suicide (1997)

The blurb on the video jacket for *The Last Time I Committed Suicide*, which was directed by Stephen T. Kay (*Boogeyman*), exclaims: "Meet Neal Cassady, a cool, happening guy who has a poet's soul, a dreamer's heart and choices to make that just may lead him down the road to happiness . . . Journey with Neal, the original 'wild one,' as he learns about love, lust, friendship and how to be a 'beat' ahead of the rest."

The opening credits of this excruciatingly dull film make the claim that the movie is based entirely on a letter written by Neal Cassady to Jack Kerouac, presumably the fabled "Joan Anderson Letter" (which was discovered in the fall of 2014 amid a file of forgotten papers). The film's introduction refers to Cassady as the "Avatar of American Hipness." Unfortunately, it all goes downhill from there. Thomas Jane (*The Mist*) portrays twenty-year-old Cassady (the film actually focuses on his life before he even hit the road with Kerouac in 1947), who works the night shift at a tire factory in Denver, Colorado, and precariously balances his rather complicated love life, which includes his relationship with the suicidal "Joan" (Claire Forlani).

The film also stars Keanu Reeves, who does not portray Kerouac as you might expect but appears for about ten minutes as Cassady's pal, "Harry," a sleazy, alcoholic pool-hall hustler. To be honest, most of the film details Cassady's various attempts to get laid. He even goes after an underage girl dubbed "Cherry Mary" (Gretchen Mol), much to the chagrin of her parents. Cassady also befriends a shy poet named "Ben" (Adrien Brody), who develops a crush on the wild-eyed hipster.

In a review of the film for the *New York Times* (June 20, 1997), critic Stephen Holden wrote, "At 20, the man who became a guiding light of the Beat Generation, inspiring Jack Kerouac's *On the Road* and later joining Ken Kesey's psychedelic troupe the Merry Pranksters, is portrayed as a hunky mixed-up kid with too many hormones roiling around in his body . . . As evocatively as it evokes the late 1940s, *The Last Time I Committed Suicide* has little dramatic momentum."

Howl (2010)

"There's no Beat Generation. It's just a bunch of guys trying to get published." In *Howl*, James Franco stars as Allen Ginsberg, "poet, counterculture adventurer, and chronicler of the Beat Generation." Ginsberg recounts the "road trips, love affairs, and search for personal liberation" that led to the creation of his landmark poem "Howl" in 1955 (sections of the famous work are even interpreted through somewhat awkward animated sequences). The film also depicts the landmark Six Gallery Reading in 1955 when Ginsberg read "Howl" for the first time, as well as the famous obscenity trial over *Howl and Other Poems* that provided a victory for freedom of expression against the backdrop of the stifling conformity rampant throughout the United States during the 1950s.

The team of Rob Epstein and Jeffrey Friedman directed *Howl*, which features the cast of Aaron Tveit as Peter Orlovsky, Jon Prescott as Neal Cassady, Todd Rotondi as Jack Kerouac, Andrew Rogers as Lawrence Ferlinghetti, Jon Hamm as defense attorney Jake Ehrlich, David Strathairn as prosecuting attorney Ralph McIntosh, Bob Balaban as Judge Clayton W. Horn, Jeff Daniels as Professor David Kirk, Mary-Louise Parker as prosecution witness Gail Potter, and Alessandro Nivola as defense witness Luther Nichols.

Howl received mixed reviews, with Rene Rodriguez of the *Miami Herald* (October 22, 2010) calling it a "disappointingly mundane movie about a vibrant, iconoclastic subject," while David Edelstein of *New York Magazine* raved, "It's a celebration, an analysis, a critical essay, an ode." Interestingly, Shig Murao (1926–99), City Lights Bookstore manager, who played a central role in the obscenity trial, was mysteriously omitted from the film's narrative.

Big Sur (2013)

"Some souls never stop searching." Arguably the most successful film adaptation of any of Jack Kerouac's novels to date, *Big Sur* was directed by Michael Polish and features beautiful cinematography, solid acting, and compelling voice-over narration such as "I was surrounded and outnumbered and had to get away to solitude again or die." *Big Sur* made its debut at the 2013 Sundance Film Festival.

Big Sur details a burnt-out, alcoholic Kerouac as he retreats to Lawrence Ferlinghetti's secluded cabin in Bixby Canyon three years after the publication of *On the Road*, which turned him into a reluctant celebrity to say the least: "No booze, no drugs, no binges, no bouts with beatniks and drunks and junkies and everybody." The film strays from the novel (in a good way!) by using the actual names of characters instead of pseudonyms. The *Big Sur* cast features Jean-Marc Barr as Kerouac, Josh Lucas as Neal Cassady, Radha Mitchell as Carolyn Cassady, Anthony Edwards as Ferlinghetti, Stana Katic as Lenore Kandel, Balthazar Getty as Michael McClure, Kate Bosworth as Billie Dabney, Henry Thomas as Philip Whalen, Patrick Fischler as Lew Welch, and Jason W. Wong as Victor Wong.

According to Polish in a November 1, 2013, *Slant* magazine interview, "I really wanted to make a movie where you really hear [Kerouac]. And you can stop hearing him if you want. It almost becomes music. You can stop and be like, 'Well, I don't really know what he said, but it looks and sounds gorgeous.' I wanted to stay true. I knew other Kerouac movies were having problems. At least, if someone has a problem with this movie, it's because it's a real Kerouac movie. You're going to hate it because it's really Kerouac."

Barr commented in a November 4, 2013, *Metro* interview that he had read *On the Road* in college and "it was like someone had opened the door to something I had always been thinking about . . . When they offered me this part I started reading more of his work and I realized there was nothing to play . . . I was living that. I was just playing myself and how Kerouac has inspired my soul and my passion about life, love, literature."

Kill Your Darlings (2013)

Loosely based on true events, *Kill Your Darlings* follows Allen Ginsberg (Daniel Radcliffe of *Harry Potter* fame) as he leaves the quiet confines of his hometown of Paterson, New Jersey, and heads to Columbia University in bustling New York City during the early 1940s. Ginsberg soon becomes fascinated with fellow student Lucien Carr (Dane DeHaan), who is eccentric, charming, handsome, and a like-minded, freethinking intellectual. Carr introduces him to William S. Burroughs (Ben Foster) and "hanger-on" David Kammerer (Michael C. Hall from *Dexter*), who is obsessed with Carr and quickly becomes envious of Ginsberg's role as his idol's new sidekick. Jack Kerouac (Jack Huston) is also a leading member of this early "Libertine Circle." Tragedy strikes when, following a drunken argument, Carr stabs Kammerer to death early one morning in Riverside Park and dumps his body into the Hudson River. Ginsberg has to decide whether to defend his friend's story of self-defense or discover the truth of what happened that night.

Kill Your Darlings was directed by John Krokidas in his feature directorial debut and scripted by Austin Bunn. The solid cast includes comedian David Cross (Louis Ginsberg), Jennifer Jason Leigh (Naomi Ginsberg), Elizabeth Olsen (Edie Parker), and Kyra Sedgwick (Marian Carr). The film premiered at the 2013 Sundance Film Festival. Lucien Carr's son, Caleb, publicly denounced the film as inaccurate, describing it as "a tired, ludicrous reading of the story of the murder case; and like all the other terribly inaccurate readings that have been put out there, it was based almost entirely on Allen Ginsberg's versions of events. And Allen had an awful lot of reasons for revising the facts to suit a narrative that served his ego and his agenda far more effectively than it did the truth."

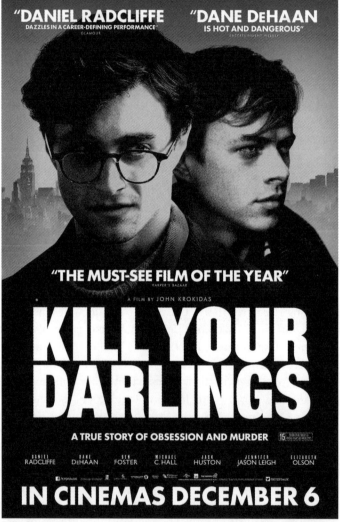

Billed as "A True Story of Obsession and Murder," the 2013 film *Kill Your Darlings* was loosely based on Lucien Carr's killing of David Kammerer in 1944.

Author's collection

On the Road (2013)

"The best teacher is experience." A curiously uninvolving adaptation of Jack Kerouac's 1957 novel, *On the Road* stars Sam Riley as "Sal Paradise," Garrett Hedlund as "Dean Moriarty," Kristen Stewart as "Marylou," Tom Sturridge as "Carlo Marx," Kirsten Dunst as "Camille Moriarty," Viggo Mortensen as "Old Bull Lee," and Amy Adams as "Jane." Walter Salles (*The Motorcycle Diaries*) directed the film, while Francis Ford Coppola served as executive producer. *On the Road* premiered at the 2012 Cannes Film Festival where it was nominated for the Palme d'Or.

In preparation for the filming of *On the Road*, Salles spent six years, on and off, filming a documentary called *Searching for On the Road*, during which time he immersed himself in the world of the Beat Generation by retracing the journeys of Kerouac and Neal Cassady in the novel. Along with crisscrossing the country, Salles met with the likes of Lawrence Ferlinghetti, Michael McClure, Diane di Prima, Amiri Baraka, and others to get a real sense of the Beat perspective.

The film garnered mixed reviews, with critic Peter Bradshaw of the *Guardian* calling it a "good-looking but directionless and self-adoring road movie." In *Time*, critic Richard Corliss wrote, "Though there's plenty of cool

The '49 Hudson used in the 2013 film version of *On the Road* is on permanent display at the Beat Museum in North Beach, San Francisco.   *Author's collection*

jazz in the background, the movie lacks the novel's exuberant syncopation—it misses the beat as well as the Beat . . . This trip goes nowhere."

Plans to make a film adaptation of *On the Road* have been in the works since the book was published in 1957. In fact, Kerouac even wrote a letter to Marlon Brando suggesting that he play the role of "Dean Moriarty" opposite the author's "Sal Paradise." Brando never responded to the letter, much to the chagrin of Kerouac. Coppola bought the rights to *On the Road* in 1979 and made several abortive attempts to get it filmed. At one point in the late 1990s, Ethan Hawke and Brad Pitt were suggested for the roles of "Sal Paradise" and "Dean Moriarty," respectively, and later the rumors had Billy Crudup cast as "Paradise" with Colin Farrell as "Moriarty."

In a 1997 interview, author Harry Crews (*A Feast of Snakes*) remarked, "Francis Ford Coppola put in for me to write the screenplay for Kerouac's *On the Road*, which he's got the rights to. I didn't tell him yes; I didn't tell him no. I went down to the end of the street and bought the damn book and read it again, and said 'I don't want to write this.' And I didn't. And I called him, and I said, 'No, I don't think I want to write it' . . . You know, you travel all the hell over in the book . . . He said, 'Hey, you rent yourself a big coach, get a couple of friends, put one in the driver's seat, just go, follow the route, whatever, do it that way.' I said, 'Man, you know how long you're talking about taking out of my life? I mean, I'd be on the road for X number of weeks, then I'd be on the set.'"

25

The Shadow Cast by Our Imaginations

Beat Generation Documentaries

A plethora of quality Beat Generation documentaries have been produced over the years that include in-depth and revealing interviews, re-creations of key moments in the literary movement's history, live readings, and little-known insights into Beat culture. Other quality documentaries in addition to the ones listed here include *Kerouac: The Movie* (1985), *Gang of Souls: A Generation of Beat Poets* (1989), *William S. Burroughs: Commissioner of Sewers* (1991), *Crazy Wisdom: The Jack Kerouac School of Disembodied Poetics* (2008), *One Fast Move or I'm Gone: Jack Kerouac's Big Sur* (2008), and *William S. Burroughs: A Man Within* (2010), among others.

West Coast: Beat and Beyond (1984)

A public television documentary, *West Coast: Beat and Beyond* was directed by Chris Felver and Gerald Nicosia, who also provided the narration. Highlights of the film include rare footage and compelling interviews with the likes of Ken Kesey, Bob Kaufman, Philip Lamantia, Jack Micheline, Harold Norse, Jan Kerouac, Joanne Kyger, Bobbie Louise Hawkins, and Howard Hart to "illuminate the imagination and inspire a torrential indictment against American mediocrity."

According to Felver (www.chrisfelver.com), "Filmed on location in San Francisco's North Beach neighborhood, and at Naropa Institute in Boulder, Colorado, this film is a tribute to the ongoing vision of America's renegade minds, as well as a salute to the visionary power of Jack Kerouac."

In a 1984 review of the film for the *Oakland Tribune*, "Beat Era Writers are Lively Survivors," critic Diana Ketcham wrote, "Despite its title, the film is not a look back at the '50s, so much as a reminder of how many of that era's legendary characters are still very much with us. Poet and publisher Lawrence

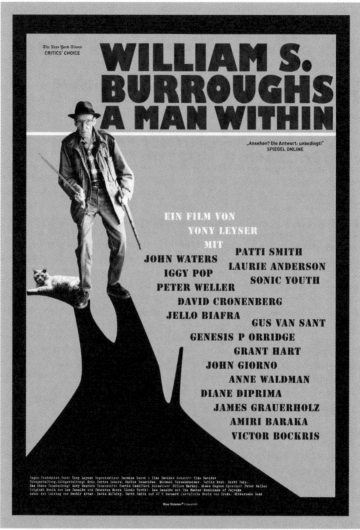

Directed by Yony Leyser, *William S. Burroughs: A Man Within* premiered at
the Slamdance Film Festival and later won the Van Gogh Award for Best
Biography at the Amsterdam International Film Festival.   *Author's collection*

Ferlinghetti is shown presiding at his City Lights bookstore, the locus of Beat
publishing in the '50s. Ferlinghetti reads from his poem 'Look Homeward,
Jack,' dedicated to Jack Kerouac, while Beat historian Nicosia talks about
Kerouac's affinity with novelist Thomas Wolfe . . . Jazz drummer Howard
Hart, one of Kerouac's New York roommates, nurses a beer in a North Beach
bar."

West Coast: Beat and Beyond was one of several notable films to come out of the 1982 Naropa "On the Road" Twenty-Fifth Anniversary Celebration that included Constanzo Allione's *Fried Shoes and Cooked Diamonds* and Robert Frank's *This Song for Jack*. A noted filmmaker and photographer, Felver has published several Beat-related books, including *The Poet Exposed* (1986), *Angels, Anarchists and Gods* (1996), *Lawrence Ferlinghetti Portrait* (1998), *The Late Great Allen Ginsberg* (2003), and *Beat* (2007). Felver also directed the documentaries *The Coney Island of Lawrence Ferlinghetti* (1996) and *Ferlinghetti: A Rebirth of Wonder* (2009). Nicosia is the author of several Beat biographies, including *Memory Babe: A Critical Biography of Jack Kerouac* (1994), *Jan Kerouac: A Life in Memory* (2009), and *One and Only: The Untold Story of On the Road* (coauthored by Anne Marie Santos, 2011).

Burroughs: The Movie (1983)

One of the best Beat Generation documentaries, *Burroughs: The Movie* began its life as director Howard Brookner's twenty-minute senior thesis at NYU Film School and then was expanded into a feature-length film five years later. Brookner enlisted fellow NYU classmates and close friends Tom DiCillo (*When You're Strange*), who served as cinematographer, and Jim Jarmusch (*Stranger than Paradise*), who was sound recordist on the project. *Burroughs: The Movie* provides an intimate glimpse of William S. Burroughs never before seen, along with interviews with many of his contemporaries, such as Allen Ginsberg, Herbert Huncke, Brion Gysin, Francis Bacon, Patti Smith, and Terry Southern, as well as rare footage of Burroughs's tormented, self-destructive son, Billy Jr.

In his three-star review of *Burroughs: The Movie*, critic Roger Ebert commented, "*Burroughs* is a documentary portrait of a man who was willing to try everything, and who has so far survived everything. The one thing you miss in the film is the sound of laughter." Reviewing *Burroughs: The Movie* in the *New York Times* (October 8, 1983), critic Janet Maslin wrote, "The quality of discovery about Burroughs is very much the director's doing, and Mr. Brookner demonstrates an unusual degree of liveliness and curiosity in exploring his subject." Brookner's directorial credits include *Robert Wilson and the Civil Wars* (1986) and *Bloodhounds of Broadway* (1989). Tragically, Brookner died of AIDS on April 27, 1988, at the age of thirty-four. In the final year of his life, Brookner left a letter that read, "If I live on it is in your memories and the films I made."

In 2012, Brookner's nephew, Aaron Brookner, launched a campaign to remaster and rerelease *Burroughs: The Movie*, which had been out of print for almost two decades. The restored documentary was rereleased in 2014 to coincide with the one hundredth anniversary of Burroughs's birth. In a 2014 interview posted on Indiewire (www.blogs.indiewire.com), Aaron Brookner remarked, "The films that Jim Jarmusch and others were making at this time, they sort of applied the total lack of respect for rules that Burroughs and Ginsberg had laid in literature, and applied it to cinema. They took what they saw around them and put it in their work. And in the case of Howard making *Burroughs: The Movie*, with Jim and also Tom DiCillo who was doing camera,

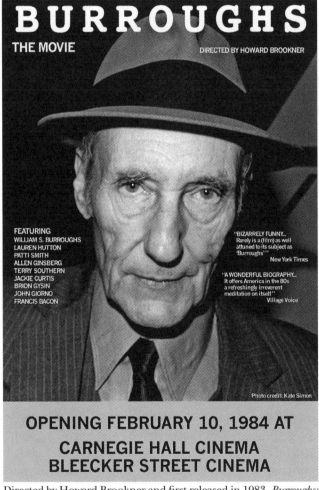

BURROUGHS
THE MOVIE
DIRECTED BY HOWARD BROOKNER

FEATURING
WILLIAM S. BURROUGHS
LAUREN HUTTON
PATTI SMITH
ALLEN GINSBERG
TERRY SOUTHERN
JACKIE CURTIS
BRION GYSIN
JOHN GIORNO
FRANCIS BACON

"BIZARRELY FUNNY...
Rarely is a (film) as well
attuned to its subject as
'Burroughs'"
New York Times

"A WONDERFUL BIOGRAPHY...
It offers America in the 80s
a refreshingly irreverent
meditation on itself"
Village Voice

Photo credit: Kate Simon

OPENING FEBRUARY 10, 1984 AT
CARNEGIE HALL CINEMA
BLEECKER STREET CINEMA

Directed by Howard Brookner and first released in 1983, *Burroughs: The Movie* was remastered and rereleased by Brookner's nephew, Aaron, in 2014 to coincide with the one-hundredth anniversary of the author's birth. *Author's collection* he went straight to the source. Howard decided not only am I going to apply the lack of rules, rule to movie-making, I'm gonna turn the camera on this moment in time as it's really happening."

What Happened to Kerouac? (1986)

Directed by Richard Lerner and Lewis MacAdams—and billed as "an investigation of the king of the Beat Generation"—*What Happened to Kerouac?* is a fascinating documentary that delves into the triumphs and tragedies of the legendary Beat author. The ninety-six-minute documentary features lively and informative interviews with his contemporaries, such as William S. Burroughs; Gregory Corso; Allen Ginsberg; Carolyn Cassady; Michael McClure; Gary Snyder; Diane di Prima; Steve Allen; John Clellon Holmes; Herbert Huncke; Fran Landesman; Lawrence Ferlinghetti; Joyce Johnson; Ed White ("Tim Gray" in *On the Road*); Robert Creeley; and Edie Parker; as well as Kerouac's only child, Jan Kerouac; his first biographer, Ann Charters; and his hometown priest, Father Armand "Spike" Morrisette.

In *What Happened to Kerouac?*, Burroughs claims that *On the Road* inspired "a worldwide cultural revolution of unprecedented worldwide extent." A rather disheveled Corso sarcastically remarks that "you don't call a generation four people." (One critic claimed that Corso seemed to be doing "an imitation of Sid Caesar imitating a cracked scientist" during his interview segments.) Jan Kerouac describes one of the only two times she ever met her father: "He was just sitting in this rocking chair in front of the TV set watching *The Beverly Hillbillies*," and periodically slugging from a bottle of whisky.

What Happened to Kerouac? also includes some great footage from Kerouac's guest spot on the *Steve Allen Show* nervously reading excerpts from *On the Road* while Allen plays some soft jazz on the piano in 1959, as well as his infamous drunken appearance on William F. Buckley's *Firing Line* show in 1968 (among the other guests was Ed Sanders of the Fugs), where he claims that "a lot of hoodlums and communists jumped on my back." There's also a nice montage of San Francisco scenes accompanied by Kerouac reading "October in the Railroad Earth." An added bonus is the inclusion of some rare clips of Neal Cassady, as well as music by jazz great Thelonious Monk.

According to Lerner (www.whathappenedtokerouac.com), "In looking over some of the many film reviews from the 1980s, I was struck by a line that mirrored our own thinking. The film couldn't answer its own title question in a way that is easily put into words." Michael Sragow wrote in the *San Francisco Examiner*, "That they don't offer a definitive answer to *What Happened to Kerouac?* is true to the man himself who like Walt Whitman (one of his heroes) contained multitudes."

The Beat Generation: An American Dream (1987)

Billed as an "Investigation of the Beat Generation," this intriguing eighty-six-minute documentary was directed by Janet Forman (and cowritten by Forman and Regina Weinrich) and uses original film clips, archival footage, and interviews to present a solid overview of the Beat Generation. *The Beat Generation: An American Dream* features appearances by Jack Kerouac, Allen Ginsberg, William S. Burroughs, Gregory Corso, Lawrence Ferlinghetti, Ray Bremser, Diane di Prima, Herbert Huncke, Hettie Jones, Amiri Baraka, Robert Creeley, Carolyn Cassady, Jan Kerouac, and Steve Allen (who serves as narrator), as well as counterculture figures Timothy Leary and Abbie Hoffman.

Highlights of *The Beat Generation: An American Dream* include Jack Kerouac reading from *On the Road* with piano accompaniment by Steve Allen, Allen Ginsberg's spirited reading of "Howl," and jazz great Thelonious Monk performing in 1957, as well as a jazz score by composer David Amram, who collaborated with Kerouac on many occasions as documented in his 2003 memoir, *Offbeat: Collaborating with Kerouac.*

Over the years, *The Beat Generation: An American Dream* has been screened in art houses and on television worldwide, as well as selected for screening at international festivals such as the Berlin Film Festival, AFI Film Festival in Los Angeles and Washington, DC, Sao Paulo Film Festival in Brazil, Ghent Film Festival in Belgium, Valladolid Festival in Spain, and Venice Film Festival. The film was also included as part of the Beat Generation retrospective at New York's Whitney Museum.

In a March 8, 1988, review of *The Beat Generation: An American Dream* for the *Los Angeles Times*, Kevin Thomas wrote that the film "offers a comprehensive and engaging study of a small group of writers who had a far greater and lasting impact than they could have ever imagined . . . The film's key point is that the young people who became known as 'the beats' simply did not feet they fit into postwar America. It was a time when a renewed emphasis on conformity in the wake of military victory coincided with a soon-booming consumer economy, the dawn of the nuclear age, the Cold War and McCarthyism. The beats, whom Jack Kerouac defined simply as being 'sympathetic,' came from a wide range of backgrounds. They realized that there was much dissatisfaction in an idealized suburbia and wanted to pursue their own, anti-materialistic version of the American dream."

The Life and Times of Allen Ginsberg (1994)

In this insightful documentary directed by Jerry Aronson, who accumulated more than 120 hours of footage, Allen Ginsberg is presented as a "visionary, radical, spiritual seeker, renowned poet, founding member of a major literary movement, champion of human rights, Buddhist, political activist and teacher," whose "remarkable life challenged the very soul of America."

The Life and Times of Allen Ginsberg traces the poet's life from his early childhood in Paterson, New Jersey (where he "bore the brunt" of his mother's mental illness), to his death from liver cancer in 1997 at the age of sixty-six.

After Allen Ginsberg passed away in 1997, Jerry Aronson, the director of *The Life and Times of Allen Ginsberg*, updated the documentary in several ways, including the addition of a new recording of Paul Simon singing the poet's "New Stanzas for Amazing Grace" for the closing credits.

Author's collection

The film was first premiered at the 1993 Sundance Film Festival to positive reviews, and has been updated and rereleased several times over the years. The eighty-two-minute documentary features interviews with the likes of William S. Burroughs; Timothy Leary; Anne Waldman; Patti Smith; Joan Baez; Michael McClure; Andy Warhol; Hunter S. Thompson; Amiri Baraka; Ken Kesey; Yoko Ono; Johnny Depp; and Paul McCartney; as well as Ginsberg family members such as his brother, Eugene; stepmother, Edith; and aunt Hannah.

In addition, the film includes footage of Ginsberg appearing on William F. Buckley's *Firing Line* TV show in 1968 and *The Dick Cavett Show* in 1978, as well as a rare clip of Ginsberg and his father, Louis (an important minor lyric poet in his own right), sharing the stage at a poetry reading and his participation in a 15,000-person protest against the Rocky Flats Nuclear Weapons Plant in 1979 (Ginsberg and Daniel Ellsberg were among the 284 protesters arrested that day).

The Life and Times of Allen Ginsberg won the prestigious International Documentary Association Award of Excellence in 1994. The documentary was revised after Ginsberg's death, and the final cut was completed for the release of the 2007 tribute DVD, which contains six hours of bonus features, including extended and updated interviews, Ginsberg reading selected poems, footage of Ginsberg and Bob Dylan at Jack Kerouac's grave, Ginsberg and Burroughs at Naropa University, Ginsberg and Cassady at City Lights Bookstore, *The Making of the Music Video A Ballad of the Skeletons*, and a featurette, *The Making of The Life and Times of Allen Ginsberg*.

Aronson's filmography also includes a documentary short, *The Divided Trail: A Native American Odyssey* (1977), which was nominated for an Academy Award, and a six-hour TV miniseries documentary, *America's Music: The Roots of Country* (1996). Aronson has taught filmmaking at Columbia College in Chicago, the University of Illinois, and the University of Colorado, Boulder. He is also the producer of *Chasing Ice*, a critically acclaimed 2012 documentary on climate change.

The Source (1999)

A unique documentary about the Beat Generation directed by Chuck Workman, *The Source* blends rare footage, photographs, TV appearances, interviews, and home movies with famous passages from the works of Allen Ginsberg ("Howl"), Jack Kerouac (*On the Road*), and William S. Burroughs (*Naked Lunch*) read by actors John Turturro, Johnny Depp, and Dennis Hopper, respectively. The film premiered at the Sundance Film Festival.

The Source also features fascinating interviews with Beat writers Ginsberg, Burroughs, Gary Snyder, and Lawrence Ferlinghetti, as well as authors Ken Kesey and Norman Mailer, Jerry Garcia of the Grateful Dead, Ed Sanders of the Fugs, and political activist Tom Hayden, among others. The documentary also delves into the Beat Generation's influence on the 1960s counterculture, as well as the prevalence of beatnik caricatures in the late 1950s and early 1960s.

In addition, *The Source* includes footage from Kerouac's infamous appearance on William F. Buckley's *Firing Line* TV show in 1968 and the landmark short film *Pull My Daisy* (1959), which was directed by Robert Frank, narrated by Kerouac, and stars Ginsberg, Corso, and Peter Orlovsky. In the *New York Times* review (August 25, 1999) of *The Source*, critic Janet Maslin called the film "a stirring, kaleidoscopic documentary." However, Chuck Rudolph of *Matinee* magazine (April 5, 2001) remarked, "Watching it feels like whiplash, and afterwards it doesn't feel like you've benefited at all from sitting through it."

An award-winning director, writer, and producer, Workman is the head of Calliope Films. Previously he had edited and produced trailers for countless films, including the likes of *American Graffiti*, *Star Wars*, and *Close Encounters of the Third Kind*. Workman's 1986 documentary, *Precious Images*, won an Academy Award for Best Live Action Short and was later selected as a landmark film for preservation by the Library of Congress National Film Registry. Workman is also known for creating many of the montage segments for the televised Academy Award shows over the years, as well as the montage at the end of the Great Movie Ride at Disney's Hollywood Studios.

A great admirer of the Beat writers, Depp published an article, "Kerouac, Ginsberg, the Beats and Other Bastards Who Ruined My Life" in the July 22, 1999, issue of *Rolling Stone*. Depp stated that his older brother lent him a "dog-eared paperback, roughed up and stained with God knows what, *On the Road*, written by some goofball with a strange frog name that was almost unpronounceable for my teenage tongue, had found its way from big brother's shelf and into my greedy little paws . . . Through this introduction to Kerouac, I then learned of his fellow conspirators Ginsberg, Burroughs, Corso, Huncke, Cassady and the rest of the unruly lot. I dove into their world full on and sponged up as much as I possibly could of their works."

Words of Advice: William S. Burroughs on the Road (2007)

Produced in Denmark and directed by Lars Movin and Steen Moller Rassmussen, the obscure but intriguing (if rather disjointed) documentary *Words of Advice: William S. Burroughs on the Road* contains never-before-seen footage of Burroughs's weeklong Scandinavian tour in October 1983 that culminated with a Copenhagen reading, as well as Lawrence, Kansas, where the author resided in the last years of his life.

Interspersed with the compelling footage are interviews with the likes of James Grauerholz (Burroughs's assistant, bibliographer, and archivist), music producer Hal Willner, poet and performance artist John Giorno, Burroughs biographer Jennie Skerl, author and Beat historian Ann Douglas, singer-songwriter and Burroughs disciple Patti Smith, and Beat Generation scholar Regina Weinrich. One of the highlights of the documentary occurs when Burroughs has a brief, awkward televised meeting with popular (and highly eccentric!) Danish writer Dan Turell, a Beat aficionado known for his 1975 autobiographical novel, *Vangede Billeder* ("Images of Vangede"). With a grimace on his face from the outset of the forced meeting, it's quite obvious that Burroughs disliked Turell from the start and would have rather been anywhere else. *Words of Advice* premiered at the Copenhagen International Documentary Festival in 2007. Rasmussen received the Roos Award from the Danish Film Institute for "outstanding efforts in documentary filmmaking" on the basis of the film.

In a July 5, 2010, review of *Words of Advice* posted on the *Film Threat* website (www.filmthreat.com), Phil Hall wrote, "For those who are well versed in Burroughs' life and writing, the film offers a rich enhancement to his remarkable canon—especially the Copenhagen footage, which has never been released before . . . Yet the depth of research and presentation in the film leaves much to be desired. Despite much talk about his late-life painting, the filmmakers fail to provide any glimpses of his canvases. Even worse, significant aspects of his biography that shaped his career and public recognition (his disastrous domestic life, his late-life heroin problems, even his celebrated narration of the re-release of the silent film *Witchcraft Through the Ages*) never receive mention. Burroughs fans may be able to overlook that, but anyone coming to the subject for the first time will only get a half-told story."

Corso: The Last Beat (2009)

Showcasing the fascinating and turbulent life of poet Gregory Corso—billed here as "the most colorful of the Beats"—*Corso: The Last Beat* presents an unexpurgated look at the poet between the year 1997 and his death in 2001. Directed by Gustave Reininger (1950–2012) and narrated by Ethan Hawke, the cinéma vérité–style documentary follows Corso on a trip to France (where he returns to the site of the "Beat Hotel" and also visits Jim Morrison's grave at Père Lachaise Cemetery), Italy (where he searches for information about his long-lost mother), and Greece. In addition, Reininger manages to track down Corso's mother, Michelina, who was forced to abandon him as a baby. In a highly emotional scene, Corso is reunited with his mother, who had been living the entire time in Trenton, New Jersey, where she worked as a waitress.

Other dramatic footage includes Corso trying to cope with the death of Allen Ginsberg in 1997 and visiting Clinton State Correctional Facility, a maximum-security prison in New York, where he served three years at the age of seventeen for stealing a $50 suit. During his prison stint (once behind bars he told everyone that he was doing time for "gang-related activity" in order to project a tougher image), Corso was protected by Mafia inmates and embarked on a process of self-education in the prison library. Finally, the film depicts Corso's battle with cancer, which forced him to face his own mortality. Corso's powerful poetic voice is woven throughout the documentary.

In a 2008 interview with the *Chicago Maroon* (the student newspaper of the University of Chicago), Reininger remarked, "It's a delicate film . . . It's hilarious, but it's terribly poignant. It's poignant when [Corso is] reunited with his mother; it's poignant when Allen [Ginsberg] dies. It deserves careful handling."

Corso met Reininger through Ginsberg, and upon their first meeting a reluctant Corso quizzed the director about the *Epic of Gilgamesh*. After the director provided some answers that satisfied Corso, he was given permission to go ahead with the documentary. However, Ginsberg died on April 5, 1997, just a month after Corso had decided to go ahead with the documentary. Corso was despondent over the death of his friend, and when Beat fans would come up to him and remark, "Hey, you're the last Beat" (William S. Burroughs had died less than six months after Ginsberg on August 2, 1997), he would angrily respond, "Is that your myth or mine?"

According to Reininger in a February 4, 2009, interview with *CityBeat Cincinnati*, "Corso in person was fascinating, funny and sometimes overwhelming . . . He was the youngest of the inner circle of the Beats, so he lived later. But he's less celebrated much because he was adverse to publicity. He just wanted to be a poet and explore truth." *Corso: The Last Beat* won the Audience Jury Award at Italy's Taormina Film Festival and captured Best Film honors at the Festival Litteratura in Mantua.

Ferlinghetti: A Rebirth of Wonder (2009)

"He opened up the doors for all of us to celebrate the rights of our First Amendment—freedom of speech." *Ferlinghetti: A Rebirth of Wonder* provides a fascinating portrait that highlights the amazing life of Lawrence Ferlinghetti—poet, artist, publisher, activist, pacifist, "literary mercenary," civil libertarian, and anarchist.

Lawrence Ferlinghetti as Charlie Chaplin in 1982, as
seen in FERLINGHETTI: A REBIRTH OF WONDER, a film by Chris Felver.
A First Run Features release. Photo by Chris Felver.

The 2009 documentary *Ferlinghetti: A Rebirth of Wonder* features insightful interviews with Ferlinghetti, Gary Snyder, Dennis Hopper, Anne Waldman, Bob Dylan, Amiri Baraka, Michael McClure, and others.

Author's collection

A highly insightful documentary directed by Christopher Felver, *Ferlinghetti: A Rebirth of Wonder* features interviews with not only Ferlinghetti but also Gary Snyder, Dennis Hopper, Anne Waldman, Michael McClure, Amiri Baraka, George Whitman of Shakespeare and Company bookstore, former US poet laureate Billy Collins, Bob Dylan, and many others.

In a February 8, 2013, review of the documentary for the *New York Post*, V. A. Musetto wrote, "With Americans' civil liberties under constant threat, it's comforting to know that Ferlinghetti is still with us." However, in a February 7, 2013, review in the *New York Daily News*, Joe Neumaier commented that the film "peaks in its terrific early sequences, as the poet ('Coney Island of the Mind'), publisher and City Lights bookstore owner's world and the long, protective wing he extends over other writers is detailed. Sadly, the film gets mired in traditionalism, something the man himself always railed against. But worth a look for seeing intellectual bravery (still) at work."

The Beat Hotel (2012)

"1957. The Latin Quarter, Paris. A No-Name Hotel for Artists Fleeing the Conformity and Censorship of America." In the late 1950s and early 1960s, a rundown hotel at 9 rue Git-le-Coeur in Paris known as the "Beat Hotel" became a refuge for several of the most prominent members of the Beat Generation (sans Jack Kerouac, who was living with his mother in Orlando, Florida, and later Northport, Long Island, during this period).

The "Beat Hotel" served as a true creative community for the likes of Allen Ginsberg (and his lover, Peter Orlovsky), William S. Burroughs, and Gregory Corso, as well as other influential writers and artists, including Brion Gysin (who introduced Burroughs to the "cut-up technique"), engineer Ian Sommerville (who developed the "Dreamachine" with Gysin), and poet Harold Norse, who later wrote a cut-up novel called *The Beat Hotel* that was published in 1983. It was here at the "Beat Hotel" that Burroughs finished *Naked Lunch*, which was published by Olympia Press in Paris in 1959.

A fascinating documentary directed by Alan Govenar, *The Beat Hotel* captures a special moment in time when these amazing creative forces gathered in the now-legendary hotel run by the extremely tolerant Madame Rachou. Highlights include interviews with other former "Beat Hotel" residents, including British photographer Harold Chapman, Scottish artist Elliot Rudie, English author Barry Miles, French artist Jean-Jacques Lebel, British book dealer "Cyclops" Lester, and George Whitman, eccentric owner of the Shakespeare and Company bookstore.

Chapman, whose fascinating photographs served to document the whole crazy "Beat Hotel" scene, referred to the "Beat Hotel" as "an entire community of complete oddballs, bizarre, strange people, poets, writers, artists, musicians, pimps, prostitutes, policemen and everybody you could imagine." Chapman's book of images, *The Beat Hotel*, was first published in 1984 with forewords by Burroughs and Gysin. The world premiere of *The Beat Hotel* took place at the Danish Film Institute in Copenhagen on December 8, 2011.

A writer, folklorist, photographer, and filmmaker, Govenar is the author of more than twenty books, including *Osceola: Memories of a Sharecropper's Daughter* (2000), which won First Place for Children's Nonfiction in the New York Book Festival, and *Stoney Knows How: Life As a Sideshow Tattoo Artist* (2003). In addition to *The Beat Hotel*, Govenar's filmography includes *Cigarette Blues* (1985), *Battle of the Guitars* (1985), *Master Qi and the Monkey King* (2010), and *You Don't Need Feet to Dance* (2013), a moving documentary about New York City performing artist Sidiki Conde, an African immigrant who lost the use of his legs to polio at the age of fourteen.

26

Strange Unexpected Acts

Artists Influenced by the Beat Generation

The Beat Generation has strongly influenced American culture, and diverse musical artists such as Bob Dylan, the Beatles, the Doors, Tom Waits, Kurt Cobain, Jerry Garcia, and many others have all paid tribute to the movement in one form or the other. William S. Burroughs cultivated his image as the "Godfather of Punk" in the late 1970s in New York City by hanging out with the likes of Mick Jagger, Lou Reed, Patti Smith, and Deborah Harry during the 1970s, as documented in the 1981 book *With William Burroughs: A Report from the Bunker.*

Bob Dylan

Bob Dylan once remarked, "[*On the Road*] changed my life like it changed everyone else's." In a 1985 interview (quoted in the *New Yorker*, August 13, 2010), Dylan elaborated, "It was Jack Kerouac, Ginsberg, Corso, Ferlinghetti . . . I got in at the tail end of that and it was magic . . . it had just as big an impact on me as Elvis Presley." According to cultural historian Douglas Brinkley in *The Majic Bus: An American Odyssey* (1993), "It's hard to imagine Bob Dylan writing the lyrics to his album *Highway 61 Revisited* without first having devoured Kerouac's opus."

Two of Dylan's song titles, "Desolation Row" and "Visions of Joanna," were reportedly inspired by Kerouac's novels, *Desolation Angels* and *Visions of Gerard*, respectively. According to Allen Ginsberg, "When I got back from India, and got to the West Coast, there was a poet Charlie Plymell at a party in Bolinas, played me a record of this new young folk singer Bob Dylan. And I heard 'Hard Rain,' I think. And wept . . .'Cause it seemed that the torch had been passed."

Ginsberg befriended Dylan during the 1960s and toured with him on the Rolling Thunder Revue in 1975 (William S. Burroughs declined an invitation to join the tour). During the tour, Ginsberg and Dylan visited Jack Kerouac's grave in Edson Cemetery in Lowell, Massachusetts. Ginsberg later appeared in Dylan's 1978 film *Renaldo and Clara*, along with Ramblin' Jack Elliott, Arlo Guthrie, Joan Baez, T-Bone Burnett, Joni Mitchell, Sam Shepard, and Harry Dean Stanton. The film, which was composed of concert footage, interviews, and fictional vignettes, received widespread negative reviews.

Dylan was born Robert Allen Zimmerman in Duluth, Minnesota, on May 24, 1941. According to rock critic Richard Goldstein in *The Poetry of Rock*, Dylan "demolished the narrow line and lean stanzas that once dominated pop, replacing them with a more flexible organic structure. His rambling ballads killed the three-minute song and helped establish the album as a basic tool for communication in rock." Dylan appeared alongside Ginsberg, Michael McClure, and Robbie Robertson of the Band posing in the alley (later known as "Jack Kerouac Alley") next to City Lights Bookstore in a famous photograph taken by Larry Keenan in 1965.

The Beatles

During the late 1950s, teenager John Lennon formed a band with his friend Paul McCartney in Liverpool, England, called the Quarrymen. By 1960, the band's name had been changed to the Beatles. Some Beat scholars have suggested that the name change reflected a sly tribute to the influence of the Beat Generation.

In *Jack Kerouac: Angelheaded Hipster* (1996), author Steve Turner commented, "[Lennon's] fellow student Bill Harry specifically remembers Lennon reading *On the Road* and the short story 'The Time of the Geek,' which was published in an anthology called 'Protest' in 1960. 'He loved the ideas of open roads and travelling,' says Harry. 'We were always talking about this Beat Generation thing.'" In a 1964 interview, Lennon remarked, "It was beat and beetles, and when you said it people thought of crawly things, and when you read it, it was beat music."

Burroughs's companion during the 1960s, Ian Sommerville, who helped develop the Dreamachine with Brion Gysin, also operated Paul McCartney's studio at 34 Montagu Square. Burroughs recorded his experimental "Hello, Yes Hello" tapes at the studio. According to McCartney, "[Burroughs] was very interesting but we never really struck up a huge conversation. I actually felt you had to be a bit of a junkie, which was probably not true." In *With William Burroughs: A Report from the Bunker* (1981), Burroughs remarked, "Ian met Paul McCartney and Paul put up the money for this flat which was at 34

Montagu Street . . . I saw Paul several times. The three of us talked about the possibilities of the tape recorder. He'd just come in and work on his 'Eleanor Rigby.' Ian recorded his rehearsals. I saw the song take shape."

William S. Burroughs appears on the cover of the Beatles' 1967 album, *Sgt. Pepper's Lonely Hearts Club Band*, along with the likes of English illustrator and author Aubrey Beardsley (1872–98); American actress Mae West (1893–80); American comedian W. C. Fields (1880–1946); English writer Aldous Huxley (1894–1963); Welsh poet Dylan Thomas (1914–53); American writer Edgar Allan Poe (1809–49); German philosopher, social scientist, communist and revolutionary Karl Marx (1818–83); American stand-up comedian and social critic Lenny Bruce (1925–66); and English occultist Aleister Crowley (1875–1947); among others.

Allen Ginsberg is mentioned in the lyrics to John Lennon's 1969 antiwar anthem "Give Peace a Chance." In addition, one of Ginsberg's last major projects was a collaboration with Paul McCartney on a musical adaptation of his poem "The Ballad of the Skeletons."

The Doors

In his 1998 autobiography, *Light My Fire*, Ray Manzarek of the Doors stated, "If Jack Kerouac had never written *On the Road*, the Doors would never have existed . . . It opened the floodgates . . . That sense of freedom, spirituality and intellectuality in *On the Road*—that's what I wanted in my work." Both Manzarek and and Doors lead singer-songwriter Jim Morrison (a.k.a. "The Lizard King") devoured the works of Beat Generation writers such as Kerouac, Allen Ginsberg, and William S. Burroughs while growing up during the 1950s. In addition, the Doors got their start in Venice Beach, California, a favorite Beatnik haunt of the late 1950s and early 1960s, as highlighted in Lawrence Lipton's 1959 book, *The Holy Barbarians*. According to Manzarek, the Doors were originally conceived as a merging of poetry and rock 'n' roll, "just as the beats a decade before us married poetry and Jazz."

The Doors derived their name from English Romantic poet William Blake, who wrote in *The Marriage of Heaven and Hell* (1790–93), "If the doors of perception were cleansed, everything would appear to man as it truly is, infinite." In addition to Morrison and Manzarek (keyboardist), the Doors consisted of Robby Krieger (guitarist and songwriter), and John Densmore (drummer). Essential Doors albums include *The Doors* (1967, featuring the band's first No. 1 hit, "Light My Fire), *Strange Days* (1967), *Waiting for the Sun* (1968), *The Soft Parade* (1969), *Morrison Hotel* (1970), and *L.A. Woman* (1971). In 1993, the Doors were inducted into the Rock and Roll Hall of Fame.

Ray Manzarek, keyboardist for the Doors, acknowledged the influence of the Beat Generation on the band in his autobiography when he wrote, "If Jack Kerouac had never written *On the Road* the Doors would never have existed . . . It opened the floodgates."   *Author's collection*

In 1969, Morrison collaborated with Beat poet Michael McClure on several writing projects and readings, including an appearance at Sacramento State College Gallery on May 1, 1969. They also collaborated on a screenplay called *The Adept* that was based on one of McClure's unpublished novels. McClure, who was instrumental in encouraging Morrison to publish his poetry, later referred to Morrison as "the best poet of his generation." The self-destructive, alcoholic Morrison died under mysterious circumstances in Paris on July 3, 1971, and is buried in Père Lachaise Cemetery.

In his afterword to the first Morrison biography, *No One Here Gets Out Alive* (1980) by Jerry Hopkins and Danny Sugerman, McClure wrote: "Jim was a metamorphic hero who thrilled us with his energy and daring . . . Jim was one of the brightest spirits that I've ever known, and one of the most complex." McClure went on to perform many spoken-word poetry concerts with Manzarek at colleges, music festivals, coffee houses, and outdoor music festivals during the 1980s through the 2000s.

Burroughs himself performed "Is Everybody In?" on *Stoned Immaculate*, a 2000 Doors tribute album. A fan of Morrison's poetry, Burroughs stated in the album's liner notes that the "Lizard King's" poems were "very much in the tradition, not necessarily imitated, of Rimbaud and Saint-Jean Perse particularly. It's very pure poetry."

Thomas Pynchon

One of several noted postmodern novelists to emerge from the 1960s, Thomas Pynchon has acknowledged the influence of the Beat Generation on his work. In the introduction to his 1984 collection of short stories, *Slow Learner*, Pynchon wrote, "Against the undeniable power of tradition, we were attracted by such centrifugal lures as Norman Mailer's essay 'The White Negro,' the wide availability of recorded jazz, and a book I still believe is one of the great American novels, *On the Road*, by Jack Kerouac."

Thomas Ruggles Pynchon Jr. was born on May 8, 1937, in Glen Cove, Long Island, New York. He attended Cornell University and received a bachelor of arts degree in English in 1959 (one of his professors was Vladimir Nabokov). At Cornell, Pynchon roomed with Richard Farina, who would later write the cult classic *Been Down So Long It Looks Like Up to Me* (1966). Published in 1963, Pynchon's first novel, *V.*, won the William Faulkner Foundation Award for "Best First Novel of the Year." His second novel, *The Crying of Lot 49* (1966), won the Richard and Hilda Rosenthal Foundation Award from the National Institute of Arts and Letters.

Gravity's Rainbow (originally titled *Mindless Pleasures*), Pynchon's next novel, was published in 1974 to critical acclaim and ended up sharing the National Book Award for Fiction with Isaac Bashevis Singer's *A Crown of Feathers*. Pynchon dedicated his award to Farina, who had died in a motorcycle accident just two days after *Been Down So Long It Looks Like up to Me* was published. *Gravity's Rainbow* features the famous opening line "A screaming comes across the sky." Pynchon's other works include *Vineland* (1990), *Mason & Dixon* (1997), *Against the Day* (2006), *Inherent Vice* (2009), and *Bleeding Edge* (2013). His complicated novels are characterized by their strange characters, dark sense of humor, and obscure references. In addition, Pynchon is known for his reclusiveness, and few if any photos of him actually exist in public.

Jerry Garcia

Grateful Dead lead singer, guitarist, and songwriter Jerry Garcia (1942–95) grew up in San Francisco and was heavily influenced by the Beat scene that centered on North Beach in the late 1950s. In a 1993 *Rolling Stone* interview, Garcia remarked, "The arts school I went to was in North Beach, and in those days the old Co-Existence Bagel Shop was open and the Place; notorious beatnik places where these guys—Lawrence Ferlinghetti, Kenneth Rexroth— would get up and read their poetry." According to Garcia, "As soon as *On the Road* came out, I read it and fell in love with it, the adventure, the romance of it, everything."

The Grateful Dead traced their history from a jug band called Mother McCree's Uptown Jug Champions. Formerly known as the Warlocks, the Grateful Dead served as house band during Ken Kesey and the Merry Pranksters' infamous Acid Trips. As the Grateful Dead's leader, Garcia was known as "Captain Trips." LSD "changed everything" for the band, according to Garcia.

The Grateful Dead made their debut at the Avalon Ballroom in San Francisco on May 19, 1966. The group had a communal home at 710 Ashbury Street. They performed along with Quicksilver Messenger Service and Jefferson Airplane at the "First Human Be-In," the prelude to the "Summer of Love" that attracted twenty thousand attendees at Golden Gate Park in San Francisco on January 14, 1967. Over the years, the Grateful Dead evolved into the ultimate cult band with their dedicated fans, known as Deadheads.

In addition to driving the Merry Pranksters' bus, Neal Cassady took the stage before early Grateful Dead concerts to deliver "free-associational monologues." Garcia referred to Cassady as "the ultimate *something*—the ultimate person as art." According to Garcia, Cassady "was a huge influence on me in ways I can't really describe . . . Neal was a master of timing. He was a twelfth-dimensional Lenny Bruce in a way, some kind of cross between a great stand-up comedian like Lenny Bruce and somebody like Buster Keaton. He had this great combination of physical poetry and an incredible mind. He was a model for the idea that a person can become art by himself, that you don't necessarily even need a forum."

Lou Reed

In a September 18, 1997, *Rolling Stone* interview, Lou Reed remarked, "When I read Burroughs, it changed my vision of what you could write about, how you could write. He broadened people's conception of what makes humanity." In a separate interview, Reed commented, "Modern rock lyrics would be inconceivable without the work of Allen Ginsberg. It opened them up from the really mediocre thing they'd been to something more interesting and relevant" (*Text and Drugs and Rock 'n' Roll: The Beats and Rock Culture*, 2014).

Lewis Allan "Lou" Reed was born in Brooklyn, New York, on March 2, 1942. He attended Syracuse University, where he studied journalism, creative writing, and film directing. Acclaimed poet and creative writing professor Delmore Schwartz mentored Reed (following Schwartz's death in 1966, Reed dedicated his song "European Son" to his former teacher). In the mid-1960s, Reed and classically trained violinist John Cale formed a band called the Primitives that later became the Warlocks. After adding guitarist Sterling Morrison and drummer Maureen Tucker to the lineup, the band became

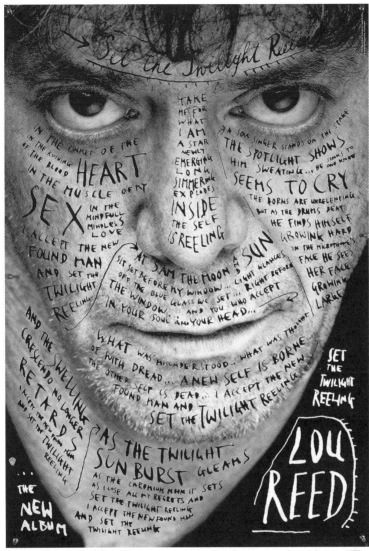

Cofounder of the Velvet Underground Lou Reed was a regular visitor to "The Bunker," William S. Burroughs's apartment in the Bowery in New York City during the late 1970s, and once remarked that the Beat author "broadened people's conception of what makes humanity."   *Author's collection*

the Velvet Underground and soon became featured performers (joined by German singer-songwriter Nico) in Andy Warhol's series of multimedia events called the Exploding Plastic Inevitable.

The band released its debut album, *The Velvet Underground & Nico*, in 1967, featuring the classic songs "I'm Waiting for the Man," "Heroin,"

"Femme Fatale," "Venus in Furs," "The Black Angel's Death Song," and others. Although a financial failure that was greeted with indifference upon its release, *The Velvet Underground & Nico* has since been acknowledged as a landmark album—with *Rolling Stone* placing it at No. 316 on its list of "500 Greatest Albums of All Time" in 2003.

After recording three more albums with the Velvet Underground—*White Light/White Heat* (1968), *The Velvet Underground* (1969), and *Loaded* (1970)—Reed left the band to embark on a solo career. His solo debut, *Transformer* (1972), which was produced by David Bowie, featured the controversial hit single "Walk on the Wild Side." Reed visited Burroughs several times at his "Bunker" apartment in the Bowery during the late 1970s as documented in the book of interviews *With William Burroughs: A Report from the Bunker* by Victor Bockris.

In 1996, the Velvet Underground were inducted into the Rock and Roll Hall of Fame by Patti Smith. Reed, who was called "rock's answer to Charles Baudelaire . . . a street-smart, sexually ambiguous paradigm of cool" by *The Outlaw Bible of American Literature*, passed away on October 27, 2013, at the age of seventy-one (he had received a liver transplant earlier that year).

Lester Bangs

"Good rock 'n' roll is something that makes you feel alive." Rock critic Lester Bangs was a true iconoclast known for his often outrageous opinions (such as his championing of Lou Reed's 1975 *Metal Machine Music* album of pure feedback). He was born Leslie Conway Bangs in Escondido, California, December 14, 1948, and grew up in a household with a mother who was a devout Jehovah's Witness and an alcoholic father who disappeared regularly on epic drinking binges (finally disappearing for good in 1957).

Bangs was heavily influenced by the Beat Generation growing up, especially Jack Kerouac's novels *On the Road* and *The Subterraneans*. "Kerouac came roaring down each new highway hollering tokay haikus like a man possessed, moving on not from a sense of disenchantment but with a voracious and insatiable hunger for experience," he would later write (as quoted in *Let It Blurt: The Life and Times of Lester Bangs*, 2000). In high school, Bangs attempted to write short stories in the style of William S. Burroughs's *Naked Lunch*. He also reportedly recited Allen Ginsberg's "Howl" in a speech class, much to the chagrin of his English teacher.

In addition, Bangs became obsessed with the jazz albums of Miles Davis, especially *Birth of the Cool* (1957), *Miles Ahead* (1957), and *Sketches of Spain* (1960), as well as Charles Mingus's *The Black Saint and the Sinner Lady* (1963), which is today considered one of the finest jazz albums ever recorded. In the mid-60s Bangs switched his allegiance from jazz to rock 'n' roll with the arrival of the Beatles and the Rolling Stones to American shores.

Bangs's album reviews started appearing in *Rolling Stone* in 1969 (his first being a negative review of the MC5's *Kick Out the Jams*). He also pleaded with the editors to write the obituary of Kerouac for the magazine (which appeared in the magazine's November 29, 1969, issue): "Jack was in so many ways a spiritual father of us all, as much as Lenny Bruce or Dylan or any of them . . . He was the first and greatest of those to write literature akin to the sound and feeling and spirit of rock . . . Good night, Jack—may Gerard and all your white-robed angels sing you tenderly upward-borne forever." Bangs's friend and fellow critic Richard C. Walls remarked, "We were both unreasonably bugged about being born too late to be Beatniks—I mean, hippies were okay, sure, but Beatniks, man, they had *culture*—and we were both world-class lushes" (*Let It Blurt*, 2000).

Bangs subsequently served as editor of *Creem*—"America's Only Rock 'n' Roll Magazine"—for five years between 1971 and 1976. Tragically, Bangs died of an accidental drug overdose on April 30, 1982, at the age of thirty-three. *The Outlaw Bible of American Literature* (2004) acclaimed Bangs as "the most influential critic of rock and roll ever to appear in newsprint." A collection of Bangs's essays, *Psychotic Reactions and Carburetor Dung*, edited by Greil Marcus, was published in 1987. A full-length biography of Bangs, *Let It Blurt: The Life and Times of Lester Bangs, America's Greatest Rock Critic*, was published in 2000 by Jim DeRogatis, who referred to Bangs as "the great gonzo journalist, gutter poet, and romantic visionary of rock writing—its Hunter S. Thompson, Charles Bukowski and Jack Kerouac all rolled into one."

In Cameron Crowe's 2000 film, *Almost Famous*, Philip Seymour Hoffman portrays Bangs, who dishes out some great lines such as "Great art is about guilt and longing and, you know, love disguised as sex, and sex disguised as love." The documentary *A Box Full of Rocks: The El Cajon Years of Lester Bangs*, directed by Raul Sandelin, appeared in 2013.

Tom Waits

In a 1976 *Newsweek* article, gravel-voiced singer-songwriter Tom Waits was quoted as saying, "There's a common loneliness that just sprawls from coast to coast. It's like a common disjointed identity crisis. It's the dark, warm narcotic American night." Thomas Alan Waits was born on Pearl Harbor Day, December 7, 1949, in Ponoma, California, to Alma Johnson McMurray and Jesse Frank Waits (both schoolteachers). According to Waits, the writings of

Singer-songwriter Tom Waits has acknowledged *Kerouac/Allen* as one of his all-time favorite albums and also penned a bittersweet tribute to Jack Kerouac and Neal Cassady called "Jack & Neal," which appears on his 1977 album, *Foreign Affairs.*   *Author's collection*

Jack Kerouac made a "tremendous impression" on him growing up in Southern California. "I started wearing dark glasses and got myself a subscription to *DownBeat*," remarked Waits in a 1975 *New Musical Express* interview. "I was a little late. Kerouac died in 1969 in St. Petersburg, Florida, a bitter old man." Waits listed *Kerouac/Allen*, a jazz poetry recording with Steve Allen on piano, as one of his all-time favorite albums.

Waits's first paid gig ($25) was at the Heritage in San Diego, and he released his first album, *Closing Time*, in 1973, followed by *The Heart of Saturday Night* (1974). In a press release for the latter album, Waits listed Kerouac, Charles Bukowski, Lawrence Ferlinghetti, Gregory Corso, and John Rechy (*City of Night*) among his favorite writers. In 1975, Waits took up residence at the legendary Tropicana Motel on Santa Monica Boulevard. In *Wild Years: The Music and Myth of Tom Waits* (2006), Jay S. Jacobs refers to Tom Waits as "the poet laureate of homesick sailors, down-on-their-luck salesmen, dance-hall girls—anyone seeking refuge from life's disappointments at the bottom of a glass. Waits's vision is an American Gothic of three-time losers, lost souls, and carnival folk."

A bittersweet tribute to Kerouac and Neal Cassady, Waits's song "Jack & Neal" was featured on his 1977 album, *Foreign Affairs*. The song includes the lines "Jack was sitten poker faced with bullets backed with bitches / Neal hunched at the wheel puttin everyone in stitches." Included on Waits's 1977 *Foreign Affairs* album, "Jack & Neal" features the legendary buddies embarking on one of their cross-country road trips with a nurse ("A red head in uniform will always get you horny"). *Foreign Affairs* also included such Waits classics as "A Sight for Sore Eyes," "Burma Shave," and "I Never Talk to Strangers," a duet with Bette Midler. "Jack & Neal" can also be found on *The Beat Generation Box Set* (1992). Other memorable Waits songs include "Warm Beer and Cold Women," "The Piano Has Been Drinking (Not Me)," "Bad Liver and a Broken Heart," "Christmas Card from a Hooker in Minneapolis," and "Looks Like I'm Up Shit Creek Again," among many others.

Waits turned to acting in the late 1970s and 1980s and made memorable appearances in several cult films, including as "Mumbles" the piano player in Sylvester Stallone's *Paradise Alley* (1978), disheveled DJ "Zack" in Jim Jarmusch's *Down by Law* (1986), and the down-and-out "Rudy" in Hector Babenco's *Ironweed* (1987) opposite Jack Nicholson. In addition, Waits collaborated with William S. Burroughs and Robert Wilson on the stage production of *The Black Rider: The Casting of the Magic Bullets*, which premiered at the Thalia Theater in Hamburg, Germany, in 1990. In a 1992 interview, Waits remarked, "Yeah, I love Burroughs. He's like a metal desk. He's like a still, and everything that comes out of him is already whiskey."

In 2000, Waits was awarded a Grammy Award for Best Contemporary Folk Album for his album *Mule Variations*. In 2011, Waits was inducted into the Rock and Roll Hall of Fame along with Alice Cooper, Neil Diamond, Dr. John, Darlene Love, Jac Holzman, Art Rupe, and Leon Russell. According to his Hall of Fame biography, Waits "is to songwriting what Charles Bukowski is to poetry, Jack Kerouac is to prose and Edward Hopper is to painting."

Jim Jarmusch

"Life has no plot, why must films or fiction?" A native of Akron, Ohio, critically acclaimed independent filmmaker Jim Jarmusch was born on January 22, 1953. After briefly studying journalism at Northwestern University, Jarmusch moved to New York City in 1971 and studied American and English literature at Columbia University. After a period of overseas travel, Jarmusch attended film school at New York University but dropped out to film his first feature, *Permanent Vacation* (1980).

As a teenager, Jarmusch was a big fan of the Beats but admitted in an interview that he didn't really appreciate Jack Kerouac's style until he heard a recording of the author reading his own work, and "then it made perfect sense to me and then I went back and re-read it and re-read it . . . Breathing and phrasing and bebop and sound influenced his way about language." Jarmusch also enjoyed the early works of Allen Ginsberg and Gregory Corso, as well as New York School poets such as John Ashbery and Frank O'Hara. In addition, Jarmusch was greatly influenced by Robert Frank's short Beat film, *Pull My Daisy* (1959)—which featured Ginsberg and Corso in the cast, along with narration by Kerouac—referring to it as "the poetic heart of the Beat movement . . . captured on film."

In 1980, Jarmusch made his directorial debut with the low-budget film *Permanent Vacation* (cost: approximately $15,000); however, Jarmusch's Beat-influenced sensibilities are strongly evident in his next two films: *Stranger Than Paradise* (1984) and *Down by Law* (1986). In *Stranger Than Paradise*, dull "Willie" (John Lurie) and his even duller buddy "Eddie" (Richard Edson), along with Willie's Hungarian cousin "Eva" (Eszter Balint), attempt to liven up their excruciatingly boring lives by taking a vacation . . . to Cleveland in the dead of winter. Cecilia Stark practically steals the show as "Aunt Lotte," who sits in her chair and exclaims, "Son of a beetch." The trio eventually travels to Florida and ends up in a cheap motel in the middle of nowhere. Somehow, Willie ends up taking a one-way journey to Hungary. Nothing much happens and that's the brilliance of this static, black-and-white film. The soundtrack features Screamin' Jay Hawkins's classic tune "I Put a Spell on You." Cinematographer Tom DiCillo later went on to write and direct his own films, including the 2009 Doors documentary, *When You're Strange*.

Another offbeat, black-and-white, dark comedy, *Down by Law* tells the tale of three diverse characters who end up in a Louisiana jail and leisurely plot an escape. Roberto Benigni (as "Roberto," an eccentric Italian tourist who speaks little English), Tom Waits (as "Zack," a radio DJ), and John Lurie of the Lounge Lizards (as "Jack," a pimp) star in what Jarmusch described as a "neo-beat-noir-comedy." The trio escapes from jail, only to end up in a shack with bunk beds that looks exactly like their cell. The film's tagline read, "It's not where you start—It's where you start again." The film also stars Ellen Barkin as "Laurette"; Benigni's wife, Nicoletta Braschi, as "Nicoletta"; and Rockets Redglare as "Gig." Filmed in and around New Orleans, *Down by Law* also features excellent cinematography by Robby Muller (*Barfly*). The film's soundtrack includes "Jockey Full of Bourbon" and "Tango Till They're Sore," both by Waits. *Stranger Than Paradise* won the Camera d'Or at the Cannes Film Festival.

Jarmusch's eclectic filmography includes *Mystery Train* (1989), *Night on Earth* (1991), *Dead Man* (1995), *Ghost Dog: The Way of the Samurai* (1999), *Coffee and Cigarettes* (2003), *Broken Flowers* (2005), *The Limits of Control* (2009), and *Only Lovers Left Alive* (2013). Jarmusch once remarked, "My aesthetic is minimal. I make films about little things that happen between human beings."

Kurt Cobain

Nirvana singer-guitarist Kurt Cobain (1967–94) paid a visit to William S. Burroughs's Lawrence, Kansas, home in October 1993. The "Father of Grunge" and the "Godfather of Punk" reportedly chatted cordially for several hours and then exchanged gifts: Burroughs handed Cobain one of his shotgun paintings, while Cobain gave Burroughs a Leadbelly biography that he had signed. Burroughs later described Cobain (quoted in *Nirvana: The Day-By-Day Eyewitness Chronicle* by Carrie Borzillo, 2000) as "very shy, very polite, and obviously enjoyed the fact that I wasn't awestruck at meeting him. There was something about him, fragile and engagingly lost."

The previous year, Cobain and Burroughs had actually collaborated on a spoken-word album, *The "Priest" They Called Him*, which consisted of Burroughs's reading overdubbed with Cobain's guitar accompaniment. As Cobain remarked in an interview included in *Kurt Cobain: The Cobain Dossier* (2006), it "was a long distance recording session" with Burroughs recording his portion at Red House Studios in Lawrence and Cobain recording his portion at Laundry Room Studio in Seattle. Cobain subsequently wrote in his journal, "I've collaborated with one of my idols William Burroughs and I couldn't feel cooler."

Cobain had first discovered Burroughs's work as a high school student in Aberdeen, Washington, often skipping classes to spend long hours perusing the books at the Aberdeen Timberland Library. In a 1993 interview (*Kurt Cobain: The Cobain Dossier*, 2006), Cobain remarked, "I really don't care what anyone thinks about my past drug use—I mean, I'm definitely not trying to glorify it in some way. Maybe when I was a kid, when I was reading some of [Burroughs's] books, I may have got the wrong impression. I might have thought at that time it might be kind of cool to do drugs . . . As I expected before I started heroin, I knew at the beginning that it would become just as boring as marijuana does. All drugs, after a few months, it's just as boring as breathing air."

In August 1992, Cobain faxed a letter to Burroughs asking if he would make a cameo in a music video for Nirvana's upcoming "Heart-Shaped Box" single from the group's third and final studio album, *In Utero* (working title: *I Hate Myself and Want to Die*), which was released in 1993. Cobain wrote, "As a fan and student of your work, I would cherish the opportunity to work directly with you." Burroughs declined the request. With the image of an old codger in a Santa's hat being crucified (was this supposed to be Burroughs's role?), human fetuses hanging from a tree, and other unpleasant imagery, the resulting "Heart-Shaped Box" video turned out to be very surreal, disturbing, and controversial even without the presence of Burroughs.

In early April 1994, less than six months after his meeting with Burroughs in Lawrence, Cobain committed suicide with a shotgun. His suicide note quoted from "My My, Hey Hey," a 1979 song by Neil Young: "It's better to burn out than fade away." After hearing of Cobain's death, Burroughs remarked, "The thing I remember about him is the deathly grey complexion of his cheeks. It wasn't an act of will for Kurt to kill himself. As far as I was concerned, he was dead already" ("William S. Burroughs and Kurt Cobain: A Dossier," www.realitystudio.org).

27

The Next Crazy Venture

Beat Tributes and Landmarks

A nyone truly interested in the Beat Generation needs to make at least one pilgrimage to bustling North Beach in San Francisco and visit landmarks like City Lights Bookstore, Jack Kerouac Alley, Vesuvio Café, and, of course, the fascinating Beat Museum, among other sites. The Jack Kerouac School of Disembodied Poetics at Naropa University in Boulder, Colorado, serves as a living tribute to the author. Last but not least, don't miss the chance to enjoy poetry readings and live music at Jack Kerouac Night held twice a year in March and October at the Flamingo Sports Bar (one of Kerouac's favorite hangouts during his later years) in St. Petersburg, Florida.

City Lights Bookstore

Nestled in the heart of North Beach in San Francisco at 261 Columbus Avenue, City Lights is a true Beat Generation landmark. The first all-paperback bookstore, City Lights was founded in 1953 by Lawrence Ferlinghetti and Peter D. Martin (each of whom invested $500 into the business). Martin named the bookstore in homage to the classic 1931 Charlie Chaplin film *City Lights* and had briefly published a magazine of the same name in the early 1950s. Ferlinghetti often remarked that City Lights was "kind of a library where books are sold." Over the years, City Lights has served as a beacon for free speech, championing First Amendment rights (a huge banner in the window once read "Banned Books").

Martin (1923–88) sold his interest in City Lights two years after the bookstore opened and headed east to launch the New Yorker Bookstore in New York City. In 1955, Ferlinghetti founded City Lights Publishers with the Pocket Poets Series. Ferlinghetti's own *Pictures of the Gone World* was the first book published in the series, followed by *Thirty Spanish Poems of Love and Exile* translated by Kenneth Rexroth and *Poems of Humor and Protest* by Kenneth Patchen.

Allen Ginsberg's controversial *Howl and Other Poems* was published in 1956 as the No. 4 book in the Pocket Poets Series, leading to the arrest of Ferlinghetti and bookstore manager Shig Murao, followed by a landmark obscenity trial. Kerouac himself name-dropped City Lights in the first chapter of his 1960 novel *Big Sur*: "I've bounced drunk into . . . City Lights bookshop at the height of Saturday night business, everyone recognized me . . . and 't'all ends up a roaring drunk in all the famous bars the bloody 'King of the Beatniks' is back in town buying drinks for everyone."

During the Iraq War, City Lights featured a banner that read, "Dissent is not Un-American." Nancy Peters, formerly a librarian at the Library of Congress, joined City Lights as an editor in 1971 and became co-owner of the bookstore in 1984. After retiring as executive director in 2007, Peters remarked, "When I started working here we were in the middle of the Vietnam War, and now it's Iraq. This place has been a beacon, a place of learning and enlightenment" (*Los Angeles Times*, April 22, 2007). In 2001, City Lights was named a local landmark by the San Francisco Board of Supervisors for its "seminal role in the literary and cultural development of San Francisco and the nation, for stewarding and restoring City Lights Bookstore, for championing First Amendment protections, and for publishing and giving voice to writers and artists everywhere."

Today, City Lights, which is billed as a "Literary Meeting Place," features three floors of books, including an extensive selection of Beat-related poetry and fiction. The *Los Angeles Times* has called City Lights "a beacon of avant-garde literature and left-wing political thought." A member of the American Booksellers Association, City Lights is located adjacent to Vesuvio Café, a legendary beat hangout that first opened its doors in 1948. As Ferlinghetti remarked in *The Beat Generation in San Francisco* (2003), "In a time when the dominant TV-driven consumer culture would seem to result in the 'dumbing down' of America, City Lights is a finger in the dike holding back the flood of unknowing."

Jack Kerouac School of Disembodied Poetics

In 1974, Allen Ginsberg and Anne Waldman founded the Jack Kerouac School of Disembodied Poetics in the writer's honor at the Naropa Institute (now Naropa University), a private Buddhist-inspired university in Boulder, Colorado. Ginsberg, Waldman, Diane di Prima, Gregory Corso, William S. Burroughs, Amiri Baraka, Michael McClure, and Robert Creeley all taught classes at Naropa over the subsequent years. In addition, many Beat literary events and poetry readings have been held at the Jack Kerouac School, such as the 1982 Jack Kerouac Conference to celebrate the twenty-fifth anniversary of *On the Road.*

The self-described goal of the Jack Kerouac School is to cultivate "contemplative and experimental approaches to writing," and consists of the undergraduate Core Writing Seminars, a BA in creative writing and literature, a residential MFA in creative writing and poetics, an MFA in creative writing, and the Summer Writing Program. Founded by Chogyam Trungpa Rinpoche (1939–87), who was born in Tibet, Naropa is the first fully accredited Buddhist-inspired university in the United States. Naropa's motto is "Transform Yourself. Transform the World." In addition, Naropa is home to the Allen Ginsberg Library, which was dedicated in 1994 and features a collection of more than thirty thousand books, periodicals, and audiovisual materials.

According to historian and Beat scholar Douglas Brinkley in *The Majic Bus: An American Odyssey* (1993), the Kerouac School "has become, in my opinion, the most innovative, rigorous, and constructive creative-writing program in the United States and the most conspicuous crossroads for our nation's poets. The Kerouac School has adopted Ezra Pound's belief that aspiring writers should take criticism only from one who has written a notable work of literature."

The very first student at the Jack Kerouac School during the late 1970s, Sam Kashner, wrote an entertaining, illuminating, and often amusing memoir in 2005 called *When I Was Cool: My Life at the Jack Kerouac School.* The 2008 documentary *Crazy Wisdom: The Jack Kerouac School of Disembodied Poetics* highlights the program's history, the integration of Buddhism into the writing curriculum, and the many changes the program has undergone over the years. *Crazy Wisdom* features interviews with students and faculty members, as well as archival footage from an offbeat 1978 documentary about Naropa titled *Fried Shoes, Cooked Diamonds.*

In an October 14, 2011, Indiewire interview, *Crazy Wisdom* director Kate Linhardt commented, "I think ultimately the film is about how countercultural movements evolve and mutate over time . . . The main question I had going into this was 'how do you institutionalize creativity?'"

Flamingo Sports Bar

During the last few years of his life, Jack Kerouac resided in St. Petersburg, Florida, with his third wife, Stella, and mother, Gabrielle in a modest brick house in a quiet neighborhood. Kerouac spent a lot of time hanging out at the Flamingo Bar, a local dive at 1230 Ninth Street North where he shot pool and drank heavily from his corner barstool. According to legend, Kerouac even took his last drink at the Flamingo the night before his death on October 21, 1969.

Today, the Flamingo Sports Bar is little changed from Kerouac's day, but the establishment has made several efforts to celebrate Kerouac's legacy, such as adding a massive framed poster of Kerouac in the window and featuring a lively "Jack Kerouac Night" with folk music and Beat poetry twice a year near the dates of the writer's birth (March 12) and death (October 21). In addition, Kerouac-related photos and magazines cover the walls of the bar. The Flamingo even features a "Jack Kerouac Special"—a shot of whisky and a beer wash for $2.25. In addition, visitors can purchase a T-shirt with Kerouac's image on the front and the famous "mad to live" line from *On the Road* on the back. Indeed, the Flamingo has become somewhat of a Mecca for Kerouac fans over the years.

Flamingo owner Dale Nichols, a Vietnam veteran, purchased the bar in 1969. Nichols enjoys giving tours of the bar and will even show visitors Kerouac's favorite barstool in the southwest corner of the center bar that has an easy view of all exits. As soon as Nichols opened the bar at 8:00 a.m., Kerouac would come in and read the newspaper. He would also sneak a bottle of liquor into the bar "and he would take swigs of his liquor in between sips of beer when he thought I wasn't looking," according to Nichols.

Two local musicians, Pat Barmore and Pete Gallagher (a.k.a. "Sunset Beach Pete"), were instrumental in the creation of the biannual Jack Kerouac Night at the Flamingo. The event features the talents of local musicians, such as the legendary Ronny Elliott, who penned a moving tribute to Kerouac titled "Jack's St. Pete Blues," which features the lyrics "I drink cause I can't write and I can't write because I'm drinking." Money raised at Jack Kerouac Night helps support Friends of the Jack Kerouac House (www.kerouachouse .com), which has three stated goals: preserve the integrity of the Jack Kerouac house at 5169 Tenth Avenue North as a historic resource connected to twentieth-century literature; educate the public and facilitate study of Jack Kerouac and his style of writing; and link St. Pete and Kerouac on the world's literary stage permanently.

Most of the other bars Kerouac once frequented in the St. Petersburg/ Tampa area, such as the Wild Boar near the University of South Florida, are long gone, but the Flamingo still endures and remains a living legacy of Kerouac's last years in St. Petersburg. The Flamingo Sports Bar is located at 1230 Ninth Street North.

Nova Convention (1978)

In 1974, William S. Burroughs returned to New York City after living the past twenty-six years abroad in Tangier, Paris, and London. Allen Ginsberg had helped him get a contract to teach creative writing at City College of New York for a semester. Burroughs eventually moved into an apartment at 222 Bowery on the Lower East Side of Manhattan nicknamed "The Bunker" since it was a former YMCA locker room with no windows. Whenever Burroughs exited the Bunker, he armed himself with a cane, tube of tear gas, and a blackjack. The Bunker was also located just around the block from CBGB (formerly Hilly's on the Bowery), which opened in 1973 and quickly became a forum for upcoming punk and new wave bands such as the Ramones, Misfits, Television, the Dead Boys, Blondie, the Dictators, Patti Smith Group, the Cramps, and Joan Jett.

During the Bunker years, Burroughs held court with a slew of musicians such as Richard Hell, Jim Carroll, Joe Strummer, Lou Reed, Mick Jagger, Debbie Harry, David Bowie, Tom Waits, Laurie Anderson, and others. The Nova Convention was a logical result of Burroughs's newfound cult hero status as the so-called "Godfather of Punk." Organized by literary critic and cultural theorist Sylvere Lotringer, poet and performance artist John Giorno, and Burroughs's assistant and bibliographer James Grauerholz, the three-day Nova Convention was held at various New York City locales (including the Entermedia Theatre, now Village East Cinema) between November 30 and December 2, 1978, and served as a multimedia retrospective of Burroughs's life and work.

Highlights of the Nova Convention included film showings; readings from Allen Ginsberg, Terry Southern, and Frank Zappa (a last-minute replacement for Keith Richards, who bowed out due to legal issues stemming from his heroin bust in Toronto); panel discussions with Burroughs, Brion Gysin, Robert Anton Wilson, and Timothy Leary; and concerts featuring Debbie Harry and Chris Stein, Patti Smith, legendary composer Philip Glass, the B-52s (before they had even released their debut album!), and Suicide. In addition, poet Eileen Myles reportedly caused quite a stir when she and a friend reenacted Burroughs's fatal "William Tell" shooting of his wife, Joan, in Mexico City in 1951.

In an interview featured in *Please Kill Me: The Uncensored Oral History of Punk* (1997), Grauerholz remarked, "The Nova Convention . . . was considered a summit meeting of the New York avant-garde, in William Burroughs' honor . . . Keith Richards had been an early promised appearance . . . so the next day [there] was like a mob scene for tickets . . . So anyway, [Richards] bailed . . . [Zappa agreed to] read 'The Talking Asshole' piece from *Naked Lunch* . . . So Patti [Smith] is one of my stars, right? The big night comes around, and Patti is very sick, supposedly with a flu. Her voice was shot . . . It was a nightmare . . . Pandemonium backstage . . . Meanwhile the audience is screaming 'Keith! Keith! Keith!' through everything."

In a retrospective of the Nova Convention for the *New York Times* (December 4, 1978), music critic Robert Palmer wrote, "If Saturday night's performers had anything in common, it was the debt they owe to Mr. Burroughs for his sheer audacity. In the 60s he challenged the structure of the novel and the very foundation of the English language by publishing prose that worked in association blocks, not linear fashion . . . Although [Burroughs] has created some enduring characters, he is his own most interesting character, and he was in rare form, sitting at a desk in a business suit and bright green hat, shuffling papers and reading in his dry Midwestern accent."

In a 2012 interview posted on www.realitystudio.org, Lotringer reflected, "We didn't realize that this huge event would be an adieu to the American avant-garde. No other event after that gathered so many of the artists, poets, musicians of the underground scene. The whole idea of an artistic avant-garde collapsed in the '80s." *With William Burroughs: A Report from the Bunker* (1996) by Victor Bockris (who served as Burroughs's aide during the Nova Convention) provides an excellent oral history of Burroughs's Bunker years and features the writer's fascinating interactions with the likes of Andy Warhol, Tennessee Williams, Susan Sontag, Terry Southern, and others.

Jack Kerouac Alley

Nestled between City Lights Bookstore and the Vesuvio Café in San Francisco, Jack Kerouac Alley (formerly Adler Place) connects Columbus Avenue in North Beach with Grant Avenue in Chinatown. Whenever he was in town, Kerouac often frequented both of these legendary establishments (as described in his 1962 novel, *Big Sur*).

Lawrence Ferlinghetti first presented the idea of renaming the alley next to City Lights in honor of Kerouac to the San Francisco Board of Supervisors in 1988, as well as naming other streets to honor the likes of Kenneth Rexroth, Ambrose Bierce, Richard Henry Dana, Jack London, Frank Norris, Mark Twain, Dashiell Hammett, and Isadora Duncan. According to Ferlinghetti, the alley was formerly "a place for fish trucks and garbage" that "smelled pretty bad on a warm day" (*SFGate*, March 30, 2007).

On October 2, 1988, City Lights hosted a gala party to mark its thirty-fifth anniversary and celebrate the unveiling of the first signs: Kerouac Street and

Dedicated in 2007, Jack Kerouac Alley features stone-and-metal plaques with poetry from the likes of Jack Kerouac, Maya Angelou, John Steinbeck, Li Po, and Confucius. It is located between City Lights Bookstore and Vesuvio Café in North Beach.

Author's collection

William Saroyan Place (across Columbus Avenue at the entrance to Specs' Twelve Adler Museum Café). However, it wasn't until the spring of 2007 that the sixty-foot-long Jack Kerouac Alley was truly transformed and rededicated in honor of the Beat Generation author into a pedestrian-only thoroughfare under the funding and direction of the Chinatown Alleyway Improvement Project. Jasmine Kaw, a landscape architect, came up with a new design that involved repaving the alley, banning motor vehicles, and adding new streetlights.

In addition, new stone-and-metal plaques inscribed with poetry were added—Chinese poems by Li Po and Confucius on the Chinatown end and Western literature by Jack Kerouac, Maya Angelou, and John Steinbeck on the North Beach end. The Kerouac quote was taken from *On the Road*: "The air was soft, the stars so fine, the promise of every cobbled alley so great I thought I was in a dream." The Angelou quote reads, "Without courage, we cannot practice any other virtue with consistency," while the Steinbeck quote states, "The free exploring mind of the individual human is the most valuable thing in the world." The Li Po quote reads, "In the company of best friends, there is never enough wine." Messages on most of the stones featured in Jack Kerouac Alley are written in English and Chinese.

In addition, the colorful mural *Vida y suenos de la canada Perla* (*Life and Dreams of the Perla River Valley*) adorns the wall of the City Lights Bookstore that faces Jack Kerouac Alley. It is a reproduction of Mexico City artist Sergio Valdez Rubalcaba's original work that was destroyed in 1998 when armed forces attacked the village of Taniperla, a Zapatista community in Chiapas, Mexico.

Lowell Celebrates Kerouac! Festival

During the first weekend of October each year, Jack Kerouac aficionados from around the world descend upon the author's hometown of Lowell, Massachusetts, for Lowell Celebrates Kerouac! (LCK!). A nonprofit organization founded in 1985, LCK! has a self-described mission "to promote a better understanding and appreciation of Kerouac's life and literature."

Featured LCK! guests over the years have included writers Allen Ginsberg, Lawrence Ferlinghetti, Gregory Corso, Michael McClure, Anne Waldman, Robert Creeley, Diane di Prima, Herbert Huncke, Ann Charters, and Joyce Johnson, as well as composer-author David Amram (who collaborated with Kerouac on jazz poetry readings), poet-rocker Patti Smith, keyboardist Ray Manzarek of the Doors, author-historian Douglas Brinkley, Sterling Lord (Kerouac's literary agent), and writer-musician John Sinclair of the MC5.

Before the LCK!, there were simply no traces of Kerouac's presence in Lowell besides his simple gravestone in Edson Cemetery. LCK! was originally organized to work in conjunction with the Lowell Historic Preservation Commission (LHPC) in an effort to raise funds for the Jack Kerouac Commemorative in downtown Lowell. The first LCK! event took place in the spring of 1986, drew more than three hundred attendees, and featured readings by Ginsberg and Corso, along with several local poets.

In December 1986, the Lowell City Council voted 8–1 (the lone dissenter felt that Kerouac was not a proper "role model" for American youth) to work with the LHPC to establish the Jack Kerouac Commemorative at a budget of $100,000. Ben Woitena, a sculptor from San Antonio, Texas, was chosen as artist on the commemorative after winning a design competition. A contemplative sculpture park located on Bridge Street, the Jack Kerouac Commemorative, which was dedicated in June 1988, features passages from some of the Beat author's best-loved works—including *On the Road*, *Mexico City Blues*, and *Visions of Cody*—etched into Carnelian granite. The dedication of the Jack Kerouac Commemorative served as the culmination of a week-long series of Kerouac-related festivities, including "An Evening of Poetry and Music," which featured spirited poetry readings from the likes of Ginsberg, Ferlinghetti, Creeley, and McClure and Manzarek, among others.

Today LCK! has grown immensely and highlights of the popular festival include tours of important Kerouac sites throughout Lowell (including a lively Kerouac Pubs Tour, A Walk in Doctor Sax's Woods, and a "Kerouac's Lowell" Birthplace-to-Gravesite Bus Tour), readings and panel discussions, live music, haiku/art exhibits, film showings, open mike events, book signings, Jack Kerouac Poetry & Prose Competition (held at Lowell High School), and Jack Kerouac 5K Road Race. In addition to the annual festival, LCK! sponsors literary programs year round, as well as a spring program tied to Kerouac's March 12 birthday. For more information about LCK!, visit www. lowellcelebrateskerouac.org.

First New York City Conference on the Beats (1994)

Hosted by the New York University School of Education, "The Beat Generation: Legacy and Celebration" took place May 17–22, 1994, and featured poetry reading, lectures, and concerts. Allen Ginsberg, Gregory Corso, Lawrence Ferlinghetti, Michael McClure (accompanied by Ray Manzarek of the Doors on piano), Anne Waldman, Ed Sanders of the Fugs, and others all gave readings during the event.

The New York University Beat celebration was designed to celebrate the fiftieth anniversary of the meeting of Ginsberg, Burroughs, and Jack Kerouac in the spring of 1944 in New York City that led to the formation of the early Beat circle (Gregory Corso joined them later in the early 1950s). Several thousand people from all over the United States and as far away as France and Germany attended the lively six-day New York University event.

William S. Burroughs appeared via telephone from Lawrence, Kansas, offering his own unique advice for young writers: "Be a bullfighter, not a bullshitter. Writing a universe, a writer makes a universe possible, vitalizing the characters." In addition, acclaimed Russian poet Andrei Voznesensky made a surprise visit, introducing himself to the audience by saying, "Greetings to the Beat Generation from us Red Cats." Another special guest was composer David Amram, who had collaborated on jazz poetry readings with Kerouac in the late 1950s. Amram also scored the landmark Beat short film, *Pull My Daisy*, in 1959. Amram recounted his days working with Kerouac and the other Beat writers, as well as playing jazz with such legends as Miles Davis, Thelonious Monk, and Charlie Parker, among others.

After someone shouted out a request for the poem, "Marriage," Corso amused the audience when he commented, "My peers will be known for *On the Road*, *Naked Lunch*, and 'Howl,' but I'm stuck being remembered for this damn 'Marriage' poem." Ferlinghetti read several poems, including "In Goya's Greatest Scenes We Seem to See," from his immensely popular

1958 poetry collection, *A Coney Island of the Mind*. One of the panels, titled "Woman and the Beats," featured poets Hettie Jones and Joyce Johnson, as well as Carolyn Cassady, the second wife of Neal Cassady, and Jan Kerouac, the daughter of Joan Haverty and Kerouac. Jan read from her mother's then-unpublished memoir, *Nobody's Wife*.

Hunter S. Thompson also made an appearance at the conference, reminiscing about the sixties, a time when "if you didn't get tear-gassed at least once a week there was something wrong. You felt guilty that you weren't doing your job."

Kerouac Project

As the publication of *On the Road* quickly evolved into a national sensation in the fall of 1957, Jack Kerouac was living quietly in College Park, a sedate neighborhood in northwest Orlando, Florida. He had rented the back porch of the cottage for $45 a month. It was also here that Kerouac typed up the original manuscript for *The Dharma Bums*, which would be published the following year.

Although Kerouac lived in the circa 1926 cottage at 1418½ Clouser Avenue for less than a year during 1957–58, the house has been transformed into a living tribute to Kerouac. The Kerouac Project odyssey started in 1996 when local TV reporter and freelance writer Bob Kealing investigated Kerouac's Orlando roots and published an article in the *Orlando Sentinel* on his findings. The Kerouac Project was soon established in an effort to purchase the then-rundown house, refurbish it, and turn it into a writer-in-residence retreat. The house is now listed on the National Register of Historic Places.

The Kerouac Project has gained national attention over the years, and visitors to the house have included the late actor, talk show host, and musician Steve Allen; Kerouac's friend and musical collaborator David Amram; Beat poet and City Lights Bookstore owner Lawrence Ferlinghetti; historian Douglas Brinkley; actor and author Michael York; and Carolyn Cassady, widow of Neal Cassady; among others. On October 22, 2014, a special ceremony was held at the Kerouac House to dedicate a permanent marker in front of the house that explains the goals of the Kerouac Project, the author's importance, and the dwelling's historical significance. The plaque, which is the only literary history marker in Orlando, reads:

> Writer Jack Kerouac (1922–1969) lived and wrote in this 1920s tin-roofed house between 1957 and 1958. It was here that Kerouac received instant fame for publication of his bestselling book, *On the*

Road, which brought him acclaim and controversy as the voice of the Beat Generation. The Beats followed a philosophy of self-reliance and self-expression. The unedited spontaneity of Kerouac's prose shocked traditional writers, yet it brought attention to a legion of emerging poets, musicians, and artists who lived outside the conventions of post–World War II America. Photographs show Kerouac in the house's back bedroom, with piles of pocket notebooks in which he scrawled thoughts and dreams while traveling. In April 1958, following completion of his follow-up novel, *The Dharma Bums*, and a play, the *Beat Generation*, Kerouac moved to Northport, New York. He died in 1969 at the age of forty-seven. In 1996, author Bob Kealing discovered the house's significance while researching an article to mark Kerouac's seventy-fifth birthday. In 1998, the Kerouac Project established a retreat here for aspiring writers in tribute to him. In 2013, the house was listed on the National Register of Historic Places.

The Beat Museum

"Experience the era that changed the world! Kerouac, Ginsberg, Burroughs . . ." Nestled in the heart of San Francisco's bustling North Beach neighborhood at 540 Broadway (near the intersection of Broadway and Columbus Avenue) and just across the street from City Lights Bookstore and Vesuvio Café, the Beat Museum is home to an extensive collection of Beat-related memorabilia, including original manuscripts, cultural ephemera, photos, rare books, paintings, records, posters, letters, and personal effects. The self-described mission of the Beat Museum "is to spread the values of the Beat Generation—Tolerance, inclusiveness, and having the courage to live your own individual truth."

Founded by Beat enthusiast Jerry Cimino in 2003 (the original site was in Monterey), the Beat Museum features five thousand square feet of interesting artifacts spread over two floors, such as Jack Kerouac's plaid jacket, Neal Cassady's referee shirt from his period as driver of the Merry Pranksters' "Further" bus, and the 1949 Hudson used in the 2012 film version of *On the Road* (donated by director Walter Salles). The Beat Museum also features an amazing collection of Beat-related books for sale, as well as posters, postcards, memorabilia, T-shirts, DVDs, and more. Outside the Beat Museum stands a dynamic, twelve-foot-high, six-foot-wide painting of Jack Kerouac and Neal Cassady in their heyday. According to Cimino in a 2013 interview posted on the Contemporary Jewish Museum blog (www.cjmvoices.blogspot.com), "We are authentic. Our theme is Beat. People dig it because it's the heart of North Beach."

Before the Beat Museum opened at its new site in North Beach, Cimino took the show on the road with the Beat Museum on Wheels (a.k.a. "Beatmobile") in 2004. A mobile performance center and museum exhibition, the Beatmobile traveled from California to Maine to Florida and back two school years in a row. During this time, Cimino and Neal Cassady's son, John Allen, delivered customized ninety-minute live performances to thousands of students and fans at high schools, colleges, and community arts centers. The Beat Museum also hosts an annual Neal Cassady Birthday Bash in February with poetry readings, live music, and special appearances.

Regularly scheduled walking tours can be arranged at the Beat Museum that take place every Wednesday and Saturday afternoon at 1:00 p.m. where visitors can "tour North Beach in the footsteps of the Beat Generation." The Beat Museum is open daily from 10:00 a.m. to 7:00 p.m. (10:00 a.m. to 10:00 p.m. on Friday and Saturday). For more information about the Beat Museum, visit www.kerouac.com.

Founded by Beat enthusiast Jerry Cimino in 2003 and dedicated to "spreading the spirit" of the Beat Generation, the Beat Museum is located in the heart of North Beach, San Francisco.

Author's collection

Beat Musical Tributes

A diverse array of musical artists have paid tribute to the inspiration of the Beat Generation over the years. One of the most notorious examples is the jazz rock band Steely Dan, which was founded by Donald Fagen and Walter Becker, and named after a steam-powered dildo described in William S. Burroughs's *Naked Lunch*: "Mary is strapping on a rubber penis: 'Steely Dan III from Yokohama,' she says, caressing the shaft. Milk spurts across the room." Fagen met Becker while attending Bard College in New York, where he was studying English literature. According to Becker (quoted in *Steely Dan: Reelin' in the Years*, 2008), "It seemed like a good name to us at the time. In fact, it turned out the name had a certain zing to it and helped the band become popular at the beginning, I think." In addition, the British progressive rock band Soft Machine was named after the 1961 Burroughs cut-up novel.

Alternative rock band Sonic Youth was also strongly influenced by the Beat Generation. According to Sonic Youth's Lee Ranaldo (quoted in *The Beats and Rock Culture*, 2014), "Ever since reading *On the Road* in '74, just out of college and on my first road trip, NY–California, at the same time, the 'Beat' writers have had a strong influence on me. I just loved the way Kerouac in particular wrote, the muscular energy and enthusiasm for life and love and travel. Ginsberg and Burroughs, Snyder, etc. came later as more acquired tastes, but Kerouac was so easy to read and so simple to identify with." Sonic Youth is featured on Burroughs's 1990 album, *Dead City Radio* ("Dr. Benway's House"). Interestingly, Sonic Youth's original drummer, Richard Edson, portrayed "Eddie" in Jim Jarmusch's 1984 cult film *Stranger Than Paradise* opposite John Lurie ("Willie"). He also played the part of the sleazy parking garage attendant in *Ferris Bueller's Day Off* (1986).

Ranaldo was one of the musicians involved in the production of the 1997 tribute album *Kerouac: Kicks Joy Darkness*, which features Kerouac's work performed by various artists, including Burroughs, Allen Ginsberg, Lawrence Ferlinghetti, Hunter S. Thompson, Johnny Depp, Matt Dillon, Patti Smith, Eddie Vedder, Jim Carroll, Lydia Lunch, Steven Tyler, Warren Zevon, and Michael Stipe.

One of the best-known song tributes to the Beats is the catchy 10,000 Maniacs song "Hey Jack Kerouac," on the band's 1987 album, *In My Tribe*. "Hey Jack Kerouac" features the lyrics "Hip flask slinging madmen / Steaming cafe flirts / They all spoke through you . . ." 10,000 Maniacs lead singer Natalie Merchant admitted in a 1987 interview, "I'm suspicious of a lot of the Beat Generation's activities . . . they led a lifestyle that was pretty incredible for the time—to be leaping in a car and driving across the country high on amphetamines . . . talking about philosophy and writing books is a real experimental way of life."

Singer-songwriter John Gorka's song "The Ballad of Jamie Bee," which can be found on his 1991 album, *Jack's Crows*, tells the tale of an aimless drifter and features the lines "Jamie's from the last great breed of roadmen / Woody [Guthrie], Jack [Ramblin' Jack Elliott] and Kerouac and such." Weezer's song "Holiday" from the band's 1994 debut album, *Weezer*, name-drops Kerouac as well: "We will write a postcard . . . In free verse on the road with Kerouac . . . On this road we'll never die." In addition, New Zealand singer Brooke Fraser wrote "Jack Kerouac" ("I'm on the road like Jack Kerouac"), which appears on her 2010 album, *Flags*. Morrissey included a song called "Neal Cassady Drops Dead" on his 2014 album, *World Peace Is None of Your Business*.

Legendary folk singer Ramblin' Jack Elliott named his 1981 album *Kerouac's Dream*. According to an interview with Elliott posted at www .ramblinjack.com, Kerouac came by Elliott's house in 1954 and read the entire manuscript of *On the Road* to him in "three days and three bottles of wine. I think he had a thing for my girlfriend. He came around many times to visit, along with other authors and poets." Also in 1981, Allen Ginsberg performed his punk poem, "Capital Air" ("I don't like dictatorship of the rich . . ."), with the Clash at the Bonds Club in Times Square. Joe Strummer introduced the poet as "President Ginsberg."

Last but not least, laid-back singer-songwriter Jimmy Buffett first discovered Key West, Florida, on a bar-hopping adventure with fellow musician Jerry Jeff Walker along the Overseas Highway from Miami. According to Buffett in his 1998 autobiography, *A Pirate Looks at Fifty*, "This was Kerouac stuff and I loved it." Although Walker soon departed for Texas, Buffett made his home in the Florida Keys, where he penned some of his most memorable tunes, including "Margaritaville," "Come Monday," "A Pirate Looks at Forty," "Trying to Reason with Hurricane Season," "Changes in Latitudes, Changes in Attitudes," and others.

28

Nothing Behind Me

Eclectic Beat Generation Biographies and Autobiographies

From the academic to the sensational and totally outrageous, Beat Generation biographies and autobiographies have run the gamut over the years. However, the sampling listed here is by no means a comprehensive or definitive sampling of Beat Generation works—just a very eclectic selection of books that have entertained, informed, and amused the author in the course of researching *The Beat Generation FAQ*. For a good representative listing of essential works associated with the Beat Generation, please refer to the Selected Bibliography at the back of this book.

The Holy Barbarians (1959) by Lawrence Lipton

In his unconventional, eminently readable 1959 book about the Beat Generation, *The Holy Barbarians*, Lawrence Lipton wrote, "When the barbarians appear on the frontiers of a civilization it is a sign of a crisis in that civilization. If the barbarians come, not with weapons of war but with the songs and ikons of peace, it is a sign that the crisis is one of a spiritual nature. In either case the crisis is never welcomed by the entrenched beneficiaries of the status quo."

Billed as "the first complete inside story of the Beat Generation," *The Holy Barbarians* focuses primarily on the then-burgeoning Beat scene in Venice, California. A well-known poet, novelist, and critic, Lipton (1898–1975) was a true insider to Venice's literary scene and a mentor to many of the younger Beat poets there. He was also blessed with the gift of self-promotion (fellow Venice poet Stuart Perkoff reportedly remarked that the book should have been titled "Holy Horseshit"). Throughout the fast-paced book, Lipton comes across as deeply ingrained in the Venice beatnik scene and spouts off some great lines such as "The squares had discovered beatville and were beginning to sniff and nibble around the edges." According to Lipton, the Beat poets all shared a "sense of absurd, the role of the clown, the Holy Fool."

Perhaps the most memorable passage in *The Holy Barbarians* revolves around Allen Ginsberg's legendary poetry reading at a private home in Los Angeles on Halloween night, October 31, 1956, where he confronted a heckler by removing all of his clothes and standing there stark naked in front of a stunned audience (which included author Anaïs Nin). As Lipton describes it, "Allen showed up high—mostly on wine . . . he launched into a vigorous rendition of Howl . . . When Allen got to the poem America, the drunken square was visibly aroused. He began to heckle . . . Ginsberg got up and went forward to meet the drunk. 'All right,' he said . . . 'You want to do something big, don't you? . . . *Take off your clothes?* . . . [Ginsberg] flung his pants down at the champ's feet and then his shorts, shoes and socks, with a curious little hopping dance as he did so. He was stark naked now. The drunk had retired to the back of the room . . . The audience just sat there, mute, staring, fascinated, petrified."

According to Lipton, who was an eyewitness to the incident, the drunken heckler approached Ginsberg after the reading and told him that "he was sorry he has made such an ass of himself and where could he buy a copy of Howl? . . . Through it all Anaïs Nin, faithful to the role in which the poets had cast her, sat imperiously still, only slightly disdainful of the hubbub, like a queen on a throne." Perkoff, who also attended the reading, later wrote a sarcastic poem about the incident titled "The Barbarian from the North."

Lipton also made a humorous cameo as "King of the Beatniks" in *The Hypnotic Eye* (1960), a low-budget horror film that also featured Eric "Big Daddy" Nord as "Bongo Drummer." Lipton's son, James, is the host of Bravo TV's *Inside the Actors Studio*. In an interview posted at www.bigthink.com, James Lipton remarked, "I became an actor by accident, not by design. My father was a poet, a rather famous American Beatnik poet . . . He also left when I was very young . . . I associated my father's profession with my father's behavior. And as a result, I ran as far away from it as possible." In the 2003 "Swan Song" episode of *Gilmore Girls*, Rory shows Jess a copy of *The Holy Barbarians*, remarking that the author is "the father of the guy that does those Actors Studio interviews," whereupon Jess responds, "It's weird that a beatniky guy would have a conservative son like that."

The First Third (1971) by Neal Cassady

"All the city was to become my playground . . ." Although Neal Cassady served as an inspiration to other Beat writers and was a prolific letter writer (just consider his recently rediscovered, sixteen-thousand-word "Joan Anderson Letter" that Jack Kerouac described as "the greatest piece of writing I ever

Held each February, the Neal Cassady Birthday Bash celebrates the birth and life of Neal Cassady, who described himself as "Denver's unnatural son." Cassady's *The First Third* was first published in 1971—three years after his death.

Author's collection

saw"), he never had anything published during his lifetime. In addition to his frantic, spontaneous letters to Kerouac and others, Cassady attempted to write an autobiography, fragments of which were published by his widow, Carolyn, as *The First Third* in 1971, three years after his death (the second third was reportedly to have been an account of his days on the road with Kerouac, while the final part would have covered his stint with the Merry Pranksters).

As one might expect, Cassady's picaresque work is raw, unstructured, and factually unreliable but full of some fascinating passages anyway. One such anecdote stands out as being truly bizarre and disturbing: A young Cassady lived with his wino father in a cheap Denver flophouse, along with a roommate nicknamed "Shorty," who slept on a three-foot-long ledge since "both of his legs had been amputated at the thigh many years previously." Shorty would drink himself into a stupor on a daily basis and Neal and his dad would invariably scour skid row searching for him and wheel him home on his makeshift cart with roller-skate wheels.

When Shorty wasn't getting inebriated (which was most of the time) he spent the majority of his hours furiously masturbating in the room: "Now and again, quietly, but with child-energy, I would burst into the room to catch Shorty playing with himself. Even though he was past forty, any preoccupation with this form of diversion was justified, I'm sure, since, judging from his appearance, he must not have had a woman since his youth, if then. Encrusted with dirt, he stank of body smell and was very ugly, with a no-forehead face full of grinning rubber mouth that showed black stubbed teeth."

Just before he collapsed alongside railroad tracks and died in Mexico in 1968, Cassady had completed a jacket blurb for *The First Third* that read, "Seldom has there been a story of a man so balled up. No doubt many readers will not believe the veracity of the author, but I assure these doubting Thomases that every incident, as such, is true."

In his editor's note to *The First Third*, Lawrence Ferlinghetti referred to Cassady as "an early prototype of the urban cowboy who a hundred years ago might have been an outlaw on the range." A tagline for the 2001 edition of *The First Third* announced, "Real-life adventures of JACK KEROUAC'S hero." In addition to *The First Third*, *Neal Cassady: Collected Letters, 1944–1967* was published in 2005 with an introduction by Carolyn Cassady.

According to LuAnne Henderson in *One and Only* (2013), "Whether or not [Cassady] had [writing] talent is something we'll probably never know . . . He wrote [*The First Third*] . . . my God, a hundred years ago—but he never finished it. It was unfinished, like his whole life."

Whitman's Wild Children (1989) by Neeli Cherkovski

"Whitman didn't throw a pebble into the literary pond; he pushed a boulder over the cliff." A clever blend of biography, literary criticism, and colorful personal anecdotes, *Whitman's Wild Children* is a rousing, gritty collection of essays profiling twelve poets, all of whom were acquaintances of Cherkovski: Michael McClure, Charles Bukowski, John Wieners, James Broughton, Philip

Lamantia, Bob Kaufman, Allen Ginsberg, William Everson, Gregory Corso, Harold Norse, Jack Micheline, and Lawrence Ferlinghetti.

According to Cherkovski in the book's introduction, "*Whitman's Wild Children* has been described as a critical memoir. I hope that it reflects the spirit of Walt Whitman—'perfect personal candor' . . . I wrote much of it in a white heat back in the mid-1980s when North Beach was still a wild kingdom. I could always find a tribe of poets up there, wandering in and out of cafes and bars and bookstores and ruling the street corners. We were gregarious folk. Whitman grew up on the streets—raucous, muddy, dusty, often dangerous."

Whitman's Wild Children is packed with great anecdotes, such as when Cherkovski recounts his first meeting with Allen Ginsberg: "The first thing Allen Ginsberg ever said to me was 'You're fat.' I answered: 'And you're bald.' Things were never smooth between us after that." Cherkovski also recounts a bad LSD trip that caused him to take shelter with Lawrence Ferlinghetti for a night. A gifted poet in his own right, Cherkovski was born in 1945 in Santa Monica, California. He has also written biographies of Ferlinghetti, Bob Kaufman, and Charles Bukowski. In addition, Cherkovski produced the first San Francisco Poetry Festival (now known as the San Francisco International Poetry Festival).

Cherkovski's other works include *Don't Make a Move* (1974), *The Waters Reborn* (1975), *Public Notice* (1975), *Ferlinghetti, A Biography* (1979), *Love Proof* (1980), *Hank: The Life of Charles Bukowski* (1991), *Elegy for Bob Kaufman* (1996), *Leaning Against Time* (2004), *Naming the Nameless* (2004), *From the Canyon Outward* (2009), *From the Middle Woods* (2011), and *Manila Poems* (2013).

Guilty of Everything: The Autobiography of Herbert Huncke (1990) by Herbert Huncke

Times Square hustler, drug addict, and petty thief Herbert Huncke's memoir, *Guilty of Everything*, was written in a straightforward manner similar to William S. Burroughs's first published novel, *Junkie* (1953). In fact, Burroughs himself wrote the book's foreword, comparing *Guilty of Everything* to the "picaresque tradition" of Petronius' *Satyricon* and Thomas Nashe's *The Unfortunate Traveller*, "a series of adventures and misadventures that befall a protagonist who is so immersed in the process of living that moral preconceptions are irrelevant." According to Burroughs, "*Guilty of Everything* is an honest, readable, informative book which incidentally mirrors the human condition." The book was dedicated to Huncke's longtime companion, Louis Cartwright.

In *Guilty of Everything*, Huncke details his adventures riding boxcars during the Great Depression, shipping out to sea during World War II, introducing the young Beat writers to the Times Square underworld, meeting sexologist Alfred Kinsey and taking part in his groundbreaking sex research, growing marijuana on Burroughs's Texas farm, doing time at Rikers Island, and appearing on *The David Susskind Show*, where he horrified the host and his audience by announcing that he had just "shot up a cooker full of heroin just before the show, and on top of that I'd taken a hefty shot of amphetamine."

Along the way, Huncke describes some of the more colorful characters he encounters, such as "Elsie John, the hermaphrodite . . . He was working West Madison Street in a freak show—half man, half woman. He was a strange creature, as you can well imagine." Huncke also details some of the more notorious Beat gathering places, such as a seedy bar dubbed the Bucket of Blood, "where petty crooks, fags, hustlers, and people of every description hung out."

In one of the more memorable chapters, Huncke actually gets nostalgic about the junk scene of the 1940s and 1950s that "was never as hectic and cold-blooded as today's drug scene, never in its worst days." In the old days, according to Huncke, "a junkie used to be a role model of a sort." Huncke also calls alcohol "one of the rottenest drugs man has ever discovered," while describing marijuana as "a harmless drug."

Publishers Weekly called *Guilty of Everything* a "sordid, ill-written memoir," while critic Jan Herman in the *Los Angeles Times* (June 10, 1990) wrote that the book "reads like an oral history of urban survival and offers an uncommon tale of the streets from which the 75-year-old author is lucky to have emerged . . . Although too many details of Mr. Huncke's life remain maddeningly vague, this is an honest book."

With William Burroughs: A Report from the Bunker (1981) by Victor Bockris

"If you weren't surprised by your life you wouldn't be alive. Life is surprise." A fascinating history of William S. Burroughs's years living in "The Bunker" in the Bowery of New York City between 1974 and 1980 as documented by Victor Bockris, *With William Burroughs: A Report from the Bunker* consists entirely of transcripts of taped conversations as the "Godfather of Punk" interacts with a revolving guest list of celebrities, including the likes of Andy Warhol, Lou Reed, Patti Smith, Debbie Harry of Blondie, Joe Strummer, Susan Sontag, Terry Southern, Tennessee Williams, and John Giorno. The book also includes a treasure trove of photos of Burroughs interacting with these celebrities.

The results are often pretty offbeat and compelling (with a few dry stretches along the way), as when Burroughs discusses his views of the Kennedy assassination with Harry, remarking, "Of course it has all the earmarks of the CIA and Mafia job combined. There's all these stories about De Santo Traficante. Santo Traficante! What a character! Imagine anybody being called Saint Trafficker, Saint Pusher! That's exactly what it means, and somebody was talking he said 'What are we gonna do if Kennedy gets elected?' He said 'He isn't gonna get elected, he's going to be hit.' So Kennedy had contracts out on him apparently from several sources."

According to Bockris in "King of the Underground: The Magic World of Williams Burroughs" (*Gadfly*, August 1999), "Burroughs always said he was not a gregarious person and did not like parties, but from what I could see there was a nearly constant party going on around him, at least in the evenings. The great thing about going to the Bunker—his starkly lit, three-room, white-on-white windowless cavern of a space at 222 Bowery, in the bowels of that grimy necropolis the Lower East Side—was that Burroughs and [his assistant James] Grauerholz had created one of the very few real literary salons in New York . . . Like Andy Warhol's Factory, the Bunker was hermetic and individual, and it ran on the same principles of love and tension."

With William Burroughs was first published in London in 1981 and republished in 1996 with some additional material. Bockris's other works include *NYC Babylon: From Beat to Punk* (1998), *Beat Punks* (2000), *Up-Tight: The Velvet Underground Story* (2003), *Warhol: The Biography* (2003), and *Transformer: The Complete Lou Reed Story* (2014), among others.

When I Was Cool: My Life at the Jack Kerouac School (2005) by Sam Kashner

The very first student at the Jack Kerouac School of Disembodied Poetics at the Naropa Institute (now known as Naropa University) in Boulder, Colorado, during the late 1970s, Sam Kashner wrote an entertaining, illuminating, and often amusing memoir of his bizarre and ultimately rewarding experiences there called *When I Was Cool: My Life at the Jack Kerouac School* (2005). The Jack Kerouac School was founded by Allen Ginsberg and Anne Waldman in 1974 at Naropa, which was the brainchild of Chogyam Trungpa Rinpoche, a Buddhist meditation master, scholar, teacher, poet, and artist.

In addition to attending the occasional lecture, Kashner spent much of his time doing odd jobs, such as typing Ginsberg's poems, cleaning Rinpoche's home, trying to prevent Gregory Corso (who reminded him of "Charles Schulz's cartoon character Pigpen") from scoring drugs, and serving

Naropa University, a private Buddhist-inspired liberal arts university in Boulder, Colorado, is home to both the Jack Kerouac School of Disembodied Poetics and the Allen Ginsberg Library. Sam Kashner's 2005 memoir, *When I Was Cool: My Life at the Jack Kerouac School*, provides his amusing perspective as the very first student at the school.

Photo by David Shankbone/Wikimedia Commons

as mediator between William Burroughs and his troubled son Billy Jr., whom he describes as "kind of a sweaty, unhappy, dead-end kid." Kashner very quickly came to understand that he was not going to be in for a conventional college experience. For instance, the main topic of the very first faculty meeting Kashner attended revolved around Peter Orlovsky's announcement "that he had gone for thirty straight days without masturbating; he told the faculty that this was a record for him."

Kashner also got the opportunity to meet some of the other Beat characters, like Herbert Huncke, "who seemed to love the idea that he was a criminal, or that people thought of him as one . . . He seemed like the kind of person who could have murdered someone once, somewhere . . . I remember thinking it didn't seem worth it—to live so desperately just to come up with the word 'beat' and be remembered for it." According to Kashner, "Ginsberg was always fighting with his ego. After all, hadn't Allen written once in a poem that he wanted to be the most brilliant man in America? I think he *did* want that. He also wanted to be rid of his ego. But he craved attention."

A contributing editor at *Vanity Fair* magazine, Kashner is the author of the 1999 novel *Sinatraland*, as well as three books of poetry, including *Driving at Night* (1976), *No More Mr. Nice Guy* (1979), and *Don Quixote in America* (1997).

Cursed from Birth: The Short, Unhappy Life of William S. Burroughs, Jr. (2006), Edited by David Ohle

A tragic casualty of the Beat Generation, the troubled son of William S. Burroughs was referred to as "the last beatnik" by poet John Giorno. Born in 1947 to Burroughs, a heroin addict, and his common-law wife, Joan Vollmer, a Benzedrine addict, William S. Burroughs Jr. (known as Billy Jr.) would later sign off a letter to his father as "your cursed-from-birth son."

Billy Jr. was born on July 21, 1947, in Conroe, Texas. After Burroughs accidentally shot and killed Vollmer in Mexico City in 1951, Billy Jr. was raised by his paternal grandparents in St. Louis, Missouri, and Palm Beach, Florida. Two of Billy Jr.'s autobiographical novels were published during his lifetime: *Speed* (1970) and *Kentucky Ham* (1973), which includes, among other incidents, Billy Jr.'s accidental shooting of his friend in the neck with a rifle (the friend survived).

In between various run-ins with the law, Billy Jr. attended the Green Valley School in Orange City, Florida, where he met his future wife, Karen Perry (the marriage only lasted from 1969 to 1974). Billy Jr.'s alcoholism and drug addiction led to serious health issues and, after he developed cirrhosis, he became one of the first patients in the United States to receive a liver transplant at Colorado General Hospital in 1976 at the age of twenty-nine. Unfortunately, Billy Jr., who often had the appearance of an unkempt derelict, kept drinking (and reportedly later stopped taking his antirejection drugs) and died of "acute gastrointestinal hemorrhage associated with micronodular cirrhosis" on March 3, 1981, at the age of thirty-three. Footage of Billy Jr. appears briefly in Howard Brookner's 1983 documentary, *Burroughs: The Movie*.

A collage-type novel, *Cursed from Birth: The Short, Unhappy Life of William S. Burroughs Jr.* was compiled by author David Ohle from Billy Jr.'s third and unfinished novel, *Prakriti Junction*, as well as his last journals, poems, interviews, medical reports, and correspondence with the likes of his father and Allen Ginsberg. Billy Jr. could often be vicious in his letters to his father, as when he wrote, "From one who has intensely studied your work all his life, let it be known that in this one's opinion, everything since *Naked Lunch* is tripe. The worst con artist stuff—as far as art goes it's your only kind—Con."

Bottom line: *Cursed from Birth* is a rather depressing but compelling read about a creative, self-destructive individual often estranged and alienated from his extremely aloof father.

The Beats: A Graphic History (2010) by Harvey Pekar

The Beats: A Graphic History provides a solid general overview of the Beat Generation in graphic novel style that features the talents of underground comic book legend Harvey Pekar (*American Splendor*), along with his frequent collaborator Ed Piskor, and a diverse array of artists and writers, including *Mad* magazine artist Peter Kuper and feminist comic creator Trina Robbins. In the book's introduction, Pekar wrote, "There was never anything like them in American literature and American culture, and it is unlikely that there will ever be anything much like them again . . . the Beats offered wild sex, recreational drug use, determined uprootedness, and most important, experimental writing of all kinds."

A decidedly mixed bag of biographical profiles with the occasional casual disregard for the facts, *The Beats: A Graphic History* is not for all tastes. For instance, the book features occasionally irreverent captions, such as a description of Allen Ginsberg as "a nerd . . . a social fuckup." In addition, some of the art is laughable, as with the depiction of Kerouac's third wife, Stella Sampas, as a ravishing beauty. Highlights include Joyce Brabner (Pekar's third wife) on "Beatnik Chicks," Jeffrey Lewis's story on eccentric poet/musician Tuli Kupferberg, and writer/editor Nancy Peters's spirited tour through the history of City Lights Bookstore.

The Beats: A Graphic History is particularly strong when dealing with more overlooked Beat figures such as Kenneth Patchen, who was a major influence on young writers such as Allen Ginsberg in the early 1950s. One of the most interesting features contained in *The Beats: A Graphic History* concerns the little-known story of D. A. Levy, a working-class poet from Cleveland, who was harassed and arrested multiple times by authorities for distributing "obscene" poetry, and committed suicide at the age of twenty-six.

Publishers Weekly called *The Beats: A Graphic History* "a superficial *Cliffs Notes* on the beats . . . Much of this volume feels like leftovers from coauthor Pekar's *American Splendor*, and one wonders if that magazine's 'drab and normal' style of illustration is appropriate for the more adventurous/experimental/flamboyant beats."

Popularly known as the "Poet Laureate of Cleveland," Pekar (1939–2010) received the American Book Award in 1987 for his *American Splendor* anthology. According to Pekar, as quoted in a July 13, 2010, *Washington Post* obituary of the writer, "The humor of everyday life is way funnier than what the comedians do on TV. It's the stuff that happens right in front of your face when there's no routine and everything is unexpected. That's what I want to write about."

Pekar's life story was brilliantly captured in the 2003 film *American Splendor*, which follows the legendary comic curmudgeon (expertly portrayed by Paul Giamatti) in his day-to-day drudgery as a file clerk at Cleveland's VA hospital, obsessively collecting obscure comic books and jazz records at garage sales, befriending Robert Crumb (James Urbaniak), starting his own comic book writing career (he leaves the drawing itself to other underground artists like Crumb), arguing with buddy and self-proclaimed "Genuine Nerd" Toby Radloff (Judah Friedlander) about the merits of *Revenge of the Nerds*, meeting his future wife Joyce Brabner (Hope Davis), and sparring with David Letterman. *American Splendor* captured the Grand Jury Prize for Dramatic Film at the 2003 Sundance Film Festival.

In a 1994 interview with the *Cleveland Plain-Dealer*, R. Crumb called Pekar "the soul of Cleveland . . . He's passionate and articulate. He's grim . . . I appreciate the way he embraces that darkness." Pekar, who died in 2010 at the age of seventy, is buried in Lake View Cemetery in Cleveland. His epitaph reads, *"LIFE IS ABOUT WOMEN, GIGS, AN' BEIN' CREATIVE."*

Another entertaining graphic novel–style book, *The Big Book of Weirdos* (1995)—which was billed as "True Tales of the World's Kookiest Crackpots and Visionaries!"—features an offbeat profile of William S. Burroughs, along with the likes of Franz Kafka, Edgar Allan Poe, Aleister Crowley, Fyodor Dostoevsky, Alfred Jarry, and Andy Warhol, among others. The book contains the work of "67 of the world's top comic artists," and was written by Carl Posey, who introduces "The Written Weird" section with the line "Writing—like suicide—is a solitary pursuit."

Beat Atlas: A State by State Guide to the Beat Generation in America (2011) by Bill Morgan

Written by celebrated Beat historian Bill Morgan, *The Beat Atlas: A State by State Guide to the Beat Generation in America* provides an indispensable state-by-state guide to significant Beat-related locales for those who want to study the minutiae of the Beat Generation, as well as inquisitive travelers who desire to hit the road in search of Beat-related landmarks. Indeed, Morgan has found a Beat presence in all of the fifty states and also offers a wealth of information concerning the movements of Beat contemporaries such as the San Francisco Renaissance, as well as the Black Mountain School and New York School of poets. The incredibly comprehensive guide even includes ALL of Kerouac's boyhood homes in Lowell, Massachusetts.

In the guidebook's introduction, Morgan writes, "It's fun to imagine just what building Dashiell Hammett had in mind when he wrote about

Sam Spade's office, or whether Melville was looking at the whale-like form of Mt. Greylock when he wrote *Moby Dick*, but with the Beat writers there is no need to speculate. When Kerouac wrote about the Stations of the Cross at the grotto in *Doctor Sax*, he was describing an actual spot that still exists in Lowell. The 'houseless brown farmland plains rolling heavenward in every direction' that inspired a Ginsberg poem can still be seen in Kansas today. All you need is a map and the desire to get out there and see it yourself. This guide is designed to help you follow your own interests to some unusual parts of the literary landscape."

Sprinkled liberally throughout the guidebook are rare photos depicting Beat figures and locales. *The Beat Atlas* serves as a companion to Morgan's previous, also highly recommended, guidebooks: *The Beat Generation in New York: A Walking Tour of Jack Kerouac's City* (1997) and *The Beat Generation in San Francisco: A Literary Tour* (2003), which appeared during the fiftieth anniversary of City Lights Bookstore.

A true authority on the Beat Generation, writer, editor, and painter Bill Morgan has served as an archivist and bibliographer for Allen Ginsberg, Lawrence Ferlinghetti, Abbie Hoffman, and Timothy Leary. In addition to his Beat-related guidebooks, Morgan is also the author of *Lawrence Ferlinghetti: A Comprehensive Bibliography* (1982), *The Works of Allen Ginsberg, 1941–1994: A Descriptive Bibliography* (1995), *The Response to Allen Ginsberg, 1926–1994: A Bibliography of Secondary Sources* (1997), *I Celebrate Myself: The Somewhat Private Life of Allen Ginsberg* (2006), *The Letters of Allen Ginsberg* (2008), *The Typewriter Is Holy: The Complete, Uncensored History of the Beat Generation* (2010), and *The Civil War Lover's Guide to New York City* (2013).

One and Only: The Untold Story of On the Road (2013) by Gerald Nicosia and Anne Marie Santos

One and Only features Beat historian Gerald Nicosia's fascinating interviews with LuAnne Henderson, who inspired the character of "Marylou" from Jack Kerouac's *On the Road*. In the process, Nicosia highlights the importance of Henderson in the Beat saga in contrast to her usual characterization as a "teenage slut." For instance, in *On the Road*, Kerouac first described "Marylou" as "a pretty blond" who was "awfully dumb and capable of doing horrible things." *One and Only* was coauthored by Henderson's daughter, Anne Marie Santos.

Henderson first met Neal Cassady in Denver in 1945 when she was just fifteen years old. The two married the following year and traveled east to New York City, where (through mutual friend Hal Chase) they befriended the early Beat circle that included Jack Kerouac, Allen Ginsberg, and William S.

Burroughs. Henderson played a central role in the cross-country trips that she made with Cassady and Kerouac between 1947 and 1950, as documented in *On the Road*. According to Henderson in *One and Only*, "I went on that trip solely as an adventure . . . I loved to go anyway; I was always ready. I was like Neal in that respect—it didn't take very much to move me." Henderson later became a thrice-married heroin addict and died in 2009 at the age of seventy-nine. Nicosia first interviewed Henderson in 1978 when she was forty-seven years old. The book features the never-before published transcript of Nicosia's taped interview with Henderson, as well as fifty-five rare photos.

A biographer, historian, poet, playwright, and novelist, Nicosia has also authored several other Beat biographies, including *Memory Babe* (1983), which was called "by far the best of the many books published about Jack Kerouac's life and work" by William S. Burroughs. Nicosia also served as an advisor on the 2012 film *On the Road*, becoming the first instructor of director Walter Salles's "Beat Boot Camp," which educated the young cast, including Kristen Stewart (*The Twilight Saga*), who portrayed Henderson. Nicosia was also involved in the production of the public television documentary *West Coast: Beat and Beyond* (1983).

29

Even the Stars Will Fade Out

Whatever Happened To . . .

Steve Allen

The first host of *The Tonight Show* (1954–57), Allen invited Jack Kerouac on *The Steve Allen Show* in 1959 and provided piano accompaniment as the author read from *On the Road*. He also collaborated with Kerouac on his debut album, *Poetry for the Beat Generation* (1959). Allen died of a massive heart attack on October 30, 2000, at the age of seventy-eight.

David Amram

The critically acclaimed composer, who collaborated with Jack Kerouac at jazz poetry readings during the 1950s, also scored the landmark Beat film *Pull My Daisy* (1959). Amram continues to travel the world as a conductor, soloist, bandleader, and visiting scholar.

Alan Ansen

A poet and playwright, Ansen was closely associated with several members of the Beat Generation, such as Jack Kerouac, Allen Ginsberg, and William S. Burroughs. He served as the model for the character "Rollo Greb" in Jack Kerouac's *On the Road*. Ansen died in his sleep on November 12, 2006, a few days after suffering a stroke at the age of eighty-three in Athens, Greece.

Ken Babbs

The best friend of Ken Kesey and one of the most famous Merry Pranksters (he even claimed to have coined the name), Babbs lives on a farm in Dexter,

Oregon, with his wife, Eileen. He is the author of the 2011 novel *Who Shot the Water Buffalo?*

Amiri Baraka

The celebrated and often controversial poet, playwright, writer, political activist, actor, and teacher died on January 9, 2014, from complications after surgery following a long illness at the age of seventy-nine.

Paul Bowles

An expatriate composer and author (*The Sheltering Sky*) who settled in Tangier, Morocco, with his wife, Jane, in the late 1940s, Bowles later befriended Brion Gysin and William S. Burroughs. He died of a heart attack at the age of eighty-eight on November 18, 1999.

Richard Brautigan

The eccentric writer of *Trout Fishing in America* (1967), Brautigan was caught between the Beat Generation and hippie counterculture, and his eclectic works defied easy labels. An alcoholic who suffered from frequent bouts of depression, Brautigan died of a self-inflicted gunshot wound to the head in 1984.

Ray Bremser

An ex-con and jazz poet who inspired Bob Dylan, Bremser died of lung cancer in Utica, New York, on November 3, 1998. In accordance with Bremser's wishes, his ashes were scattered at Allen Ginsberg's farm in Cherry Valley, New York.

Charles Bukowski

The so-called "Poet Laureate of Skid Row" and occasional friend but usual foe of the Beats died of leukemia on March 9, 1994. Bukowski is buried in Green Hills Memorial Park in Rancho Palos Verdes, California. His epitaph reads, "Don't Try."

William S. Burroughs

Several posthumous collections of Burroughs's work have been published since he died in 1997, such as *Word Virus: The William Burroughs Reader* (1998) and *Last Words: The Final Journals of William S. Burroughs* (2000).

William S. Burroughs Jr.

The troubled son of Joan Vollmer and William S. Burroughs published two novels, *Speed* (1970) and *Kentucky Ham* (1973), and received one of the first liver transplants in the United States in 1976. He died of an acute gastrointestinal hemorrhage associated with micronodular cirrhosis in DeLand, Florida, on March 3, 1981, at the age of thirty-three.

Herb Caen

A celebrated San Francisco journalist who was honored as the city's "voice and conscience," Caen coined the term "beatnik" in 1958 and helped popularize the term "hippie" during the 1967 "Summer of Love." He died of lung cancer at the age of eighty on February 2, 1997.

Bill Cannastra

An original member of the early Beat scene (reportedly the "wild man" of the group), Cannastra was living with Jack Kerouac's future wife Joan Haverty when he died in a bizarre subway accident on October 12, 1950, at the age of twenty-eight.

Mary Carney

The model for the title character in Jack Kerouac's 1959 novel *Maggie Cassidy*, Carney lived her whole life in Lowell, Massachusetts, got married twice, and died circa 1993.

Lucien Carr

A key member of the early Beat scene, Carr spent two years in prison for killing David Kammerer in 1944. He then embarked on a distinguished career with United Press International. Carr died of bone cancer on January 28, 2005, at the age of seventy-nine.

Carolyn Cassady

Neal Cassady's second wife (and the model for "Camille" in Jack Kerouac's *On the Road*), Cassady died on September 20, 2013, at the age of ninety after slipping into a coma following an emergency appendectomy.

Neal Cassady

The legendary "Joan Anderson Letter" written by Cassady that inspired Jack Kerouac to change his writing style for *On the Road* was discovered in the fall of 2014. Plans to auction the letter were postponed when both the Cassady and Kerouac estates made claims to the famous Beat artifact.

Gregory Corso

The youngest of the inner circle of Beat writers, Corso died of prostate cancer on January 17, 2001, and was the subject of the award-winning 2009 documentary *Corso: The Last Beat.*

Elise Cowen

A talented poet who was briefly Allen Ginsberg's girlfriend in the early 1950s, Cowen, who suffered from severe bouts of depression, committed suicide by jumping through a closed window at her parents' apartment and falling seven stories to the street below on February 27, 1962. *Elise Cowen: Poems and Fragments* was published by Ahsahta Press in 2014.

Henri Cru

Jack Kerouac's good friend from the Horace Mann School days in New York City, Cru served as the model for "Remi Boncoeur" (the guy obsessed with the "Banana King") in *On the Road*. He died in 1992 at the age of seventy-two.

Diane di Prima

A feminist Beat poet and author of *Memoirs of a Beatnik* (1969), di Prima was named Poet Laureate of San Francisco in 2009. Her latest work, *The Poetry Deal*, was published by City Lights in 2014.

Kirby Doyle

A San Francisco Renaissance poet heavily involved in the North Beach scene, Doyle died on April 5, 2003, at the age of seventy after a long illness.

Robert Duncan

Singled out by none other than Kenneth Rexroth as "one of the most accomplished, one of the most influential" of the postwar American poets and a fearless advocate for gay rights, Duncan died in San Francisco on February 3, 1988, after a long battle with kidney disease.

Kells Elvins

A childhood friend and Harvard University classmate of William S. Burroughs (the two had collaborated on the short story "Twilight's Last Gleamings" in 1938), Elvins died of a heart attack in 1961.

William Everson

Also known as Brother Antoninus, Everson was a major figure of the San Francisco Renaissance who died of Parkinson's disease on June 3, 1994, at the age of eighty-one, in his rustic cabin known as "Kingfisher Flat" (just north of Santa Cruz).

Lawrence Ferlinghetti

The legendary poet, painter, activist, and cofounder of City Lights Bookstore published a new book in 2015 titled *Writing Across the Landscape: Travel Journals (1950–2013)*.

Bea Franco

The inspiration for the migrant worker "Terry," who had a brief relationship with "Sal Paradise" in Jack Kerouac's *On the Road*, Franco died at the age of ninety-two in 2013 (she was reportedly unaware of her role in the novel until just three years before she died). Franco is the subject of Tim Z. Hernandez's 2013 book, *Manana Means Heaven*.

Robert Frank

An acclaimed photographer (*The Americans*) and filmmaker (*Pull My Daisy*), Frank turned ninety years old in 2014, and remarked in a November 7, 2014, interview with the *Guardian*, "The kind of photography I did is gone . . . There are too many pictures now. It's overwhelming. A flood of images that passes by, and says, 'why should we remember anything?' There is too much to remember now, too much to take in."

Jerry Garcia

Beat aficionado and lead singer of the Grateful Dead, which provided live music for the "Acid Tests" hosted by Ken Kesey and the Merry Pranksters, Garcia died of a heart attack on August 9, 1995, at the age of fifty-three.

Allen Ginsberg

Author of the landmark poem "Howl," Ginsberg died of liver cancer on April 5, 1997, at the age of seventy. Ginsberg was the subject of a 1993 documentary, *The Life and Times of Allen Ginsberg*, as well as the 2010 feature film *Howl*, starring James Franco.

James Grauerholz

A writer and editor best known as the bibliographer and literary executor of the estate of William S. Burrroughs, Grauerholz edited *Last Words: The Final Journals of William S. Burroughs* (2000).

Brion Gysin

An artist, traveler, writer, and alchemist, Gysin introduced William S. Burroughs to the use of permutations and cut-ups in writing at the "Beat Hotel." He died of lung cancer on July 13, 1986, in Paris, France.

Joan Haverty

Jack Kerouac's second wife died of breast cancer in 1990 and was survived by the couple's only child, Jan Michelle Kerouac. Published posthumously in 2000, Haverty's memoir, *Nobody's Wife*, "delivers colorful portraits of Jack's dependence on his mother, his friendship with Neal Cassady and his struggle to write *On the Road*," according to a February 4, 2001, review in the *New York Times*.

Wally Hedrick

Considered the "Godfather of Funk Art," Hedrick helped organize the landmark Six Gallery Reading in 1955. He died of congestive heart failure on December 17, 2003, at the age of seventy-five.

LuAnne Henderson

Neal Cassady's first wife and the inspiration for "Marylou" in *On the Road*, Henderson died on September 25, 2009, at the age of seventy-nine.

John Clellon Holmes

The author of the first Beat novel, *Go* (1952), Holmes died of cancer on March 30, 1988, in Middletown, Connecticut, at the age of sixty-two.

Herbert Huncke

The inspiration for "Herman" in William S. Burroughs's *Junkie* and "Elmer Hassel" in Jack Kerouac's *On the Road*, Huncke died on August 8, 1996, in New York City at the age of eighty-one. His autobiography, *Guilty of Everything*, was published in 1990.

Ted Joans

A true original, Joans was a jazz poet, Beat writer, musician, and Surrealist whose work defies classification with any specific group or school. Joans died from complications of diabetes on April 25, 2003, in Vancouver, Canada.

Joyce Johnson

A prolific author, Johnson won the National Book Critics Circle Award for her 1987 memoir, *Minor Characters: A Beat Memoir*. Her most recent work is *The Voice Is All: The Lonely Victory of Jack Kerouac* (2012).

Hettie Jones

The first wife of Amiri Baraka, Jones is the author of *How I Became Hettie Jones*, which was published by Grove Press in 1990. *Booklist* has called her "a potent and fearless poet."

Lenore Kandel

Affiliated with both the Beat Generation and hippie counterculture, Kandel authored the controversial book of poetry *The Love Book* (1966) and was the only woman to speak from the stage during the 1967 Human Be-In in San Francisco. She died of lung cancer on October 18, 2009. *Collected Poems of Lenore Kandel* was published in 2012.

Bob Kaufman

Known as the "black American Rimbaud," Kaufman was a highly entertaining Beat poet influenced by both Surrealism and jazz music. He died from emphysema on January 12, 1986, at the age of sixty in San Francisco.

Jack Kerouac

In 2014, a new three-thousand-pound memorial stone was added at Kerouac's gravesite in Edson Cemetery, Lowell, Massachusetts, inscribed with the words "The Road is Life" taken from *On the Road*.

Jan Kerouac

The daughter of Jack Kerouac and his second wife, Joan Haverty, Kerouac published two novels: *Baby Driver* (1981) and *Trainsong* (1988). She had only met her famous father on two brief occasions at the ages of nine and fifteen. Kerouac, who had suffered kidney failure and had been on dialysis for several years, died a day after getting her spleen removed on June 5, 1996, at the age of forty-four in Albuquerque, New Mexico.

Ken Kesey

The author of *One Flew Over the Cuckoo's Nest* (1962), proponent of psychedelic drugs, and leader of the Merry Pranksters, Kesey died of complications after surgery for liver cancer on November 10, 2001, at the age of sixty-six in Eugene, Oregon.

Tuli Kupferberg

A bohemian poet, author, cartoonist, anarchist, and cofounder of the Fugs, Kupferberg died on July 10, 2012, in New York City at the age of eighty-six.

Philip Lamantia

A popular San Francisco poet who embraced Surrealism, Lamantia died of heart failure on March 7, 2005, at the age of seventy-seven. He was survived by his wife, Nancy Peters—a writer, editor, publisher, and president of the Board of Directors at City Lights Foundation.

Robert LaVigne

A celebrated artist whose subjects included many Beat writers (including a nude portrait of Peter Orlovsky that caught Allen Ginsberg's eye in 1954), LaVigne died in 2014 at the age of eighty-five. He was the model for "Robert Browning" in *Big Sur* (1962) and "Levesque" in *Desolation Angels* (1965).

Timothy Leary

Once described by President Richard Nixon as "the most dangerous man in America," the guru of psychedelia died of prostate cancer on May 31, 1996, at the age of seventy-five. The 1996 documentary *Timothy Leary's Dead* provided a bizarre journal of the last year of the cult figure's life as he prepared for the "ultimate trip." Some of Leary's ashes were sent into space in an air-launched Pegasus rocket on April 21, 1997, that also carried the cremated remains of *Star Trek* creator Gene Roddenberry, physicist and space enthusiast Gerard K. O'Neill, and others.

Lawrence Lipton

The Venice Beach Beat poet who penned *The Holy Barbarians* (expertly dissecting the Beat scene in Southern California) in 1959, Lipton died on July 9, 1975, at the age of seventy-six. He was the father of *Inside the Actors Studio* host James Lipton.

Adelbert Lewis Marker

The inspiration for "Allerton" in William S. Burroughs's 1985 novel, *Queer*, Marker, a retired small business owner, passed away on April 25, 1998, at the age of sixty-seven in St. Petersburg, Florida.

Michael McClure

Called "one of our best and wisest bard/scholars" by Anne Waldman, McClure was the subject of the documentary *Abstract Alchemist of Flesh*, which premiered at the 2013 Berkeley Video and Film Festival and features cameos by Allen Ginsberg, Dennis Hopper, Ray Manzarek of the Doors, Peter Coyote, and others.

Fred W. McDarrah

A legendary *Village Voice* photographer who documented the Greenwich Village/Beat Generation scene during the 1950s and came up with the notorious "Rent-A-Beatnik" service, McDarrah died in his sleep at the age of eighty-one on November 6, 2007.

David Meltzer

Described by Lawrence Ferlinghetti as "one of the greats of the post–World War II San Francisco poets and musicians," Meltzer has published a dozen poetry books, including his latest, *When I Was a Poet* (2011), which was No. 60 in the City Lights Publishers' Pocket Poets Series.

One of the key poets of the Beat Generation, David Meltzer was described by Lawrence Ferlinghetti as "one of the greats of post–World War II San Francisco poets and musicians. He brought music to poetry and poetry to music!"

Courtesy of Beyond Baroque Literary Arts Center/ Wikimedia Commons.

Jack Micheline

A San Francisco poet, painter, and true iconoclast who once referred to the Beat Generation as a "media hustle," Micheline died of a heart attack while riding a BART subway train on February 27, 1998.

Gillbert Millstein

The *New York Times* reviewer who gave Jack Kerouac's *On the Road* an incredible boost and put the Beat Generation on the map in September 1957, Millstein died of kidney failure at the age of eighty-three in 1999.

Harold Norse

Author of the 1983 experimental cut-up novel *The Beat Hotel*, Norse was called "the best poet of [his] generation" by William Carlos Williams. He died in San Francisco on June 8, 2009, at the age of ninety-two.

Peter Orlovsky

Allen Ginsberg's longtime companion and the author of *Clean Asshole Poems & Smiling Vegetable Songs* (1978), Orlovsky died of lung cancer on May 30, 2010, at the age of seventy-six.

Edie Parker

Jack Kerouac's first wife, Parker appeared as "Judie Smith" in *The Town and the City* (1950). She died from complications of diabetes in 1993. Parker wrote a memoir, *You'll Be Okay: My Life with Jack Kerouac*, which was published posthumously in 2007.

Kenneth Patchen

A highly talented San Francisco Renaissance poet, painter, and anarchist who was lauded by Henry Miller as "the living symbol of protest," Patchen suffered from a chronic spinal injury for most of his life and was bedridden in his later years. He died of a heart attack on January 8, 1972.

Stuart Perkoff

One of the central figures in the Beat scene that centered on Venice Beach, Perkoff died of cancer at the age of forty-four on June 24, 1974.

Charles Plymell

A noted writer and small press publisher who shared a house with Neal Cassady and Allen Ginsberg in the early 1960s, Plymell founded Cherry Valley Editions with his wife, Pam. He is the author of *Benzedrine Highway* (2013), which revisits his early writings, including *The Last of the Moccasins* and *Apocalypse Rose*.

Kenneth Rexroth

The so-called "Grandfather of the Beats" (a title he despised!) died on June 6, 1982, at the age of seventy-six and is buried in the Santa Barbara Cemetery (his grave is the only one that faces the sea).

Barney Rosset

The founder of both the *Evergreen Review* and Grove Press, which published *Naked Lunch* in the United States for the first time in 1962, Rosset died after a double-heart-valve replacement on February 21, 2012, at the age of eighty-nine. A critically acclaimed documentary about Rosset, *Obscene*, was released in 2008.

Ed Sanders

Poet, singer, social activist, and cofounder of the Fugs, Sanders lives in Woodstock, New York, where he publishes the online *Woodstock Journal* (www .woodstockjournal.com) with his wife, Miriam.

Gary Snyder

Known as the "Poet Laureate of Deep Ecology," Snyder has published more than twenty books, the latest being *Tamalpais Walking: Poetry, History, and Prints* (2009, with Tom Killion). Snyder also took part in a 2010 documentary called *The Practice of the Wild* with fellow writer Jim Harrison.

Allan Temko

The inspiration for "Roland Major" in Jack Kerouac's *On the Road*, Temko became a Pulitzer Prize–winning architecture critic for the *San Francisco Chronicle*. He died of congestive heart failure in 2006 at the age of eighty-one.

Joan Vollmer

The common-law wife of William S. Burroughs and model for "Jane" in Jack Kerouac's *On the Road*, Vollmer was accidentally shot and killed by her husband during a drunken William Tell act on September 6, 1951. She is buried in Panteón Americano cemetery in Mexico City.

Anne Waldman

A poet, scholar, and activist, Waldman cofounded with Allen Ginsberg the Jack Kerouac School of Disembodied Poetics, which is located at Naropa University in Boulder, Colorado. Her latest book of poetry, *The Iovis Trilogy*, was published in 2011.

Writer, editor, teacher, performer, and cultural/poltical activist Anne Waldman cofounded with Allen Ginsberg the Jack Kerouac School of Disembodied Poetics at the Naropa Institute (now Naropa University) in 1974.

Courtesy of Miami-Dade College Archives/Wikimedia Commons

Helen Weaver

The model for "Ruth Heaper" in Kerouac's 1965 novel, *Desolation Angels*, Weaver was briefly Jack Kerouac's girlfriend during the mid-1950s. She is the author of *The Awakener: A Memoir of Kerouac and the Fifties* (2009).

Lew Welch

The new and expanded edition of Welch's *Ring of Bone: Collected Poems*, which features an afterword by Gary Snyder, was published by City Lights in 2012.

Philip Whalen

The celebrated San Francisco poet and Zen Buddhist monk passed away at the age of seventy-eight on June 26, 2002, after a long illness.

Phil White

A drug addict and thief, White served as the inspiration for "Roy" in *Junkie* (1953), the lowlife who "rolled drunks" in the subway with William S. Burroughs, as well as "Sailor" in *Naked Lunch* (1959). He hanged himself in the "Tombs" (the nickname for New York City's municipal jail) in 1952.

William Carlos Williams

A highly influential poet from Rutherford, New Jersey, who wrote the introduction to Allen Ginsberg's *Howl and Other Poems* (1956), Williams died in his sleep of a cerebral hemorrhage on March 4, 1963. He was posthumously awarded the Pulitzer Prize for Poetry for *Pictures from Brueghel and Other Poems* (1962), as well as the Gold Medal for Poetry from the National Institute of Arts and Letters.

Victor Wong

An artist and actor who befriended poet Lawrence Ferlinghetti in the 1950s, Wong served as the model for "Arthur Ma" in Kerouac's *Big Sur* (1962) and later appeared in a series of feature films, including *Dim Sum: A Little Bit of Heart* (1985), *Big Trouble in Little China* (1986), and *The Joy Luck Club* (1993). He died of heart failure on September 12, 2001, at the age of seventy-four.

Each Stolen Moment
A Beat Generation Timeline

1914

- *Naked Lunch* author William Seward Burroughs is born on February 5 in St. Louis, Missouri, to Laura Lee and Mortimer Burroughs.

1915

- Times Square hipster and hustler Herbert Edwin Huncke is born on January 9 in Greenfield, Massachusetts.

1922

- *On the Road* author Jack Kerouac is born Jean Louis Lebris de Kerouac on March 12 in Lowell, Massachusetts, to Gabrielle and Leo Kerouac.
- Kerouac's first wife, Frankie Edith Parker, is born on September 20 in Grosse Pointe, Michigan.

1923

- Neal Cassady's second wife, Carolyn Elizabeth Robinson, is born on April 28 in East Lansing, Michigan.
- Poet Philip Whalen is born on October 20 in Portland, Oregon.
- Burroughs's common-law wife, Joan Vollmer, is born on February 4 in Loudonville, New York.

1925

- A key member of the early Beat circle, Lucien Carr, is born on March 1 in New York City, New York.
- Poet Bob Kaufman is born on April 18 in New Orleans, Louisiana.

1926

- "Howl" poet Allen Ginsberg is born on June 3 in Newark, New Jersey.
- The inspiration for "Dean Moriarty" in *On the Road*, Neal Leon Cassady is born on February 8 in Salt Lake City, Utah.
- John Clellon Holmes is born on March 12 in Holyoke, Massachusetts.
- Lew Welch is born on August 16 in Phoenix, Arizona.
- Kerouac's older brother, Gerard, dies of rheumatic fever at the age of nine in Lowell, Massachusetts.

1928

- Carl Solomon is born on March 30 in the Bronx, New York City.
- Ted Joans is born on July 4 in Cairo, Illinois.

1930

- Gregory Corso is born on March 26 in New York City.
- Gary Snyder is born on May 8 in San Francisco, California.

1932

- Michael McClure is born on October 20 in Marysville, Kansas.
- Burroughs attends Harvard University and majors in English literature.

1934

- Ray Bremser is born on February 22 in Jersey City, New Jersey.
- Diane di Prima is born on August 6 in Brooklyn, New York City.
- Everett LeRoi Jones (later Amiri Baraka) is born on October 7 in Newark, New Jersey.

1935

- *One Flew Over the Cuckoo's Nest* author and Merry Prankster Ken Kesey is born on September 17 in La Junta, Colorado.

1936

- Burroughs attends medical school at the University of Vienna.

1938

- Kerouac scores the winning touchdown in the Thanksgiving Day football game for Lowell High School against rival Lawrence High School.
- Burroughs and his childhood friend Kells Elvins collaborate on the short story "Twilight's Last Gleamings."

1939

- Kerouac travels to New York City to attend the Horace Mann School.

1940

- Kerouac attends Columbia University on a football scholarship.

1942

- Kerouac signs up for the Merchant Marine and serves on the *SS Dorchester*.

1943

- Kerouac enlists in the US Navy but is quickly discharged with a diagnosis of "indifferent character."
- Kerouac works on a novel called *The Sea Is My Brother*, based on his merchant marine experience.

1944

- Kerouac meets Lucien Carr, who introduces him to Allen Ginsberg and William S. Burroughs.
- Carr kills David Kammerer, claiming self-defense.
- Kerouac marries his first wife, Edie Parker.

1945

- Kerouac and Burroughs collaborate on a novel, *And the Hippos were*

After a brief stint in the merchant marine, Jack Kerouac joined the US Navy in 1943 but was honorably discharged on psychiatric grounds after just ten days of active duty. *Author's collection*

Boiled in Their Tanks (that remains unpublished until 2008), based on the Carr/Kammerer case.
- Ginsberg is expelled from Columbia University.

1946

- Cassady marries LuAnne Henderson.
- Burroughs purchases a ninety-six-acre farm in New Waverly, Texas, with the intention of growing marijuana.
- Corso begins a three-year stint at Clinton Correctional Facility for grand theft.

1947

- Kerouac meets Cassady in New York City, and over the next three years they embark on a series of cross-country trips that will be featured in *On the Road*.
- Naomi Ginsberg receives a prefrontal lobotomy at Pilgrim State Hospital in Brentwood, New York.
- Cassady writes the "Great Sex Letter" in a Kansas City bar.
- William Burroughs Jr. ("Billy") is born on July 21 in Conroe, Texas.

1948

- Burroughs and his family move to Algiers, Louisiana.
- Ginsberg undergoes a series of life-changing visions relating to English Romantic poet William Blake.
- Kerouac casually mentions the term "Beat Generation" in conversation with Holmes.

1949

- Ginsberg is sent to New York State Psychiatric Institute where he meets fellow patient Carl Solomon.
- Burroughs and his family move to Mexico City.

1950

- Harcourt Brace publishes Kerouac's first novel, *The Town and the City* (under the name "John Kerouac").
- Kerouac's friend Bill Cannastra dies in a freak subway accident in New York City.
- Kerouac marries his second wife, Joan Haverty.
- Cassady marries his third wife, Diana Hansen, in Newark, New Jersey.

Neal Cassady and Jack Kerouac embarked on a series of cross-country road trips between 1947 and 1950 that would serve as the basis for *On the Road*. Cassady's frantic lifestyle and stream-of-consciousness-style letters to Kerouac helped the author move toward the "spontaneous prose" of *On the Road*.   *Courtesy of Photofest*

- Kerouac receives the fabled "Joan Anderson Letter" from Cassady and reevaulates the writing style for his "road novel."

1951

- Burroughs accidentally shoots and kills his wife, Joan, in Mexico City during a drunken William Tell routine.
- Kerouac (re)writes a version of *On the Road* on a single roll of tracing paper during three weeks in April.

1952

- The first Beat Generation novel, *Go* by John Clellon Holmes, is published.
- Haverty gives birth to Jan Kerouac on February 16 in Albany, New York.
- Holmes's seminal article, "This Is the Beat Generation," appears in the *New York Times Magazine.*

1953

- Ferlinghetti and Peter Martin open City Lights Bookstore, the first paperback bookstore in the United States.
- Ace Books publishes Burroughs's first novel, *Junkie*, in a two-in-one deal with *Narcotic Agent* by Maurice Helbrant.
- Burroughs travels in South America in search of the hallucinogen yage.

1954

- Robert Creeley edits the first issue of *Black Mountain Review.*

1955

- The Six Gallery Reading takes place on October 7 in San Francisco, featuring Rexroth as master of ceremonies and readings by Allen Ginsberg ("Howl"), Philip Lamantia, Michael McClure, Philip Whalen, and Gary Snyder.
- Ferlinghetti launches the Pocket Poets Series at City Lights Books by publishing one of his own collections of poetry, *Pictures of a Gone World.*
- Corso publishes his first poetry collection, *The Vestal Lady on Brattle and Other Poems.*

1956

- Ginsberg's *Howl and Other Poems* is published as part of City Lights' Pocket Poets Series.
- Kerouac works as a fire lookout for the Forest Service at Desolation Peak in Washington.
- Ginsberg challenges a heckler by getting naked during a poetry reading in Los Angeles.
- Ginberg's mother, Naomi, dies at Pilgrim State Hospital.
- Burroughs travels to London and undergoes apomorphine treatment with Dr. Yerbury Dent in an effort to cure his heroin addiction.
- Snyder leaves for Japan to study Zen Buddhism.

1957

- Norman Mailer's groundbreaking essay "The White Negro" appears in *Dissent* magazine.
- Judge Clayton Horn rules "Howl" not obscene during a landmark obscenity trial.
- Kerouac, Ginsberg and Orlovsky, and Alan Ansen visit Burroughs in Tangier and assist with the typing and editing of *Naked Lunch*.
- The *Evergreen Review* publishes its landmark "San Francisco Scene" issue.
- Viking Press publishes Kerouac's novel *On the Road*.

Founded in 1957 by Grove Press publisher Barney Rosset, the legendary Evergreen Review consistently published the works of Beat writers, such as William S. Burroughs's classic treatise "Deposition: Testimony Concerning a Sickness."

Courtesy of Evergreen Review/evergreenreview.com

San Francisco Chronicle columnist Herb Caen first coined the word "beatnik" in an April 2, 1958, article by coming up with a play on words based on the Russian satellite Sputnik. Use of the term quickly spread across the country.

Photo by Nancy Wong/Wikimedia Commons

1958

* Kerouac makes an appearance on *The Steve Allen Show* reading selections from *Visions of Cody* and *On the Road* to Allen's piano accompaniment.
* Herb Caen coins the word "beatnik" in the *San Francisco Chronicle.*
* Cassady starts a two-year jail term in San Quentin State Prison for marijuana possession.
* Kerouac's *The Dharma Bums* and *The Subterraneans* are published.
* LeRoi and Hattie Jones publish *Yugen*, a Beat-related magazine.
* City Lights publishes Corso's poetry collection *Gasoline.*

1959

* Olympia Press (Paris) publishes Burroughs's novel *Naked Lunch.*
* Brion Gysin accidentally discovers the cut-up technique while residing in the "Beat Hotel" in Paris and shares his discovery with an extremely enthusiastic Burroughs.
* Kerouac's first album, *Poetry for the Beat Generation*, features piano accompaniment by Steve Allen.
* The popular TV show *The Many Loves of Dobie Gillis* makes its debut featuring the Beatnik character "Maynard G. Krebs" (Bob Denver).

- Kerouac's article "The Origins of the Beat Generation" appears in the June edition of *Playboy* magazine and includes the memorable line "Who knows, my God, but that the universe is not one vast sea of compassion actually, the veritable holy honey, beneath all this show of personality and cruelty?"
- Directed and produced by Roger Corman, *A Bucket of Blood*, the definitive beatnik satire, is released by American International Pictures.
- *Life* magazine publishes "Squaresville USA vs. Beatsville" article.
- Directed by Robert Frank and Alfred Leslie, the landmark short film *Pull My Daisy*, is released—starring Ginsberg, Orlovsky, Corso, artist Larry Rivers, and musician David Amram.
- Kerouac's *Doctor Sax* and *Maggie Cassidy* are published.
- A "Rent-A-Beatnik ad appears in the *Village Voice*.
- Gysin and Ian Sommerville create the "Dreamachine" at the "Beat Hotel" in Paris.

1960

- Ferlinghetti offers Kerouac the use of his cabin in Bixby Canyon, California.
- The TV series *Route 66* makes its debut, with many similarities to *On the Road*.
- Kerouac's *Tristessa* is published.
- MGM's film version of *The Subterraneans* is released, starring Leslie Caron and George Peppard.
- *Mad* magazine features the satire "Beatnik: The Magazine for Hipsters."
- Neal Cassady is released from San Quentin Prison.
- *Minutes to Go*, the first cut-up book, by Burroughs, Gysin, Corso, and Sinclair Beiles, is published in Paris.

1961

- Olympia Press publishes Burroughs's *The Soft Machine*, the first novel in his Nova Trilogy.
- Ginsberg's *Kaddish and Other Poems* is published.
- Diane di Prima and LeRoi Jones publish *The Floating Bear* newsletter.

1962

- Kerouac's novel *Big Sur* is published.
- Grove Press (New York) publishes Burroughs's *Naked Lunch*.
- Burroughs's novel *The Ticket That Exploded* is published.

1963

- Kerouac's novel *Visions of Gerard* is published.
- Ginsberg's *Reality Sandwiches* is published.
- The "Beat Hotel" in Paris closes for good.

1964

- Diane di Prima founds Poets Press.
- Ken Kesey and the Merry Pranksters make their way across the United States in a bus called "Further," promoting the use of psychedelic drugs.

1965

- The word "hippie" is coined by *San Francisco Examiner* writer Michael Fallon.
- Kerouac's novel *Desolation Angels* is published.
- Burroughs' *Naked Lunch* is declared obscene during a Boston trial.
- The first "Acid Test" takes place at Merry Prankster Ken Babbs's ranch near Santa Cruz, California.
- Ginsberg is declared the "King of May" in Prague, Czechoslovakia.

1966

- Kerouac's novel *Satori in Paris* is published.
- Kerouac marries his third wife, Stella Sampas.
- The Massachusetts Supreme Judicial Court reverses the earlier decision by the Boston courts and declares that *Naked Lunch* is not obscene.
- The Psychedelic Shop opens in Haight-Ashbury.

1967

- The Human Be-In takes place at Golden Gate Park in San Francisco, a precursor to the "Summer of Love."

1968

- Neal Cassady dies on February 4 in San Miguel de Allende, Mexico.
- Ginsberg and Burroughs, along with Jean Genet and Terry Southern, cover the Democratic National Convention in Chicago for *Esquire* magazine.
- Kerouac makes a drunken appearance on the *Firing Line* TV show hosted by William F. Buckley.
- Tom Wolfe's *The Electric Kool-Aid Acid Test* is published, detailing the various antics of Ken Kesey and the Merry Pranksters.

- Ginsberg's *Planet News* is published.
- Kerouac's *Vanity of Duluoz* is published.

1969

- Kerouac dies of an abdominal hemorrhage on October 21 in St. Petersburg, Florida.

1971

- Cassady's autobiography, *The First Third*, is published posthumously.
- Burroughs's *The Wild Boys* is published.

1972

- Ginsberg's *The Fall of America: Poems of These States* is published.

1973

- Burroughs's collection of short stories titled *Exterminator!* is published.
- Ginsberg wins the National Book Award for *The Fall of America: Poems of These States.*

1974

- After twenty-six years abroad, Burroughs returns to New York City and eventually makes his residence in "The Bunker" at 222 Bowery.
- Ginsberg and Anne Waldman cofound the Jack Kerouac School of Disembodied Poetics at the Naropa Institute (now Naropa University) in Boulder, Colorado.

1975

- Ginsberg and Bob Dylan visit Jack Kerouac's grave in Edson Cemetery in Lowell, Massachusetts, during the Rolling Thunder Revue tour.

1978

- Ginsberg's *Mind Breaths* is published.
- The Nova Convention is held in New York City to honor Burroughs's life and work.

1980

- *Heart Beat*, a film adaptation of Carolyn Cassady's memoir, is released starring Sissy Spacek, Nick Nolte, and John Heard.

1981

- Burroughs Jr. dies on March 3 in DeLand, Florida.
- Burroughs moves to Lawrence, Kansas, where he will reside for the rest of his life.
- Burroughs appears on *Saturday Night Live* and reads from "Twilight's Last Gleamings."
- Burroughs's *Cities of the Red Night* is published.

1982

- The Naropa Institute hosts a twenty-fifth anniversary celebration of *On the Road*.

1983

- Directed by Howard Brookner, the documentary *Burroughs: The Movie* is released.
- Burroughs is elected to the American Academy and Institute of Arts and Letters.

1984

- Burroughs's *The Place of Dead Roads* is published.

1985

- Burroughs's collection of essays *The Adding Machine* and novel *Queer* are published.

1986

- Ginsberg's *White Shroud Poems* is published.

1987

- Burroughs's *The Western Lands* is published.

1988

- Holmes dies at the age of sixty-two in Middletown, Connecticut.

1989

- Burroughs appears as "Old Tom the Junkie Priest" in the Gus Van Sant's cult movie *Drugstore Cowboy*.

In 1982, William S. Burroughs moved into a stone farmhouse five miles outside of Lawrence, Kansas, where he continued to write, engage in other pursuits such as shotgun art, and act in cult movies such as *Drugstore Cowboy* (1989).   *Courtesy of Photofest*

1990

- Burroughs releases *Dead City Radio*, a spoken-word album.
- The *Jack Kerouac Collection* is released.
- Burroughs collaborates on the play *The Black Rider* with singer-songwriter Tom Waits and director Robert Wilson.

1991

- David Cronenberg's adaptation of *Naked Lunch* is released, starring Peter Weller as "William Lee."

1993

- Ginsberg is awarded the medal of the Chevalier des Arts et des Letters (the Order of Arts and Letters) by the French Minister of Culture.
- Burroughs and Kurt Cobain of Nirvana collaborate on an album, *The "Priest" They Called Him.*

1994

- Burroughs appears in a series of Nike TV commercials.

Jack Kerouac referred to Herbert Huncke as "the greatest story-teller I know." The true personification of "beat," Huncke lived out his last years in a small room in the legendary Chelsea Hotel in New York City.   *Photo by Chris Felver/Getty Images*

1995

- New York University sponsors "The Writings of Jack Kerouac Conference."
- Burroughs's *My Education: A Book of Dreams* is published.

1996

- Jan Kerouac dies in an Albuquerque, New Mexico, hospital on June 5 at the age of forty-four.
- Huncke dies from congestive heart failure on August 8 in New York City.

1997

- Ginsberg dies of liver cancer on April 5 in New York City.
- Burroughs dies of a heart attack on August 2 in Lawrence, Kansas.

1999

- Ginsberg's *Death and Fame* is published posthumously.

2001

- Corso dies from prostate cancer on January 17 in Minnesota.

2003

- The Beat Museum opens its doors in North Beach, San Francisco, across the street from City Lights Bookstore.

2009

- Helen Weaver publishes *The Awakener: A Memoir of Kerouac and the Fifties.*

2012

- The documentary *The Beat Hotel* is released.
- The film version of *On the Road* is released.

2013

- The film version of *Big Sur* is released.

2014

- The fabled "Joan Anderson Letter" written by Cassady is discovered in a pile of decades-old files.

Selected Bibliography

Abbott, Keith. *Downstream from Trout Fishing in America*. Santa Barbara, CA: Capra Press, 1989.

Agee, James. "The Great American Roadside." *Fortune* (September 1934).

Allen, Donald M., ed. *The New American Poetry, 1945–1960*. New York: Grove Press, 1960.

Bald, Margaret, Nicholas J. Karolides, and Dawn B. Sova. *100 Banned Books: Censorship Histories of World Literature*. New York: Checkmark Books, 1990.

Bangs, Lester. *Psychotic Reactions and Carburetor Dung*. New York: Anchor Books, 2003.

Baraka, Amiri. *Dutchman & The Slave*. New York: William Morrow and Company, 1964.

———. *Preface to a Twenty Volume Suicide Note*. New York: Totem Press, 1961.

———. *The System of Dante's Hell*. New York: Grove Press, 1965.

Beiles, Sinclair, William S. Burroughs, Gregory Corso, and Brion Gysin. *Minutes to Go*. San Francisco: Beach Books, 1968.

Bianco, Anthony. *Ghosts of 42nd Street: A History of America's Most Infamous Block*. Scranton, PA: William Morrow, 2004.

Bird, Christiane. *The Da Capo Jazz and Blues Lover's Guide to the U.S.* Boston: Da Capo Press, 2001.

Black, Jack. *You Can't Win: The Autobiography of Jack Black*. New York: AMOK Press, 1988.

Bockris, Victor. *With William Burroughs: A Report from the Bunker*. New York: St. Martin's Press, 1996.

Borzillo, Carrie. *Nirvana: The Day-By-Day Eyewitness Chronicle*. New York: Thunder's Mouth Press, 2000.

Bowles, Paul. *Without Stopping: An Autobiography*. New York: Ecco Press, 1972.

Brautigan, Richard. *The Abortion: An Historical Romance 1966*. New York: Simon and Schuster, 1971.

———. *Trout Fishing in America*. Boston: Mariner Books, 2010.

Bremser, Ray. *Blowing Mouth: The Jazz Poems 1958–1970*. Cherry Valley, NY: Cherry Valley Editions, 1978.

———. *Poems of Madness*. New York: Paperback Gallery, 1965.

Brinkley, Douglas. *The Majic Bus: An American Odyssey*. New York: Thunder's Mouth Press, 2003.

Brinkley, Douglas, ed. *Windblown World: The Journals of Jack Kerouac.* New York: Viking Press, 2004.

Buehle, Paul, ed. *The Beats: A Graphic History.* New York: Farrar, Straus and Giroux, 2009.

Buffett, Jimmy. *A Pirate Looks at Fifty.* New York: Random House, 1998.

Bukowski, Charles. *Hollywood.* New York: Ecco Press, 2002.

——. *Notes of a Dirty Old Man.* San Francisco: City Lights Publishers, 2001.

——. *Screams from the Balcony.* Boston: Black Sparrow Press, 1993.

Burroughs, William S. *The Adding Machine: Selected Essays.* New York: Grove Press: 2013.

——. *Cities of the Red Night.* New York: Picador, 1981.

——. *Exterminator!* New York: Penguin Books, 1979.

——. *Ghost of a Chance.* New York: High Risk Books, 2002.

——. "Heart Beat: Fifties Heroes as Soap Opera." *Rolling Stone* (January 24, 1980).

——. *Interzone.* New York: Penguin Books, 1990.

——. *Junky: The Definitive Text of "Junk."* New York: Grove Press, 2012.

——. *The Last Words of Dutch Schultz: A Fiction in the Form of a Film Script.* New York: Arcade Publishing, 1993.

——. "Letter from a Master Addict to Dangerous Drugs." *British Journal of Addiction* (January 1957).

——. *My Education: A Book of Dreams.* New York: Penguin Books, 1996.

——. *Naked Lunch.* New York: Grove Press, 2013.

——. *Nova Express.* New York: Grove Press, 1994.

——. *The Place of Dead Roads.* New York: Picador, 1983.

——. *Queer.* New York: Viking Penguin, 1985.

——. *The Soft Machine.* New York: Grove Press, 1992.

——. *The Ticket That Exploded.* New York: Grove Press, 1994.

——. *The Western Lands.* New York: Penguin Books, 1987.

——. *The Wild Boys: A Book of the Dead.* New York: Grove Press, 1994.

Burroughs, William S., and Allen Ginsberg. *The Yage Letters Redux.* San Francisco: City Lights Publishers, 2006.

Burroughs William S., and Jack Kerouac. *And the Hippos Were Boiled in Their Tanks.* New York: Grove Press, 2008.

Burroughs, William S. Jr. *Speed/Kentucky Ham.* New York: Overlook Press, 1993.

Calonne, David. *Charles Bukowski: Sunlight Here I Am, Interviews and Encounters 1963–1993.* Northville, MI: Sun Dog Press, 2003.

Cassady, Carolyn. *Off the Road: My Years with Cassady, Kerouac and Ginsberg.* London: Black Spring Press, 1990.

Cassady, Neal. *The First Third and Other Writings*. San Francisco: City Lights Publishers, 1971.

———. *Neal Cassady: Collected Letters 1944–1967*. New York: Penguin Books, 2005.

Challis, Chris. *Quest for Kerouac*. London: Faber & Faber, 1984.

Charters, Ann, ed. *The Beats, Literary Bohemians in Postwar America*. Farmington Hills, MI: Gale, 1983.

———. *The Portable Beat Reader*. New York: Viking, 1992.

Cherkovski, Neeli. *Whitman's Wild Children: Portraits of Twelve Poets*. South Royalton, VT: Steerforth Press, 1999.

Cherry, Jim. *The Doors Examined*. Birmingham, UK: Bennion Kearny Limited, 2013.

Christy, Jim. *The Long Slow Death of Jack Kerouac*. Toronto: ECW Press, 1998.

Coleman, Joe. *Cosmic Retribution: The Infernal Art of Joe Coleman*. Seattle: Fantagraphics Books, 1993.

Cook, Bruce. *The Beat Generation*. New York: Charles Scribner's Sons, 1971.

Corman, Roger. *How I Made a Hundred Movies in Hollywood and Never Lost a Dime*. Cambridge: Da Capo Press, 1998.

Corso, Gregory. *Gasoline*. San Francisco: City Lights Publishing, 2001.

———. *The Happy Birthday of Death*. New York: New Directions Publishing, 1960.

———. *Mindfield: New and Selected Poems*. New York: Thunder's Mouth Press, 1998.

———. *The Vestal Lady on Brattle and Other Poems*. San Francisco: City Lights Publishing, 1969.

Crowther, Hal. *Unarmed but Dangerous*. Atlanta: Longstreet Press, 1995.

Davis, Francis. *Bebop and Nothingness: Jazz and Pop at the End of the Century*. New York: Schirmer Books, 1996.

DeRogatis, Jim. *Let It Blurt: The Life & Times of Lester Bangs, America's Greatest Rock Critic*. New York: Broadway Books, 2000.

Di Prima, Diane. *Memoirs of a Beatnik*. New York: Penguin Books, 1998.

———. *Recollections of My Life as a Woman: The New York Years*. New York: Penguin Books, 2001.

Dickey, Christopher. *Summer of Deliverance*. New York: Touchstone, 1998.

Dittman, Michael J. *Masterpieces of Beat Literature*. Santa Barbara, CA: Greenwood Publishing Group, 2006.

Dostoevsky, Fyodor. *Notes from Underground*. New York: Tribeca Books, 2010.

Doyle, Kirby. *Sapphobones*. New York: Poets Press, 1966.

Duncan, Robert. *Selected Poems*. New York: New Directions Publishing, 1997.

Elger, Dietmar. *Dadaism*. Los Angeles: Taschen, 2004.

Evans, Mike. *The Beats: From Kerouac to Kesey, an Illustrated Journey through the Beat Generation*. London: Running Press, 2007.

Feldman, Gene, and Max Gartenberg, eds. *The Beat Generation and the Angry Young Men*. New York: Citadel Press, 1958.

Felver, Christopher. *The Late Great Allen Ginsberg*. New York: Thunder's Mouth Press, 2002.

Ferlinghetti, Lawrence. *A Coney Island of the Mind*, 50th Anniversary Edition. New York: New Directions, 2008.

———. *Pictures of the Gone World*. San Francisco: City Lights Publishing, 2001.

———. *The Secret Meaning of Things*. New York: New Directions, 1968.

Fields, Rick. *How the Swans Came to the Lake: A Narrative History of Buddhism in America*. Boston: Shambhala Publications, 1992.

Frank, Robert. *The Americans*. New York: Grove Press, 1959.

French, Warren. *Jack Kerouac: Novelist of the Beat Generation*. Boston: Twayne Publishers, 1986.

George-Warren, Holly, ed. *The Rolling Stone Book of the Beats: The Beat Generation and American Culture*. New York: Hyperion, 1999.

Gifford, Barry, and Lawrence Lee. *Jack's Book: An Oral Biography of Jack Kerouac*. New York: St. Martin's Press, 1978.

Gilmore, Mikal. *Stories Done: Writings on the 1960s and Its Discontents*. New York: Free Press, 2008.

Ginsberg, Allen. "A Definition of the Beat Generation." *Friction* no. 1 (Winter 1982).

———. *Death and Fame: Poems 1993–1997*. New York: Harper Perennial, 2000.

———. *Deliberate Prose: Selected Essays 1952–1995*. New York: HarperCollins Publishers, 2000.

———. *Empty Mirror: Early Poems*. San Bernardino, CA: Bookslinger, 1961.

———. *The Fall of America: Poems of These States 1965–1971*. San Francisco: City Lights Publishers, 2001.

———. *Howl and Other Poems*. San Francisco: City Lights Publishers, 2001.

———. *Kaddish and Other Poems*, 50th Anniversary Edition. San Francisco: City Lights Publishers, 2010.

———. *Mind Breaths 1972–1977*. San Francisco: City Lights Publishers, 2001.

———. *Planet News*. San Francisco: City Lights Publishers, 2001.

———. *Reality Sandwiches 1953–1960*. San Francisco: City Lights Publishers, 2001.

———. *Snapshot Poetics: Allen Ginsberg's Photographic Memoir of the Beat Era*. San Francisco: Chronicle Books, 1993.

———. *White Shroud Poems 1980–1985*. New York: Harper & Row, 1986.

Goulart, Ron. *Cheap Thrills: An Informal History of the Pulp Magazines*. New Rochelle, NY: Arlington House, 1972.

Grauerholz, James, ed. *Last Words: The Final Journals of William S. Burroughs.* New York: Grove Press, 2000.

Hackett, Pat, ed. *The Andy Warhol Diaries.* New York: Warner Books, 1989.

Harris, Oliver, ed. *Everything Lost: The Latin American Notebooks of William S. Burroughs.* Columbus: The Ohio State University Press, 2008.

Haverty, Joan. *Nobody's Wife.* Berkeley, CA: Creative Arts Book Company. 2000.

Hernandez, Tim Z. *Manana Means Heaven.* Tucson: University of Arizona Press, 2013.

Hibbard, Allen. *Conversations with William S. Burroughs.* Jackson: University Press of Mississippi, 2000.

Hofmann, Albert. *LSD: My Problem Child.* New York: McGraw-Hill, 1980.

Holmes, John Clellon. *Go.* New York: Thunder's Mouth Press, 2002.

———. *Gone in October: Last Reflections on Jack Kerouac.* Boise, ID: Limberlost Press, 1985.

———. *Horn.* New York: Thunder's Mouth Press, 1988.

———. *Passionate Opinions: The Cultural Essays of John Clellon Holmes.* Fayetteville: University of Arkansas Press, 1988.

———. "This Is the Beat Generation." *New York Times Magazine* (November 16, 1952).

Hopkins, Jerry and Danny Sugerman. *No One Here Gets Out Alive.* New York: Warner Brothers, 1980.

Hughes, Evan. *Literary Brooklyn.* New York: Holt Paperbacks, 2011.

Humphrey, Mark. *The Jimmy Buffett Scrapbook.* New York: Citadel Press, 1993.

Huncke, Herbert. *Guilty of Everything: The Autobiography of Herbert Huncke.* New York: Paragon House, 1990.

Jacobs, Jay S. *Wild Years: The Music and Myth of Tom Waits.* Toronto: ECW Press, 2006.

Javna, John. *Cult TV.* New York: St. Martin's Press, 1985.

Joans, Ted. *The Hipsters.* New York: Corinth Books, 1961.

———. *Teducation: Selected Poems.* Minneapolis: Coffee House Press, 1999.

Johnson, Joyce. *Minor Characters.* Boston: Houghton Mifflin, 1983.

———. *The Voice Is All: The Lonely Victory of Jack Kerouac.* New York: Penguin Books, 2012.

Jones, Hettie. *How I Became Hettie Jones.* New York: Penguin Books, 1991.

Kashner, Sam. *When I Was Cool: My Life at the Jack Kerouac School.* New York: HarperCollins Publishers, 2004.

Kaufman, Alan, Neil Ortenberg, and Barney Rosset. *The Outlaw Bible of American Literature.* New York: Thunder's Mouth Press, 2004.

Kemp, Harry. *Tramping on Life.* New York: Garden City Press, 1927.

Kerouac, Jack. "After Me, the Deluge." *Chicago Tribune* (September 28, 1969).

———. *Big Sur.* New York: Farrar, Straus, and Cudahy, 1962.

———. *Book of Blues*. New York: Penguin Books, 1995.

———. *Desolation Angels*. New York: Coward-McCann, 1965.

———. *The Dharma Bums*. New York: Penguin Books, 2005.

———. *Doctor Sax*. New York: Grove Press, 1994.

———. *Maggie Cassidy*. London: Penguin Books, 1993.

———. *Mexico City Blues*. New York: Grove Press, 1994.

———. *On the Road*. New York: Penguin Books, 1998.

———. *On the Road: The Original Scroll*. New York: Penguin Books, 2007.

———. "The Origins of the Beat Generation." *Playboy* (June 1959).

———. *Satori in Paris & Pic*. New York: Grove Press, 1988.

———. *The Subterraneans*. New York: Grove Press, 1994.

———. *The Town and the City*. New York: Harcourt Brace, 1950.

———. *Tristessa*. New York: Penguin Books, 1992.

———. *Vanity of Duluoz*. New York: Penguin Books, 1994.

———. *Visions of Cody*. New York: Penguin Books, 1993.

———. *Visions of Gerard*. New York: Penguin Books, 1991.

Kerouac, Jack, Albert Saijo, and Lew Welch. *Trip Trap*. San Francisco: Grey Fox Press, 1973.

Kerouac, Jan. *Baby Driver*. New York: St. Martin's Press, 1981.

———. *Trainsong*. New York: Henry Holt & Co., 1988.

Kerouac-Parker, Edie. *You'll Be Okay: My Life with Jack Kerouac*. San Francisco: City Lights Publishers, 2007.

Kesey, Ken. "The Day After Superman Died." *Esquire* (October 1979).

———. *The Further Inquiry*. New York: Viking Press, 1990.

———. *One Flew Over the Cuckoo's Nest*. New York: Signet Books, 1963.

Knight, Arthur and Kit Knight, eds. *The Beat Vision*. New York: Paragon House Publishers, 1987.

Lamantia, Philip. *Bed of Sphinxes: New & Selected Poems 1943–1993*. San Francisco: City Lights Publishers, 1997.

———. *Erotic Poems*. New York: Bern Porter, 1946.

Landesman, Jay, ed. *Neurotica: Authentic Voice of the Beat Generation*. London: Jay Landesman Ltd., 1981.

Lawlor, William. *The Beat Generation: A Bibliographical Teaching Guide*. Lanham, MD: Scarecrow Press, 1998.

Lipton, Lawrence. *The Holy Barbarians*. New York: Grove Press, 1959.

London, Jack. *The Road*. New York: Macmillan, 1907.

Lord, Sterling. *Lord of Publishing: A Memoir*. New York: Open Road Media, 2013.

Lutz, Tom. *Doing Nothing: A History of Loafers, Loungers, Slackers, and Bums in America*. New York: Farrar, Straus and Giroux, 2006.

Mailer, Norman. *Advertisements for Myself.* Cambridge: Harvard University Press, 1992.

———. "The White Negro." *Dissent* (1957).

Manzarek, Ray. *Light My Fire: My Life with the Doors.* New York: Berkeley Boulevard, 1998.

Mariani, Paul. *William Carlos Williams: A New World Naked.* New York: W. W. Norton & Company, 1990.

McCarthy, Kevin M. *The Book Lover's Guide to Florida.* Sarasota, FL: Pineapple Press, 1992.

McClure, Michael. *The Beard.* New York: Grove Press, 1967.

———. *Ghost Tantras.* San Francisco: City Lights Publishers, 2013.

———. *Scratching the Beat Surface.* Boulder, CO: North Point, 1992.

McDarrah, Fred W. *Kerouac & Friends: A Beat Generation Album.* New York: William Morrow and Company, 1985.

McDarrah, Fred W., and Gloria S. McDarrah. *Beat Generation: Glory Days in Greenwich Village.* New York: Schirmer, 1996.

McKinnon, Gina. *500 Essential Cult Books: The Ultimate Guide.* New York: Sterling, 2010.

McNeil, Legs, and Gillian McCain. *Please Kill Me: The Uncensored Oral History of Punk.* New York: Penguin Books, 1997.

Meltzer, David. *San Francisco Beat: Talking with the Poets.* San Francisco: City Lights Publishers, 2001.

Mersmann, James F. *Out of the Vietnam Vortex: A Study of Poets and Poetry Against the War.* Lawrence: University Press of Kansas, 1974.

Micheline, Jack. *River of Red Wine.* Sudbury, MA: Water Row Press, 1986.

Miles, Barry. *Hippie.* New York: Sterling Publishing Co., 2005.

Miller, Beverly Gray. *Roger Corman: Blood-Sucking Vampires, Flesh-Eating Cockroaches, and Driller Killers.* Santa Monica, CA: AZ Ferris Publications, 2004.

Mitchell, Ted. *Thomas Wolfe: An Illustrated Biography.* New York: Pegasus Books, 2006.

Montandon, Mac, ed. *Innocent When You Dream: The Tom Waits Reader.* New York: Thunder's Mouth Press, 2005.

Montgomery, John. *Kerouac at the "Wild Boar" and Other Skirmishes.* San Anselmo, CA: Fels & Firn, 1986.

Morgan, Bill. *Beat Atlas: A State by State Guide to the Beat Generation.* San Francisco: City Lights Publishers, 2011.

———. *Beat Generation in New York: A Walking Tour of Jack Kerouac's City.* San Francisco: City Lights Publishers, 2001.

———. *The Beat Generation in San Francisco: A Literary Tour.* San Francisco: City Lights Publishers, 2003.

Morgan, Bill, ed. *Rub Out the Words: The Letters of William S. Burroughs 1959–1974.* New York: HarperCollins Publishers, 2012.

———. *The Letters of Allen Ginsberg.* Cambridge, MA: Da Capo Press, 2008.

Morgan, Ted. *Literary Outlaw: The Life and Times of William S. Burroughs.* New York: Henry Holt and Company, 1988.

Nash, Jay Robert. *Bloodletters and Badmen: A Narrative Encyclopedia of American Criminals from the Pilgrims to the Present.* New York: M. Evans and Company, Inc., 1973.

Nashawaty, Chris. *Crab Monsters, Teenage Caveman, and Candy Stripe Nurses: Roger Corman: King of the B Movie.* New York: Harry N. Abrams, 2013.

Newlove, Donald. *Those Drinking Days, Myself and Other Writers.* New York: Horizon Press, 1981.

Nicosia, Gerald. *Memory Babe: A Critical Biography of Jack Kerouac.* New York: Grove Press, 1983.

Nicosia, Gerald, and Anne Marie Santos. *One and Only: The Untold Story of On the Road.* Berkeley, CA: Viva Editions, 2012.

Norse, Harold. *The Beat Hotel.* San Diego: Atticus Press, 1983.

Ohle, David. *Cursed from Birth: The Short, Unhappy Life of William S. Burroughs, Jr.* New York: Soft Skull Press, 2006.

O'Neill, Paul. "Sad but Noisy Rebels." *Life* (November 30, 1959).

Orlovsky, Peter. *Clean Asshole Poems & Smiling Vegetable Songs.* San Francisco: City Lights Publishers, 1978.

Patchen, Kenneth. *The Collected Poems of Kenneth Patchen.* New York: New Directions, 1968.

———. *The Journal of Albion Moonlight.* New York: New Directions: 1961.

———. *The Memoirs of a Shy Pornographer.* New York: New Directions, 1999.

Peck, Abe. *Uncovering the Sixties: The Life & Times of the Underground Press.* New York: Pantheon Books, 1985.

Perry, Charles. *The Haight-Ashbury: A History.* New York: Rolling Stone Press, 1984.

Perry, Paul. *On the Bus.* New York: Thunder's Mouth Press, 1990.

Petry, David. *The Best Last Place: A History of the Santa Barbara Cemetery.* Seattle: Olympus Press, 2006.

Phillips, Lisa. *Beat Culture and the New America: 1950–1965.* New York: Whitney Museum of American Art in association with Flammarion, 1995.

Plimpton, George. *Beat Writers at Work: The Paris Review.* New York: The Modern Library, 1999.

Podhoretz, Norman. *Ex-Friends: Falling Out with Allen Ginsberg, Lionel and Diana Trilling, Lillian Hellman, Hannah Arendt, and Norman Mailer.* New York: The Free Press, 1999.

———. "The Know Nothing Bohemians." *Partisan Review* (Spring 1958).

Pynchon, Thomas. *Slow Learner.* New York: Penguin Press, 2012.

Rexroth, Kenneth. *Bird in the Bush/ Obvious Essays.* New York: New Directions, 1959.

Rieff, David, ed. *Susan Sontag: Essays of the 1960s & 70s.* New York: Library of America, 2013.

Rumaker, Michael. *Robert Duncan in San Francisco.* San Francisco: City Lights Publishers, 2013.

Saroyan, Aram. *Genesis Angels: The Saga of Lew Welch and the Beat Generation.* New York: Morrow, 1979.

Schafer, Ben, ed. *The Herbert Huncke Reader.* New York: Harper Perennial, 1998.

Shaffer, Andrew. *Literary Rogues: A Scandalous History of Wayward Authors.* New York: HarperCollins Publishers, 2013.

Shinder, Jason. *The Poem That Changed America: "Howl" Fifty Years Later.* New York: Farrar, Straus & Giroux, 2006.

Silverberg, Ira, ed. *Everything Is Permitted: The Making of Naked Lunch.* New York: Grove Wiedenfield, 1992.

Snyder, Gary. *The Real Work: Interviews & Talks, 1964–1979.* New York: New Directions, 1980.

———. *Turtle Island.* New York: New Directions, 1974.

Solomon, Carl. *Mishaps, Perhaps.* San Francisco: City Lights Publishers, 1966.

Stevens, Jay. *Storming Heaven: LSD and the American Dream.* New York: Grove Press, 1998.

Suiter, John. *Poets on the Peaks: Gary Snyder, Philip Whalen and Jack Kerouac.* Berkeley, CA: Counterpoint, 2003.

Sweet, Brian. *Steely Dan: Reelin' in the Years.* New York: Omnibus Press, 2008.

Theado, Matt. *Dictionary of Literary Biography: The Beats: A Documentary Volume.* Farmington Hills, MI: Gale, 2000.

Theado, Matt. *Jack Kerouac.* Columbia: The University of South Carolina Press, 2000.

Trigilio, Tony, ed. *Elise Cowen: Poems and Fragments.* Boise, ID: Ahsahta Press, 2014.

Tully, Jim. *Beggars of Life.* New York: Albert and Charles Boni, 1924.

Turner, Steve. *Jack Kerouac: Angelheaded Hipster.* New York: Viking Press, 1996.

Tytell, John. *Paradise Outlaws: Remembering the Beats.* New York: William Morrow, 1999.

Updike, John. "On the Sidewalk." *New Yorker* (February 21, 1959).

Vale, V., ed. *William Burroughs, Brion Gysin, Throbbing Gristle (Re/ Search #4/ 5).* San Francisco: RE/Search Publications, 1982.

Waldman, Anne, ed. *The Beat Book: Poems & Fiction from the Beat Generation.* Boston: Shambhala Publications, Inc., 1996.

Wallis, Michael. *Route 66: The Mother Road.* New York: St. Martin's Griffin, 1990.

Watson, Steven. *The Birth of the Beat Generation: Visionaries, Rebels, and Hipsters 1944–1960.* New York: Pantheon Books, 1995.

Weaver, Helen. *The Awakener: A Memoir of Kerouac and the Fifties.* San Francisco: City Lights Publishers, 2009.

Weddle, Jeff. *Bohemian New Orleans: The Story of the Outsider and Loujon Press.* Jackson: University Press of Mississippi, 2007.

Welch, Lew. *Ring of Bone: Collected Poems.* San Francisco: City Lights Publishers, 2012.

Weldon, Michael. *The Psychotronic Encyclopedia of Film.* New York: Ballantine Books, 1983.

Whitman, Walt. *Leaves of Grass: The Original 1855 Edition.* Mineola, NY: Dover Publications, 2007.

Williams, William Carlos. *Paterson.* New York: New Directions, 1995.

Wolfe, Thomas. *Look Homeward, Angel.* New York: Charles Scribner's Sons, 1929.

Wolfe, Tom. *The Electric Kool-Aid Acid Test.* New York: Farrar, Straus and Giroux, 1968.

Wormser, Richard. *Hoboes: Wandering in America, 1870–1940.* New York: Walker Publishing Company, Inc., 1994.

Zott, Lynn M., ed. *The Beat Generation: A Gale Critical Companion.* Farmington Hills, MI: Gale, 2003.

Index

THE FAQ SERIES

AC/DC FAQ
by Susan Masino
Backbeat Books
978-1-4803-9450-6 .... $24.99

Armageddon Films FAQ
by Dale Sherman
Applause Books
978-1-61713-119-6 .... $24.99

Lucille Ball FAQ
*by James Sheridan
and Barry Monush*
Applause Books
978-1-61774-082-4 .... $19.99

The Beach Boys FAQ
by Jon Stebbins
Backbeat Books
978-0-87930-987-9 .... $22.99

Black Sabbath FAQ
by Martin Popoff
Backbeat Books
978-0-87930-957-2 .... $19.99

Johnny Cash FAQ
by C. Eric Banister
Backbeat Books
978-1-4803-8540-5 .... $24.99

Eric Clapton FAQ
by David Bowling
Backbeat Books
978-1-61713-454-8 .... $22.99

Doctor Who FAQ
by Dave Thompson
Applause Books
978-1-55783-854-4 .... $22.99

The Doors FAQ
by Rich Weidman
Backbeat Books
978-1-61713-017-5 .... $24.99

The Eagles FAQ
by Andrew Vaughan
Backbeat Books
978-1-4803-8541-2 .... $24.99

Fab Four FAQ
*by Stuart Shea and
Robert Rodriguez*
Hal Leonard Books
978-1-4234-2138-2 .... $19.99

Fab Four FAQ 2.0
by Robert Rodriguez
Backbeat Books
978-0-87930-968-8 .... $19.99

Film Noir FAQ
by David J. Hogan
Applause Books
978-1-55783-855-1 .... $22.99

Football FAQ
by Dave Thompson
Backbeat Books
978-1-4950-0748-4 .... $24.99

The Grateful Dead FAQ
by Tony Sclafani
Backbeat Books
978-1-61713-086-1 .... $24.99

Prices, contents, and availability
subject to change without notice.

Jimi Hendrix FAQ
by Gary J. Jucha
Backbeat Books
978-1-61713-095-3 .... $22.99

Horror Films FAQ
by John Kenneth Muir
Applause Books
978-1-55783-950-3 .... $22.99

James Bond FAQ
by Tom DeMichael
Applause Books
978-1-55783-856-8 .... $22.99

Stephen King Films FAQ
by Scott Von Doviak
Applause Books
978-1-4803-5551-4 .... $24.99

KISS FAQ
by Dale Sherman
Backbeat Books
978-1-61713-091-5 .... $22.99

Led Zeppelin FAQ
by George Case
Backbeat Books
978-1-61713-025-0 .... $19.99

Modern Sci-Fi Films FAQ
by Tom DeMichael
Applause Books
978-1-4803-5061-8 .... $24.99

Morrissey FAQ
by D. McKinney
Backbeat Books
978-1-4803-9448-3 .... $24.99

3 1901 05811 7831

0515